Who's Who in Shakespeare's England

ALAN & VERONICA PALMER

Methuen

Published by Methuen 2000

1 3 5 7 9 10 8 6 4 2

First published in hardback in the United States by St Martin's Press in 1981
First published in the United States in paperback (with revisions) by St Martin's
Griffin in 1999

First published in Great Britain in 2000 by Methuen Publishing Limited
215 Vauxhall Bridge Road, London SW1V 1EJ

Copyright © Alan and Veronica Palmer, 1981, 1999

The authors have asserted their rights under the Copyright, Designs
and Patents Act, 1988, to be identified as the authors of this work

Methuen Publishing Limited Reg. No. 3543167

A CIP catalogue record for this book is available from the British Library

ISBN 0 413 74710 7

Printed in Great Britain by St Edmundsbury Press Ltd,
Bury St Edmunds, Suffolk

Contents

Preface

No period in English history is so richly varied in interest as the third of a century which separates the publication of Spenser's *Faerie Queen* in 1590 from the printing of Shakespeare's First Folio in 1623. At first sight this generalization may seem tendentious. Politically, these were not exciting years. The fireships which scattered the Spanish Armada in 1588 left no afterglow to inspire later combatants in the long war; and, for once, home affairs were less memorable for legislation than litigation. Yet the "golden decade" which rounded off the sixteenth century, and the early years of Stuart rule in England which followed it possess a threefold historical fascination: they show the social classes blending together as never before; they abound in masterpieces of literature and drama; and they look outward to a wider world across the oceans which stirred the mind and filled the merchant's coffers. This epoch encompasses the adult life of William Shakespeare, the Warwickshire man who came to London to act and who returned to his native Stratford-upon-Avon as the most popular of living dramatists and a man of property. In his person and through his works Shakespeare reflected the dominant themes of the time.

When my late wife Veronica and I first planned to write *Who's Who in Shakespeare's England,* we did not want to add "just another book about the Bard" to an already long list in library catalogues. Our intention was to provide readers with a fresh insight into Shakespeare's world by presenting a verbal portrait gallery of some seven hundred of his contemporaries in England, from royalty down to shadowy figures whose notoriety lifted them momentarily from the darkest depths. Many of our entries were people whom Shakespeare did not know personally; and there are some of whom he had probably never heard. We did, however, include the actors, writers, publishers, patrons and printers with whom Shakespeare was acquainted as well as the public figures of the time. And we also added some of the better-known people in Stratford-upon-Avon and neighbouring Warwickshire, for it is obvious that many of Shakespeare's acquaintances, both in Stratford and London, suggested characters for his plays: there have long been candidates for Malvolio, and for Justice Shallow, and the gentlemen whose wives made merry with Falstaff at Windsor. Attempts to identify the "dark lady," "Mr. W. S.," or "the rival poet" have for many years prompted scholars to study some at least of Shakespeare's contemporaries; and this book includes the men and women suggested as solutions for these traditional academic puzzles: the entries note the champions of each name, and when their claims were in fashion. We hoped to produce a biographical dictionary which would stimulate an interest in other men and women of Shakespeare's day, people whom he may have met, whose books he read, whose plays he knew, or whose adventures and misfortunes reached him by word of mouth in what was still a compact community.

Three points of general interest struck us while we were compiling *Who's Who in Shakespeare's England.* The first was the artificiality of that conventional division in historical teaching that falls like a curtain on the day of Elizabeth I's death in March 1603 so as to separate "Tudor" from "Stuart" times. The recurrence of similar names in the Essex conspiracy of 1601 and the Gunpowder Plot of 5 November 1605 emphasizes that these dramatic events, though threatening different dynasties, were less than five years apart. It is hard to accept that some recognisable "Stuart" figures—John Donne, for example—were swaggeringly Elizabethan in their youth. The second point which impressed us was the impact of women at court and in society. Their influence was monstrously ignored by the Victorian editors of the original *Dictionary of National Biography* and subsequently by authors of many standard books; fortunately, over the last twenty years of historical writing, this omission has been largely rectified. Finally we noticed that, although London clearly remained a magnet attracting ambitious social climbers, many regions distant from the capital were politically less remote than earlier in the sixteenth century, notably during the changing uncertainties of the Reformation. Stratford-upon-Avon and Warwickshire in particular were not backwaters, as the Gunpowder Plot showed; and city worthies in Plymouth and Exeter, Bristol and Norwich exerted greater influence on political life than do their successors four centuries later. If, as A. F. Pollard once memorably suggested, "Tudor despotism consisted largely of London's dominance over the rest of the country," the capital's hold on affairs was being challenged by 1597 when Shakespeare chose to invest his London earnings in Warwickshire real estate.

Inevitably we found we had to impose limits on our selection of candidates for inclusion in a reference book of this character. We confined ourselves almost entirely to men and women with national or local influence during the years 1590 to 1623. This led us to exclude such familiar figures as John Foxe, Thomas Gresham, and Archbishops Parker and Grindal at one end and Queen Henrietta Maria and Richard Baxter at the other; nor did we include eminent foreigners such as Philip II of Spain, Henri IV of France, or Galileo Galilei, who was born ten weeks ahead of Shakespeare, or Cervantes who died on that same day in 1616. The length of the biographies should not be seen as a yardstick by which to assess the relative importance of the entries; it is always easier to condense the lives of well-known people than of fringe figures of general interest. Thomas Coryat, for example, has a longer entry than Sir Francis Drake; but no one should assume that the "Odcombian Leg-Stretcher" therefore possesses greater historical significance than the Devonian circumnavigator.

We added to the bottom of our entries a few titles of books or articles which we thought the reader would find as useful and stimulating as we did ourselves. In the last twenty years there have been several important publications which challenge older preconceptions and invite revision of judgement from the fresh material they present. Outstanding among them are: Park Honan, *Shakespeare: A Life* (Oxford and New York, 1998), the most detailed of many biographies; two scholarly studies by Robert Bearman, *Stratford-upon-Avon: A History of its Streets and Buildings* (Nelson, Lancs, 1988) and *Shakespeare in the Stratford Records* (Stratford-upon-Avon, 1994); L. Barroll, *Politics, Plague and Shakespeare's Theater* (Ithaca, N.Y., 1991). Barry Day, *This Wooden 'O', Shakespeare's Globe Reborn* (London, 1996) is an account of how Sam Wannamaker ensured that "the Shakespearean theatrical experience" could be re-created in modern Southwark. Antonia Fraser's *The Gunpowder Plot* (London, 1996) broadens our understanding of the challenge of "faith and reason" in the post-Elizabethan decade.

I remain grateful to John Spires, of the Harvester Press, who first suggested that Veronica and I should compile a book of this nature. Over the years, we received ready assistance from the staffs of the Bodleian Library, Oxford, and the London Library, which we much appreciated.

ALAN PALMER
Woodstock, Oxon, January 1999

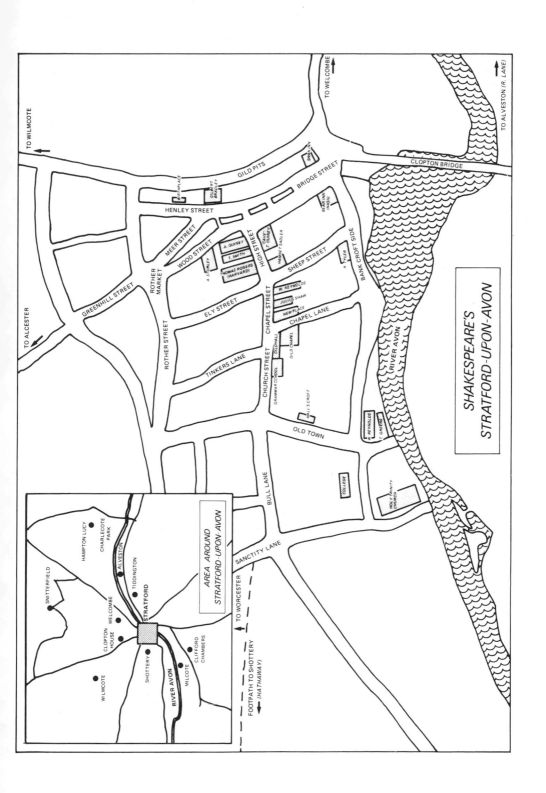

SHAKESPEARE'S
STRATFORD-UPON-AVON

AREA AROUND
STRATFORD-UPON-AVON

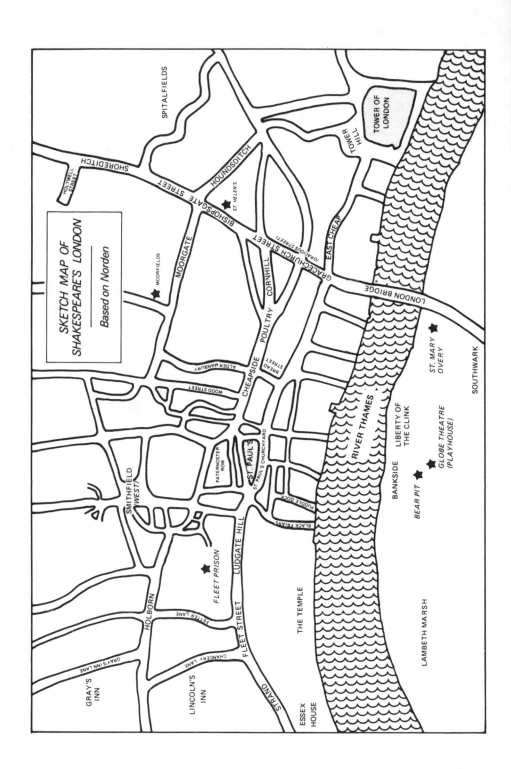

SKETCH MAP OF
SHAKESPEARE'S LONDON

Based on Norden

Classified List of Entries
DIVISIONS OF CLASSIFICATION SYSTEM

Artists, Architects and Sculptors
Churches: Anglican Clergy; Dissenting Ministers; Roman Catholic Priests and Religious
Colonialists
Court and Society Women
Courtiers
Diplomats
Explorers
Government and local officials
Judges and Lawyers
Landowners and countrymen
Mathematicians
Merchants, Bankers, Manufacturers
Musicians and composers
Occult
Physicians and surgeons
Politicians
Printing, Booksellers, Publishers
Rebels and conspirators
Royalty, etc.
Scholars
Scientists
Seamen
Secret Service
Shakespeare, the Man: Family; Legends; London connections; Stratford connections; Stratford contemporaries
Shakespeare, the Works: Alleged authors; "Dark Ladies"; "Mr W.H."; Performances witnessed by –; Possible originals of characters or allusions
Soldiers
Statesmen
Theatre: Actors; Company patrons; Managers and theatre owners; Miscellaneous connections with the Theatre
Underworld
Writers: Antiquarians, Topographers; Critics; Diarists and letter writers; Dramatists; Essayists, Philosophers, Theologians, etc.; Historians and biographers; Novelists; Poets and anthologists; Satirists; Translators, Writing-Masters etc.; Travel writers

Classified Entries
Artists, Architects and Sculptors

Droeshout, Martin
Evesham, Epiphanius
Gheeraerts, Marcus
Hilliard, Nicholas
Janssen, Cornelis
Janssen, Gheerart
Jones, Inigo
Mytens, Daniel

Oliver, Isaac
Smythson, John
Smythson, Robert
Spicer, William
Stone, Nicholas
Thorpe, John
White, John

Churches
Anglican Clergy

Abbot, George, Abp.
Alabaster, William
Andrewes, Lancelot, Bp.
Aylmer, John, Bp.
Bancroft, Richard, Abp.
Barlow, William
Barton, Richard
Bretchgirdle, John
Bright, Timothy
Brooke, Samuel
Byfield, Richard
Carlton, Richard
Corbet, Richard, Bp.
Daborne, Robert
Donne, John
Fletcher, Giles, II
Fletcher, Phineas
Fletcher, Richard
Gilbard, William
Goodman, Gabriel

Goodman, Godfrey, Bp
Hall, Joseph, Bp.
Harrison, William
Harsnet, Samuel, Abp.
Heicroft, Henry
Heton, Martin, Bp.
Hooker, Richard
King, John, Bp.
Laud, William, Abp.
Mathew, Tobias, Abp.
Montagu, Richard, Bp.
Morgan, William, Bp.
Nowell, Alexander
Overall, John, Bp.
Roche, Walter
Rogers, John
Ussher, James, Abp.
Watts, Richard
Whitgift, John, Abp.
Willis, John

Dissenting Ministers

Barrow, Henry
Bradford, William
Browne, Robert
Cartwright, Thomas

Hooker, Thomas
Perkins, William
Ward, Samuel

Roman Catholic Priests and Religious

Allen, William, Cdl.
Garnet, Henry
Gerard, John

Parsons, Robert
Southwell, Robert
Ward, Mary

Colonialists

Digges, Dudley
Gates, Thomas
Gorges, Ferdinando
Jourdain, Sylvester
Pory, John
Ralegh, Walter
Rolfe, John
Rolfe, Thomas
Sandys, Edwin

Sandys, George
Sidney, Robert
Smith, John
Smith, Thomas
Somers, George
Southampton, Henry, 3rd Earl of
White, John
Yardley, George

Court and Society Women

Bacon, Alice, Lady
Bacon, Ann, Lady
Bedford, Lucy, Countess of
Burghley, Mildred, Lady
Carey, Elizabeth (Lady Hunsdon)
Carey, Elizabeth (Lady Berkeley)
Carlisle, Lucy, Countess of
Cary, Elizabeth, Lady
Clifford, Anne
Cumberland, Margaret, Countess of
Fitton, Mary
Hardwick, Elizabeth ('Bess')
Hatton, Elizabeth, Lady
Howard, Catherine, Lady
Howard, Catherine, Countess of Suffolk
Howard, Frances, Countess of Essex and
    Somerset
Kildare, Frances, Lady
Lanier, Emilia
Leicester, Lettice, Countess of
Lincoln, Elizabeth, Countess of

Parry, Blanche
Pembroke, Mary, Countess of
Percy, Dorothy, Countess of
    Northumberland
Rainsford, Anne, Lady
Ralegh, Elizabeth, Lady
Ratcliffe, Margaret
Rich, Penelope, Lady
Russell, Anne
Russell, Elizabeth, Lady
Sheffield, Douglas, Lady
Southampton, Elizabeth, Countess of
Southampton, Mary, Dowager Countess of
Southwell, Elizabeth
Spencer, Alice (Countess of Derby)
Stuart, Arbella
Talbot, Mary, Countess of Shrewsbury
Vere, Elizabeth (Countess of Derby)
Walsingham, Frances (Countess of Essex)
Warwick, Anne (Countess of)

Courtiers

Alexander, William
Armstrong, Archibald
Berkeley, Thomas
Buck, George
Buckingham, George, Duke of
Carey, George, 2nd Lord Hunsdon
Carey, Henry, 1st Lord Hunsdon
Carey, Robert
Carr, Robert
Derby, Henry, 4th Earl of
Essex, Robert, 2nd Earl of
Harington, John
Hatton, Christopher

Hay, James
Heneage, Thomas
Home, George
Knollys, Francis
Knollys, William
Lee, Henry
Leicester, Robert, Earl of
North, Roger, Baron
Oxford, Edward, 17th Earl of
Pembroke, Philip, 4th Earl of
Pembroke, William, 3rd Earl of
Ralegh, Walter
Rutland, Francis, 6th Earl of

Greene, Thomas
Lambarde, William
Lucas, Thomas
Noy, William
Peryam, William

Popham, John
Replingham, William
Selden, John
Underhill, William, I
Walter, John

Landowners and Countrymen
Bedford, Francis, 4th Earl of
Boyle, Richard, Earl of Cork
Brydges, Giles, 3rd Baron Chandos
Dover, Robert
Greville, Edward
Greville, Fulke, I
Greville, Lodowick
Herbert, Henry (of Chepstow)
Hertford, Edward, Earl of
Hoby, Edward
Hoby, Thomas Posthumous
Howard, Thomas, Earl of Arundel
Huntingdon, Henry Hastings, Earl of
Kytson, Thomas (Sir)
Lee, Henry

Cecil, Thomas, Earl of Exeter
Cholmeley, Richard
Cromwell, Oliver (Sir)
Lincoln, Henry, 2nd Earl of
Lucy, Thomas, I, II and III
Lumley, John
Pembroke, Henry, 2nd Earl of
Pembroke, Philip, 4th Earl of
Sandys, William, Baron
Shrewsbury, George, 4th Earl of
Sidney, Robert
Spencer, Robert
Tresham, Thomas
Vaughan, Rowland

Mathematicians
Barlow, William
Briggs, Henry
Hariot, Thomas
Hood, Thomas

Napier, John
Savile, Henry
Wright, Edward

Merchants, Bankers, Manufacturers
Boyle, Richard, Earl of Cork
Bulmer, Bevis
Cokayne, William
Courten, William
Cranfield, Lionel
Hobson, Thomas
Leveson, William
Middleton, Hugh

Mompesson, Giles
Palavicino, Horatio
Ridolfi, Roberto di
Smith, Thomas
Spencer, John
Spencer, Robert
Sutton, Thomas

Musicians and Composers
Bull, John
Byrd, William
Campion, Thomas
Carlton, Richard
Dowland, John
Farnaby, Giles

Ferrabosco, Alfonso
Gibbons, Orlando
Jones, Robert
Kirbye, George
Lanier, Nicholas
Milton, John

Pavier, Thomas
Purfoot, Thomas
Roberts, James
Short, Peter
Simmes, Valentine
Smethwick, John
Stafford, Simon
Stansby, William

Thorpe, Thomas
Tottel, Richard
Trundell, John
Walkley, Thomas
Walley, Henry
White, Edward
White, William
Wise, Andrew

Rebels and Conspirators

Baynham, Edmund
Brooke, George
Brooke, Henry, Lord Cobham
Catesby, Robert
Cromwell, Edward
Cuffe, Henry
Danvers, Charles
Essex, Robert, 2nd Earl of
Fawkes, Guy
Lee, Thomas
Meyrick, Gelly
Monteagle, Lord
Northumberland, Henry, 9th Earl of

Blount, Christopher
Percy, Thomas
Ridolfi, Roberto di
Rookwood, Ambrose
Rutland, Francis, 6th Earl of
Rutland, Roger, 5th Earl of
Sandys, William, Baron
Seymour, William
Somerville, John
Southampton, Henry, 3rd Earl of
Tresham, Francis
Tyrone, Hugh o'Neill, Earl of
Winter, Thomas

Royalty etc.

Anne of Denmark, Queen
Charles, Prince (later King Charles I)
Elizabeth I, Queen
Elizabeth, Princess
Frederick, Elector Palatine

Henry, Prince of Wales
James I, King
Pocahontas, Princess
Stuart, Arbella

Scholars

Bodley, Thomas
Cartwright, Thomas
Dee, John
Digges, Leonard
Gager, William
Gwinne, Matthew

Harvey, Gabriel
Legge, Thomas
Mulcaster, Richard
Ruggle, George
Savile, Henry

Scientists

Barlow, William
Digges, Thomas
Gilbert, William
Hood, Thomas

Lobel, Mathias de
Northumberland, Henry, 9th Earl of
Ridley, Mark
Tradescant, John

Salusbury, John
Savage, Thomas
Smith, William (of Waltham Cross)

Southampton, Henry, 3rd Earl of
Walker, Henry
Wayte, William

Stratford Connections
Addenbrooke, John
Barton, Richard
Bradley, Gilbert
Bretchgirdle, John
Collins, Francis
Combe, John
Combe, Thomas, I
Combe, Thomas, II
Combe, William, I
Combe, William, II
Lane, John
Lane, Richard
Lucas, Thomas
Mainwaring, Arthur
Nash, Anthony
Nash, John
Nash, Thomas
Quiney, Adrian
Quiney, George
Quiney, Richard
Replingham, William

Reynolds, William
Richardson, John
Robinson, John
Rogers, John
Rogers, Philip
Russell, Thomas
Sadler, Hamnet
Sadler, Judith
Sandells, Fulke
Shaw, Julius
Smith, Ralph
Sturley, Abraham
Tyler, Richard
Underhill, William, II
Walker, William
Watts, Richard
Whatcott, Robert
"Whateley, Anne"
Wheeler, Margaret
Whittington, Thomas

Stratford Contemporaries
Aspinall, Alexander
Bott, William
Brownsword, John
Byfield, Richard
Carew, George
Catesby, William
Clopton, William
Cottam, John
Field, Richard
Gilbard, William
Greville, Edward

Greville, Fulke, I
Greville, Lodowick
Harvard, Catherine
Heicroft, Henry
Jenkins, Thomas
Jones, Davy
Roche, Walter
Rookwood, Ambrose
Smith, William (of Stratford)
Somerville, John

Shakespeare: The Works
Alleged authors
Bacon, Francis
Derby, William, 4th Earl of
Marlowe, Christopher

Oxford, Edward, 17th Earl of
Rutland, Roger, 5th Earl of
Shirley, Anthony

'Dark Ladies'

Davenant, Jane
Fitton, Mary
Hatton, Elizabeth

Lanier, Emilia
Morgan, Lucy
Rich, Penelope

"Mr W. H."

Hall, William
Hatcliffe, William
Hervey, William

Pembroke, William, 3rd Earl of
Southampton, Henry, 3rd Earl of
Willoughby, Henry

Performances witnessed by:-

Forman, Simon
Keeling, William

Manningham, John
Platter, Thomas

Possible originals of characters, or allusions

Annesley, Cordell
Aspinall, Alexander
Danvers, Charles
Gardiner, William
Garnet, Henry
Gilbard, William
Hoby, Thomas Posthumous

Jenkins, Thomas
Knollys, William
Lopez, Roderigo
Orsini, Virginio
Wayte, William
Whittington, Thomas
Williams, Roger

Soldiers

Blount, Christopher
Buckingham, George, Duke of
Carew, George
Carey, George
Cecil, Edward
Cecil, Thomas
Danvers, Charles
Danvers, Henry
Essex, Robert, 2nd Earl of
Essex, Robert, 3rd Earl of
Grey of Wilton, Thomas, Lord
Hervey, William
Lee, Thomas
Leicester, Robert, Earl of

Mountjoy, Charles, Lord
Norris, John
Ormonde, Thomas, Earl of
Oxford, Edward, 17th Earl of
Russell, William
Rutland, Roger, 5th Earl of
Sidney, Philip
Sidney, Robert
Smith, John
Southampton, Henry, 3rd Earl of
Stanley, William
Warwick, Ambrose Dudley, Earl of
Williams, Roger
Willoughby, Lord Peregrine

Statesmen

Buckingham, George, Duke of
Burghley, William, Lord
Cecil, Robert

Walsingham, Francis
Wentworth, Thomas, Earl of Strafford

Theatre

Actors

Alleyn, Edward
Armin, Robert

Barksted, William
Beeston, Christopher

Benfield, Robert
Browne, Robert
Bryan, George
Burbage, Richard
Condell, Henry
Cooke, Alexander
Cowley, Richard
Crosse, Samuel
Dutton, Lawrence
Ecclestone, William
Field, Nathan
Fletcher, Lawrence
Gilburne, Samuel
Goughe (Goffe), Robert
Green, John
Heminges, John
Jones, Richard
Kempe, William
Knell, William
Lowin, John
Ostler, William
Pallant, Robert, senior
Pallant, Robert, junior
Pavy, Solomon
Phillips, Augustine

Pollard, Thomas
Pope, Thomas
Reynolds, Robert ("Pickleherring")
Rice, John
Robinson, Richard
Rowley, William
Sackville, Thomas
Sands, James
Shakespeare, Edmund
Shank, John
Sharpe, Richard
Sinckler, John
Singer, John
Slater, Martin
Sly, William
Spencer, Gabriel
Spencer, John ("Hans Stockfisch")
Swanston, Elliard
Tarlton, Richard
Taylor, Joseph
Tooley, Nicholas
Underwood, John
Wilson, Jack
Wilson, Robert

Company Patrons
Anne of Denmark, Queen
Brydges, Grey, 5th Baron Chandos
Carey, George, Lord Chamberlain
Carey, Henry, Lord Chamberlain
Charles, Prince
Derby, Henry, 4th Earl of
Derby, William, 6th Earl of
Elizabeth, Queen
Elizabeth, Princess
Frederick, Elector Palatine
Henry, Prince of Wales

Hertford, Edward, Earl of
Howard, Charles, Lord High Admiral
James I, King
Leicester, Robert, Earl of
Lincoln, Henry, 2nd Earl of
Oxford, Edward, 17th Earl of
Pembroke, Henry, 2nd Earl of
Strange, Ferdinando, Lord
Sussex, Robert, 5th Earl of
Warwick, Ambrose, Earl of
Worcester, Edward, 4th Earl of

Managers and Theatre Owners
Beeston, Christopher
Burbage, Cuthbert
Burbage, James
Evans, Henry (boys)
Farrant, Richard (boys)
Giles, Nathaniel (boys)

Giles, Thomas (boys)
Henslowe, Philip
Hunnis, William (boys)
Keysar, Robert (boys)
Langley, Francis
Lanman, Henry

Porter, Henry
Rowley, Samuel
Rowley, William
Ruggle, George
Sackville, Thomas, 1st Earl of Dorset
Shakespeare, William

Essayists, Philosophers, Theologians, etc.
Bacon, Francis
Breton, Nicholas
Bryskett, Lodowick
Burton, Robert
Cornwallis, William
Hall, Joseph
Herbert, Edward, Lord, of Cherbury
Hooker, Richard

Tomkis, Thomas
Tourneur, Cyril
Webster, John
Wilkins, George
Wilson, Arthur
Wilson, Robert

Mulcaster, Richard
Overbury, Thomas
Peacham, Henry
Perkins, William
Pound, Thomas
Scott, Reginald
Stubbes, Philip

Historians and Biographers
Camden, William
Greville, Fulke
Hayward, John
Holinshed, Raphael

Moffet, Thomas
Ralegh, Water
Wilson, Arthur

Novelists
Deloney, Thomas
Greene, Robert

Lodge, Thomas
Wilkins, George

Poets and Anthologists
Alexander, William
Allot, Robert
Barnes, Barnabe
Barnfield, Richard
Basse, William
Bodenham, John
Breton, Nicholas
Brooke, Christopher
Browne, William
Campion, Thomas
Chapman, George
Chester, Robert
Churchyard, Thomas
Constable, Henry
Corbet, Richard
Daniel, Samuel
Davenant, William
Davies, John (of Hereford)
Davies, Sir John
Davison, Francis
Digges, Leonard

Donne, John
Drayton, Michael
Drummond, William
Dyer, Edward
Fletcher, Giles, II
Fletcher, Phineas
Freeman, Thomas
Gorges, Arthur
Greville, Fulke, II
Griffin, Bartholomew
Holland, Hugh
Jonson, Ben
Kyffin, Maurice
Lodge, Thomas
Markham, Gervase
Nashe, Thomas
Peele, George
Percy, William
Ralegh, Walter
Scoloker, Antony
Shakespeare, William

A Prospect of LC

THAMESIS FLVVIVS.

D. Loggan fec.

Loggan's Panorama of London, 1620. The Globe Theatre (36), in the Bear Garden (37) and the Swan Theatre (38) can be seen in the foreground.

Note on Sources

We have cited books or articles of particular relevance to a specific person under the appropriate entry so as to suggest material which may be read for fuller treatment of a subject. Five major works we have used extensively and we mention them, by abbreviated initials, where they are of especial interest. These five works are:

G.E. Bentley, *The Jacobean and Caroline Stage* (1941–68), cited as G.E.B.

E.K. Chambers: *The Elizabethan Stage* (1923), cited as E.K.C., *E.S.*

    : *William Shakespeare* (1930), cited as E.K.C., *W.S.*

M. Eccles, *Shakespeare in Warwickshire* (1961), cited as M.E.

S. Schoenbaum, *William Shakespeare: A Documentary Life* (1975), cited as S.S.

Throughout the book we have also used the following basic reference sources:

E. Arbor (ed), *Transcript of the Registers of the Company of Stationers of London 1554–1640* (1875–94)

Dictionary of National Biography (1885–1913)

Dictionary of Welsh Biography (1959)

J. Foster, *Alumni Oxonienses, 1500–1714* (1891–2)

V. Gibbs, et al., *Complete Peerage* (1910–59)

R.B. McKerrow, *Dictionary of Printers and Booksellers* (1910)

J. and J.A. Venn, *Alumni Cantabrigienses* (1922–7)

Our debt to these works, to the scholarship of such distinguished historians as Sir John Neale and Dr A.L. Rowse, and to other authors cited in the text, must be apparent in the pages that follow.

A.W.P.
V.M.P.

Acknowledgements

The illustrations on pages 28 and 270 are reproduced with kind permission of the Heather Professor of Music, Oxford University; and on pages 188 and 189 with kind permission of the National Trust, London.

Ashmolean Museum, Oxford 252

Bodleian Library, Oxford 28, 31, 181, 270

Courtauld Institute of Art, London 188, 189

Mary Evans Picture Library, London 3, 6, 9, 19, 34, 37, 43, 54, 55, 63, 67, 69, 70, 76, 78, 79, 82, 87, 109, 115, 119, 124 left, 124 right, 125, 139, 151, 154, 162, 170, 177, 182, 210, 212, 215, 216, 225, 230, 240, 243, 259, 261, 267, 273

The Mansell Collection, London xxiv-xxv, 5, 16, 30, 40, 47, 48, 75, 107, 135, 193, 201, 222, 227, 234, 245

The National Trust, London 103, 104

Royal College of Music, London 33, 92

A

ABBOT, George (1562—1633), archbishop: born at Guildford, educated at Balliol College, Oxford, becoming Master of University College in 1597 and subsequently serving as Vice-Chancellor. While at Oxford he wrote *A Briefe Description of the Whole World* (1599), which contains one of the earliest topographical studies of America. His Calvinistic zeal made him unpopular in Oxford, where he was responsible for the public burning of religious pictures. In 1605 he ordered the imprisonment of more than a hundred students who had declined to remove their hats in his presence at the University Church. Abbot was consecrated Bishop of Lichfield in 1609, translated to London a few months later and became Archbishop of Canterbury in 1611. He strongly supported contacts with the German Protestants, personally conducting the marriage service between Princess Elizabeth (q.v.) and the Elector Palatine in February 1613. Abbot, however, angered James I by opposing the attempt of the Countess of Essex (Frances Howard, q.v.) to have her marriage ended by a decree of nullity (September 1613). He recovered his influence by introducing George Villiers (the later Buckingham, q.v.) to the Court in 1615, taking advantage of royal favour to secure for his brother, Robert Abbot (1560—1617), the see of Salisbury. In July 1621 the Archbishop accidentally killed a gamekeeper while hunting in Hampshire. This misfortune was exploited by Abbot's enemies among the High Churchmen, especially Laud, and he was arraigned as a "man of blood" before a commission of six bishops and four laymen. Ultimately he was granted a dispensation by James I at Christmas in 1622. Archbishop Abbot presided over Charles I's coronation in 1625 but his hostility to what he regarded as "Romish" tendencies led the King to order his suspension in October 1627. Although the suspension was lifted within a few weeks, Abbot spent the last years of his archiepiscopate in virtual retirement.

Paul Welsby, *George Abbot* (1962)

ADDENBROOKE, John (fl. 1608—9), Warwickshire resident: sued by Shakespeare in Stratford Court of Record for a debt of £6, August 1608. He was arrested, freed on the surety of Thomas Hornby, blacksmith of Henley Street, and then appears to have left Stratford. The court decided in Shakespeare's favour in June 1609, and ordered Hornby to show cause why, in Addenbrooke's absence, he should not pay the debt, together with costs and damages.

ALABASTER, William (1567—1640), writer and priest: born Hadleigh, Suffolk, educated at Westminster School and Trinity College, Cambridge, for whom he wrote *Roxana*, a Latin tragedy, in 1592. Alabaster was Essex's chaplain on the Cadiz expedition of 1596 but was then converted to Roman Catholicism and imprisoned in the Clink. In 1598 he escaped but was recaptured at La Rochelle. An essay in mystical theology was condemned by the Holy Office and by 1614 he had reverted to Anglican beliefs, becoming a Doctor of Divinity (Cambridge) and a King's chaplain. In 1618 he married Katherine Fludd, widowed mother of the Rosicrucian Robert Fludd (q.v.). Alabaster, who had written some notable Latin poems as a young man, was also the author of some of the earliest metaphysical sonnets of devotion, which remained unpublished until 1959. The last twenty years of his life were devoted to

1

theological studies: he died as Vicar of Therfield, Hertfordshire.

E. K. C., *E.S.*

ALEXANDER, William (1567/8 – 1640), poet: was educated in Glasgow and Leyden. He was already tutor to Prince Henry before James VI succeeded to the English throne; after 1603 he became Gentleman Extraordinary of the Privy Chamber to both Princes, Henry and Charles. In 1604 Alexander published a sonnet sequence, *Aurora*, and in 1614 *Doomsday*, a long poem. He also wrote a poem to Prince Henry and four tragedies, probably never acted, on classical subjects: Darius, Croesus, Alexander and Caesar. In 1630 he became a viscount, in 1633 Earl of Stirling, and was Secretary for Scotland from 1626 to his death. The King also granted him "Nova Scotia" in North America (1621), an area soon overrun by the French. Alexander was given the patent to print James I's metrical version of the Psalms for twenty-one years from 1628. He was a friend of Drayton and Drummond of Hawthornden (qq.v.).

ALLDE, Edward (? – 1628), printer: son of John Allde, printer, of London. He became a freeman of the Stationers' Company in 1584 and worked at first from his father's old shop, the "Long Shop" in the Poultry. He then had shops at the sign of the "Gilded Cup" Cripplegate, in Aldersgate (1597), on Lambert Hill (1604) and near Christ Church (1615). Allde printed mainly poetry and plays, but in 1597 his press was seized and he was banned by the Stationers' Company for printing a "Popish Confession". The Archbishop of Canterbury removed the ban; however, Allde was in trouble again in 1599 for printing condemned books. In 1611 he printed Shakespeare's *Titus Andronicus* for Edward White. After his death Allde's widow carried on the business.

ALLEN, Giles (fl. 1555 – 1601), land-owner in the Finsbury Fields and Shoreditch area of London: with his father Allen is mentioned as purchaser of land in the Liberty of Holywell (1555), part of which he leased in 1576 to James Burbage (q.v.) for twenty-one years, with the option of a new lease after ten. Allen received an annual rent of £14 from Burbage for this land. Relations between the two men were strained: Burbage proposed a new lease in 1585, which included the stipulation that the Allen family should have free seats in the Theatre, provided they arrived before the playhouse was full; but Allen refused to sign the new lease. When renewal of the lease became due, Allen wished to double the rent and take possession after five years in order to use the building for other purposes. On James Burbage's death in January 1597, his son, Cuthbert (q.v.), continued negotiations with Allen, who travelled up from Hasely, Essex, each quarter to collect his rents. Although Cuthbert accepted Allen's terms, Allen then refused to allow Richard Burbage as surety, threatening to pull down the Theatre and convert the materials to "better use". The Burbages forestalled Allen on 28 December 1598 by pulling down the Theatre themselves and moving it across the river. Allen brought an action against their carpenter, Street (q.v.), claiming £800 damages, including 40 shillings for trampling on his grass. Allen's suit failed: he then instituted a second action against Cuthbert Burbage and took a complaint of perjury to the Star Chamber in 1601, but again without success, for Bacon was asked to arbitrate, and gave his opinion against Allen.

E. K. C., *E.S.*

S.S.
C. W. WALLACE, "First London Theatre", (*Nebraska University Studies*, XIII (1913)

ALLEN, William (1532–94), English cardinal: born at Rossall, Lancashire, and became a Fellow of Oriel College, Oxford, at the age of eighteen. He was elected Principal of St Mary's Hall, Oxford, in 1556 retaining the post for the first two years of Elizabeth's reign, even though he was an uncompromising Catholic. He left Oxford for Louvain in 1561, returned a year later to his native Lancashire but finally emigrated in 1565, thereafter concentrating on the training of priests for the conversion of England. He founded colleges at Douai (1568), Rome (1575) and Valladolid (1589). In 1587 he was created a cardinal and, in the following year, signed an "admonition" urging English Roman Catholics to rise in support of the Spanish Armada. As a scholar, he took a large part in the preparation of the 'Douai Bible' (New Testament published 1582; Old Testament published 1609), the traditional translation in use among English-speaking Roman Catholics.

M. Haile, *An Elizabethan Cardinal* (1914)

ALLEYN, Edward (1566–1626), actor: born in Bishopsgate, London and known to have appeared with Earl of Worcester's Company, 1583, and Lord Admiral's Company, 1589. From 1592 to 1594 he played with the combined Lord Admiral's Company and Lord Strange's Men at the Rose Theatre, Southwark, under Philip Henslowe's (q.v.) management, and on tour during the plague of 1593. He married Henslowe's step-daughter, Joan, on 22 October 1592, and was associated with Henslowe in running theatres and bear-gardens. They became joint Masters of the Royal Game of Bears, Bulls and Mastiff Dogs in 1604. By 1594 Alleyn was the leading actor of the Admiral's Men, retiring in 1597 but returning three years later to build, with Henslowe, the Fortune Theatre in Cripplegate. He finally left the stage soon after Henry, Prince of Wales, took over the company in 1604, his last public appearance being in James I's coronation procession. Alleyn kept his financial interest in the Fortune and inherited Henslowe's share of the Hope in

Edward Alleyn

1616. His principal roles were: Tamburlaine, the Jew of Malta, and Faustus (Marlow); Orlando (Greene); Hieronimo in Kyd's *Spanish Tragedy*. Although famous for his tragic style, "Roscius for a tongue", he was also a notable musician. In retirement he bought the manor of Dulwich where he settled in 1613 to found "the college of God's Gift" which was incorporated in 1619 (Alleyn publicly reading the deed) and endowed with the freehold of the Fortune Theatre. He remained a philanthropist and patron of the arts. In 1623 he took as his second wife Constance, daughter of John Donne, Dean of St Paul's.

G. L. Hosking, *Life and Times of Edward Alleyn* (1952)

ALLOT, Robert (fl. 1599–1600), editor: edited *England's Parnassus* (1600), a collection of over 2,000 fragments of poetry arranged under subjects from "Albion" to "Youth". Spenser is the most represented poet; Shakespeare is included. The book was published in October 1600, probably in order to compete with the two anthologies appearing earlier in the year under the patronage of Bodenham (q.v.). Allot used the same printer, Nicholas Ling (q.v.) and is the most likely editor of *Wits Theater* (1599), an anthology of moral sayings, anecdotes and epitomes from classical times onwards. Bodenham's name was connected with this collection also.

D. E. L. Crane, (ed.), *England's Parnassus* (1970)

ANDERSON, Edmund (1530–1605), judge: born in Flixborough, Lincolnshire, of Scots descent, educated at Lincoln College, Oxford, and became a member of the Inner Temple. He was knighted in 1582 when he became Lord Chief Justice of Common Pleas. His bullying manner made him feared, especially by the Puritans (whom he detested). He presided over the trials of Babington (1586), Essex (1601) and Ralegh (1603), and in 1602 he won wide respect while on circuit in Somerset for snatching a sword from one of his escort and personally quelling a disturbance. Natural parsimony and shrewd investment enabled him to live sumptuously at Harefield Place, Middlesex, and later at Eyworth, Bedfordshire, where he is buried.

A. L. Rowse, *The England of Elizabeth* (1950)

ANDREWES, Lancelot (1555–1626), bishop and theologian: born in east London, educated at Merchant Taylors' School and Pembroke Hall, Cambridge, of which he was Master from 1589 to 1605. As a prebendary of St Paul's Cathedral he became famous for his preaching during the 1590s, his sermons rejecting the rigid Calvinism of the Puritans in favour of a reasoned Anglicanism with its ceremonial basically Catholic in tradition. Andrewes was Dean of Westminster from 1601 to 1605, when he became successively Bishop of Chichester, Ely (1609) and Winchester (1619). He was a generous benefactor and scholar who knew at least fifteen languages, his writings — like his sermons — playing elegantly with words, in a fashion which appealed to the Jacobean Court. In effect he was general editor of the Authorised Version of the Bible, and he took a prominent part in the Hampton Court Conference of 1604.

Paul Welsby, *Lancelot Andrewes, 1555–1626* (1958)

ANNE OF DENMARK (1574–1619), Queen Consort: born at Skanderborg Castle, the daughter of Frederick II of Denmark and Norway. Her mother, Sophia of Mecklenburg, ensured that she was educated as a tolerantly-minded Lutheran and in later years she showed some sympathy for the Roman Catholics, accepting gifts from Pope Clement VIII. She was married by proxy to James VI of Scotland in 1589, meeting her husband in November of that year in Oslo and accompanying him back to Leith in the following spring. Her first child, Henry (q.v.), was born in February 1594: she had six other children, of whom only Elizabeth and Charles (qq.v.) survived infancy. In June 1603 she followed her husband south to London and was crowned at Westminster with him in July. Her vanity and frivolity aroused criticism, but she took a lively interest in the theatre, becoming patron of Worcester's Men in the winter of 1603–4 and they were then known as Queen Anne's Men until her death. In 1604 Burbage mounted a revival of *Love's Labour's Lost* for her at Southampton House because, as he said, he had "no new play that the Queen has not seen". She was also

Anne of Denmark. Portrait by Van Somer

an enthusiastic patron of a series of masques, written by Ben Jonson and designed by Inigo Jones. The best known of these were the *Masque of Blackness* (1605), the *Masque of Beauty* (1608) and the Candlemas entertainment, *Masque of Queens* (1609). She danced in all these masques. Anne patronised other masque writers, too, notably Samuel Daniel (q.v.). Over political questions, the Queen championed Ralegh, favoured a Spanish mar-

riage for her eldest son, but was strongly opposed to Elizabeth's marriage to the Elector Palatine since she had little liking for the German Protestants. Her relations with her husband were strained. From 1607 onwards they came together only on state occasions. As Bishop Goodman (q.v.) commented, "They did love as well as man and wife could do, not conversing together."

E. C. Williams, *Anne of Denmark* (1970)

ANNESLEY, Cordell (or Cordelia) (?– 1636): daughter of Sir Brian Annesley, a Kentish landowner who had been a Gentleman Pensioner to Queen Elizabeth. In October 1603 Sir Brian's two older daughters, Lady Sandys and Lady Wildgoose, tried to have their father certified insane so as to obtain his estate. Cordell, his youngest daughter, protested against this proposal in a letter to the principal Secretary of State, Sir Robert Cecil, urging, as an alternative, that a guardian should be appointed for her father. On Sir Brian's death the Wildgooses contested his will, but they failed in their attempt to overturn Cordell's interests. In 1608 she became the wife of Sir William Hervey (q.v.), widower of the dowager Countess of Southampton (q.v.). Cordell's story may have given Shakespeare some of his plot for *King Lear*.

ARDEN, Mary (c. 1540–1608) see SHAKESPEARE, Mary.

ARMIN, Robert (c. 1570–1615), writer and comic actor: came from Norfolk, but was apprenticed to a London goldsmith in 1581. He first made a reputation as the author of prefaces, letters and collections of anecdotes (notably *Foole upon Foole, or Six Sortes of Sottes*, published in 1600). He was also a playwright (*The Two Maids of*

Moreclake, 1609, and other plays) and produced a verse adaptation of an Italian story, *Phantasma*, in 1609. Tarlton (q.v.) encouraged him to go on the stage and he was performing at the Globe before 1600. He was originally one of Lord Chandos's Men, but he became established in the Chamberlain's Men between 1599 and 1603, when he is mentioned in the first Royal Patent. He succeeded Kemp (q.v.) as principal clown and is thought to have created Feste, Autolycus, and the Fool in *Lear*, as well as playing Dogberry. There is no mention of his playing any roles after 1610, but his name appears on the First Folio list.

ARMSTRONG, Archibald (or Archie) (?–1672), court jester: came of a Scottish

Archibald Armstrong

family, but was probably born in Arthuret, Cumberland. The tradition that he started life as a sheep-stealer seems doubtful, as he was regular Court Fool to James I from 1603; he was already part of the King's household in Scotland, presumably from a very early age in view of his date of death. Armstrong's jokes were fairly crude and involved horseplay, but he was a favourite of James and became wealthy. The King granted him a pension of two shillings a day from 1611 and a patent to make tobacco pipes in 1618, and he received gifts from many noblemen. James even sent Armstrong to join Prince Charles and the Duke of Buckingham in Spain; his letter to the King, dated 28 April 1623, claims he had more access to the Spanish royal family than the Prince and the Duke; he was "better and more fool than all the fools here". Buckingham had to write the letter, as Armstrong could only make his mark. He kept his position under Charles I, but fell foul of Archbishop Laud; among other jests he is supposed to have said as grace at a banquet "Great praise be given to God and little *laud* to the devil." The Archbishop, a small man, was present. Armstrong was finally dismissed in disgrace in 1637, and retired to Arthuret to transform his wealth into land. He married in 1646 and was buried on 1 April 1672. Armstrong was credited with the authorship of a joke book, the *Banquet of Jests* (1630), many of which are found in earlier works.

John Doran, *History of Court Fools* (1858)

ASPINALL, Alexander (?1546–1624), schoolmaster: a Lancastrian by birth and a graduate of Brasenose College, Oxford (1572–5). He served as Master of Stratford Grammar School from 1582 until his death, living at first in the "Schoolmaster's Chamber" within the gild hall, later in the Old School, where he was a neighbour of

Shakespeare at New Place. In 1594 he married Ann, widow of Ralph Shaw. During their betrothal, Aspinall sent her a pair of gloves with a verse:

> The gift is small
> The will is all
> Alexander Aspinall

A seventeenth-century tradition attributes this simple verse to Shakespeare. Marriage brought Aspinall a substantial interest in the wool trade. In 1602 he became an Alderman of Stratford and in 1613, Deputy Town Clerk, often keeping the Council minutes. Although he came to Stratford too late to teach Shakespeare it is thought he may have inspired Holofernes in *Love's Labour's Lost*.

M. E.
E. I. Fripp, *Shakespeare Studies* (1930)

ASPLEY, William (d. 1640), bookseller: son of William Aspley of Cumberland. He served his apprenticeship in London for nine years from February 1588 and became a freeman of the Stationers' Company in April, 1597. Aspley sold books in London until the year of his death, first at the "Tiger's Head" in St Paul's Churchyard, then at the "Parrott". He published his first book in 1598; *Much Ado About Nothing* and *Henry IV*, part 2 appeared in 1600, published by Aspley together with Andrew Wise (q.v.). Aspley also joined in publishing the First Folio of 1623. He printed plays by other authors, including Chapman and Dekker, and was Master of the Stationers' Company in 1640, dying in office.

AYLMER, John (1521–94), bishop: a member of a Norfolk gentry family, educated at Queen's College, Cambridge, served as tutor to Lady Jane Grey and attracted the attention of Elizabeth for his courteously comprehensive criticism of the Scottish Calvinist, Knox, in a book entitled *An Harbour for True Faithful Subjects* (1559). Aylmer was consecrated Bishop of London in 1577: he was a strict disciplinarian, impartially hard on "papists" and Puritans (notably Cartwright, q.v.; whom he gaoled). He was the father of seven sons and three daughters, and was remembered both for his concern over money matters and for a quarrelsome temper.

B

BACON, Alice (1592–1650), wife of Sir Francis: born Alice Barnham, second daughter of an Alderman and M.P. who died in 1597, leaving each daughter £6,000 and £300 a year in land. Alice was thus a good match for the financially embarrassed Bacon (q.v.), who married her in 1606. The marriage was not very happy; Alice found consolation in her steward, John Underhill, a relative of William Underhill (q.v.) who sold Shakespeare New Place. Bacon does not seem to have resented this conduct until he made the last part of his will in December 1625 and revoked all previous bequests to his wife "for just and great causes". Alice married Underhill in April 1626, eleven days after her husband's death. She was separated from him in 1639 and spent the rest of her life mainly with her mother, who had by then been married four times herself.

D. Du Maurier, *The Winding Stair* (1976)

BACON, Ann (1528–1610): mother of Francis and Anthony Bacon. She was born Ann Cooke, second of the clever daughters of Sir Anthony Cooke of Gidea Hall, Essex (v. *Lady (Mildred) Burghley, Elizabeth Russell*). She accompanied her father to Court when he was tutor of the later Edward VI, and in 1553 became the second wife of Nicholas Bacon, who was a friend of her brother-in-law, William Cecil. She had already served as a companion to Bacon's first wife and looked after her children. Ann lost two daughters in infancy but she was more fortunate with her sons, Anthony (born in 1558) and Francis, two years his junior. She kept up her studies, translating Bishop Jewel's *Apology for the Church of England* from Latin into English in 1564. After her husband's death in 1579, Ann lived in retirement on the family estate at Gorhambury, her peace of mind disturbed by anxiety about her sons. She worried most about Anthony: his health, his religion — for all the Cookes were strong Protestants — and his disreputable friends (especially Essex, q.v.) caused her great pain. Francis was less sickly, but equally worrying; Ann bombarded both her sons with letters of good advice. After the shock of Anthony's death and the Essex conspiracy (1601) she began to fail and became senile some years before she died.

D. Du Maurier, *Golden Lads* (1975)
S. Barnes, "Cookes of Gidea Hall", *Essex Review*, XXI (1912)

BACON, Anthony (1558–1601), spymaster: son of Sir Nicholas Bacon, Queen Elizabeth's Keeper of the Great Seal, and his wife Ann (*supra*), elder brother of Francis (q.v.). Anthony's health was always weak, and the brothers were educated at home until they went together to Trinity College, Cambridge in 1573, and Gray's Inn in 1576. On Sir Nicholas's death (1577) Anthony inherited his estates, but Lady Bacon remained at Gorhambury, the family's chief establishment, for her lifetime. Anthony travelled abroad from the autumn of 1579 to February 1592. He visited Geneva and Italy, but spent most of his time in France and Navarre, whose King, the future Henri IV of France, became his friend. Anthony lived in Montauban from 1585; he enjoyed the friendship of many Huguenots, but made enemies as well. In 1586 they secured his arrest on a charge of sodomy with a page, but Henry of Navarre was able to arrange his release. By this time Anthony's debts were so great that he was forced to stay in Montauban till they were cleared; he moved to Bordeaux in 1590. In this year Sir Francis Walsingham (q.v.) died; Anthony Bacon had been sending him confidential reports on the countries he visited from the first. He now began to employ an agent on his own account, Anthony Standen, (q.v.), whom he helped to free from prison. During his stay in Bordeaux, Bacon also became friendly with the essayist Montaigne and contracted the severe gout from which he continued to suffer. In 1592 he returned to England, in poor health but with useful contacts in France and Spain established. He settled down in a house in Bishopsgate and his manor of Redbourne, Hertfordshire. His companions now consisted mainly of Roman Catholics, some homosexuals, greatly to the disgust of his mother and aunt, Lady Russell; many of them were professional associates in his business of collecting information. Anthony became an M.P. (Wallingford 1593, Oxford 1597) but never appeared in Parliament. His health did not permit much activity and his abilities were not of the public kind. After his brother had introduced him to the Earl of Essex, Anthony transferred his spy network to the Earl's service and moved to Essex House in 1595. For Essex he employed agents in Scotland; his main European operators were Standen and Antonio Perez. The expense of maintaining his agents forced Anthony to sell Redbourne; he lived in Essex House, increasingly ill with gout and stone, during 1599, while Essex went to Ireland and returned in disgrace. In March 1600, all the Earl's followers, including Bacon, were ejected from the house so that Essex might remain alone under arrest. Anthony was now poor. He sold more land and even thought of selling Gorhambury. But he was saved from disgrace at Essex's fall in 1601. Although one of the Earl's most trusted servants, he was not charged or called to give evidence, and his name was

mentioned only once at Essex's trial. This instance was struck from the official record afterwards. Whether his brother Francis's influence or his state of health was responsible is unknown. Anthony Bacon became bedridden during the trial and died soon after. He was buried at St Olave's, Hart Street on 17 May 1601.

D. Du Maurier, *Golden Lads* (1975)

BACON, **Francis** (1561–1626), knighted 1603, created Baron Verulam 1618 and Viscount St Albans 1621), statesman and writer: born at York House

Francis Bacon

in the Strand, London, second son of Ann Bacon (q.v.) and nephew of Burghley. Accompanied his elder brother, Anthony (*supra*) to Trinity College, Cambridge, in 1573 and Gray's Inn (1576). He served as a diplomat in France for three years but was called to the Bar in 1582. He was a member of five Elizabethan Parliaments, representing Melcombe Regis in 1584, Taunton 1586–7, Liverpool, 1589, Middlesex 1593 and Ipswich 1597–8.

From 1592 onwards he was a political ally of Essex (q.v.), but he spoke against a Crown grant in 1593—4 and fell out of favour with the Queen. His hopes of becoming Attorney-General were disappointed (cv. *Coke*) and he failed in his efforts to secure the posts of Solicitor-General or Master of the Rolls. He also failed to gain Elizabeth Hatton (q.v.) as a wife, and in 1598 was arrested for debt. His successes included appointment as a Queen's Counsel in 1596 and the publication of the first ten of his famous *Essays* in 1597. Bacon turned against his former benefactor Essex in 1600—1, helping to prosecute him for his misdemeanours in Ireland, and later writing a pamphlet denouncing the Earl's "practices and treasons". His career flourished under James I: Bacon's *Advancement of Learning* (1605) was dedicated in flattering terms to the King; and in 1607 he at last became Solicitor-General. Marriage in 1606 to Alice Barnham, daughter of a London merchant, improved his financial position, and in 1608 he received the remunerative post of Clerk of the Star Chamber. He was appointed Attorney-General in 1613, prosecuted Somerset (Carr, q.v.) and was Lord Chancellor from 1618 until 1621 when a Parliamentary committee found him guilty on twenty-three counts of corruption. He was fined £40,000 and sent to the Tower: both penalties were remitted by the King, who recognised and admired the great intellect of Bacon. For the last five years of his life Bacon devoted himself to study and writing. His major philosophical work, the *Novum Organum* (on which he was engaged for thirty years) had already been presented to James I in 1620, but Bacon saw it as only the first instalment of a major reassessment of all knowledge, the *Instauratio Magna*, which he never completed. *A History of Henry VII* appeared in 1622 and an ambitious *History of Life and Death* a year later as well as legal

maxims, literary studies and the final and much extended edition of the *Essays* in 1625. Increasingly, Bacon concerned himself with experimental research and an attempt to assess the antiseptic properties of snow cost him his life, for he caught a chill while stuffing a fowl with snow at Highgate in the cold March of 1626, and died on 9 April. He left £22,000 worth of debts. From 1769 onwards claims were made that Bacon was the real author of Shakespeare's plays. Lack of evidence for this assertion prompted the Minnesota congressman Ignatius Donnelly (1835—1901) to publish in 1888 his thousand-page work, *The Great Cryptogram, Francis Bacon's Cipher in the So-Called Shakespeare Plays*. Such speculation obscures the true value of Bacon's scholarship.

F. H. Anderson, *Francis Bacon, his Cipher and his Thought* (1962)
C. Hill, *Intellectual Origins of the English Revolution* (1965)

BACON, Matthias (or Matthew) (fl. 1590—1615): owned the Blackfriars Gatehouse before Henry Walker (q.v.) who sold it to Shakespeare in 1613. Bacon acquired it from his mother, Ann, in 1590, and she inherited it from her mother, Margaret Campion, a relative of Edmund Campion. During this family's ownership the Gatehouse was a refuge for priests and recusants. Father John Gerard (q.v.) is alleged to have sought to use the Gatehouse for the Gunpowder Plotters, but by 1604 Bacon had sold the building to Walker for £100. Bacon retained the title deeds and other documents until 1615 when he was ordered to surrender them after a bill of complaint against him was laid by Shakespeare and others.

E. K. C. *W.S.*

BALES, Peter (1547—?1610), writing master: probably educated at Gloucester

Hall, Oxford. He lived in the Old Bailey district of London, where he taught penmanship and practised miniature writing; he is said to have produced a bible that would fit into a walnut. Bales also worked for Hatton and Walsingham, partly as a decipherer but also in order to forge passages which were added to letters between spies and conspirators, notably in the years of uncertainty which preceded the execution of Mary, Queen of Scots, and the coming of the Spanish Armada. He was employed as a forger again in 1599, to copy incriminating letters from the Earl of Essex (v. *Frances Walsingham*). In 1590 he published *The Writing Schoolmaster* which described his method of shorthand, called "Brachygraphy". This he presented in revised version as *A New Year's Gift for England* in January 1600 (v. also *Timothy Bright, John Willis*). Bales's position as foremost penman in England was confirmed in 1595, when he won a gold pen worth £20 in a contest against his nearest rival.

W. J. Carlton, *Timothe Bright* (1911)

BANCROFT, Richard (1544–1610), archbishop: born at Farnworth, educated at Christ's and Jesus College, Cambridge. Between 1586 and 1597, as a Canon of Westminster, he became well known for his sermons against Puritanism and Presbyterianism. He was consecrated Bishop of London in 1597, where he maintained a vigorous campaign against the Puritan underground press, and was principal spokesman for the bishops in the Hampton Court Conference of 1604, rejecting all Puritan demands for reform in the nature of the episcopate. In 1604 he succeeded Whitgift as Archbishop of Canterbury, subsequently helping to re-establish bishops in Scotland.

Stuart Babbage, *Puritanism and Richard Bancroft* (1962)

BARCLAY, John (1582–1621), satirist: son of William Barclay, Scottish lawyer and writer and his French wife, John Barclay was born at Pont-à-Mousson, Lorraine, where his father was Professor of Civil Law. He went to England in 1603, but soon returned to France and was married in Paris in 1605. In the same year he published the first part of his *Satyricon*, a satirical Latin novel attacking the Jesuits and his father's patron, the Duke of Lorraine; the second part appeared in 1607. Barclay and his wife lived in London again from 1606 to 1616. Here he published *Sylvae*, a collection of Latin poems, (1606) *Apologia* (1611) vindicating *Satyricon*, and *Icon Animorum* (1614), a character sketch of the European nations. Although Barclay's works were proscribed by the Holy Office, he remained a Catholic and decided to settle in Rome from 1616. He obtained a pension from the Pope, tried writing anti-Protestant theology, then devoted the rest of his life to his major work, *Argenis*, published a month before his death in 1621. *Argenis* is a political and historical novel in Latin, in which real characters are disguised under fictitious names.

BARKER, Christopher (c. 1529–99) Queen's Printer: was associated with the Walsingham family at the start of his career, hence the tiger's head on his title pages and in the names of two of his shops: this was part of the Walsingham arms. In 1577 he obtained his first patent as Queen's Printer, entitling him to a monopoly in printing the Bible, the Book of Common Prayer, the Statutes of the Realm and all proclamations. Next year Barker circularised the City companies, offering them copies of the Bible at cheap rates. In 1589 his patent was renewed for his lifetime and that of his son Robert (*infra*). Barker's press was noted for its beautiful productions.

11

BARKER, Robert (1570–1645), royal printer: born near Datchet, Buckinghamshire, son of Christopher Barker (*supra*). He was made a freeman of the Stationers' Company in June 1589 and shared in the Royal Patent until his father's death in 1599, when he became sole patentee. Barker married the daughter of William Day, later Bishop of Winchester, and had a large family: two of his sons were King's Printers after him. He was Master of the Stationers' Company in 1605 and 1606. The most famous product of the royal printing house under Barker was the new translation of the Bible (1611), known as the *Authorized Version*. Barker was supposed to bear the cost of printing the Bible, but was partly financed by others who took a share in the profits of his office as recompense. This led to much litigation, and after 1616, Barker was forced to share his imprint with his backers. He died a debtor in the King's Bench Prison. Barker had inherited a fine printing house from his father, but his own work was spoiled by carelessness.

BARKSTED, William (fl. 1606–29), actor and writer: was associated with the Children of the Revels in 1609, later appearing with Lady Elizabeth's (1611) and Prince Charles's Men (1616). Barksted wrote two poems, *Myrrha* (1607) and *Hiren* (1611) and either collaborated with Marston (q.v.) on the tragedy *The Insatiate Countess* (published 1631) or finished it. *Myrrha* contains a reference to Shakespeare as a greater poet than himself.

BARLOW, William (?–1625), Anglican priest and mathematician: was a son of William Barlow, the extreme Erastian Bishop of Chichester from 1559 to 1569. He was also a nephew of Roger Barlow, who had sailed with Sebastian Cabot to the River Plate and who was much respected as a navigator at Henry VIII's court. The younger William Barlow was educated at Balliol College, Oxford, and became a Prebendary of Winchester in 1581, later holding prebends at Lichfield, Southwell and York before spending his last years as Archdeacon of Salisbury. All four of his sisters married bishops, but Barlow himself was more interested in problems of science and mathematics than in clerical advancement. From his youth, as he said, he "altogether abhorred the sea" but he spent much of his time on improving the construction and use of the marine compass. At Winchester he had his own workmen, who made navigational instruments to his instructions and specifications. He published his theories in 1616 under the title *Magnetical Advertisements concerning the Nature and Property of the Loadstone*. The book was based on work done with William Gilbert (q.v.), whom Mark Ridley (q.v.) accused him of plagiarising, a charge which led to an exchange of polemics between Barlow and Ridley. In 1612 Barlow presented an inclinatory instrument to Prince Henry, to whom he was for seven years a tutor in mathematics.

E. G. R. Taylor, *Mathematical Practitioners of Tudor and Stuart England* (1967)

BARNES, Barnabe (c. 1569–1609), poet: born in Yorkshire, younger son of a Bishop of Durham. He was an undergraduate at Brasenose College, Oxford, in 1586 but took no degree and accompanied Essex (q.v.) to Dieppe in 1591. With the encouragement of Gabriel Harvey (q.v.) Barnes published his first book of poems, *Parthenophil and Parthenophe* (1593), dedicating the book to William Percy, son of the Earl of Northumberland. *Spiritual Sonnets* followed two years later. His anti-papist tragedy *The Devil's Charter*, loosely based on episodes in the life of Pope Alexander VI, was played before James I in

1607. A play by Barnes on the Battle of Hexham — or, less probably, the Battle of Evesham — has disappeared. Barnes was charged with attempted poisoning in 1598 but escaped from prison, returned to the north and was buried at Durham. Campion and Nashe (qq.v.) disliked Barnes and were hostile to his poetry, perhaps because of his friendship with Harvey. Sir Sidney Lee, in the 1890s, thought Barnes was Shakespeare's "rival poet", but he seems an unlikely candidate.

BARNFIELD, Richard (1574–1627), poet: son of Richard Barnfield, gentleman, of Norbury in Shropshire. He was educated at Brasenose College, Oxford (1589–92), although rusticated for a time in 1591. Barnfield was allowed to return to college if he delivered a declamation in hall or paid a fine of 6s 8d. He produced several collections of poems. *The Affectionate Shepherd* (1594) is a series of variations on Vergil, *Eclogues II*, dedicated to Penelope, Lady Rich. In 1595 he published *Cynthia, with certain sonnets* and in 1598 *The Encomion of Lady Pecunia*, a satirical poem on the power of wealth. Two of Barnfield's poems, "If music and sweet poetry agree" and "As it fell upon a day" were long attributed to Shakespeare. Barnfield spent most of his life as a country gentleman on his estate at Stone, Staffordshire. He was a friend of the writers Drayton, Thomas Watson, and Meres (qq.v.).

BARRETT, William (?–1624), bookseller: son of Thomas Barrett, yeoman, of Lincolnshire. He was apprenticed for eight years from 1597 and became a freeman of the Stationers' Company in 1605. Barrett had shops at the "Green Dragon" (1608) and the "Three Pigeons" (1614), both in St Paul's Churchyard. During 1608 he was in partnership with Edward Blount (q.v.). Barrett published Francis Bacon's works, but seems to have specialised in travel books. In 1610 he published an account of the Virginia colony. Barrett acquired the copyright of Shakespeare's *Venus and Adonis* in 1617 and brought out an edition that year. He transferred many of his copyrights to John Parker (q.v.) in 1620.

BARROW (or BARROWE), Henry (c. 1550–93), Puritan separatist: born in Shipdam, Norfolk, a distant kinsman of Francis Bacon. He was educated at Clare Hall, Cambridge, becoming a member of Gray's Inn in 1576. Barrow experienced a dramatic conversion, at the age of thirty, while "walking in Lord's Day". Thereafter, he abandoned his gambling and other "profligate ways", becoming an extreme Protestant who was critical of Calvin and his fellow Congregationalist, Browne (q.v.), as well as of kings, bishops and the priesthood. Barrow was detained, under suspicion of spreading seditious views, while visiting his colleague, John Greenwood, in the Fleet Prison in October 1586. He was examined on at least five occasions, his interlocutors including Archbishop Whitgift, Bishop Aylmer and Burghley, (before whom Barrow appeared on the day the Spanish Armada was first sighted off the Scilly Isles). There seems to have been some reluctance to act against a determined Protestant at such a time of Catholic menace. While he was in detention, two important works by Barrow *A True Description of the Visible Congregation of the Saints*, 1589, and *A Brief Discovery of the False Church*, 1590, were printed in Amsterdam. He was charged with encouraging the circulation of seditious literature in March 1593 and, together with Greenwood, hanged a month later.

R. W. Dale, *History of English Congregationalism* (1907)

BARTON, Richard (fl. 1584–1601), Vicar of Stratford-upon-Avon: came from

13

Coventry and served as Vicar in Stratford, 1584−9. A Puritan survey described him as "a preacher, learned, zealous and godly". He baptised Shakespeare's children, Hamnet and Judith, on Candlemas 1585. The local community seem to have thought highly of Barton, for he received several gifts from the Corporation and he was invited back in 1597 and 1601 to preach special sermons.

M. E.

BASSE, William (?1583−?1653), poet: came from Moreton, Oxfordshire. He probably served Lord Norris, later Earl of Berkshire, and lived in his house at Rycote, eight miles from Oxford. In 1602 Basse published two long poems, *Sword and Buckler* and *Three Pastoral Elegies of Anander, Anetor and Muridella*, and in 1613 an elegy on Prince Henry, *Great Britain's Sunset, bewailed with a Shower of Tears*. Few of Basse's shorter poems were printed apart from his *Angler's Song*, praised by Izaak Walton and included in the *Compleat Angler* (1653). Basse is best known for his *Epitaph on Shakespeare*, printed with Donne's poems in 1633 and thought then to be by Donne. The poem appeared again in the second edition of Shakespeare's Sonnets (1640), signed "W.B.". Basse must have written it before 1623, as his suggestion that Beaumont, Chaucer and Spenser should move up in their tombs in Westminster Abbey so as to make room for Shakespeare is gently mocked by Jonson's eulogy in the First Folio.

BASTARD, Thomas (1566−1618), cleric and satirist: born at Blandford, Dorset, and educated at Winchester and New College, Oxford (1586). While at Oxford Bastard contributed to memorial volumes on Sir Philip Sidney (q.v.) and Anne, Countess of Oxford (Burghley's daughter). He was made perpetual Fellow of New College in 1588, but deprived of his Fellowship in 1590/1 for "libelling". Bastard eventually became chaplain to Thomas Howard, Earl of Suffolk (q.v.) who provided him with the livings of Bere Regis and Hamer. In 1598 he published *Chrestoleros, Seven Books of Epigrams*, Bastard's writing is very bitter, and his life was hard. He had a small income, a large family, and (apparently) an improvident wife. He died in a debtors' prison at Dorchester.

BAYNHAM (or BAINHAM), Edmund (1577−post 1642), conspirator: son of William Baynham of Kent. He may have been educated at Balliol College, Oxford (1594−6) and certainly entered the Middle Temple in 1596. Baynham was a follower of Essex, spent some time in Ireland, and was knighted by the Earl just before his return. He became notorious in London as one of the leaders of a drunken riot which began at the Mermaid Tavern, Bread Street on the night of 18 March 1600, and ended with the arrest of Baynham and his friends after a pitched battle with the watch, some of whom were severely wounded, in St Paul's Churchyard. The case came to Star Chamber and Baynham was fined £200. Next year he was arrested again for joining in Essex's rebellion, and this time condemned to death, but pardoned by the end of the year, largely at the intercession of Ralegh. Ralegh's steward and Baynham's brother-in-law were granted the administration of his confiscated estates; some lands were sold and the rest restored to Baynham by 1602. Ralegh was said to have been well rewarded for his help. Baynham now proclaimed himself a Roman Catholic and an opponent of James' succession to the English throne. He was imprisoned in the Marshalsea for a time in 1603 and after his release was often in the company of the Gunpowder conspirators. In July 1605 Father Garnett (q.v.) suggested that a letter should be sent to ask advice from the Pope, and Baynham was chosen as the messenger. Whether by intention or design, Baynham did not arrive in Rome until the end of October 1605, too late for the Pope's views to affect the execution of the Gunpowder Plot. He lingered in Rome and was not tried with the other conspirators, although mentioned frequently at the trial as one of the "damned crew", the anti-government hooligans who made London's night life hideous. Baynham never returned to England, but wandered about in Spain and the Low Countries, often passing as an Italian or a Frenchman. In 1608 he killed his opponent in a duel that arose from an argument over the Gunpowder Plot. He was still alive and in Rome again in 1642.

S. E. Sprott, "Sir Edmund Baynham" *Recusant History*, 10 (1969–70)

BEAUMONT, Francis (1584–1616), dramatist: third son of Justice Beaumont of Grace Dieu Priory, Leicestershire. He entered Broadgates Hall, Oxford (1587) but did not take his degree and was admitted to the Inner Temple (1600). Poems, which were published posthumously, and a comic lecture for the Inner Temple Christmas Revels were followed by a comedy, *The Woman Hater*, written for Paul's Boys about 1606. His most famous comedy, *The Knight of the Burning Pestle*, was produced in 1607. In that same year he and John Fletcher (q.v.) both wrote commendatory verses for Jonson's *Volpone*, and the Beaumont-Fletcher collaboration began soon afterwards. Together they wrote at least seven plays for the Revels and Lady Elizabeth's Companies, tragi-comedies like *Philaster* and *The Maid's Tragedy*. In about 1613 he married an heiress, Ursula Isley, and seems thereafter to have stopped writing drama. The later plays attributed to the partnership are now believed to have been written either by Fletcher alone, or in collaboration with others. Beaumont wrote the Inner Temple and Gray's Inn masque for Princess Elizabeth's wedding (20 February 1613). He died on 6 March 1616, and was buried in Westminster Abbey.

E. K. C., *E.S.*

BEDFORD, Francis Russell, fourth Earl of Bedford (1593–1641): son of William, Lord Russell of Thornhaugh (q.v.) and grandson of the second Earl. Russell served with his father in Ireland in his youth, and was knighted in 1607. In 1609 he married Catherine Brydges, daughter of Lord Chandos. He succeeded his father in 1613 and his cousin as Earl of Bedford (1627), and was Lord Lieutenant of Devon from 1623 to his death. As Earl of Bedford he owned large estates in the Fen country. An Act of Parliament for "the recovering . . . of the Marshes" had been passed in 1600, but Bedford was the first of the landowners to begin draining the Fens on a large scale, in 1630. The resulting farmland is called the "Bedford Level". Bedford was also responsible for the first square in London, planned like an Italian piazza by Inigo Jones (q.v.) on the Bedford land in Covent Garden. Although he inclined to the Parliamentary side against Charles I, Bedford tried to save the life of Strafford and compromise with the King. He died of smallpox.

BEDFORD, Lucy, Countess of (1580/1 –1627), patron of poets: daughter of John, first Lord Harington of Exton, and his wife Anne (Kelway) who was a considerable heiress. Lucy was a distant cousin of Sir Philip Sidney. On 12 December 1594, she married Edward Russell, third Earl of Bedford, who had succeeded his grandfather in 1585. The marriage, possibly in conjunction with that of Lord

Derby and Elizabeth Vere (qq.v.), has been considered a likely occasion for the first performance of Shakespeare's *Midsummer Night's Dream*. When Lucy was three, Claude Desainliens (or Holyband, who may have been her tutor) dedicated to her his *Campo di Fior*, a manual of Latin, French, English and Italian. In later years

Lucy, Countess of Bedford

she was reckoned learned and could read and speak French, Italian and Spanish. All her life Lucy Bedford was a patron of the arts: Drayton, who was "bequeathed to her service" by his first patron Sir Henry Goodere, dedicated poems to her from 1594 to 1597; some jealousy of a rival poet estranged him from her after 1606. She was patron also of John Florio, Samuel Daniel, Ben Jonson and John Donne (to whom she once gave £30 to discharge his debts), and she was able to take "her" poets, Jonson and Daniel, with her into the Court of James I. Lucy was in favour from the beginning of the new reign, being reckoned the most beautiful of Queen Anne's ladies and appearing in many Court masques. From 1620 onwards the illness of the Earl of Bedford enabled his wife to control the Russell political interest, generally in opposition to the Buckingham faction. She was a member of the Virginia Company and served on its Council. She was also a regular correspondent, and thus an adviser on English political affairs, to the former Princess Elizabeth (q.v.) after she became titular Queen of Bohemia. The Earl and Countess had no surviving children, and both died in the same year, at Moor Park, Hertfordshire.

B. H. Newdigate, *Drayton and his Circle* (1961)

BEESTON, Christopher (alias Hutchinson) (?–1638) actor and theatre manager: started as a servant to Phillips (q.v.) in the Lord Chamberlain's Company. In 1602 he joined Worcester's Men, later Queen Anne's, and he remained connected with them until the Queen's death in 1619. He contributed verses to Heywood's *Apology for Actors*, published in 1612. By 1617 he had acquired the Cockpit, in Drury Lane, and remodelled it so as to form a new theatre, the Phoenix. Both Beeston's house and the Phoenix were vandalised in a riot of apprentices on Shrove Tuesday, 4 March 1617. Beeston nevertheless continued to manage the Phoenix successfully: from 1622 onwards he presented the Lady Elizabeth's Men, Queen Henrietta's Men, and finally his own children's company, "Beeston's Boys". He grew wealthy at the expense of his actors. His son, William Beeston (who lived in Shoreditch until his death in 1682) told the antiquarian, John Aubrey, that Shakespeare had been a schoolmaster before he became an actor.

E. K. C., *E.S.*
G.E.B.

BELOTT, Stephen (fl. 1602–13), London tiremaker: son of a French widow who later married a king's trumpeter, Humphrey Fludd. Belott was bound apprentice by Fludd to the tiremaker, Christopher Mountjoy (q.v.), in whose house Shakespeare lodged in 1604. During this year Belott, by now working for a salary, courted the Mountjoy's daughter, Mary, Shakespeare acted as a matchmaker and persuaded Belott to the marriage, which took place on 19 November 1604 in St Olave's Church, Silver Street. The Belotts established their own tiremaking business but moved back to Mountjoy's house after his wife died in 1606. They left again after arguments between Belott and his father-in-law and in 1612 Belott sued Mountjoy for the residue of Mary's marriage portion. Shakespeare was a witness in this suit (for details, v. *Mountjoy*).

S. S.

BENFIELD, Robert (?–?1649), actor: a member of Lady Elizabeth's Company in 1613. By 1616 he had joined the King's Men, replacing Ostler (q.v.) as Antonio in *The Duchess of Malfi* between 1619 and 1623. He specialised in dignified roles, playing kings and old men; and he stayed with the King's Company until its end, being listed in the First Folio. He petitioned for a share in the profits, 1635.

E. K. C., *E.S.*
G. E. B.

BERKELEY, Thomas (1575–1611), courtier: son of Henry, Lord Berkeley and his wife Catherine (Howard). Berkeley was educated at Magdalen College, Oxford (1590) and Gray's Inn (1598). He suffered a fall in youth which left his head and neck awry, and at Oxford he contracted a recurring fever. On 19 February 1596 Berkeley married Elizabeth Carey, daughter of Sir George Carey and granddaughter of the Lord Chamberlain, Lord Hunsdon (qq.v.). Their wedding has been con-

sidered a possible occasion for the first performance of Shakespeare's *Midsummer Night's Dream* at the Lord Chamberlain's house in Blackfriars. Berkeley was one of the courtiers who brought James I the official news of Queen Elizabeth's death. James made him a Knight of the Bath and he was M.P. for Gloucestershire from 1604 till his death. Berkeley was so extravagant that he overspent the annual income of his wife and himself by £1,500 a year; in 1609 they signed a detailed agreement to economise, listing the number of horses and servants they could afford. Berkeley was too fond of foreign travel to save much. He was in Europe for long periods in 1600, 1608 and 1610, and died shortly after his last journey abroad, leaving many debts.

John Smythe, *Lives of the Berkeleys* (1883 edition)

BERTIE, Peregrine (1555–1601) see WILLOUGHBY, Lord.

BLOUNT, Charles (1563–1606) see MOUNTJOY, Charles, Lord.

BLOUNT, Christopher (1556–1601), soldier: born at Kidderminster, Worcestershire, the younger son of Thomas Blount, a member of the Catholic gentry, conforming as a recusant. Christopher was educated at Hart Hall, Oxford, served as Master of the Horse to Leicester in the Netherlands, and appears to have acted as an agent in ferreting out the Babington conspiracy and the role therein of Mary, Queen of Scots. He was knighted in the winter of 1587–8. Within a few weeks of Leicester's death in 1588, Blount married his widow, Lettice (Countess of Leicester, q.v.). She had originally been married to the first Earl of Essex and Blount thus became stepfather to the second Earl, the Queen's favourite. This second Earl of Essex (q.v.) materially assisted his stepfather, securing his return as Member for the county of Staffordshire in the Parliament of 1593. Sir Christopher served as Colonel of Land Forces on the expedition of Essex to Cadiz in 1596 and was Master of the Field for Essex's army in Ireland in 1599, identifying himself thereafter closely with his step-son's cause. He was heavily involved in the conspiracy and revolt of Essex on 7-8 January 1601 and was subsequently charged with treason and executed. Sir Christopher Blount was a distant kinsman of Essex's successor in Ireland, Lord Mountjoy (q.v.), who was born Charles Blount. The two men were not brothers, as has sometimes been stated.

A. J. Perret in *Transactions of the Worcestershire Archaeological Society* for 1942.

BLOUNT, Edward (?–1632), printer and bookseller: apprenticed to William Ponsonby for ten years from 1578 and became a freeman of the Stationers' Company in 1588. His shops were at the north door of St Paul's and the "Black Bear", St Paul's Churchyard. Blount had a good reputation and showed consideration to his authors; he particularly admired Marlowe, as apparent in his preface to *Hero and Leander* (1598). In 1608 Blount took a partner, William Barrett (q.v.) and registered Shakespeare's *Pericles* and *Anthony and Cleopatra* for publication, but the plays were never printed by him. However, he was associated in the production of the First Folio in 1623. Blount regarded printer's errors as inevitable in his books, but apologised for them. In his Preface to John Earle's *Microcosmographie* (1628) he wrote "If any faults have escaped the press (as few books can be printed without) impose them not on the author, I entreat thee, but rather impute them to mine and the printer's oversight."

BODENHAM (or BODNAM), John (1558/9–1610), anthologist: the son of a London grocer, educated at Merchant Taylors' School from 1570, and made freeman of the Grocers' Company in 1580. His father left him comfortably off, and he became a patron of literature. Bodenham was originally thought to have edited four anthologies, but is now regarded as the inspiration behind them. *Politeuphuia, Wits Commonwealth* (1597) was edited by the printer, Nicholas Ling and dedicated to Bodenham. *Wits Theater* (1599), also dedicated to Bodenham, was probably edited by Allot, (q.v.) who signed the dedication in one copy. *Belvedere or the Garden of the Muses* (1600) lists Shakespeare among the contributors, but quotes only a little of *Romeo and Juliet*, Act II. The most likely editor for this work is Antony Munday (q.v.). *England's Helicon* (1600) edited by "L. N." (possibly Ling again) has been considered the best contemporary collection of Elizabethan lyric poetry. Bodenham was certainly patron of all four books.

H. C. Rollins, ed., *England's Helicon* (1935)

BODLEY, Sir Thomas (1545–1613), diplomat and bibliophile: born at Exeter, spending much of his childhood at Geneva in order to escape the Marian persecution. He entered Magdalen College, Oxford at the age of thirteen, and became a Junior Fellow of Merton in 1564, lecturing on Greek and Hebrew. His linguistic proficiency led the Queen to employ him as confidential envoy, principally in Denmark and France in the period 1576–87, and he was ambassador in the Netherlands, 1589–96. In 1598 the University of Oxford accepted his offer to restore the fifteenth-century library. In seven years the library trebled in size, partly through his purchases and partly through his powers of persuading his friends to act as benefactors. He was knighted by James I in 1603. Bodley's prejudices reflected early years as a Marian exile in Calvin's Geneva; he was hostile to any "Romish" works and he disliked all printed plays. His library thus strengthened the influence of the Copernican and

Sir Thomas Bodley

Paracelsan scientific revolutions in a conservatively-minded university. Bodley gained from the Stationers' Company in 1610 the right to receive a gift copy of every book they printed, thereby making the University a nucleus for the first national library in England. His considerable personal fortune was left to the University library, partly to purchase books and partly to build the quadrangle which has, ever since, formed the centre of the "Bodleian Library".

BONIAN, Richard (fl. 1598–1611), bookseller: was the son of Richard Bonyon, of Hayes, Middlesex. He was first apprenticed to a printer, Richard Watkins, for eight years from Christmas 1598, but Watkins died next year, so Bonian transferred to Simon Waterson for eight

years and a half. He became a freeman of the Stationers' Company in August, 1607, and from then till 1611 sold books in London at three different shops: the "Spread Eagle", near the north door of St Paul's, 1607–10, the "Red Lion" on London Bridge, 1609 and the "Fleure de Luce and Crown" in Paul's Churchyard, 1611. Bonian and Henry Walley (q.v.) together published the First Quarto of *Troilus and Cressida* in 1609; two editions were issued during the year. The title-page of the first edition attributes the play to Shakespeare and states that it was performed by the King's Men at the Globe, whereas the Preface to the second edition proclaims *Troilus* a new and unperformed play.

BOTT, William (fl. 1560–7), resident of Stratford: was occupying New Place as a tenant in 1560 when the owner, William Clopton, died. The heir, William Clopton (q.v.) wished to raise money on the property; Bott therefore acquired the title to New Place in 1563. A year later Clopton unsuccessfully sued Bott in Star Chamber for fraud. Rumour in the town maintained that Bott had poisoned his own daughter, Isabella, a month after her marriage to John Harper in order to acquire land from the Harper family. Feeling ran high against Bott who, in 1565, was expelled from the office of Alderman for declaring that his fellow civic dignitaries were all dishonest. Two years later he sold New Place to William Underhill (q.v.) whose son sold it to Shakespeare. Bott seems to have disappeared from Stratford after 1567, leaving behind him an unsavoury reputation. A witness in the Star Chamber action of 1564 summed up his character by declaring, "If Bott had had his right, he had been hanged long ago."

M. E.

19

BOWES, Jerome (c. 1550–1616), ambassador: probably born in County Durham. He was present at Court in the middle of the 1570s. In April 1577 he is known to have made representations to the Queen "touching on plays" and in the following August was temporarily banished from Court, allegedly for having slandered Leicester (q.v.). In 1583 he was knighted and sent on a special embassy to Russia with the double objectives of urging peace between Russia and Sweden and confirming the trade monopoly for English vessels using northern Russian ports — privileges already accorded to the Muscovy Company were being eroded by Dutch and French traders. Bowes, a giant of a man, "three storeys high" (as a contemporary said), sought to overawe the Court of Ivan the Terrible by a show of fearless arrogance. He achieved nothing, however, by the time of Ivan's death (March 1584) and was imprisoned by the new Tsar, Feodor Ivanovich. Threats of a terrible vengeance induced Feodor to release Bowes, who returned home to find himself a popular hero. Tales of Bowes's national pride lingered long after his death; they were recorded, with embellishments, by Pepys in his diary as late as September 1662. He founded a company for the manufacture of drinking glasses, using (from 1597) a specially constructed warehouse, which appears to have been in the crypt of St Anne's Church, Blackfriars. He was M.P. for Lancaster in the Parliament of 1601. In January 1602 the Queen appointed him personal escort to a Russian ambassador, Gregory Mikulin, who attended the Court festivities on Twelfth Night. A month later there was widespread interest taken in London at news of a robbery at his Charing Cross home in which his personal servant was murdered. Sir Jerome represented Reading in the first Parliament of King James, 1604–11.

L. Hotson, *The First Night of Twelfth Night* (1948)

BOWES, Robert (1535–97), ambassador: born at Aske, Yorkshire, serving for many years in the defence of the Scottish border, under his father, Sir Richard Bowes. He served in the Commons as M.P. for Knaresborough in 1563 and 1566, for Appleby in Westmorland in 1586–7, and for Cumberland in 1589. His principle service was as ambassador in Scotland during the difficult years, 1577–83. He remained one of the Queen's closest contacts with James VI through the 1590s when he was Treasurer of Berwick.

BOYLE, Richard (1566–1643, created Earl of Cork in 1620), Anglo-Irish landowner: born in Canterbury, educated at King's School there and at Bennet's College, Cambridge. He was subsequently admitted to the Middle Temple but was forced to leave through poverty, becoming an adventurer and land-grabber in Ireland in 1588. Marriage to an heiress in 1595 enabled him to purchase large estates in Munster, but his fortunes suffered a setback with the Irish revolt in 1598. Queen Elizabeth encouraged him to assist in the restoration of order and he acquired Ralegh's Irish lands at a cheap price. He was knighted in 1603 and for the following forty years successfully built up the Protestant ascendancy in Munster, winning the backing of Buckingham who was largely responsible for his elevation to the peerage. He improved communications, founding harbours and small towns, many of which he fortified for the first time. His estates provided work for 4,000 people, and he made a steady fortune from his ironworks, ruling with such natural grandeur that people automatically called him "the great Earl". He was virtual ruler of Ireland from 1629 to 1633 but his methods were called in question by Thomas Wentworth as Lord Deputy, a conflict won ultimately by the Earl. Among his thirteen children was the famous chemist and physicist, Robert Boyle (1627–91).

BRADFORD, William (1590–1656), "Pilgrim Father": born at Ansterfield, near Doncaster, and became associated with a group of Puritan separatists who emigrated from the Midlands and East Anglia to Amsterdam in 1608, soon settling at Leyden. In 1620 the Leyden refugees crossed back to England and were joined by other separatists from London and Southampton before sailing from Plymouth, Devon, in the *Mayflower*, (16 September 1620) anchoring off Cape Cod after a rough voyage of sixty-six days. Bradford served as Governor of the new "pilgrim" colony in New England from 1621 until his death, apart from an interlude of a few weeks. He showed great skill in handling relations with the merchants who had invested in the *Mayflower* undertaking (v. *Edwin Sandys*) as well as in establishing good relations with the Indians. Bradford's narrative of the early years of the colony is an historical document of great importance.

C. M. Andrews, *The Colonial Period in American History*, I (1934)
S. E. Morison, ed., *William Bradford's Of Plymouth Plantation* (1952)

BRADLEY, Gilbert (fl. 1561–5), glover of Stratford: lived in Henley Street (in what is now the Public Library) three houses away from the Shakespeare family. He was a burgess, 1565, and may have been Gilbert Shakespeare's godfather a year later.

M. E.

BREND, Matthew (1598/9–?), gentleman: son of Sir Nicholas Brend (*infra*), original lessor of the Globe site. Matthew

was less than two years old when he succeeded his father. His original trustee, Collett, was bought out by Sir John Bodley who, in October 1613, granted a new lease of the Globe, which had recently been burned down and was being rebuilt at the time. The revised terms extended the lease from 1629 to 1635. In February 1614 Matthew Brend and his mother received a deputation of Heminges, Condell and the two Burbages (qq.v.) and signed a promise to extend the lease to 1644 when he came of age. In 1624, however, Sir Matthew settled the land on his wife and sought to repudiate his promise but was held to it by the Court of Requests in 1633. When Brend finally regained possession of the site, two years after the formal closing of the theatres, he ordered the Globe to be pulled down (15 April 1644).

E. K. C., *E.S.*
G. E. B.

BREND, Sir Nicholas (?–1600), lawyer and gentleman: was the son of Sir Thomas Brend of West Molesey, and became a member of the Inner Temple. His father had disinherited him for a secret marriage, but by 1598 he had come into his inheritance. His properties included land on the Bankside, south of Maiden Lane (now Park Street) which Brend leased to the Burbages (qq.v.) for their new theatre, the Globe. The lease, which was signed on 21 February 1599, ran for thirty-one years from Christmas 1598, at an annual rent of £14-10s., £7-5s for each of the half shares. Before he died in the autumn of 1600 Brend had transferred his estate to his baby son, Matthew (*supra*), and a trustee, John Collett.

C. W. Wallace, *Nebraska University Studies*, X (1910)

BRETCHGIRDLE, John (fl. 1561–5), Vicar of Stratford: educated at Christ

Church, Oxford (B.A., 1545, M.A., 1547), Curate of Witton in Cheshire, serving as Master of the School there. He became Vicar at Stratford in January 1561, remaining there until his death in 1565. One of Bretchgirdle's Witton pupils, John Brownsword (q.v.), followed him to Stratford as Schoolmaster. Bretchgirdle left an extensive library, much of it to the Smith family (cf. *William Smith*) and he bequeathed a Latin-English dictionary to Stratford school. Bretchgirdle baptised Shakespeare.

M.E.

E. I. Fripp, *Shakespeare Studies* (1930)

BRETON, Nicholas (?1545–?1626), poet, essayist: son of William Breton, a London merchant; the Bretons were originally an old Essex family. William Breton died in 1559 and left his family well provided for, but by 1568 his widow had married the poet George Gascoigne who spent most of the inheritance. Breton is said to have been at Oriel College, Oxford, but there is no record of this. By 1577 he was living in Holborn. He became one of the writers patronised by the Countess of Pembroke (q.v.). Breton had a ready pen, he produced works in verse and prose — religious, romantic, pastoral and gently satirical. His best known lyrics are in *England's Helicon* (1600) and his own collection, *The Passionate Shepheard* (c. 1604). He was the first writer after Sir Thomas Overbury (q.v.) to produce essays on characters, a type of work which became very popular. Breton published two such collections: *Characters upon Essays Moral and Divine* (1615) and *The Good and the Bad* (1616). In 1593 he was married to Alice Sutton and was father to two sons and two daughters.

BRIGGS, Henry (1561–1630), mathematician: born near Halifax, Yorkshire and educated at St John's College, Cambridge

(B.A., 1581). From 1596 to 1620 he was Professor of Astronomy at Gresham College, London. In 1602 he published a *Table to find the height of the Pole* but his main work was the simplifying of the logarithms of Napier (q.v.). Briggs had lectured on Napier's work, and in 1615 he spent a month with Napier in Edinburgh. Together they agreed on the revised system, and in 1617 Briggs published his first 1,000 new logarithms, based on Napier's but more convenient to use, and in 1624 he produced *Arithmetica Logarithmica* containing 30,000 more. The table of his logarithms published after his death in *Trigonometrica Britannica* (1633) was employed for 200 years. Briggs also wrote works on astronomy and navigation; from 1619 he was Savilian Professor of Astronomy at Oxford University and Fellow of Merton College; he died in Oxford.

E. G. R. Taylor, *Mathematical Practitioners of Tudor and Stuart England* (1967)

BRIGHT, Timothy (1550/1–1615), physician, clergyman, inventor of shorthand: born in Cambridge and educated there at Trinity College (1561–8). He was studying in Paris in 1572 and escaped the massacre of St Bartholomew's Day, finding shelter in Walsingham's house. He then returned to Cambridge, took his medical degrees, married, and began to practise medicine. A treatise on preserving health, *Hygieina* (1582) was followed by one on restoring health, *Therapeutica* (1583). By 1585 he had become a physician at St Bartholomew's Hospital, Smithfield, largely owing to Walsingham's influence. Here he produced his *Treatise of Melancholy* (1586), in which he distinguishes between the mental and physical causes of sorrow. Shakespeare is thought to have used the book and may even have derived from it the phrase "discourse of reason" for Hamlet's first soliloquy. About the same time

Bright invented his shorthand system; he offered to teach it to Robert Cecil, sending the Cecils' secretary, Hickes, Paul's *Epistle to Titus* in shorthand. By 1588 he had a royal patent for his system and published a book, *Characterie*, in which he described his revised method. Bright's shorthand, though justly acclaimed as the first system devised in Britain, was cumbersome; it involved the use of alphabetic symbols with different terminations representing 537 words while an elaborate table of synonyms was intended to supply other words; and it had to be written vertically, from top to bottom of a page, rather than horizontally. Peter Bales (q.v.) and John Willis (q.v.) soon challenged Bright's *Characterie* system. Bright's shorthand studies and his *Epitome of Foxe's Book of Martyrs* absorbed so much of his time that in 1591 he was dismissed from St Bartholomew's Hospital, after repeated warnings, for neglecting the care of the poor. Already Walsingham's patronage had brought him the curacy of Christ Church, Newgate, and he was now presented to the livings of Methley (1591) and Barwick-in-Elmet (1594) in the West Riding of Yorkshire. Disputes with his parishioners at Methley led to his being summoned before the Ecclesiastical Commission; he was ordered to contribute to the relief of the parish poor and to repair his parsonage. By 1615 he had left Yorkshire, moving to Shrewsbury where he lived with his brother William, Curate of St Mary's Church. Here he died and was buried in St Mary's.

W. J. Carlton, *Timothe Bright* (1911)

BROOKE, Christopher (?–1628), poet: son of Robert Brooke, twice Lord Mayor of York. He may have gone to Trinity College, Cambridge, like his brother Samuel (q.v.), and was certainly a member of Lincoln's Inn in the 1590s. There he became a great friend of John Donne, with whom he shared lodgings. Donne addressed two verse letters to Brooke, and Brooke left Donne his portrait of the Countess of Southampton in his will. Brooke also witnessed Donne's secret marriage, in 1601; both brothers were afterwards imprisoned with Donne. In 1614 Christopher Brooke became a Bencher of Lincoln's Inn. Three of his poems were published in the same year, *Eclogue*, *Ghost of Richard III*, and *Epithalamium*. He also wrote an elegy for Henry, Prince of Wales (1613) and another for the funeral of Sir Arthur Chichester (1624) as well as sharing in the general revival of pastoral poetry, particularly associated with Wither and William Browne (qq.v.). He was six times M.P. for York between 1604 and 1624. His friends included the poets John Davies of Hereford, Drayton and Jonson.

BROOKE, George (1568–1603), conspirator: a younger son of the tenth Lord Cobham. He was educated at King's College, Cambridge. In the winter of 1602–3 he believed Queen Elizabeth promised him the Mastership of St Cross at Winchester. On the Queen's death the post was conferred by James I on one of his favourites. In disappointment, George Brooke plotted with Lord Grey of Wilton (q.v.) to seize the King and induce him to change his council, appointing to it men more sympathetically inclined towards the Roman Catholics. Brooke hoped he would himself become Lord Treasurer. Knowledge of the plot reached Robert Cecil (q.v.), Brooke's brother-in-law. Brooke was arrested in July 1603, imprisoned in the Tower and subsequently executed at Winchester. Investigation of this so-called "Bye Plot" produced evidence of a further conspiracy in which his elder brother Henry (*infra*), was heavily involved.

BROOKE, Henry, Lord Cobham (1564–1619), Lord Warden of the Cinque Ports, and conspirator: was the eldest son of the Kentish landowner, William Brooke, tenth Baron Cobham, who was Lord Warden of the Cinque Ports and Lord Chamberlain in the early 1590s. The Brookes were descended from the Lollard rebel, Sir John Oldcastle, (alias "the good Lord Cobham") who was executed in 1414 and regarded by the Puritans as an early Protestant martyr. Shakespeare's representation of Sir John Oldcastle as the boisterous and craven companion of Prince Hal in *Henry IV* led to complaints at Court, either by the tenth Lord Cobham or by his son, Henry, who succeeded to the title in 1597; and Shakespeare substituted Falstaff for Oldcastle in the play. For the last six years of Elizabeth's reign, Henry Brooke (the eleventh Baron) was much in favour at Court, enjoying influence through the support of his brother-in-law, Robert Cecil (q.v.), and being treated as a personal enemy by Essex (q.v.), whom he had defeated in a contest for succession to the Lord Wardenship on his father's death. Soon afterwards Cobham married the widowed Lady Kildare (q.v.). When not in Kent they lived in Blackfriars, close to the theatre. Cobham, unlike his brother-in-law, was not prepared to welcome James's succession. In the summer of 1603 he was arrested after the discovery of the so-called "Bye Plot", concocted by his brother, George (*supra*). Cobham under interrogation admitted he had discussed with Ralegh (q.v.) and with the Spanish ambassador a plan for placing Arbella Stuart (q.v.) on the throne in place of James I. For this conspiracy Cobham was sentenced to death, but he was reprieved on the scaffold in December 1603 and imprisoned in the Tower as an attainted traitor for the following fourteen years, his wife deserting him from loyalty to the new dynasty. In 1617 Cobham was allowed to leave the Tower in order to take the waters at Bath but he collapsed soon afterwards, lingering in broken health until January 1619.

BROOKE, Samuel (c. 1574–1631), Anglican priest: born in York, and was brother to the poet, Christopher Brooke (q.v.). Samuel went up to Trinity College, Cambridge (1592–5). Like Christopher, he was a friend of John Donne (q.v.) and was briefly imprisoned in 1601 for having officiated at Donne's secret marriage. Later he became a royal chaplain under both James I and Charles I, and Master of Trinity for the last two years of his life. Between 1613 and 1615 he wrote three plays for his college: the first two were performed before Prince Charles and the Elector Palatine, the third before James I. Brooke was also Professor of Divinity at Gresham College in London from 1612 to 1629.

BROWNE, Robert (c. 1550–1633), Puritan writer and preacher, a distant cousin of Burghley: born at Tolethorpe, Rutland, and educated at Corpus Christi College, Cambridge. By 1580 Browne was head of an austerely Protestant congregation in Norwich. These religious separatists — familiarly known as "Brownists" — denied episcopacy, Presbyterianism and ordination. Browne's schismatic views and hot temper led to his imprisonment but, through Burghley's intervention, he was freed and allowed to emigrate to Holland, later crossing back to Scotland. After a formal reconciliation with the Church of England he came to London. He was Master of St Olave's School, Southwark, from 1586 to 1591 when he was ordained by the Bishop of Peterborough and served as Rector of Achurch, Northamptonshire, until his death. The violence of his language and temper led to occasional imprisonment, and he died in Northampton Gaol. The Brownists were subsequently called "Congregationalists".

R. W. Dale, *History of English Congregationalism* (1907)

BROWNE, Robert (fl. 1583–1620), actor: known to have acted with Worcester's Men in 1583 and Derby's Men in 1599–1601, but spent most of his career on the Continent. He toured Holland, although he was best known in Germany where he played in most years between 1590 and 1607, appearing at the Frankfurt Fair and at Court in Cassel under the patronage of the Landgrave. At Frankfurt in 1592 Browne's company performed *Gammer Gurton's Needle* and plays by Marlowe. During the following year while he was acting on the European mainland, his whole family was wiped out by the plague in London. By 1595, however, Browne had married again and was father of a second family (v. *Sly*). Browne was a patentee of the Queen's Revels Company in 1610; he had returned to touring in Germany by 1618, and his last noted appearance was at the Frankfurt Fair of 1620. (Cf. *Green, Jones, Reynolds, Sackville, Spencer.*)

E. K. C., *E.S.*
G. E. B.

BROWNE, William (?1591–?1643), poet: born in Tavistock, Devon, educated at the local grammar school and Exeter College, Oxford, entering the Inner Temple in 1613, and producing the Inner Temple masque, *Ulysses and Circe* in 1615. It was in order to see this masque that people climbed up the outside walls of the hall, peering through the windows; the chief cook's room was badly damaged by them, its chimney broken down. Browne's fame rests on his pastoral poetry (*Britannia's Pastorals*, 1613 and 1616) which contained political criticism effectively veiled from any censor. He is best remembered for his succinct epitaph on Mary Herbert, dowager Countess of Pembroke ("Sidney's sister, Pembroke's mother"). He returned to Oxford in 1624, taking his Master's degree, and spent his last years in the Herbert household at Wilton. Browne was never an active political radical, like his friend George Wither (q.v.).

BROWNSWORD, John (c. 1540–89), schoolmaster and poet: came from Witton, Cheshire, where he was taught by Bretchgirdle (q.v.) to whom he addressed three Latin poems. He was Master of Macclesfield School from 1561, serving as Schoolmaster in Stratford from 1565 to 1567, but he returned to Macclesfield after Bretchgirdle's death and taught there for twenty-one years. He was considered a good Latin poet.

BRYAN, George (fl. 1586–1613), actor: was a member of the touring company which, at the recommendation of the Earl of Leicester, visited Denmark and the German states, playing at the Courts of Elsinore and Dresden (1586–7). He was one of Strange's Men, 1590–3, and was in the Chamberlain's Company in 1596. It is possible that he may not have acted much, since he held a household post as Groom of the Chamber, certainly from 1603 to 1613. His name, however, is listed as an actor in the First Folio.

E. K. C., *E.S.*

BRYDGES, Giles, third Baron Chandos (1547–94): married Lady Frances Clinton and was M.P. for Gloucestershire in 1572, becoming Lord Lieutenant in the 1580s and entertaining Elizabeth I at Sudeley in 1592. He was succeeded as fourth Baron by his brother, William.

BRYDGES, Grey, fifth Baron Chandos (1579–1621): succeeded his father, William, to the barony in 1602. Grey Brydges was a close friend of the Earl of Essex and was implicated in the conspiracy of 1601. He remained a friend of Henry Wriothesley, the Earl of Southampton (q.v.), and played an active part in the masques and tournaments of James I's reign, with a company of actors of his own. The lavish entertainment which he maintained at Sudeley Castle led him to be dubbed the "King of the Cotswolds".

BRYSKETT, Lodowick (1546/7–?1612), government official, writer: son of Antonio Bruschetto, a Genoese merchant settled in England. Bryskett was probably born in Hackney, but went to Tonbridge School, Kent. He entered Trinity College, Cambridge in 1559 with the idea of studying medicine, but left without a degree when his father began to lose his money. By 1565 Bryskett had joined the household of Sir Henry Sidney, and accompanied his son Philip (q.v.) on his European tour (1572–4). When Sir Henry was reappointed Lord Deputy of Ireland in 1575, he took Bryskett with him as Clerk to the Irish Privy Council. From 1579 to 1580, Bryskett was in England, renewing his friendship with Philip Sidney and probably making a new friend, Spenser (q.v.). Soon after returning to Ireland, Bryskett acquired an estate in County Wexford. When he was disappointed of the position of Irish Secretary of State (1582) he retired there, living on the income from various minor posts, and £200 a year as Clerk of the Council of Munster (from 1583) with Spenser doing most of the work as his deputy. Bryskett wrote two elegies on Sidney, published in Spenser's *Astrophel*, and *A Discourse of Civil Life* (published 1606). This work, adapted from an Italian original, is a discussion between Bryskett and his friends in Ireland on the ideal behaviour and conversation of gentlemen. It includes a brief account by Spenser of his purpose in writing the *Faerie Queene*. In 1598 Bryskett had to fly to England from Tyrone's rebellion. He was given a pension by Queen Elizabeth and sent to Flanders on a secret mission for Sir Robert Cecil. For about two years Bryskett was a prisoner of the Spaniards, who hoped to exchange him for some Jesuits held in England; his ransom had first been fixed at 8,000 French gold pieces. By 1603 he was free and trying to settle in Chelsea, where he became involved in a long dispute with his landlord, Henry Clinton, Earl of Lincoln (q.v.). Bryskett eventually returned to Ireland and may have died there.

M. R. Plomer and T. P. Cross, *Life and Correspondence of Lodowick Bryskett* (1927)

D. Jones, "Lodowick Bryskett and his Family", *Thomas Lodge and other Elizabethans*, ed., C. J. Sisson (1966)

BUCK (or BUC), George (1562/3–1622), antiquarian, historian, Master of Revels: son of Robert Buck. The Bucks were an old family whose fortunes "withered with the White Rose", as Buck himself wrote; his grandfather fought for Richard III at Bosworth, was wounded and afterwards attainted and executed. The family was rescued by the Duke of Norfolk, who settled them at Long Melford, Suffolk. Buck was born at Ely and educated by his step-sister's husband, Henry Blaxton, first privately, then at Chichester School of which Blaxton became Master in 1570. Buck taught there himself in 1578, Blaxton being Chancellor of the Cathedral by then. His education was completed at Thavies Inn and the Middle Temple (1585) in London. By 1587 he was employed on errands between Sir Edward Stafford, Ambassador in Paris, and Walsingham (q.v.). He fought against the Armada under his family's patron,

Lord High Admiral Howard (q.v.), who found him a pocket borough, Gatton in Surrey. Buck was M.P. for Gatton in 1593 and 1597–8. He accompanied Howard and Essex to Cadiz (1596) and was sent by them to report to the Queen on the expedition. About 1597 he was given the reversion of the Mastership of the Revels, although the office had been promised to Lyly (q.v.). Meanwhile he was employed again as envoy, notably to Flanders (1601). In 1603 Buck became a much richer man, as he won possession of his aunt's lands in Lincolnshire. He was knighted by James I and began to act as deputy Master of the Revels under Sir Edmund Tilney (q.v.). In this capacity he went with Lord Howard to Spain (1605) to celebrate the peace treaty with shows and entertainments. Buck started the licensing of plays by the Revels Office, and his signature, or his deputy's, appears on the licence for all Shakespeare's plays after 1606, although Buck did not succeed Tilney as Master until 1608. After Tilney's death in 1610 Buck persuaded the government to buy a house on St Peter's Hill as Revels Office and residence for the Master, and here he wrote his major historical works — Buck had already published poetry — greatly pleasing James I with *Daphnis Polystephanos* (1605) which traced the royal genealogy in verse from the first English Kings to the Stuarts. Now he wrote *The Third University of England*, describing the "Colleges Schools and Houses of Learning" in London. It was dedicated to Coke (q.v.), and published as an appendix to Stow's *Annales* in 1615. He also produced the *Art of Revels* (now lost) and a vindicatory history of Richard III, containing the story of the Bucks. This was finished in 1619, but not published until 1646, when his great-nephew, George Buck issued it under his own name with alterations. In March 1622 Buck went mad; he died in the following December.

M. Eccles, "Sir George Buck", *Thomas Lodge and other Elizabethans*, ed., C. J. Sisson (1966)
George Buck, *History of the Life and Reign of Richard III*, ed., A. R. Myers (1973)

BUCKHURST, Lord (1536–1608) see SACKVILLE, Thomas.

BUCKINGHAM, Duke of (1592–1628, born George Villiers), courtier and politician: son of Sir George Villiers of Brooksby, Leicestershire, where he was born. James I met him for the first time on 7 August 1614 when he was a guest of Sir Anthony Mildmay at Apethorpe. Within a month he was recognised at Court as the King's favourite: James knighted him in April 1615, created him Viscount Villiers in 1616, Earl of Buckingham in 1617 and Marquis in 1618. He succeeded Howard of Effingham as Lord High Admiral in 1619 and received from the King other remunerative offices. So great was Buckingham's influence that he began to promise honours in return for payment and in the four years 1619–22 is known to have made over £24,000 from the sale of nine peerages in Ireland and eleven baronetcies. The King encouraged a close friendship between his heir, Charles, and Buckingham, whom he affectionately nicknamed "Steenie". Buckingham unsuccessfully sought a Spanish marriage for Charles, the two men going secretly to Madrid in 1623. The King made Buckingham a duke and Lord Warden of the Cinque Ports on his return from Spain, and he was by then virtual chief minister. He continued to enjoy great influence after the accession of Charles I, despite impeachment proceedings initiated in the Commons by Dudley Digges (q.v.) and John Eliot, but rejected by the King. Buckingham's conduct of an expedition to the Isle of Rhé, intended to relieve the Huguenots besieged in La Rochelle, was so inept that, despite his personal bravery, he became as unpopular with the soldiery as with the politicians. He was assassinated at Portsmouth on 23 August 1628 while fitting out a second expedition to France.

K. Sharpe, ed., *Faction and Parliament* (1978)

BULL, John (1563–1628), musician: born in Somerset. As a "Child of the Chapel Royal", from about 1572 onwards,

John Bull

he was a boy actor as well as a chorister. He returned to the Chapel Royal as a "Gentleman" in 1586, becoming organist in 1591. The Queen recommended him as first Professor of Music in the newly-founded Gresham College in Bishopsgate, 1596. He became, officially, organist to James I in 1607 but, as a Roman Catholic, he fled to the southern Netherlands in 1613 and spent the last eleven years of his life as organist of Antwerp Cathedral. Bull was one of the earliest composers of contrapuntal keyboard music, and the air of "God Save the Queen" is attributed to his composition. The use of "John Bull" as a generic name for Englishmen has nothing

to do with him, it dates from about 1712.

L. Henry, *Dr John Bull* (1937)

BULMER, Bevis (c. 1540–1615), entrepreneur and mining engineer: his origins are unknown. There is a reference to his undertaking lead mining in Scotland as early as 1566. In the 1580s and 1590s he was mainly concerned with activities in the west of England, collaborating with Sir Julius Caesar (q.v.) in promoting in Bristol (1584) a scheme to protect the coast from pirates by a system of lighthouses, and developing the Mendip lead mines by a drainage scheme. From 1587 to 1591 he supervised the mining of silver at Combe Martin in Devon. Three years later he established an experimental pumping system at Blackfriars which was intended to provide water for the western districts of the city. He then returned to Scotland where he extracted gold from Glengonner Water. His wealth and enterprise tempted him to seek from the Queen the right to farm certain taxes, notably the impost on Newcastle sea-coal, a monopoly he seems to have enjoyed in 1599–1600 but which provoked such widespread opposition that it was soon revoked. The accession of James brought him a knighthood and the right to undertake a fresh search for gold in Scotland. He successfully mined silver at Hilderstone, West Lothian, from 1606 to 1610, concentrating for the last five years of his life on the silver and lead mines on Alston Moor in Cumberland, where he died.

H. M. Robertson, "Sir Bevis Bulmer", *Journal of Economic and Business History*, I (1931)

BURBAGE, Cuthbert (1567–1636), theatre builder and owner: elder son of James Burbage and brother of Richard (qq.v.). Cuthbert is known to have been a servant to Walter Cope, M.P. (q.v.) in the late 1580s. In 1589 he took over the lease of the Theatre as his father's nominee and in 1590 joined other members of his family in their fight with his uncle's widow (v. *James* and *Richard Burbage*). For this behaviour he was summoned for contempt of court. Disagreement with the ground landlord, Giles Allen (q.v.) over renewing his lease led Cuthbert to propose moving the Theatre soon after his father's death. On 28 December 1598 Cuthbert organised the complete pulling down of the building, which was then transported across the Thames to Bankside, where it was rebuilt as the Globe. Allen subsequently took Burbage and his associates to law, claiming damages; the case dragged on until 1602, finally failing in a Star Chamber hearing partly owing to the opposition of Francis Bacon (q.v.). Cuthbert owned a quarter share in the Globe and, from 1608, a seventh share in his brother's new Blackfriars. He looked after the company in many ways, even overseeing the preparation of their wills, and one actor (Nicholas Tooley, q.v.) lived in his house in Holywell Street, Shoreditch. Towards the end of his life Cuthbert had to defend himself in a series of legal actions: over the parking of patron's coaches at the Blackfriars and over the lease of the Globe (1633–4). In 1635 other members of the company successfully brought against him an action for redistribution of the Blackfriars shares.

E. K. C., *E.S.*
C. C. Stopes, *Shakespeare's Environment* (1914)

BURBAGE, Ellen (fl. 1568–98, née Brayne): married James Burbage and was mother of Cuthbert and Richard. She supported James (*infra*) in the fight against her brother's widow in 1590; and she also supported her sons in moving the Theatre across the river.

BURBAGE, James (1531–97), actor, manager and builder of theatres: was father of Cuthbert and Richard (qq.v.). James started life as a joiner but by 1572 had settled, with his wife and two sons, in Shoreditch and was a leading actor in Leicester's Men, although in 1585 he declared himself a Chamberlain's Man. In 1576 he built the Theatre in Halliwell (Holywell) Street, Shoreditch, and was later called by his son, Cuthbert, "the first builder of playhouses". He was in financial partnership with his brother-in-law, John Brayne, a grocer, an arrangement which led to litigation and, after Brayne's death, to a Chancery suit. Brayne's widow won the case (1590), but the Burbages violently repelled her and her supporters from the Theatre, and James and Cuthbert were summoned for contempt. James, who was described as "a stubburne fellow", continued to defy the courts and the case fell through at the widow's death. In 1596 James bought part of Blackfriars to turn into an indoor theatre and had begun the work when a petition by local residents, led by the dowager Lady Russell (q.v.) caused the Privy Council to forbid use of the theatre. James Burbage died soon afterwards.

E. K. C., *W.S.*
C. C. Stopes, *Shakespeare's Environment* (1914)

BURBAGE, Richard (c. 1571–1619), actor: younger son of James Burbage (*supra*). His career probably began by 1584, but he was certainly appearing in his father's Theatre in 1590, for during the quarrel between Burbage senior and his former partner's widow, Richard is known to have taken a broomstick to the opposition. From 1595 onwards Richard was prominent in the Lord Chamberlain's Company and remained with it for the rest of his life, appearing in the Royal Patent (1603) and all the acting lists, including the First Folio. Richard was associated with his brother Cuthbert (q.v.) in removing the fabric of the Theatre across the river in 1598 and rebuilding it as the Globe. The Burbages retained a half interest in the Globe's profits, the other half being shared among the chief actors in the Lord Chamberlain's Company. Richard also inherited the Blackfriars,

Richard Burbage

which he leased to Henry Evans (q.v.) for boy actors until August 1608, when a new lease shared ownership of the theatre between seven members of the King's Company, including Richard and Cuthbert Burbage, Heminges, Condell and Shakespeare. Richard Burbage and his wife, Winifred, settled in Halliwell Street, Shoreditch, in 1603 and lived there until his death. As an actor he was described as "Protean", one who lived his part and sustained it in speech and silence. His great roles were Malvolio, Richard III, Hamlet, Othello, Lear and Hieronimo (Kyd's *Spanish Tragedy*). He is not known to have appeared publicly after the water pageant to celebrate the creation of Prince Henry as Prince of Wales in 1610, but he

remained associated with the company for the remainder of his life. He was respected as a painter in oils, and in 1613 and 1616 he painted the device for the shield of Francis, Earl of Rutland (q.v.), Shakespeare writing the motto on the first occasion. Richard Burbage was a close friend as well as a colleague of Shakespeare and is mentioned in his will.

Edwin Nunzeger, *Dictionary of Actors* (1929)
E. K. C., *W.S.*

BURBAGE, Winifred (?–1655?), wife of Richard: sole executrix of her husband's will; later married the actor, Richard Robinson (q.v.).

BURBY, Cuthbert (?–1607), book-seller, son of Edmund Burbie, a Bedfordshire farmer. He was apprenticed for eight years from Christmas 1583, and became a freeman of the Stationers' Company in January 1592. Burby produced his first book in May 1592, a translation of the pseudo-Platonic dialogue, *Axiochus*, and continued to sell books at three different shops in London until his death, "The Poultry" (1592), Cornhill, near the Royal Exchange (1601–7), and "The Swan" in St Paul's Churchyard (1602–7). In 1594 Burby sold the old play *Taming of a Shrew*, regarded as the original version of Shakespeare's *Shrew*. He also published *Love's Labours Lost* (1598) and the Second Quarto of *Romeo and Juliet* (1599). Burby left money in his will to be lent to poor young booksellers, and his premises and stock to his apprentice; Mrs Burby carried on the business for two years after her husband's death.

BURGHLEY (Mildred), Lady (1526–89, née Cooke), was the eldest daughter of Sir Anthony Cooke of Gidea Hall, Essex. (For her sisters cf. *Ann Bacon, Elizabeth Russell*.) All of Cooke's daughters were scholars, Mildred herself translating the works of St Basil the Great from Greek into English. In 1546 her father, a tutor to the later Edward VI, took her to Court with him so that she could meet William Cecil (v. *Lord Burghley*), then a widower with an infant son. She married Cecil on Christmas Day, 1546. She lost several children in infancy before the birth of her daughters, Anne and Elizabeth. Her son, Robert Cecil (q.v.) was born in the seventeenth year of her marriage. Lady Burghley was a benefactress of St John's College, Cambridge, where she maintained two scholars. Soon after her death, her husband wrote a tribute to her learning and to her generosity, noting especially a succession of anonymous gifts of money "to buy bread, cheese and drink" for prisoners held in London. She is buried in Westminster Abbey.

D. Du Maurier, *Golden Lads* (1975)
S. Barnes, "Cookes of Gidea Hall", *Essex Review*, XXI (1912)

William Cecil, Lord Burghley, c. 1585

BURGHLEY, Lord (William Cecil, 1520–98, created Baron Burghley, 1571): born at Bourn, Lincolnshire, although the Cecil family was of Welsh origin, his grandfather having supported Henry Tudor in the Bosworth campaign of 1485. William Cecil was educated at grammar schools in Grantham and Stamford and at St John's College, Cambridge. He was enrolled at Gray's Inn, entering government service under Protector Somerset's patronage in 1547. Discretion enabled him to survive Somerset's disgrace, serve Northumberland (gaining a knighthood in 1551), undertake diplomatic missions for Mary I and secretly establish contact with Elizabeth before her accession. From 1558 to 1572 he was Elizabeth's principal Secretary of State, serving her thereafter until his death as Lord Treasurer. From 1561 onwards he was also Master of the Court of Wards, an influential and lucrative post in the judiciary. He was an able administrator and a conservative financier, restoring the value of the currency with a newly minted silver coinage (1561), but he also reformed the outdated statute of labourers so as to give greater elasticity to wage scales in different parts of the kingdom. In religious matters he was more distinctly Protestant than his sovereign, but he was never a zealous Puritan, like Walsingham (q.v.). At times he favoured a more vigorous policy towards Scotland than did the Queen, but in general he was in agreement with her over foreign affairs, showing caution and seeking to postpone open conflict with Spain as long as possible. In his use of agents and propaganda pamphlets he long waged an unobtrusive cold war against Spain and the Jesuits. His position in England was, on two occasions, precarious: from 1569 until 1572 he was faced with opposition from the old nobility and from Leicester (q.v.), but was consistently backed by the Queen; and in February

1587 he was, for a time, excluded from Court by Elizabeth for having despatched the death warrant for Mary, Queen of Scots, without her express command. Generally, however, he showed skill in managing his Queen, who recognised her dependence on his judgment. She called him "my Spirit" and, in his last illness, came to his bedside and fed him "with her own princely hand". Burghley's first wife, Mary Cheke, died in 1544, leaving him with one son (cf. *Thomas Cecil*). Two years later he married Mildred Cooke (*supra*). Their son, Robert Cecil (q.v.), assisted his father as Secretary of State 1596–8. Burghley's great interests were genealogy and building; he added a magnificent palace at Theobalds in Hertfordshire to the vast home created from the family fortunes at Burghley itself, near Stamford.

Conyers Read, *Mr Secretary Cecil and Queen Elizabeth* (1955); *Lord Burghley and Queen Elizabeth* (1960)

BURTON, Robert (1577–1640), writer and cleric: born in Leicestershire and educated at Nuneaton and Sutton Cold-field Grammar Schools, and Oxford (Brasenose College, 1593, transferred to Christ Church, 1599–1605). Burton wrote Latin and English verse and a Latin comedy *Philosophaster*, performed in Christ Church hall in 1617. His main work is the *Anatomy of Melancholy* (1621); this began as a medical work but Burton finally expanded it to a general commentary on the human race. It is also a storehouse of quotations, from classical authors and the Bible to Burton's contemporaries. The *Anatomy* went into five editions in Burton's lifetime. Although he was Vicar of St Thomas', Oxford, from 1616 and Rector of Burton Segrave, Leicestershire from 1630 until his death, Burton stayed in Christ Church. He "lived a silent, sedentary, solitary, private life" according to himself, but he was Librarian of his college and

Clerk of Oxford Market. He died at Christ Church and left his library of 2,000 books to the college and the Bodleian. There is a remarkable memorial to Burton — a black-gowned bust in a sculptured niche — in Christ Church Cathedral, Oxford.

R. Burton, *Anatomy of Melancholy*, ed., Holbrook Jackson (Everyman edition, 1948)

BUSBY, John (fl. 1576–1619), book-seller: was the son of William Busby of London. He was apprenticed to a printer, Oliver Wilkes, for nine years from Michaelmas, 1576, but was allowed to serve out his time under a draper, while "exercising the art of a stationer". He became a freeman of the Stationers' Company in November, 1585, and sold books in St Dunstan's Churchyard, London from 1590 to 1619. Busby was for some time in partnership with Arthur Johnson (q.v.) for whom he procured the *Merry Wives of Windsor*; Busby's name appears on the play's first edition, 1602, but it was transferred to, and printed by, Johnson. Busby also shared in publishing *Henry V* (1600) and *King Lear* (1608). (Cf. *Butter, Millington*.)

BUTTER, Nathaniel (d. 1664), book-seller: was the son of Thomas Butter, printer and bookseller in London from 1581 to 1590. Butter became a freeman of the Stationers' Company in February, 1604 and sold books from 1605 till his death, first at the "Pyde Bull", St Austin's Gate, and later in Cursitors' Alley. He published his first book in December, 1604, and Shakespeare's *King Lear* with John Busby (1608). In 1622 Butter and William Shefford published a newsheet, *News From Most Parts of Christendom*, and Butter devoted most of his time to journalism after this. He produced a series of six-monthly volumes of foreign news from 1630, and the right to publish all news and history was granted to Butter and Nicholas Bourne by Charles I. News was not profitable, however; Butter is said to have died a pauper.

BYFIELD, Richard (c. 1570–1633), Vicar of Stratford: served as incumbent at Stratford from January 1597 until 1605 but was forbidden to preach after James I's accession, except at Easter 1605 under special licence from the Bishop of Worcester after petition from some of the Aldermen. Byfield was married soon after his arrival at Stratford and two sons, Richard and Nathaniel, were born there. Both sons became prominent Sabbatarians, writing books on the subject. The citizens of Stratford thought so highly of Richard Byfield that they wished to keep him as a schoolmaster.

M. E.
E. R. C. Brinkworth, *Shakespeare and the Bawdy Court of Stratford* (1972)

BYNNEMAN, Henry (?–1583), printer: was apprenticed for eight years from 1559 to Richard Harrison, stationer and printer of Cripplegate, but Harrison died in 1563 and it is not known what happened to the rest of Bynneman's apprenticeship. He became a freeman of the Stationers' Company in 1566 and had several shops in London, two in Paternoster Row, the "Black Boy" (1566) and the "Mermaid" (1567), in Knightrider Street (1567–80), the "Three Wells" by St Paul's (1572) and in Thomas Street (1580–3). Bynneman became well known as printer and bookseller from 1572 onwards. His work was fine, with a special wood-cut border for the pages of his folios, and his patrons at Court included Sir Christopher Hatton (q.v.). He was only once in trouble during his career, when in 1580 he printed a libellous letter from one M.P. to another, but this was not a serious offence. Bynneman's

most famous work was Holinshed's *Chronicle*. He took as deputies Henry Denham and Ralph Newbery, but on his death his business passed to a syndicate of his former apprentices.

BYRD, William (c. 1543–1623), composer: probably born at Lincoln, where he was cathedral organist from 1563 to 1572. Byrd was closely associated at the Chapel Royal with Thomas Tallis (from 1572 to 1585), the two men receiving from

William Byrd

Elizabeth I in 1575 a monopoly for printing music, following the publication of their joint *Cantiones Sacrae*. Byrd was Catholic in sympathy and acted with discretion in religious observance; but his gifts as organist and composer won him the protection of a special licence from the Queen. His first collection of *Psalms, Sonnets and Songs of Sadness and Piety* was published in 1588 and dedicated to Hatton (q.v.). A second collection of songs "some of gravity and others of mirth", appeared in 1589. He continued to publish further collections of songs and madrigals until 1611, as well as composing three Masses in the 1590s. Some 250 of his motets survive. He is generally recognised as the greatest of Tudor composers, the extent and quality of his work making him the musical counterpart of Shakespeare.

E. H. Fellowes, *William Byrd* (1948)

33

C

CAESAR, Julius (1558–1636), judge and Master of the Rolls: born at Tottenham, son of Cesare Adelmare, a physician to Queen Mary I. He was appointed to judge in the Admiralty Court in 1584, was knighted by James I on his accession and appointed Chancellor of the Exchequer in 1606. From 1614 until his death he held the remunerative post of Master of the Rolls, an administrative judicial position which brought him £2,200 in his first twelve months of office. The King regarded Sir Julius as an important spokesman in the Parliament of 1621, but in 1624 the electors of St Ives declined to return him to Parliament even though he was "recommended" to them by the heir to the throne as Duke of Cornwall.

W. J. Jones, *The Elizabethan Court of Chancery* (1967)

CALVERLEY, Walter (fl. 1604–8), notorious Yorkshire murderer in 1605 see WILKINS, George.

CAMDEN, William (1551–1623), antiquary and historian: born in London, although his family owned land near Leamington, Warwickshire. He was educated at Christ's Hospital and St Paul's School and subsequently both at Magdalen College and Christ Church, Oxford, becoming Undermaster at Westminster School in 1575 and serving as Headmaster there from 1593 to 1598. He taught the boys of Westminster to compose English verse. Among his Westminster pupils were Jonson and Cotton (qq.v.). For some years he was associated with the intellectual circle around Leicester and Philip Sidney, corresponding through them with European scholars, especially the Flemish and Dutch humanists. Camden was inspired by the topographical anti-

quarianism of Lambarde (q.v.). For nearly ten years Camden made journeys of investigation through England, publishing in Latin his *Britannia* in 1586. He continued to expand and revise his work for

William Camden

the following twenty years, adding much freshly acquired material on medieval England: *Britain*, an English translation by Philemon Holland, was published in 1610. Camden was principal founder of the original Society of Antiquaries (refounded 1717), which was established soon after the publication of *Britannia* and which had twenty-four members by 1591. In 1597 Camden was appointed Clarenceux King-of-Arms and, largely through his friendship with the Cecils, was allowed access to recent state papers so as to compile his *Annals of the Reign of Elizabeth to the year 1589* which was published, again in Latin, in 1615; a second part was printed posthumously (1627). Among Camden's other works was a narrative of

34

the trials of the Gunpowder Plotters, published in 1607. He spent his last years in retirement at Chislehurst but is buried in Westminster Abbey.

S. Piggot, "William Camden and the Britannia", *Proceedings of the British Academy*, XXXVII (1951)
H. R. Trevor-Roper, *Queen Elizabeth's First Histories* (1971)

CAMPION, Thomas (1567–1620), poet and musician: son of a Chancery clerk from Hertfordshire, educated at Peterhouse, Cambridge. In 1586 he entered Gray's Inn but did not practise as a lawyer. By 1607 he was a "doctor in physic" with a medical degree. His poems were often set to music of his own composition and he collaborated with Philip Rosseter (q.v.) in *A Book of Airs* (1601). He composed over a hundred songs, published in five books. Campion wrote four masques: two of them, both in 1613, for weddings (Princess Elizabeth's and the Earl of Somerset's); another masque was written for the entertainment of James I's Queen, Anne. His association with Somerset (Robert Carr, q.v.) put him out of favour in 1613–15 because of the scandal over Frances Howard (q.v.). His *Observations in the Art of English Poesie* (1602) attacked the fashion of excessively artificial rhyming schemes in poetry. His own lyrics are marked by a judicious use of rhyme. Probably his most famous lyrics are "Follow your saint" and "There is a garden in her face". Shortly before his death Campion completed a short treatise on the technique of Counterpoint.

CAREW, George, later first Baron Clopton and first Earl Totnes (1555–1629), Warwickshire landowner: received a knighthood for military service in Ireland (1586) and was appointed Lieutenant-General of Ordnance in 1592. Although of West Country origin — he was a cousin of Sir Walter Ralegh — he had Warwickshire connections by marriage, for in 1580 he had taken as his wife Joyce Clopton, daughter of William Clopton (q.v.); and in 1592 he purchased land in Old Stratford and neighbouring Bridgetown. He served under Essex at Cadiz in 1596, commanding the *Mary Rose*, and four years later was appointed Lord President of Munster. By now he was inclined to the Cecil rather than the Essex faction, and he prospered under James I. By 1605, when he was created Baron Clopton, he had bought his wife's family home, Clopton House, north of Stratford. It was leased in that year to Ambrose Rookwood (q.v.), an associate in the Gunpowder Plot and the house was accordingly raided by the Bailiff of Stratford. Carew became Master of Ordnance in 1608 and profited from overseas enterprise, serving on the Council of the Virginia Company from 1609 onwards. Carew, who on the petition of the town was appointed High Steward of Stratford in 1610, retained his rights to tithes at Old Stratford and was a defendant in a Chancery suit over tithes brought by Shakespeare in 1610 or 1611. In 1614 he opposed the enclosure of the common fields at Welcombe, a matter of major controversy in Stratford. He was created Earl of Totnes by Charles I in 1625. The Earl and his Countess are buried in an imposing tomb in the Clopton Chapel of Holy Trinity Church at Stratford. They had no children.

E. I. Fripp, *Shakespeare's Haunts near Stratford* (1929)

CAREW, Richard (1555–1620), antiquarian: son of Thomas Carew of Antony, Cornwall, and cousin of the poet, Thomas Carew. As his father died in 1564, Carew was already in possession of his estates when he became a Scholar of Christ Church, Oxford, at the age of eleven. He had rooms in Broadgates Hall and was a contemporary of William Camden (q.v.).

Carew was a brilliant student and held his own in public disputation with Philip Sidney of Sidney's uncles, the Earls of Leicester and Warwick. He entered the Middle Temple in 1574; by 1577 he was back in Cornwall, married Juliana Arundell, and settled down to administer his estates, study the county's history, and teach himself languages. He learnt Greek, Italian, French, German and Spanish entirely from reading. Carew fulfilled several public duties: he was J.P. (1581), Sheriff (1582), M.P. for Saltash (1584) and St Michael's (1597) and Deputy Lieutenant under his friend Ralegh (q.v.). From 1589 he was a member of the Antiquarian Society and corresponded with Camden and others, as well as reading papers to the Society when he was able to come to London. One letter to Camden, on the *Excellency of the English Tongue*, was printed in Camden's *Remains* (published 1605) and contains a mention of Shakespeare as the equal of Catullus. Carew's literary works include a translation from Tasso (1594), the *Examination of Men's Wits* (1594), translated from the Spaniard Huarte, and the *Herring's Tail* (1598), a verse fantasy. His major work was his *Survey of Cornwall* (1602) dedicated to Ralegh, whose son Carew was his godson (1605). The *Survey* was well received, and he planned a second edition, but his health weakened From 1611 he was blind, though his sight was partially restored in 1615 by an operation for cataract. He remained as cheerful as ever and died suddenly at his prayers. He is buried in Antony Church. Carew has sometimes been confused with his son Richard, who wrote his own memoirs, including an account of his father's life. The younger Carew was author of a *True and Ready Way to Learn the Latin Tongue* (1654), advocating the direct method, as opposed to learning the grammar first. This work has often been wrongly attributed to his father.

A. L. Rowse, *Tudor Cornwall* (1949)
R. Carew, *Survey of Cornwall*, ed., F. E. Halliday (1969)

CAREY, Elizabeth, Lady Hunsdon (1552–?): was the second daughter of Sir John Spencer and a relative of the poet Edmund Spenser. She married Sir George Carey, later second Baron Hunsdon, in 1574. Spenser dedicated *Muiopotmos* to her and also commemorated her in one of the dedicatory sonnets to the *Faerie Queene*. Lady Hunsdon was a patron of Nashe and Dowland, and herself translated Petrarch.

CAREY, Elizabeth (1576–1635): was the daughter of Sir George Carey and his wife Elizabeth (Spencer). In 1595 she was suggested as a possible bride for William Herbert, later third Earl of Pembroke (q.v.), but he was unwilling and Elizabeth married Sir Thomas Berkeley (q.v.) the following year, possibly with the first performance of *A Midsummer Night's Dream* as part of her wedding festivities. They had two children, Theophila (1596) and George (1601) before Elizabeth was widowed in 1611. Although she had brought a portion of £1,000 in money and the equivalent in land to the marriage, the family was left a legacy of debt through Berkeley's extravagance. Elizabeth's good management helped to restore her son George's estates, however, and she arranged a prosperous match for him. She was able to buy a dower house for herself at Cranford in Middlesex, where she spent the rest of her life. Elizabeth, like her parents, was a patron of Thomas Nashe.

John Smythe, *Lives of the Berkeleys* (1883 edition)

CAREY, George, later second Baron Hunsdon (1547–1603), Lord Chamberlain: eldest son of Henry Carey (*infra*). He was educated at Trinity College, Cambridge from 1560, undertook missions to Scotland in 1566 and 1569 and served under the Earl of Sussex in suppressing the northern rebellion and in the subsequent campaign on the Scottish border (1569–71). Sussex knighted him in 1570. Carey was appointed Steward and Constable of Bamburgh Castle (1574), Steward of the royal manor of Great Saxham, Suffolk (1575), and Captain-General of the Isle of Wight (1582). As Captain-General he lived mainly in Carisbrooke Castle, improving the defences of the island and securing the enfranchisement of Newtown (1584), with the right for life of nominating one of the borough's two M.P.s. Carey had himself sat in the Commons for Hertfordshire in 1571; he represented Hampshire 1584–5, 1586–7, 1589 and 1593. He went on two more˙ diplomatic missions to Scotland, 1582 and 1589. In 1596 he succeeded as second Baron Hunsdon, a year later being appointed to his father's former post of Lord Chamberlain. This office gave him patronage of the company of Shakespeare and the Burbages, the Lord Chamberlain's Men, who were then appearing mainly at the Theatre, moving to the Globe in December 1598 (v. *Cuthbert Burbage*). Hunsdon often presented them in plays at Court or at Hunsdon House, Blackfriars, to entertain important guests. Their last appearance before Queen Elizabeth was on 2 February 1603. Hunsdon was present in Richmond Palace on 24 March when the Queen died, and he helped his younger brother Robert Carey (q.v.) to escape to Scotland with the news. He did not long survive the transformation of his acting company into the King's Men.

CAREY, Henry, first Baron Hunsdon (1524–96), Lord Chamberlain: was the son of Mary, Anne Boleyn's sister, and Sir William Carey and so first cousin to Queen Elizabeth; it was rumoured that his father was Henry VIII and he was also the

Queen's half-brother. He was M.P. for Buckingham in 1547, 1554 and 1555, but really came into prominence with Elizabeth's accession (1558), becoming one of her most reliable officials. He was knighted immediately and made Baron Hunsdon at the coronation; he was a keen

Henry Carey, first Baron Hunsdon

jouster and performed notably in the Court tournaments. In 1561 Hunsdon was made a Knight of the Garter and Privy Councillor, and in 1568 Governor of Berwick, a post which involved the defence of the border and delicate missions to Scotland about the fate of Mary, Queen of Scots. Hunsdon also took command in the field during the rebellion of the Northern Earls (1569–71) and defeated them in battle. Although the Queen was a frequent visitor to Hunsdon House in Hertfordshire (where she had spent some of her childhood) and rewarded her cousin with lands, she and Hunsdon disagreed over his post in Berwick. Hunsdon complained that his salary was not paid and he could not afford to do the work from his own resources. However, in 1583 she appointed him Lord Chamberlain. The group of players whom he had maintained intermittently since

1564 were now known as the Lord Chamberlain's Men; in 1594 the company was reconstituted under the leadership of the Burbages and included William Shakespeare. Meanwhile Hunsdon had been commissioner at the trial of the Queen of Scots and gone on one more diplomatic mission to Scotland in 1587, successfully explaining to James VI the necessity for his mother's execution. He became Lord Warden-General of the Marches towards Scotland, and in 1588 defended England against Spain as commander of Tilbury Fort. The internal security of the country was also Hunsdon's concern; from 1584 to 1594 he was commissioner at treason trials. Hunsdon married Anne, daughter of Sir Thomas Morgan; he had ten sons and kept a young mistress, Emilia Lanier (q.v.) towards the end of his life. The Queen allowed him to live in Somerset House in London, where he died. Hunsdon was buried in Westminster Abbey.

J. E. Neale, *The Elizabethan House of Commons* (1949)

CAREY, Robert, later first Earl of Monmouth (?1560–1639): tenth and youngest son of Henry Carey (*supra*). He accompanied his father on a mission to the Low Countries in 1582, escorting the Queen's rejected suitor, the Duke of Alençon. After further travel in France, Carey returned to England, spending most of his youth at Court where he was a favourite with the Queen, his father's cousin. However, he went to Scotland with Walsingham in 1583 and was well received by James VI. He represented Morpeth in the Commons of 1586, 1589 and 1593, took part in the fight against the Armada, and served in Normandy under Essex, who knighted him (1591). About 1593 he married Elizabeth Widdrington, widowed daughter of a Cornish knight, Sir Hugh Trevannion, angering the Queen,

who did not forgive Carey for some years. He served on the Scottish borders, originally as his father's deputy but succeeding him as Warden-General of the Scottish Marches in 1596. He was also Captain of Norham Castle and M.P. for Northumberland in the Parliaments of 1597–8 and 1601. Carey paid his last visit to the Queen early in March 1603. To him she admitted, "Robin, I am not well", and he remained at Court observing her illness, which he describes in his *Memoirs*. He had already forewarned James VI and on the morning of 24 March, immediately after Elizabeth's death, he slipped out of Richmond Palace behind his brother, the Lord Chamberlain. The Council tried to prevent his going but Carey reached Holyrood with his news late on 26 March, although his horse had thrown and kicked him. However, when James arrived in England, Carey was disappointed of his reward. His fortunes were low with the disappearance of the Anglo-Scottish border, but he managed to sell his Captaincy of Norham for £6,000. Lady Carey ingratiated herself with Queen Anne and was given charge of the three-year-old Prince Charles (q.v.). She helped Charles survive a weakly infancy and saved him from his father's drastic remedies, such as iron boots to harden feeble legs. Sir Robert later became the Prince's governor (1605), Master of the Rolls (1611) and Chamberlain (1617), following Charles to Spain in 1623. Upon Charles's accession Carey was given lands and created Earl of Monmouth (1626), retiring reluctantly from the royal service.

R. Carey, *Memoirs*, ed., G.H. Powell (1905)

CARLETON, Dudley (1573–1632), diplomat: born at Baldwin Britwell, Oxfordshire, and educated at Westminster School and Christ Church, Oxford, graduating in 1595. After travelling for several years abroad, he became principal secretary to the ambassador in Paris, 1602–3. He was elected M.P. for St Mawes in 1604 and was present that year at the Court's Christmas Revels, complaining that the dresses of the Queen and her ladies were "too light and courtesan-like for such great ones". He remained out of the country for several years and, as a one-time secretary to Northumberland (q.v.), was even suspected in 1606 of being an accessory to the Gunpowder Plot. He successfully cleared his name with Salisbury (Robert Cecil, q.v.) and was knighted by the King in 1610, the year in which he was sent to Venice as ambassador. Sir Dudley employed John Chamberlain (q.v.) to keep him informed of news from England, the correspondence being one of the principal surviving sources of London political gossip in this period. Carleton soon won respect as a patient and discreet diplomat. He remained ambassador at Venice until 1615 and then served for nine years at The Hague. In 1626 he represented Hastings in Charles I's second Parliament, speaking out strongly in support of the King. That autumn he was created Baron Carleton and sent back to The Hague for another two years embassy. On his return in 1628 he became Viscount Dorchester and spent the last four years of his life as Secretary of State.

N. E. McClure, ed., *The Letters of John Chamberlain* (1939)

CARLISLE, Lucy, Countess of (1599–1660, née Percy): the beautiful daughter of Henry Percy, ninth Earl of Northumberland, and his wife Dorothy (qq.v.). In 1617, while the Earl was still confined in the Tower for his role in the Gunpowder Plot, Lucy and her mother encouraged the courtship of James Hay (q.v.), one of James I's favourites. Northumberland disliked the match (he "could not endure

that his daughter should dance any Scottish jig") but could do nothing to prevent it, and Lucy Percy married Hay in October 1617. Their household became famous for its culinary extravagance, the cost of a dinner for the French ambassador in 1621 coming to well over £3000. Hay was created Earl of Carlisle in 1622. After his death in 1636, Lady Carlisle became a strong supporter and close friend of Strafford, later managing to intrigue with Pym, the Presbyterians and the French as well as keeping up her friendship with Queen Henrietta Maria. Not surprisingly, she spent some time in the Tower under the Commonwealth.

J. Richardson, *Famous Ladies of the English Court* (1899)

CARLTON, Richard (c. 1560–1638), composer: born near King's Lynn, graduating from Clare College, Cambridge in 1577, and apparently spending some thirty years at Norwich Cathedral. He published a book of madrigals in 1601, describing himself as a priest, and he became Rector of Bawsey, Norfolk, in 1612. He was one of the contributors to the *Triumph of Oriana* in 1601.

CARR, Robert, later Earl of Somerset (1585/7–1645), favourite: youngest son of Sir Thomas Kerr of Roxburghshire. He may have been at the Scottish Court as a page to George Home when Overbury (q.v.) visited Edinburgh in 1601. Carr then served King James for two years in Scotland, spending some time fortune hunting in France before coming to London in about 1606. He is said to have fallen dramatically at James's feet with a broken leg during a tourney. The King soon adopted him as chief favourite, taught him Latin and knighted him (December 1607), giving him money and the estate of Sherborne, once Ralegh's home. He was created Viscount Rochester and Lord High Treasurer of Scotland in 1611 and a Privy Councillor in the following year. Two opposing forces assisted his advancement: renewal of his acquaintance with the able Overbury, who became his secretary; and alliance with the Howards. By 1609, Carr was the lover of Frances Howard (q.v.), then Countess of Essex, encouraged by her parents and especially by her uncle, Northampton (Henry Howard, q.v.). Overbury was happy to assist by writing Carr's love letters, until the question of annulling the Essex marriage arose. How

Robert Carr, later Earl of Somerset

far Carr betrayed Overbury to his imprisonment in the Tower or planned his murder is uncertain, but he plotted with Northampton to brainwash him by correspondence during his confinement. After Overbury's death and the Essex divorce, Carr (now Earl of Somerset) and Frances Howard were married on 26 December 1613, with great festivity. The Earl was patron of many poets: Campion and Chapman wrote masques for the occasion, Donne the best known of his *Epithalamia*,

and Jonson celebratory verses; Francis Bacon produced the Gray's Inn masque, for which John Chamberlain (q.v.) alleged he received over £2,000. Within two years Somerset's fortunes had changed and all his fair-weather followers deserted him or became enemies; only Chapman still honoured him in disgrace. In 1614—15 Somerset was superseded in the King's affection by George Villiers (Buckingham, q.v.), the old nobility readily turned against Somerset as an intruder, and Lord Chief Justice Coke (q.v.) began to investigate the Overbury case. In November 1615 Somerset was sent to the Tower and six months later tried for Overbury's murder. Unlike his wife and her associates, Somerset who at first refused to attend at all, pleaded Not Guilty. The trial, with Francis Bacon prosecuting, was a great show, and seats cost up to £50. Somerset was condemned to death, but pardoned. He and his wife remained in the Tower, where their daughter Anne was born in 1616. They were released in 1622, first into the custody of Sir William Knollys, then to their own house at Chiswick. Somerset was paid an annuity by James I and survived to assist his daughter's marriage in 1637 to the heir of the Earl of Bedford, much against that nobleman's will.

B. White, *Cast of Ravens* (1965)

CARTWRIGHT, Thomas (1535— 1603), Puritan divine: born in Hertfordshire and became a Scholar of St John's College, Cambridge (1550—53). He left Cambridge and went into exile during Mary's reign, returning as a Fellow of Trinity, 1559—71. In 1569 he was elected Lady Margaret Professor of Divinity, but his vigorous championship of Scriptural purity in both worship and government of the Church led Whitgift (q.v.), the Vice-Chancellor, to deprive him of his chair in 1570. Most of the following fifteen years Cartwright spent at Geneva or in the Netherlands, although he remained in close touch with the anti-episcopalian movement in England, which he supported by his trenchant pen. In 1585, with the Earl of Leicester as protector, he returned to England and served as Master of the Earl's Hospital in Warwick, using his position to bring order into the nascent Presbyterian structure in the Midlands and the south. He was brought before the Court of High Commission in 1590 and remained in custody for two years, before being allowed to go to the Channel Islands. He returned to Warwick for the last five years of his life, enjoying considerable wealth and status in the city. After James's accession he drew up the Millenary Petition (April 1603) in which he claimed to voice the hopes of a thousand Puritan ministers who sought relief from "the common burden of human rites and ceremonies" in religious observance. Cartwright died at Christmas in the same year.

A. F. S. Pearson, *Thomas Cartwright and Elizabethan Puritanism* (1925)

CARY, Elizabeth (1586–1639, née Tanfield), dramatist: was the daughter of Lord Tanfield, M.P. for Woodstock and Chief Baron of the Exchequer. She was a precocious child, for in 1597 Drayton dedicated one of his *Heroical Epistles* to her, commending her fluent French and Italian and other learning. In 1602 she married Henry Carey of Berkhamsted. He was sent abroad on a diplomatic mission and Elizabeth was forced to continue living with her mother, who ill-treated her in many ways, making her spend most of the time on her knees. In 1613 Elizabeth published a tragedy, *Miriam the Fair, Queen of Jewry*, listed as her second play. Her husband was created Viscount Falkland in

1620, serving as Lord Lieutenant of Ireland, 1622–9, and dying in 1633. Elizabeth's son, Lucius, born at Burford in 1610, became the famous second Viscount Falkland, whose house at Great Tew in Oxfordshire was in the 1630s a natural centre for writers and scholars, including Ben Jonson and Waller. She has been confused with both Elizabeth Carey (Lady Hunsdon) and her daughter Elizabeth Carey (Lady Berkeley) (qq.v.).

E. K. Chambers, *Sir Henry Lee* (1936)

CATESBY, Robert (1573–1605), conspirator: born at Lapworth, Warwickshire, ten miles north of Stratford-upon-Avon. He was the son of the recusant, Sir William Catesby (*infra*) who was imprisoned for having given secret hospitality to the Jesuit, Edmund Campion, when Robert was seven years old. Robert went up to Gloucester Hall, Oxford, in 1586 but did not take his degree because of his Catholic religious beliefs. A rich marriage, and a sound inheritance from his father, made him a wealthy man but in 1601 he was imprisoned and heavily fined for having supported Essex (q.v.) and for taking part in an affray in a London street, in which he was wounded. The combination of resentment and religious zeal inclined Catesby to support the plot hatched by his kinsman, Thomas Winter (q.v.), for blowing up King and Parliament with gunpowder. After the arrest of Fawkes (q.v.), Catesby and Winter took refuge at Holbeach Hall, Staffordshire, where, on 8 November 1605, Catesby was shot while resisting arrest.

Joel Hurstfield, *Freedom, Corruption and Government in Elizabethan England* (1973)

CATESBY, William (1547–98), Warwickshire property owner: was Sheriff of Warwickshire in 1577, with a house known both as Bushwood Hall and Lapworth Hall within Stratford parish. He was a Roman Catholic, and a recusant from 1580 onwards. In 1581 he was imprisoned in the Fleet and tried in Star Chamber for refusing to say whether or not he had entertained the Jesuit missionary, Edmund Campion (1540–81). In the Armada year he was imprisoned at Ely but allowed to visit Bath for the sake of his health, settling finally at Milcote, near Stratford, where he lived with Sir Edward Greville (q.v.). He was a direct descendant of the William Catesby portrayed in *Richard III*, and was father of the Gunpowder Plot conspirator (*supra*).

M. E.

CAVENDISH, Thomas (1560–92), seaman: born at Trimley St Martin in Suffolk, losing much inherited wealth as a young man at Court before sailing under Grenville (q.v.) in an expedition financed by Ralegh in 1585 which attempted to colonise Virginia. From July 1586 until September 1588 Cavendish was engaged on a major expedition against Spanish and Portuguese settlements in South America, subsequently entering the Pacific, seizing a Spanish vessel off the coast of California as it was sailing home from the Philippines. He then crossed the Pacific himself, reconnoitred Manila and Java, sailed round the Cape of Good Hope and became the first Englishman to land on St Helena. His voyages made him the second English circumnavigator of the world. He was much fêted on his return. Three years later he set out in company with Captain John Davis (q.v.) in a voyage which was intended to reach China. Constant friction between Cavendish and his companions confined his activities to the coast of Portuguese Brazil. He appears to have died at sea while making for the Cape Verde islands.

CECIL, Edward (1572–1638), soldier: grandson of Burghley (q.v.) and the third son of Thomas Cecil (q.v.), Earl of Exeter. He first served in the Netherlands from 1597 to 1599 and was knighted in 1601, the year in which he was returned to the Commons as M.P. for Aldeburgh. He continued to serve as commander of the English forces helping the Dutch until 1610. His subsequent advancement owed much to the favour of Buckingham (q.v.). He was returned to the Commons as M.P. for Dover in 1624 and showed himself strongly in favour of assisting the Dutch and opposing the Spanish. As soon as Parliament was opened Sir Edward proposed a day of national fast as evidence of the determination to oppose "the Spanish religion". He was given command of the expedition which made a bungled raid on Cadiz in October 1625; but Buckingham's support saved him from disgrace upon his return home. He fought in Holland again from 1627 to 1629 and was Governor of Portsmouth for the last eight years of his life.

R. E. Ruigh, *The Parliament of 1624* (1971)

CECIL, Robert (1563–1612, created Baron Cecil 1603, Viscount Cranborne 1604, Earl of Salisbury 1605), statesman: son of William and Mildred Cecil (v. *Lord* and *Lady Burghley*) and cousin of the Bacons (qq.v.). He was educated at St John's College, Cambridge, serving briefly as a diplomat in Paris before sitting in Parliament for Westminster (1584–5 and 1586–7). He was member for Hertfordshire in the Parliaments of 1589, 1593, 1597–8 and 1601 before going to the Lords. Cecil's political skill was respected by Queen Elizabeth, even though she chaffed him for being small and roundbacked by calling him "my little man" and "my elf". Bacon, writing to Essex (q.v.) in November 1593, described Cecil as "an excellent wherryman who you know looketh towards the bridge when he pulleth towards Westminster." He was sworn of the Privy Council and knighted in 1591 and, after a period of intensive rivalry for political favours with Essex, was made Chancellor of the Duchy of Lancaster in October 1595, a post with great political patronage. From 1599 he was Master of the Court of Wards, the most remunerative office in the land. He was acting Secretary

Robert Cecil, Earl of Salisbury

of State before he was thirty and principal Secretary of State from 1596 until his death, thus controlling foreign policy for some twenty years. Towards the close of Elizabeth's reign he embarked on a secret correspondence with James VI of Scotland to ensure his smooth accession to the throne. "'Tis a great task to prove one's honesty and yet not spoil one's fortune", Cecil wrote privately soon after James arrived in London. From the King he received titles, gifts of crown lands, and rights to certain customs duties. He also received generous sums from other suitors

so that, by 1610, he could count on an income of at least £25,000 a year. Much of this he spent on works of art, music and entertainment: as early as 1594 he had played a prominent role in entertaining Queen Elizabeth at Theobalds in Hertfordshire, honouring her with an oration of his own. In 1607 he exchanged Theobalds for the royal estate at Hatfield, where in the following five years he spent £40,000 on creating the Jacobean masterpiece, Hatfield House. At the same time he was building Salisbury House in The Strand and Cranborne Manor in Dorset. His wealth and influence attracted envy at Court and his authority was undermined by Carr (q.v.), James I's Scottish favourite, who poisoned the King's mind against his chief minister (Lord Treasurer as well as Secretary of State since April 1608). James unjustly blamed Salisbury for his own inept handling of the Commons, and he fell from favour in January 1611. Salisbury's health gave way ten months later. He sought a cure at Bath but died on 12 May 1612 while returning to his new house at Hatfield, in which he never resided.

A. Cecil, *Robert Cecil* (1915)
D. Cecil, *The Cecils of Hatfield House* (1973)
J. Hurstfield, *Freedom, Corruption and Government* . . . (1973)
H. S. Reinmuth, ed., *Early Stuart Studies* (1970)

CECIL, Thomas (1542–1623), soldier: elder son of the first Lord Burghley (q.v.). After spending two years of trivial dissipation in Paris and Germany, he was returned as M.P. for Stamford — a Cecil family preserve — in 1563. Soldiery was more to his liking than politics. He served against the northern rebels in 1569 and in the siege of Edinburgh in 1573. In 1575 he was knighted. After several years of campaigning in the Netherlands, he served afloat against the Armada in 1588. His most important post came in 1599, a year after he succeeded as the second Baron Burghley: he was appointed President of the Council of the North. By chance he was in London on leave in 1601 at the time of Essex's abortive rising and he immediately took vigorous military action to crush the rebellion at its source. James I created him Earl of Exeter in 1605. He was a generous benefactor of Clare College, Cambridge. His son William (1566–1640), titular Lord Burghley from 1605 to 1623, ably headed a diplomatic mission to Florence in 1600.

CHAMBERLAIN, John (1554–1628), newsgatherer and letter-writer: born in London, the son of an Alderman and twice Master of the Worshipful Company of Ironmongers. John Chamberlain was educated at Trinity College, Cambridge, and Gray's Inn but never became a barrister. He remained a bachelor without any specific occupation, lodging with friends or relatives, and always living close to St Paul's Cathedral, which was the recognised place in the City for exchanging news and arranging business. Chamberlain described himself as a "Paul's-walker", who watched and listened for thirty years, sending news to his friend Sir Dudley Carleton, a diplomat, and occasionally to Bishop Lancelot Andrewes (q.v.) and Sir Ralph Winwood (q.v.). The letters cover the years 1597–1626.

N. McLure, ed., *Letters of John Chamberlain* (1939)

CHANDOS, Lords see BRYDGES, Giles and Grey.

CHAPMAN, George (?1559–1634), dramatist, poet: born at Hitchin, Hertfordshire, probably self-educated, served as a soldier in the Netherlands. His first poem, *The Shadow of Night*, appeared in 1594. He contributed a single poem in 1601 to the collection associated with Chester (q.v.), *The Phoenix and Turtle*. By 1598 he is known to have been writing comedies for the Admiral's Men but he was also engaged on completing Marlowe's unfinished *Hero and Leander*. In 1604 his tragedy, *Bussy d'Amboise*, was produced by Paul's Boys. The play was very popular and was later revived by the King's Men. In 1605 he collaborated with Jonson and Marston on the comedy *Eastward Ho!*, for the Children of the Chapel at Blackfriars. Scurrilous remarks about the Scots sent the authors to prison. Chapman was unrepentant, and he was again in trouble with his play, *Charles, Duke of Biron* (1608), which offended the French ambassador. Although he wrote masques and revised earlier work, Chapman never produced another new play. He devoted all his time to the poetic enterprise which he had begun in 1598, a verse translation of all Homer's works. At first his patron was Prince Henry (q.v.), who appointed him Sewer-in-Ordinary, a household post with nominal responsibility for service at table. The Prince encouraged him with a promise of £300 and a pension. Henry's death in 1612 left Chapman without patron or pension. Eventually the Homer translation was completed in 1624 under the patronage of the Earl of Somerset (Robert Carr, q.v.), but Chapman always complained of his personal poverty. Some nineteenth-century commentators regarded Chapman as a possible "rival poet", mentioned in the Shakespeare Sonnets, but there is no reason for linking him with Shakespeare's personal circle.

E. K. C., *E.S.*

CHARLES (1600–49, Duke of York 1605–16, Prince of Wales 1616–25, King Charles I 1625–49): born at Dunfermline, second son of James I and Anne of Denmark. He was a frail child, so shy that he never overcame a stammer, but he was intelligent, with an aptitude for languages and theological controversies. From 1608 to 1625 his patronage was given to a company of actors who, in his name, played in the provinces and at Court, especially before the younger members of the royal family: William Rowley (q.v.) was a leading member of the company. After 1615 this company closely collaborated with the Children of the Queen's Revels under Henslowe's financial direction, and was later associated with Alleyn and Beeston (qq.v.). Charles's personal popularity was, from time to time, weakened by rumours of a Spanish marriage which persisted from 1614 until his return from a seven-month incognito visit to Madrid (October 1623) without a bride. His subsequent betrothal to Henrietta Maria, the sister of Louis XIII of France, revived fears of "papists", only partially allayed when he sent back to France a bishop and twenty-nine priests from his wife's retinue a year after his accession. Charles's friendship with Buckingham (q.v.) aroused distrust in Parliament, a conflict with his subjects intensified by eleven years of non-Parliamentary government (1629–40) and culminating in the Grand Remonstrance of January 1642 and the Civil War (1642–46). Subsequently King Charles was put on "trial" at Westminster as a "tyrant, traitor and murderer"; he was beheaded in front of the Banqueting House of his Palace of Whitehall on 30 January 1649.

E. K. C., *E.S.*
G. E. B.
For a full account of the critical years of Charles I's reign see the two volumes by C. V. Wedgwood, *The King's Peace, 1637–1641* (1955) and *The King's War, 1641–47* (1958)

CHESTER, Robert (fl. 1586–1601), poet: author of *Love's Martyr* (1601), a long allegorical poem published in a collection which included original poems by Chapman, Jonson, Marston and Shakespeare. The collection carries the title: *Divers Poetical Essays on the former Subject: viz. The Turtle and Phoenix: done by the best and chiefest of our modern writers . . . and consecrated by them all generally to the love and merits of the true-noble Knight, Sir John Salusbury.* The identity of Chester and the occasion which caused publication of the poems have aroused scholarly speculation for over a century. The Reverend Alexander Grosart, who edited *Love's Martyr* for the Shakespeare Society in 1878, identified Chester as a knight from Royston in Hertfordshire who lived from 1566 to 1640. This identification is now discredited, for Grosart's Chester had no apparent connection with the dedicatee of the *Poetical Essays*, Sir John Salusbury (q.v.). Professor Carleton Brown, editing Salusbury's and Chester's poems in 1914, showed that there was a Robert Chester in the Salusbury household in Denbighshire and that he had written poems which indicate familiarity with Salusbury's home and private life. It is probable *Love's Martyr* was originally written by this Robert Chester to mark the marriage of John Salusbury and Ursula Stanley in December 1586; the phoenix and turtle-dove imagery would then have been appropriate, for Salusbury was the sole remaining male in a family seeking to win back, and perpetuate in a love-match, its good name — recently discredited by the execution of Salusbury's elder brother for complicity in the Babington Plot. By 1601 Salusbury was a respected public figure, a friend of better poets than Chester, and also the father of eleven children. It would therefore be apt to celebrate the Queen's conferment of a knighthood by re-furbishing Chester's *Love's Martyr* and by adding to it other poems on the phoenix and turtle theme (or "former subject") by the more gifted writers whom Salusbury had come to know in fourteen years of social advancement.

Another interpretation of Chester's allegory, and of Shakespeare's contribution to the collection, suggests that the phoenix was intended to represent Queen Elizabeth and the turtle the Earl of Essex. Professor Matchett argues that the publisher Blount (q.v.) may have assembled the volume in honour of Essex but that he was forced to change the dedication after the Earl's fall so as to render the poems politically innocuous.

Poems by Sir John Salusbury and Robert Chester, ed., Carleton Brown (1914)
W. H. Matchett, The Phoenix and the Turtle (1965)
J. Buxton, "Two Dead Birds: A Note on The Phoenix and Turtle" in English Renaissance Studies Presented to Dame Helen Gardner (1980)

CHETTLE, Henry (c. 1560–c. 1607), dramatist and printer: son of a London dyer, was apprenticed to the printer, Thomas East, in 1577 and became a freeman of the Stationers' Company in 1584. Chettle went into partnership with Danter and Hoskins from 1589 to 1591, continuing the link with Danter's press until at least 1596. In 1592 Chettle edited Robert Greene's *Groatsworth of Wit*; he later apologised for the attack in it on Shakespeare (v. *Greene*). Chettle was writing plays for the Admiral's Men, either as sole author or as a collaborator, by 1598. Meres (q.v.) mentioned Chettle as "among the best for comedy", but he also wrote tragedies. He was constantly in debt for small sums to Henslowe, and on several occasions was forced to pawn his manuscripts.

E. K. C., *E.S.*

CHOLMELEY, Sir Richard (1580–1632), landed gentleman: son of Sir Henry Cholmeley of Whitby, Yorkshire. He matriculated at Trinity College, Cambridge in 1595, but next year his father married him to an heiress, Susanna Legard

of Scarborough, and Richard refused to return to college. The couple lived at first in Sir Henry's house and Cholmeley was a father by the age of nineteen. He cost Sir Henry a good deal in fines and bribes, including £3000 to extricate him from the Essex plot (1601) and another large sum when he hit a man in the Court of Star Chamber. Cholmeley's love of a quarrel was shown in 1603 at the Blackfriars Theatre, which he apparently frequented. He arrived late and had to take one of the stools on the stage. When he stood up to stretch between scenes, another play-goer sat in his seat, and, after some words, Cholmeley pursued him from the theatre and tried to force a duel upon him; what play was so interrupted is unknown. Cholmeley, who was knighted in 1603, went to live at Whitby in 1608. Here he became a respected country gentleman and J.P., but fell out with his litigious and puritanical neighbour, Sir Thomas Hoby (q.v.). In 1611 Cholmeley's first wife died after having borne six children; he married a second wife, Margaret Cob, and decided to give up public duties, partly because he was tired of Hoby's annoyances. However he inherited his father's estate in 1617 and was persuaded to become Deputy Lieutenant of Yorkshire and sit on the Council of the North (1619). A year later he was elected M.P. for Scarborough and incurred considerable expense moving south so as to attend the Parliament, which sat from 30 January 1621 until 6 January 1622; ill health limited Cholmeley to six visits to the Commons. On his return north he became High Sheriff of Yorkshire in 1624 but this office, on top of his London trip, nearly bankrupted him and he made his estate over to his son before he died.

Sir Hugh Cholmeley, *Memoirs* (1788 edition)

CHURCHYARD, Thomas (?1520–1604), poet and pamphleteer: was once a page to the poet Henry, Earl of Surrey (1517—47). Much of his life was spent as a soldier, serving in Scotland, Ireland, France and the Netherlands. By 1553 he had published *A Mirror for Man*, and between 1560 and 1603 he continued to turn out a succession of small volumes or broadsheets of verse and prose, including autobiographical narratives (such as the *Wofull Warres in Flaunders* in 1578), most of which were comments on current affairs. Churchyard also contributed to masques for Queen Elizabeth's entertainments on progress.

CLARKE, Sampson (fl. 1583—98), bookseller: became a freeman of the Stationers' Company in 1583. His shops were by the Guildhall (1583) and behind the Royal Exchange (1589—91). Clarke sold ballads mainly, but in 1585 he had to defend himself against the assigns of Richard Day for unlawfully printing and selling the *A.B.C. and Little Catechism* for which Day held the patent. In 1591 Clarke published the *Troublesome Reign of King John*, generally regarded as the source of Shakespeare's play. Clarke was admitted to the Livery of the Stationers' Company in 1598.

CLIFFORD, Anne (1590—1676), diarist: daughter of George Clifford, third Earl of Cumberland, and his wife Margaret (qq.v.). Much of her early life was spent with her mother's sister, Lady Warwick (q.v.), whom she attended at Court during the last days of Queen Elizabeth's life. She wrote an account of the Queen's funeral and of James I's coming to England in her diary, although the fact that she was not tall enough to walk in the funeral procession rankled. Anne was well-educated, the poet Samuel Daniel being one of her tutors between 1595 and 1599, but her father would not allow her to learn foreign languages. Daniel stimulated her

interest in poetry, especially his own and that of Spenser, and she was later responsible for the monuments to both poets. She kept a day-by-day book until the end of her life and a full diary, with fairly regular entries, until 1624. Her parents were separated for some time before her father's death in 1606; his will

Lady Anne Clifford

broke the entail on his estates to leave them to his brother, the fourth Earl. Anne and her mother tried unavailingly to recover them. Although Anne was frequently at Court and popular with the Queen, James I opposed her efforts. In 1609 she married Richard Sackville who, when his father died two days after the wedding, became Earl of Dorset. He was a gambler and extravagant, and urged Anne to abandon her claims in favour of a money settlement. Their quarrel became so severe that Dorset left her, taking away their daughter, Margaret. In July 1617 the King confirmed the Earl of Cumberland in possession of the estates, awarding the Earl of Dorset £20,000 compensation. This settlement almost reconciled Dorset to

Anne, but she refused to acknowledge the King's decision. When Dorset died, heavily in debt in 1624, Anne was left with two daughters. She resolved to stay a widow but in 1630 married Philip Herbert, Earl of Montgomery and later of Pembroke (q.v.), a supporter of her claim to the Cumberland estates. These lands she finally inherited in 1643 after the deaths of her uncle and her cousin without heirs. The rest of her life was spent in northern England, repairing her castles, ordering a tenantry made unruly by civil wars (she indignantly refused an offer of help from Cromwell), entertaining her grandchildren, and journeying between her estates. She died in Brougham Castle, Westmoreland, in the room of her mother's death and her father's birth.

Lady Anne Clifford, *Diary*, ed., V. Sackville-West (1923)
Lady Anne Clifford, *Diary*, ed., G. Williamson (1967)
V. A. Wilson, *Society Women of Shakespeare's Time* (1925)
W. Notestein, *Four Worthies* (1956)

CLIFFORD, George, third Earl of Cumberland (1558–1605), admiral: through his mother, Eleanor Brandon, was a great-nephew of Henry VIII. He inherited his title at the age of twelve, and a year later went up to Trinity College, Cambridge, where his tutor was Whitgift (q.v.). He was primarily a student of mathematics, taking his Master's degree in 1576 but then going to Oxford to study geography. In 1577 he married his cousin, Lady Margaret Russell: their daughter was Anne Clifford (*supra*). Cumberland was a great champion at the tilt and as Knight of the Crown (1590) became the regular challenger for the Queen's Day Tilt, composing many of his speeches for these festivities. His main interest was in the sea. At his own expense he equipped and sailed on twelve naval expeditions between

1586 and 1598, as well as commanding Drake's former vessel, *Elizabeth Bonaventura*, in the running battle with the Armada of 1588. These expeditions, designed to harass the Spanish fleet and

George Clifford, third Earl of Cumberland

overseas possessions, finished with Cumberland's voyage to Puerto Rico in 1598, when he captured the forts of San Juan which had successfully defied Drake three years previously. Cumberland was too ill to establish a permanent settlement on Puerto Rico, as he had hoped. His expeditions were costly affairs, and Cumberland became more and more in debt, a condition aggravated by chronic gambling habits. His married life was stormy and he died separated from his wife.

CLIFFORD, Lady Margaret (1560–1616) see CUMBERLAND, Margaret Clifford, Countess of.

CLOPTON, William (1538–92), gentleman of Stratford: a great-great-great-nephew of Sir Hugh Clopton (d. 1496), Lord Mayor of London in 1491 and builder of both New Place and the Clopton Bridge at Stratford. After the death of his father and namesake in 1560, William Clopton was forced to sell or mortgage his lands in order to pay legacies to his four sisters and to continue his travels in Italy. William Bott (q.v.) acted as his agent, having moved in to New Place, which he subsequently purchased from Clopton (1563). A year later Clopton brought a Star Chamber case against Bott accusing him of forgery and of having defrauded him of rents. In 1580 George Carew (q.v.) married Clopton's daughter, Joyce, and eventually bought the family's main seat north of Stratford, Clopton House. The Clopton family recovered the house after Joyce's death, as the Carews had no children; New Place also returned to the Cloptons in the eighteenth century.

M. E.
S. S.

CLOWES, William (c. 1540–1604), surgeon and pioneer of English medical science: born in Warwickshire, served with the army in the Low Countries and as chief surgeon to the fleet in the Armada campaign. Clowes practised medicine at St Bartholomew's Hospital, later retiring to Plaistow in Essex. He wrote five important medical studies, on the treatment of wounds received from gunshot, on tuberculosis, and on the treatment of syphilis.

COBHAM, Lord (1554–1619) see BROOKE, Henry.

COKAYNE, William (?1561–1626), merchant and Lord Mayor: born in London, succeeding his father as a prominent merchant tailor and becoming a city Alderman in 1609. The Corporation of London made him responsible for the district of Derry which passed into their hands as part of the plantation of Ulster in 1612, and he is thus technically the founder of Londonderry. In 1614, James I appointed him Controller of the King's Merchant Adventurers, a company which was to have a monopoly of the cloth trade, exporting (principally to the Baltic) cloth already dressed and dyed. "Alderman Cockayne's project" was intended to steal this trade from the Dutch. In 1615 the company made a profit but within three years it collapsed entirely, partly through Dutch protectionist counter-action, but also through shortage of shipping. Cokayne, who was knighted in 1615, saved his personal funds and invested in overseas enterprises, notably a short-lived scheme for a settlement in Nova Scotia. He served as Lord Mayor of London, 1619–20.

Astrid Friis, *Alderman Cokayne's Project and the Cloth Trade* (1927)

COKE, Edward (1552–1634), jurist: born at Mileham, Norfolk, and educated at Norwich School and Trinity College, Cambridge. He entered Clifford's Inn in 1572, was called to the Bar in 1578, showing such skill as a lawyer that he was taken under Burghley's patronage, and made rapid progress, assisted by marriage in 1582 to the wealthy Bridget Paston. Coke was Recorder of Coventry (1585), M.P. for Aldeburgh (1589), Solicitor-General with a knighthood (1592), and Speaker of the House of Commons (1593). In the following years he was a constant rival, in professional and private affairs, to Francis Bacon (q.v.): Coke, and not Bacon, was chosen as Attorney-General in 1594; and in 1598 the rich Lady Elizabeth Hatton (q.v.) chose the widower Coke as her second husband rather than Bacon. He showed himself a harsh prosecutor of

Essex, Ralegh and the Gunpowder Plotters (1601, 1603, 1605). James I appointed him Chief Justice of Common Pleas in 1606 but the King found Coke showed great independence in asserting the supremacy of common law over ecclesiastical cases and in denying the power of the King to change common law by proclamation. His firm resistance to encroachments by the Crown led James to appoint him Chief Justice of the King's Bench in 1613, believing he would have less opportunity in this new post to vindicate common liberties against the Sovereign. His determination to establish the truth about Overbury (q.v.) in 1615 annoyed the King who, on trivial grounds, secured Coke's removal from the Bench in November 1617. Tension with his wife was aggravated by Coke's determination to force his daughter, Frances, to marry John Villiers, the brother of the King's favourite, Buckingham (q.v.). Coke returned to the Commons as M.P. for Liskeard in 1620 and was a forceful critic of royal policy, opposing monopolies and the proposed Spanish marriage for the future Charles I. His intemperate words induced the King to imprison him in the Tower for nine months (1621–2). By 1624 he was back in Parliament, representing Coventry and he continued to sit in the first Parliaments of Charles I's reign, assisting Pym (q.v.) in drawing up the Petition of Right (1628). Between 1600 and 1615 thirteen volumes of his Law Reports were published and in the last seven years of his life four volumes of *Institutes* clarifying the jurisdiction of the various law courts and defining disputed aspects of the criminal law.

J. E. Neale, *The Elizabethan House of Commons* (1949)
S. F. Thorne, *Sir Edward Coke* (1957)
W. J. Jones, *Politics and the Bench* (1971)

COLLINS, Francis (?– d. 1617), lawyer of Stratford: member of Clement's Inn. He held various official posts in Stratford from 1600 onwards, serving on the Town Council from 1602–8 and acting as solicitor for the Corporation, 1609–12. He drew up the indentures for Shakespeare's purchase of tithes in 1605, but by 1613, when he drafted the will of John Combe (q.v.), he was living in Warwick. Shakespeare's will of 25 March 1616 is in Collins's handwriting, and he probably wrote the first draft in January of that year. Shakespeare appointed Collins as one of the two overseers of his will, leaving him twenty marks. In April 1617 Stratford elected Collins as Town Clerk, provided he moved back to Stratford again. He did so, but died in September of that same year.

M. E.

COMBE, John (? ante 1561–1614), landowner and money-lender: member of an old Stratford family, the richest citizen of Stratford-upon-Avon in his time. In 1602, with his uncle William I, Combe sold land to Shakespeare, and in his will he left £20 to the poor of the town and "£5 to Mr Shakspere". He appears to have died a bachelor. The tomb of Combe in Holy Trinity Church has, like Shakespeare's tomb, a monument designed by Gheerart Janssen. Legend maintains that Shakespeare composed an epitaph for Combe but the verses quoted are not original and no trace of them survives on Combe's monument.

E. K. C., *W.S.*

COMBE, Thomas I (?– d. 1609), citizen of Stratford: brother of money-lender John Combe, father of the younger William and Thomas; lived at the College (the old chantry priests' house), by Holy Trinity Church.

E. K. C., *W.S.*

COMBE, Thomas II (1589–1657), lawyer of Stratford: son of Thomas I,. became member of the Middle Temple in 1608. He supported his brother William in his attempt to enclose the common fields of Welcombe, calling the Stratford Council "dogs and curs". Shakespeare left Thomas Combe his sword in his will. Combe served as Recorder of Stratford from 1648 until his death and was Sheriff of Warwickshire in 1648.

E. K. C., *W.S.*
M. E.

COMBE, William I (1551–1610), lawyer and Member of Parliament: born at Broadway, Worcestershire, and admitted to the Middle Temple in 1571. He was elected M.P. for Droitwich in 1588, for Warwick in 1593 and for Warwickshire in 1598. He lived mainly in Warwick, but acted as counsel for Stratford and held land there. Together with his nephew, the money-lender John Combe (q.v.), he sold Shakespeare 127 acres of land in Old Stratford, May 1602.

E. K. C., *W.S.*
M. E.

COMBE, William II (1586–1667), lawyer and landowner at Stratford: son of Thomas I and nephew of money-lender John (qq.v.), matriculated at Christ Church, Oxford, in 1603 and was admitted to the Middle Temple. He was one of the defendants in Shakespeare's Chancery suit over tithes (1610–11). His enclosures of land at Welcombe in 1614 were opposed by Stratford Corporation and in January 1615 led to fighting with tenants alarmed by Combe's activities. In 1616 Chief Justice Coke (q.v.) ruled against Combe, who nevertheless continued to beat and imprison his tenants. Combe's position was strengthened by the fact that he was serving as Sheriff of Warwickshire for the year 1615–16. Eventually, in 1619, he was forced to remove his enclosures by order of the Privy Council. Before and during the Civil War he was a soldier, captain of the Stratford trained band and leader of the militia for the Parliamentarian cause. By then he had become a money-lender, even richer than his uncle John.

E. K. C., *W.S.*
M. E.

CONDELL, Henry (?1562–1627), actor: one of Shakespeare's closest colleagues, mentioned in his will. Condell was a member of the Lord Chamberlain's (King's) Company from 1598 to 1625, and appears in the Royal Patent (1603). His name is not in any cast list after 1619 though in all the other official lists and the First Folio acting list. In 1603 he had a share in the Blackfriars Theatre and later (1612) the Globe, and was Churchwarden of St Mary, Aldermanbury. He and John Heminges (q.v.) were joint editors of the First Folio of Shakespeare's plays and wrote the Preface (1623). Condell was both comedian and tragedian: he acted in Jonson's comedies and also played the Cardinal in Webster's *Duchess of Malfi*. He died on his country estate in Fulham, a richer man than Shakespeare.

E. K. C., *E.S.; W.S.*
G. E. B.
E. A. B. Barnard, *New links with Shakespeare* (1930)

CONSTABLE, Henry (1562–1613), poet: son of Sir Robert Constable of Newark, Nottinghamshire, educated at St John's College, Cambridge (1578–80). Constable was a friend of Philip Sidney (q.v.) and a protégé of Sir Francis Walsingham (q.v.) whom he met in Perth in 1583. Walsingham recommended him to the English ambassador in Paris, Sir

Edward Stafford, and, from 1585 onwards Constable travelled in Europe (Germany, Poland, Italy) on Walsingham's business. He produced a pamphlet defending English intervention in the Low Countries and wrote sonnets to the Princess of Orange. On his return to England — probably in 1588–9 — Constable spent some time at Court and became a friend of Penelope Rich (q.v.) to whom he addressed sonnets. Through her he was involved in intrigues with James VI of Scotland on behalf of Essex. In 1589 also, Constable produced his *Examen Pacifique de la Doctrine des Huguenots*, a treatise written as by a Roman Catholic, but ecumenical in spirit. By 1591 Constable had definitely become a Roman Catholic; he joined Essex's expedition to Rouen and deserted the Protestant cause when he was in France. After a journey to Rome, he settled in Paris, where King Henri IV (by now a Catholic himself) paid him a small pension. Constable kept up a correspondence with Essex and Anthony Bacon (q.v.) propounding various schemes to ensure the succession of James VI to the English throne. In pursuit of his own favourite plan of converting James and his wife, Anne, to Roman Catholicism, Constable visited Scotland in 1599 and acquired some influence at the Scottish Court. In 1600 he again visited Rome, presumably for fresh instructions. He came to England in 1603 and was at first well received by James — now King James I — but a year later he was imprisoned in the Tower. After his release, he stayed in England, poor and obscure and suffering another brief spell of imprisonment in the Fleet before his deportation in 1610. He returned to Paris, where he died three years later. His works include a sonnet-sequence, *Diana* (1592), and spiritual sonnets.

Poems of Henry Constable, edited with an introduction by Joan Grundy (1964)

COOKE, Alexander (?–1614), actor: appeared with the King's Men from 1603 onwards. He had presumably been apprenticed to Heminges, whom he called "my master" and made trustee in his will. By the time of his death Cooke had become a sharer in the company, and he is mentioned in the First Folio list.

COPE, Walter (?–1614), government official: was Member of Parliament for St Mawes in 1588, Weymouth in 1601, Westminster in 1604 and Stonehenge in the year of his death. Cope served as an agent and close adviser of Burghley and remained a confidant of his son Robert Cecil. He was knighted in 1610 and became chamberlain of the Exchequer. In this capacity he assisted his friend Cotton (q.v.) to compile a catalogue of the records in all four treasuries of the Exchequer. In 1607 he built Cope Castle, Kensington, which became Holland House a few years later when Cope's daughter married Henry Rich, Lord Kensington and Earl of Holland.

CORBET (or CORBETT), Richard (1582–1635), bishop, poet: son of Vincent Corbet, of Ewell, Surrey. Vincent Corbet, praised by Ben Johnson in an elegy, seems to have been an independent nursery-man and gardener and was able to send his son to Westminster School. Corbet proceeded to Broadgates Hall, Oxford (1598) and Christ Church (B.A., 1602), where he spent most of his life. As Proctor (1613) he spoke funeral orations for Sir Thomas Bodley and Henry, Prince of Wales (qq.v.). In 1620 he became Dean of Christ Church, as well as Vicar of Cassington near Oxford. In spite of a notorious occasion in 1621 when he dried up while preaching in front of the King at Woodstock, Corbet's High Churchmanship suited the times and he was appointed Bishop of Oxford in 1628.

While at Christ Church he was noted for conviviality; he drank with his chaplain and frequently entertained Ben Jonson at the Deanery. Corbet was fond of practical joking and is said to have sung ballads outside a tavern in Abingdon, disguised as a balladmonger. Corbet's last few years, from 1632, were spent as Bishop of Norwich and he is buried in Norwich Cathedral. He was married in 1623–4 to Alice Hutten, and had two children. Corbet's poetry is mainly light and amusing; it was published after his death in two collections (1647–8). The most famous poems are *Iter Boreale*, the travels of four students in the Midlands north of Oxford, and the *Fairies Farewell*, lamenting the departure of fairies from England as a result of Puritanism.

J. A. W. Bennett and H. R. Trevor-Roper, eds., *The Poems of Richard Corbett* (1955)

CORK, first Earl of (1566–1643) see BOYLE, Richard.

CORNWALLIS, Charles (c. 1580–1629), diplomat: born in Suffolk, the second son of Sir Thomas Cornwallis (*infra*). He was knighted in 1603 and returned as M.P. for Norfolk in 1604. From 1605 to 1609 he was ambassador in Madrid, attempting to mitigate the rigours of the Inquisition so as to benefit English seamen. In December 1610 he became Treasurer of the household of the Prince of Wales (Prince Henry, q.v.), a post he held until Henry's death in November 1612. Cornwallis handled the self-willed young man with tact, and wrote a vivid memoir of the Prince in 1626 which was published by Cornwallis's nephew in 1641. Cornwallis served as Commissioner on Irish affairs in 1613, but fell into disfavour with the King a year later for encouraging members of the Commons to show hostility in their speeches to the Scots

who had accompanied James to London. This hostility to Scotsmen in general — and to Carr (q.v.) in particular — brought him twelve months imprisonment in the Tower. Thereafter he retired to his estate at Harbone in Staffordshire.

CORNWALLIS, Thomas (1519–1604), recusant: born in Suffolk, spent some of his youth at Henry VIII's Court, and was knighted in 1548. He spent several years curbing radical Protestantism in Norfolk and served Queen Mary as the last English Governor of Calais, 1554–7, returning to London as Comptroller of her household in the last year of Mary's life. He represented Suffolk as M.P. in the twelve-day Parliament of November 1558, but was dismissed from office on Elizabeth's accession. He spent most of the remaining years of his life at Brome Hall, Suffolk, briefly held under arrest in 1570 and with his name at the head of recusants in 1587, but otherwise surviving unmolested into the reign of James I.

CORNWALLIS, William (1579–1614), essayist: son of Sir Charles Cornwallis (q.v.) by his first wife, said later to have been educated at Queen's College, Oxford. He knew Latin, but not Greek, Italian and some Spanish, but no French; he read Montaigne in translation. Cornwallis was married young (1595) to Catherine Parker. The couple had eleven children and were extravagant, so that Charles Cornwallis had to help his son out of debt. By 1600 he had become a friend of Donne (q.v.) and started writing. His collected essays appeared in two parts (1600 and 1601), and his *Discourses upon Seneca* in 1601. Cornwallis then tried to enter public life. He went to Scotland to cultivate James VI before his accession, and there made friends with Overbury (q.v.). Cornwallis was M.P. for Orford, 1604 and 1614, and went with his father on his mission to

Spain (1605), but even the pamphlet on the *Miraculous and Happy Union of England and Scotland* (1604) ascribed to him did not bring him the favour of the King to any great extent; it was considered a feeble piece of writing. Cornwallis's only other work was the *Encomium of Richard III*, produced anonymously at first but published under his name after his death (1616). This was the first defence of Richard III, anticipating Sir George Buck (q.v.). Cornwallis was a popular essayist, although less original than Bacon, and his essays were reprinted in 1607 and 1610. He died, however, in poverty.

William Cornwallis, *Essays*, ed., D. C. Allen (1946); *Encomium of Richard III*, ed., J. A. Ramsden and A. N. Kincaid (1977)

CORYAT, Thomas (?1577–1617), traveller, writer: born at Odcombe, Somerset, where his father was Rector. Coryat claimed to be the fourth cousin of the Earl of Essex. He entered Gloucester Hall, Oxford in 1596, leaving in 1599 without graduating. He then returned to Odcombe where in 1606 he organized a new kind of festival, to raise money for parish funds: it involved two mock battles against the men of Yeovil and long speeches by himself. Probably he left Odcombe on his father's death in 1607 and was briefly attached to the household of Prince Henry, where his wit won him acceptance as an unofficial jester. In May 1608 he set off to cross Europe on foot, partly through lack of money for transport. By 21 June he was in Venice. Passing through Switzerland and up the Rhine he reached Cologne on 19 September and was back in London on 3 October. Coryat dedicated his shoes in Odcombe Church, and wrote an account of his journey, *Coryat's Crudities: hastily gobbled up in five months travels* (1611). More than fifty of his acquaintances, including Donne, Dray-

ton, Jonson, Inigo Jones and Wotton wrote introductory poems to the book. In October 1612 Coryat set off overland for Afghanistan and India, taking ship as far as Constantinople. He spent most of the years 1613–14 exploring the Middle East, reached India in 1615 and was received at the Court of the Great Mogul, Jahangir. After travelling on foot for several more months around India, he died at Surat, on

Thomas Coryat

the west coast. Coryat was known in London for his eccentric wit — he called himself the "Odcombian Leg-Stretcher" — and was a popular member of the group of scholars, writers and politicians who met at the Mermaid Tavern in Bread Street. Coryat is, indeed, the only source for the idea of there having been a "Mermaid Club". He sent two letters to the "fraternity" from his last journey. The first, from Aleppo in 1614, was lost; but the second, "from the town of Asmere in eastern India" was printed by Purchas (q.v.). Coryat addressed it to "The High

Seneschal of the Right Worshipful Fraternity of Sirenaical Gentleman, that meet the first Friday of every month at the sign of the Mermaid in Bread Street". He refers to the fact that they had given him a "password" at the last meeting before his departure, and he mentions by name several members of the fraternity, including Donne, Jonson and Jones, as well as sending a personal message to Sir Robert Cotton. Unfortunately he gave no details of rules or membership of the "club". (cf. *John Jackson, William Johnson*).

M. Strachan, *Life and Adventures of Thomas Coryat* (1962)

COTTAM, John (fl. 1566–81), schoolmaster: born in Lancashire, graduated from Brasenose College, Oxford, in 1566, settled in London but came to Stratford-upon-Avon in 1579 as Master of the school. In November 1581 his younger brother, Thomas Cottam, who had followed him to Brasenose and London but became a Jesuit priest, was put on trial with Edmund Campion and was executed at Tyburn on 30 May 1582. John left Stratford at the end of 1581, probably asked to resign as Schoolmaster because of his brother's activities. Subsequently John Cottam inherited his father's estate, gave up teaching and lived in Lancashire as a Roman Catholic recusant.

M. E.

COTTON, Robert Bruce (1571–1631), antiquarian: eldest son of Thomas Cotton of Conington, Huntingdonshire, the family claiming descent from King Robert Bruce. Cotton was a pupil of Camden (q.v.) at Westminster School, going on to Jesus College, Cambridge (1581–5) and the Middle Temple (1588). Together with Camden and Spelman (q.v.) he helped to found the Society of Antiquaries in about

1586. Marriage to an heiress, Elizabeth Brocas, in 1592 enabled him to find the wealth to build up a valuable collection of books and manuscripts by the end of the century. He was introduced at Court by Hunsdon (George Carey, q.v.), for whose pocket borough of Newtown he was returned to Parliament in 1601. James I knighted Cotton at his coronation, creating him a baronet in 1611. Cotton was M.P. for

Sir Robert Bruce Cotton

Huntingdonshire (1604–11), under the patronage of Henry Howard (q.v.), returning to the Commons as member for Old Sarum (1624), Thetford (1625) and Castle Rising (1628). He was a friend of Jonson and Donne and a member of the Mermaid Tavern fraternity (v. *Coryat*). Cotton allowed his library to be used by most of the leading scholars of the day. After Henry Howard's death in 1614 he became a client of the Court favourite, Carr (q.v.). In 1616 he was confined in the Tower of London for five months because of advice he had given Carr during the investigation of the death of Overbury (q.v.). Thereafter, Cotton tended to side with the opposition, looking upon Buckingham

55

especially as a political enemy. In 1622 Cotton was able to purchase a house at Westminster between the two Houses of Parliament. He housed his collection there, and Cotton House became a meeting place for scholars from all over Europe as well as of Parliamentarians searching for historical precedents in their contest with the Court. He was in trouble in 1627 for publishing a study of Henry III's reign which was interpreted as a plea to the young King to reform his government. Two years later he was imprisoned for allowing the circulation of an anti-Royalist pamphlet, and his library was closed. Although granted his liberty by the amnesty which celebrated Charles II's birth (May 1630), he was denied access to his library except upon supervision by a clerk of the council. His health gave way under the stress of these restraints, and he died on 6 May 1631. During his lifetime he had given many books and manuscripts to Bodley, Selden (qq.v.) and other private collectors, such as Robert Cecil. His grandson presented the Cottonian Collection to the nation in 1700. Although suffering loss by fire in 1730, it is now in the British Library.

K. Sharpe, *Sir Robert Cotton* (1979)

COURTEN, William (1572–1636), merchant and entrepreneur: born in London, the son of a Flemish refugee, spent some twenty years of his youth at Haarlem in the clothing industry. On his return to London he built up a company which from 1606 flourished in the silk and linen business, bringing him such wealth that he was eventually able to undertake major trading enterprises both in the West Indies and the East Indies. He was knighted in May 1622. From 1624 to 1631 he colonised Barbados, also staking a claim to all the unexplored southern lands; *"Terra Australis Incognita"*, as he called them.

Although he lent considerable sums to James I and to Charles I, conflict with the Dutch — including some of his own relatives — weakened the financial structure of his company in the 1630s.

COWLEY, Richard (?–1619), actor: played minor roles with Strange's or the Admiral's Men, 1590–3 and carried a letter to Alleyn from his wife, while the company was on tour. By 1600 he was well established with the Chamberlain's Men and is known to have played Verges in *Much Ado*. He was payee for the company in 1601. His name appears in the Royal Patent, 1603 and in the First Folio list, but he was never a sharer in the profits of the company.

CRANFIELD, Lionel (1575–1645, created Earl of Middlesex 1622), Lord High Treasurer: born in London of obscure origins, became a City merchant and was a spokesman before the Privy Council for the Mercers' Company. James I saw he was a shrewd businessman, knighted him and appointed him Surveyor General of Customs in 1613. Cranfield's skill in checking wastage of funds in the royal household and in the navy made him acceptable to both King and Commons. He was a member of the 1621 Parliament, under Buckingham's patronage, but became Lord High Treasurer before the end of the year. He checked inflation by curbing expenditure although his own fortunes flourished for three years, and in 1622 he purchased the estate of Milcote on Avon, which had belonged to Edward Greville (q.v.). Cranfield's opposition to English participation in the Thirty Years War made him unpopular with Parliament. He was impeached for alleged corruption in 1624, fined, dismissed from office and briefly imprisoned. He retired from public life in 1625, sat in the Lords during the Short Parliament of 1640, but remained uncommitted when the Civil War broke out.

R. H. Tawney, *Business and Politics under James I* (1958)
M. Prestwich, *Cranfield: Politics and Profit under the Early Stuarts* (1966)

CREEDE, Thomas (?–?1617), printer: of unknown origins. Creede became a freeman of the Stationers' Company in 1578 and had his press in London from 1593 at the "Catherine Wheel", Thames Street (to 1600) and the "Eagle and Child", Old Exchange (1600–17). His work was fine and he printed several of Shakespeare's plays: the early *Henry VI*, part 2 for Thomas Millington (1594), *Richard III* for Andrew Wise (1598, 1602) and Matthew Law (1605), *Romeo and Juliet* for Cuthbert Burby (1599), *Henry V* for John Busby and Thomas Millington (1600) and Thomas Pavier (1602), and *Merry Wives of Windsor* for Arthur Johnson (1602). In 1616 Creede took a partner, Bernard Alsop, who succeeded to the business in 1617, presumably at Creede's death.

CREWE, Ranulph (1558–1646), lawyer: son of a tanner from Nantwich, Cheshire. He was called to the Bar (Lincoln's Inn) in 1584 and was M.P. for Brackley in the Parliament of 1597–8. James I knighted him in 1614 and he was elected Speaker of the Commons that year, presiding over the so-called "Addled Parliament" (April-June 1614) which refused to vote supplies or pass measures. In 1615 Sir Ranulph became Serjeant-at-Law and he was one of the commissioners who enquired into the death of Overbury (q.v.). He became Lord Chief Justice of the King's Bench in January 1625 but was forced to resign in November 1626 because he declined to sign a document saying that forced loans were legal. He then retired to Crewe Hall, Cheshire, which he allowed the Parliamentarians to fortify during the Civil War.

CROMWELL, Edward (1559–1607), soldier: great-grandson of Henry VIII's minister, Thomas Cromwell (1485–1540), and a third cousin of Sir Oliver Cromwell (*infra*). Edward Cromwell was educated at Jesus College, Oxford. He served as a colonel under Essex (q.v.) in Normandy in 1591, took part in the "Islands Voyage" to the Azores (1597) and helped Essex in Ireland, 1599. In 1592 he succeeded his father as third Baron Cromwell. His role in the Essex insurrection of January 1601 is confused but he was thrown into the Tower and heavily fined before securing his release. James I appointed him a Privy Councillor. Soon thereafter he settled in Ireland, where he died in September 1607.

CROMWELL, Oliver (1563–1655), East Anglian landowner and uncle of the Lord Protector: born at Hinchingbrooke, the family estate outside Huntingdon, the eldest son of Sir Henry Cromwell, whose scale of entertainment for the Queen and her Court won him respect as the "Golden Knight". Oliver, himself knighted by the Queen in 1598, offered lavish entertainment to James I and his family at Hinchingbrooke on several occasions. It is probable that Sir Oliver's nephew, godson and famous namesake appeared, as a child, in a play by Tomkis (q.v.) before King James at Hinchingbrooke. Sir Oliver sat for Huntingdon in Parliament and showed interest in draining the Fens and colonising Virginia. His second marriage, to the widow of the wealthiest commoner in England, Sir Horatio Palavicino (q.v.), helped Sir Oliver enjoy life on the scale to which his father had accustomed him, but by 1627 expenditure bore so heavily on the family that Sir Oliver was forced to sell

Hinchingbrooke to Sir Sidney Montague and spend the last twenty-eight years of his long life at his smaller property, the gatehouse of Ramsey Abbey, secured for the family by his great-great uncle, Thomas Cromwell (1485–1540). Sir Oliver remained a staunch Royalist, raising men and funds for Charles I, although prepared to accept the intervention of his nephew to save his remaining possessions from sequestration in 1648.

A. Fraser, *Cromwell, Our Chief of Men* (1973)

CROSSE, Samuel, (?–?1605), actor: his name appears in the list of First Folio actors as having played in Shakespeare but he is not mentioned in other lists. It is possible that he was an actor from the previous generation (mentioned by Heywood, q.v.) who appeared in early plays by Shakespeare.

CUFFE, Henry (1563–1601), scholar: matriculated at Trinity College, Oxford in 1578, subsequently becoming a Fellow. He held tutorial posts at Merton and Queen's Colleges and was Professor of Greek from 1590 to 1596 when he accompanied Essex (q.v.) on his expedition to Cadiz. Cuffe remained as secretary to Essex throughout his Irish misadventures and disgrace; and he seems at times to have been generously rash with advice. In 1600 Cuffe completed his only literary work, *The Differences of the Ages of Man's Life*. He was arrested with the other Essex supporters after the rebellion of 1601, the Earl blaming him for instigating the attempt to raise London. Cuffe was hanged, drawn and quartered at Tyburn on 25 February 1601.

CUMBERLAND, George, third Earl of (1558–1605) see CLIFFORD, George.

CUMBERLAND, Margaret Clifford, Countess of (1560–1616): the daughter of Francis Russell, second Earl of Bedford. She and George Clifford, Earl of Cumberland (q.v.) were brought up together, as her father was Clifford's guardian. They were married in 1577 in the presence of Queen Elizabeth. Margaret was handsome and well-educated, interested in science and a good manager of the Cumberland estates, but she and Clifford could not agree, and before 1603 Margaret had separated from her husband and was living with her sister, Lady Warwick (q.v.). A daughter of the marriage, Anne Clifford (q.v.), survived. Cumberland died in 1606 and Margaret spent the last ten years of her life making great efforts to overset his will and secure the estates for Anne. She had all the family deeds copied into vast reference books for her law suits, but to no avail.

V. A. Wilson, *Society Women of Shakespeare's time* (1925)
Anne Clifford, *Diary*, ed., G. Williamson (1967)

"CUTPURSE Moll" (1570s–1650), thief, bawd, fence, prostitute: was the origin of the chief character in *The Roaring Girl*, by Middleton and Dekker (?1607). Her real name was Mary Frith or Markham, and she may have acted as well as being mentioned in several plays; women did not normally appear on stage but Moll always wore men's clothing and smoked a pipe. She was born in Aldersgate Street, London, ran a school for thieves for a time, and in 1612 did public penance at Paul's Cross. She was still pursuing her career during the Civil War, when she held up and robbed the Parliamentary commander Fairfax. Moll died of dropsy.

G. Salgado, *The Elizabethan Underworld* (1977)

D

DABORNE, Robert (?–1628), dramatist: born "a gentleman" (so he claimed), probably in Guildford, Surrey. He was a patentee for the Queen's Revels Company in 1610; he may have written for them, and certainly did so after their amalgamation with Lady Elizabeth's Men in 1613. He wrote tragedy or tragi-comedy, alone or in collaboration, selling some of his work to the King's Men. Only two of his plays survive. Daborne was often in debt to Henslowe (q.v.), generally poor, and once gaoled in the Clink. Between 1614 and 1618 he abandoned the stage in favour of ordination. By 1620 he was a prebendary of Lismore in Ireland, serving there as Dean for the last seven years of his life.

E. K. C., *E.S.*

DALLINGTON, Robert (1561–1637), author and Master of Charterhouse: born at Geddington, Northants, was a Scholar of Corpus Christi College, Cambridge (about 1575–80) and then a schoolmaster in Norfolk. Dallington travelled extensively in France and Italy before becoming secretary to Francis Manners, Earl of Rutland (q.v.). He was Gentleman of the Privy Chamber to Prince Henry and possibly after Henry's death to Prince Charles. In 1624 he was knighted and made Master of Charterhouse. He is buried in Charterhouse. Dallington wrote two travel books, *A Survey of the Great Duke's State of Tuscany* (published 1605) and *A Method of Travel* (1606), and a collection of sayings, *Aphorisms Civil and Military* (1613).

DANIEL, Samuel (1562–1619), poet and dramatist: born in Somerset, probably the son of a music master, John Daniel.

Samuel Daniel entered Magdalen Hall, Oxford, in 1579 but did not take a degree and by 1585 was serving in France as an agent of Walsingham, sending him reports on political affairs. He also went on diplomatic missions to Paris and Italy in 1586. He was a good Italian scholar and a friend of the lexicographer John Florio (q.v.), who married Daniel's sister. On returning to England Daniel became a tutor, first to William, third Earl of Pembroke, and then to Anne Clifford (q.v.); his *Poetical Essays* of 1599 include an epistle to Anne's mother, Lady Cumberland. He had already produced his sonnet sequence *Delia* and the *Complaint of Rosamund* (both 1592), as well as a Senecan tragedy, *Cleopatra* (1594) and an epic poem on the Wars of the Roses, *Civil Wars* (1595). In 1603 Daniel tactfully published a *Panegyrike Congratulatorie* in both Edinburgh and London. He was invited to provide the first masque of the reign and became a licensee for the Queen's Revels Company, who produced his *Philotas* (1604). The tragedy was thought to defend Essex's rebellion and Daniel was summoned to appear before the Privy Council. He was, however, still able to compose masques for the Court, notably the *Tethys Festival* which marked the Prince of Wales's investiture in June 1610. In 1615 he became Inspector of the Children of the Queen's Revels, his brother, John — a musician — being by now a patentee of the company. Samuel Daniel is known to have been on poor terms with Ben Jonson, who thought little of his poetry. He believed that the English language was particularly suited to rhymed verse, as he maintained in his *Defence of Rhyme*, which was published in 1602 in reply to Thomas Campion (q.v.). Drayton (q.v.) considered Daniel "too much historian in verse". His prose work, *History of England,* was widely read in the years before the Civil War. Daniel's London home was in Old Street, but he kept a farm near Beckington, in Somerset, and there he was buried. Because of his early connection with Pembroke, Daniel has been considered a possible "rival poet" in Shakespeare's sonnets.

Joan Rees, *Samuel Daniel* (1964)

DANTER, John, (?–1599), printer: son of John Danter, weaver, of Oxfordshire. He was apprenticed first to John Day in March 1582, then transferred to Robert Robinson, 1588. During his apprenticeship Danter was caught operating a secret press, reprinting books of which Richard Day owned the patents. He was barred from becoming a master printer, but the sentence was remitted by 1589 when Danter was made a freeman of the Stationers' Company. At first he was in partnership with Henry Chettle (q.v.) and William Hoskins, but in 1591 set up on his own; his presses were in Duck Lane, near Smithfield, then Hosier Lane, near Holborn Conduit (1592). Danter printed two Shakespeare Quartos, *Titus Andronicus*, sold by Thomas Millington and Edward White (1594) and *Romeo and Juliet* (pirated, 1597); no copy of the *Titus* was discovered until 1905. Both were badly printed, like all Danter's work. He was often in trouble for unauthorised printing of privileged books, and his press was seized (1596) for producing a Roman Catholic devotional work.

DANVERS, Charles (?1568–1601), soldier: son of Sir John Danvers of Dauntsey, fought in the Netherlands and was knighted in 1588, sitting in the Parliament of 1589 as M.P. for Cirencester. A long feud between Sir John Danvers and his neighbour Sir Walter Long was continued by their sons. After a series of accusations and abuse between members of the families, Charles received letters from the Longs which (so his mother later told Burghley) were "of such form as the heart of a man indeed had rather die than endure". On 4 October 1594 Sir John Danvers and his sons, Charles and Henry (*infra*), with a considerable retinue, travelled to Corsham where Sir Walter Long and his son, Henry, were at dinner. In an affray, Henry Long was killed. Charles Danvers and his brother found temporary refuge with their friend Southampton (q.v.) at Titchfield (over sixty miles from Corsham), and were smuggled to France, taking service with Henri IV until pardoned by Elizabeth in 1598. The Danvers-Long family feud created a considerable sensation and was almost certainly one of the influences on Southampton's friend, Shakespeare, during the writing of *Romeo and Juliet*. Charles Danvers, who returned to England a secret Roman Catholic, was heavily implicated in the Essex conspiracy of 1601, being given responsibility for taking possession of the guard chamber at the palace in Whitehall. He was charged with treason and beheaded on Tower Hill.

A. L. Rowse, *Shakespeare's Southampton* (1965)

DANVERS, Henry (1573–1644), soldier: second son of Sir John Danvers and therefore brother of Charles (*supra*). He was Philip Sidney's page, spending a few terms at Christ Church, Oxford, before serving in Normandy under Essex (q.v.) who knighted him in 1591. With Charles Danvers he was involved in the Long murder scandal, and may indeed have personally killed Henry Long with his dagger. After pardon in 1598 he served, with Southampton (q.v.), under Essex in Ireland, remaining there until 1602 and thus escaping involvement in the conspiracy which cost his brother's life. Henry was created Baron Danvers of Dauntsey upon James I's accession and served as Lord President of Munster from 1607 to 1615, becoming a friend of Prince Henry. His relative, John Aubrey, describes him as "tall and spare, temperate, sedate and solid", and commends his shrewd management of his estate. Charles I made him Earl of Danby in 1626 and created him a Knight of the Garter in April 1633 with great ceremony. He is best remembered for founding the Botanic Garden in Oxford in 1621, originally intending the three-acre site beside the Cherwell for the growth of herbs needed for medicine. Henry Danvers never married. His younger brother John (?1588–1655), knighted by James I and sitting for Oxford University in four Parliaments, became a colonel in the Parliamentary army and disgraced the family by signing the death warrant of Charles I.

O. L. Dick, ed., *Aubrey's Brief Lives* (1949)

DAVENANT, Jane (?–1622), alleged mistress of Shakespeare: wife of John Davenant (*infra*) of the Tavern Inn, Oxford. She was reputed, in the seventeenth century, to have been Shakespeare's mistress, but there is no evidence for this apart from the claim of her son, Sir William Davenant (q.v.), that Shakespeare was his father. In 1913 the writer Arthur Acheson sought to identify Jane Davenant as the "Dark Lady" of the sonnets and heroine, Avisa, of *Willobie His Avisa*, a poem prefaced by the first printed reference to Shakespeare's poetry (v. *Willoughby*); but Acheson's views won little acceptance.

A. Acheson, *Mistress Davenant* (1913)
J. O. Halliwell-Philipps, *Outlines of the Life of Shakespeare* (1898)

DAVENANT, John (?–1622), Oxford landlord: from 1604 he was landlord of the Tavern, a wine-house later known as the Crown, adjoining the Cross Inn, in Cornmarket Street, Oxford. Tradition held that Shakespeare often stayed there and that the landlady was his mistress (*supra*). The King's Men certainly lodged at the Tavern when they played before the Mayor and Corporation of Oxford on 9 October 1605. John Davenant, reputedly a melancholy man, was Bailiff of Oxford in 1613 and Mayor of the city at the time of his death. He was the recognised father of the dramatist and poet laureate, Sir William Davenant (*infra*).

DAVENANT, William (1606–68), dramatist, poet: son of John Davenant, landlord of the Tavern Inn, Oxford, and his wife Jane (*supra*). Davenant was said to be Shakespeare's godson and later claimed to be his natural son. Certainly an early devotion to Shakespeare led him to write an *Ode in Remembrance of Master Shakespeare* (published 1638) in 1618, when he was twelve. He was educated at Lincoln College, Oxford (from 1620), became a page to the Duchess of Richmond, and later served Fulke Greville, first Baron Brooke (q.v.). Davenant became a popular poet in Court circles, especially favoured by Queen Henrietta Maria. He also wrote plays and in 1638 was made Poet Laureate. Next year he lost his nose from syphilis, which made him the butt of many jokes. Davenant had an exciting Civil War on the King's side, full of daring exploits and hair-breadth escapes; he was knighted by Charles I at the siege of Gloucester (1643). From 1650 to 1652 he was in the Tower, where he wrote an epic poem *Gondibert* (1651); Milton is supposed to have rescued him from captivity. Before and after the Civil War, Davenant was manager of the Drury Lane Theatre, and later transferred his patent to Covent Garden. He wrote *The Siege of Rhodes* (1656), the first English opera, introduced actresses to the stage, and, with Dryden, adapted Shakespeare's *Tempest* (1667).

DAVIES, John (?1565–1618), poet and writing-master: known as "John Davies of Hereford", his native town. He published poems from 1603 (*Microcosmos*) to 1617 (*Wit's Bedlam*). *The Scourge of Folly* (undated, but appearing in the Stationers' Register for 1610) is a poem addressed to Shakespeare as "our English Terence". Marginal notes in earlier poems suggest he made other references to Shakespeare. Other epigrams in *The Scourge of Folly* mention Jonson and Fletcher. Davies's *Anatomy of Fair Writing* was published posthumously (1633). He was writing-master to Henry, Prince of Wales (q.v.).

DAVIES, Sir John (1569–1626), poet and lawyer: born at Tilsbury, Wiltshire, educated at Winchester and Queen's College, Oxford, entering the Middle Temple in 1588. He wrote sonnets, *Epigrams* (1590), the long work, *Orchestra, or a Poem of Dancing* (1596), and a collection of acrostics on the name Elizabeth, *Astraea* (1599), as well as contributing to entertainments for the Queen. His ambitious *Nosce Teipsum* (1599) resembles the later metaphysical poetry of the seventeenth century by seeking to prove the immortality of the soul, questioning scientific theories. From 1598 to 1601 he was disbarred for having assaulted a fellow member of the Middle Temple, but his legal career prospered under James I. He was knighted as Solicitor-General for Ireland (1603–6) and was Attorney-General for Ireland from 1606 to 1619 as well as Speaker of the Irish Parliament in 1613. Charles I appointed him Lord Chief Justice of England, but he spluttered his life away with apoplexy before taking up the post.

DAVIS, John (?1550–1605), seaman: born at Sandridge, Devon. He was already "well grounded... in the art of navigation" by 1585 when he was appointed by a group of London merchants to head an expedition in search of a north-west passage to China. Both this, two month, voyage and longer voyages in 1586 and 1587 explored and named points along the coast of Greenland, reaching latitude 73' North. Davis served off the Azores in 1589 and commanded *Desire* in Cavendish's last expedition of 1591–3, in which Davis discovered the Falkland Islands. He accompanied Essex to Cadiz in 1596 and the Azores in 1597, undertook two expeditions for the Dutch in the East Indies in 1598 and 1600 and then returned to the waters around Java and Sumatra for the British East India Company in 1601 and 1604–5. In December 1605 he was treacherously murdered by Japanese pirates in the Java Sea. Davis invented navigational aids, and produced several manuals of seamanship and navigation, notably his *Seaman's Secrets* (1594) and *The World's Hydrographical Description* (1595).

A. H. Markham, *The Voyages and Works of John Davis* (1880)

DAVISON, Francis (?1575–?1619), poet and lawyer: son of William Davison (c. 1541–1608), who as Secretary of State in 1587 was imprisoned in the Tower for having allowed the despatch of the death warrant for Mary, Queen of Scots without royal authority. Francis Davison entered Gray's Inn in 1593 and contributed to the Gray's Inn masque of 1595. He was a friend of the Earl of Essex, but avoided implication in the troubles of February 1601. Together with his brother Walter, Francis Davison published *A Poetical Rhapsody* (1602), a collection of poems by Ralegh, Greene, Wotton, Spenser, and others.

DAY, John (1574–1640), dramatist: a farmer's son from Norfolk. He entered Gonville and Caius College, Cambridge in 1592 but was expelled from the University a year later for stealing a book. From 1599 to 1603 Day was writing for the Admiral's and Worcester's Men, mostly in collaboration, and only *The Blind Beggar of Bethnal Green* survives from this period. His later plays were mainly written alone; they include *Law Tricks, The Isle of Gulls* and *Humour out of Breath*, all of them comedies for the Children of the Revels. He also wrote part of *The Travels of Three English Brothers*, a comedy in which Will Kempe appears as a character. His *Parliament of Bees* (?1607) is a set of allegorical dialogues, introducing different types of "bees" to illustrate various virtues and vices. Day appears to have continued to write plays after 1608, mainly in collaboration with Dekker, and for inferior companies.

E. K. C., *E.S.*

DEE, John (1527–1608) mathematician, philosopher, alchemist, astrologer: was of Welsh descent, later claiming kinship with King Arthur, but was born in London and educated at Chelmsford Grammar School and St John's College, Cambridge (1542–5). He became a Fellow of Trinity College, Cambridge, on its foundation in 1546 and there produced Aristophanes's *Peace*, with marvellous mechanical flying effects. Dee began travelling on the Continent, bringing back to Trinity the first astronomical instruments seen in England. In 1548 he became a Cambridge Master of Arts, the only degree he had, though he was called "Doctor". English universities were not sufficiently scientific for him, so he went to Louvain University and then lectured in mathematics at Paris. On his return to England in 1551 he served the Earl of Pembroke's family and tutored

the Duke of Northumberland's children, including the future Earl of Leicester. Dee enjoyed lifelong patronage from the Sidney-Herbert circle. He was in disgrace under Mary I but, favoured by Elizabeth as an astrologer, he settled at Mortlake in the intervals of travelling. There he collected

John Dee

the largest private library in England and studied philosophy, alchemy, navigation and antiquities. He gave advice to the Queen and Court, and was consulted by navigators, especially Gilbert, Frobisher and John Davis (qq.v.). With the aid of a (possibly fraudulent) medium, Edward Kelly, Dee began to hold seances and raise spirits; in 1583 the two men visited Bohemia and the Court of the Emperor Rudolf II, but the trip ended in failure, Dee and Kelly splitting up. Kelly went on to great feats of alchemy (v. *Edward Dyer*). Meanwhile Dee's house in Mortlake had been looted by a mob who regarded him as a magician and he returned to England in 1588 a poor man. A long struggle for official advancement ended, in 1595, with his appointment as Warden of Manchester College, originally founded as part of the collegiate church of St Mary, Manchester (now the cathedral) but coming under royal patronage after the Reformation. Dee introduced the organ into the church, but his relations with the Fellows of the college were strained and he resigned in 1604. His last four years of life were spent in poverty, and he was forced to sell his remaining books. He begged James I to have him tried for sorcery so that he might defend himself and re-establish his reputation, but the request was not granted. Dee wrote seventy-nine works, the majority of them never printed. Most influential were his mathematical treatises and his *General and Rare Memorials pertaining to the Perfect Art of Navigation* (1577), in which he was the first English writer to use the phrase "British Empire". He also kept a diary for the years from 1595 to 1601. Shakespeare's Glendower in *Henry IV*, Part 1, may well owe something to John Dee.

P. J. French, *John Dee: the World of an Elizabethan Magus* (1972)

DEKKER, Thomas (c. 1572–1632), dramatist: born in London; nothing is known of his education or early life. Between 1598 and 1602 he wrote, either alone or in collaboration, some forty-four plays for the Admiral's and Worcester's Men, but only six of them survive. In 1599 he completed two comedies, *Old Fortunatus*, and the famous *Shoemaker's Holiday*, which was based on a story by Thomas Deloney (q.v.). *Satiromastix* (1601), played by the Lord Chamberlain's Men and Paul's Boys, was in part a satire on Jonson and his circle. Although Jonson called Dekker "a rogue", the two men collaborated in London's entertainments for the King on the eve of his coronation in 1604. Dekker then took to writing pamphlets; his *Gull's Hornbook* of 1609 was an attack on fashionable fops, and he was also the author of six vivid pamphlets about the plague,

especially in London in 1603. He continued to write for the stage, dramatising London life among the middle and lower classes in plays like *The Roaring Girl* (1611), a comedy in which he collaborated with Middleton (q.v.). In 1612 he produced the Lord Mayor's pageant, but a year later his long personal history of poverty and debt landed him in the King's Bench Prison, where he remained until 1619. The last play of which he was sole author was a tragi-comedy, *Match Me in London*, published in 1631 but performed earlier. Together with Ford, Massinger, Rowley and Day he continued to write, mainly for Prince Charles's Men, until the last years of his life and again produced the Lord Mayor's pageant, in 1628 and 1629. He was twice a recusant, and probably died in debt. His surviving works suggest a man of cheerful temperament, well-disposed towards the poorer classes and sympathetic to animals.

DELONEY, Thomas (1543–1607), balladmonger, pamphleteer, novelist: came from Norwich and was a silk weaver by trade. In 1588 he wrote three ballads about the Spanish Armada. An indiscreet reference to Queen Elizabeth in a ballad of 1596 caused him some trouble and he turned to the writing of prose. He was the author of three loosely constructed "craft" novels: *Jack of Newbury* (1597) about weavers; *The Gentle Craft* (1597–8) about shoemakers; *Thomas of Reading* (1600) about clothiers. *The Gentle Craft* contained the stories of the shoemaker Simon Eyre who became Lord Mayor of London (v. Dekker's *Shoemaker's Holiday*) and "Long Meg of Westminster", a notorious adventuress who dressed as a man, went for a soldier and finished by keeping a tavern in Islington. Deloney's novels were noted for their scenes of London life. He died in poverty.

R. G. Howarth, *Two Elizabethan writers of fiction, Nash and Deloney* (1956)

DERBY, Ferdinando Stanley, fifth Earl of (1559/60–1594) see STRANGE, Ferdinando Stanley, Lord Strange.

DERBY, Henry Stanley, fourth Earl of (1531–93): son of Edward Stanley, third Earl, and his wife Dorothy (Howard), daughter of the Duke of Norfolk and great aunt to Queen Elizabeth. He married (1555) Margaret Clifford, daughter of the Earl of Cumberland and granddaughter through her mother of Mary Tudor, Henry VIII's sister. This marriage, which was not a very happy one, brought a tenuous claim to the English throne into the Stanley family. As Lord Strange, Henry Stanley was Gentleman of the Privy Chamber to both Edward VI and Philip II of Spain, but the family prospered more in Elizabeth's reign. Henry Stanley did not attend university, but was a member of Gray's Inn (1562). From 1572, when he succeeded to the earldom, he was Lord Lieutenant of Lancaster and Chester. In 1574 he became a Knight of the Garter, and was head of the mission which took the Garter to Henri III of France in 1585. Derby was a determined enemy of Roman Catholicism; he was one of the earls on the commission to try Mary, Queen of Scots (1586) and Lord High Steward at Arundel's trial (1589). Derby was patron of a company of actors, from 1573 to 1582; they appeared sometimes at Court, but mainly in the provinces, and were not so famous as the company of his son Lord Strange (q.v.). For the last four years of his life he was Steward of the Queen's Household. He was buried at Ormskirk; his wife, who survived him by three years, lies in Westminster Abbey.

DERBY, William Stanley, sixth Earl of (1561–1642): second son of Henry Stanley, fourth Earl (*supra*) and his wife Margaret (Clifford) great-niece of Henry VIII. He was educated at St John's College, Oxford, where he matriculated at

the age of eleven, together with his older brother, Ferdinando Lord Strange (q.v.). In 1594 he entered Lincoln's Inn and succeeded his brother as Earl of Derby. Next year (on 26 January) he married Elizabeth Vere, granddaughter of Lord Burghley (qq.v.). The marriage, which was celebrated at Greenwich in the Court, may have been the occasion for the first performance of Shakespeare's *Midsummer Night's Dream*. In 1601 Derby was made a Knight of the Garter and from 1607 until his death he served as Lord Lieutenant of Lancaster and Chester, after 1626 jointly with his son. He retained the Lordship of the Isle of Man as part of the inheritance of the Earls of Derby by buying it back from his nieces. Derby had a company of actors playing in the provinces, probably mainly with the same players as his brother's Strange's Men, from 1594 to 1618. Between 1599 and 1601 they appeared at Court, led by Robert Browne (q.v.). Derby was said to be writing comedies for them himself in 1599, a fact which led some nineteenth-century enthusiasts to claim him as the author of Shakespeare's plays. He was buried, with others of his family, at Ormskirk.

S. Schoenbaum, *Shakespeare's Lives* (1970)

DEVEREUX, Robert (1566–1601) see ESSEX, 2nd Earl of.

DEVEREUX, Robert (1591–1646) see ESSEX, 3rd Earl of.

DEWE, Thomas (?–1625), bookseller: became a freeman of the Stationers' Company in 1621. He published Shakespeare's *King John* (1622). He must have acquired the copyright from John Helme (q.v.) with whom he may have been in partnership.

D'EWES, Simonds (1602–50), antiquarian: member of a family of Flemish descent. His grandfather was a prominent London printer, Gerard d'Ewes (d. 1591) and his father, Paul, bought the manor of Stowlangtoft in Suffolk, where Simonds spent most of his boyhood. From Lavenham School he went to St John's College, Cambridge, was called to the Bar at the Middle Temple in 1623, but married an heiress with much land in Suffolk in 1626 and decided to retire, enjoying the social status of the knighthood conferred on him that summer by Charles I. His antiquarian interests attracted the attention of Cotton and Selden and he was respected as a constitutional historian and an authority on the legal force of ordinances issued without the King's consent. He sat for Sudbury, Suffolk, in the Long Parliament, was a Presbyterian in religion and politics, and was one of the most eminent muddle-heads of his generation. His greatest work was his compilation of the detailed Parliamentary journals for Queen Elizabeth's reign.

J. O. Halliwell, ed., *Autobiography and Correspondence of Sir Simonds D'Ewes* (1845)

DIGGES, Dudley (1583–1639), Member of Parliament and patron of exploration: son of Thomas Digges (q.v.) and step-son of Shakespeare's friend, Thomas Russell (q.v.). He graduated from University College, Oxford in 1601 having had the future Archbishop Abbot as his tutor. From 1604 to 1611 he was M.P. for Tewkesbury, and was knighted in 1607. Digges was interested in exploration, and was a member of the Council of the Virginia Company in 1609. He helped raise some of the money for Hudson's voyage to discover the north-west Passage and even advocated an expedition to the North Pole. In 1611 he became a Governor of the North-West Passage Company and published a book proving that the passage existed. Digges was active in the East India and Muscovy Companies as well; in 1618 he accompanied the botanist John Tradescant (q.v.) on a voyage to Russia. Throughout the 1620s Digges was one of the leaders of the Commons, taking a prominent part in the impeachment of Buckingham in 1626, when he was briefly imprisoned by Charles I in the Tower, and he spoke at length in the debates on the Petition of Right in 1628. Later he was reconciled to the King, becoming Master of the Rolls in 1636. As his main house Digges built Chilham Castle in Kent, finished in 1616.

J. L. Hotson, *I, William Shakespeare* (1937)
K. Sharpe, ed., *Faction and Parliament* (1978)

DIGGES, Leonard (1588–1635), writer: son of Thomas Digges, brother of Dudley Digges and step-son of Shakespeare's friend Thomas Russell (qq.v.). He graduated from University College, Oxford in 1606 and published his first book, a translation of Claudian, in 1617. It was dedicated to his much loved sister Ursula, who died soon afterwards. He returned to Oxford in 1621 and remained there for the rest of his life. Fluency in French and Spanish enabled him to produce notable translations, especially of Spanish literature. He was a Shakespeare enthusiast and wrote two sets of laudatory verses for the First Folio of 1623; the shorter set was printed.

J. L. Hotson, *I, William Shakespeare* (1937)

DIGGES, Thomas (d. 1595), scientist and mathematician: was Member of Parliament for Wallingford (1572–83) and Southampton (1584–5), serving under the nomination of the Earl of Leicester. Digges was reckoned one of the most eloquent debaters in the Commons. He had a good patron in Leicester, under whom he served in the Low Countries (1585). Digges was respected by Burghley as an astronomer and, in his *Alae seu Scalae mathematicae* (1573) and *Prognostication* (1576), he became the first man to explain in England the details of the Copernican system. Digges also wrote on navigation, fortification, pyrotechnics, ballistics, and the designing of ships, but most of his work was unfinished because he became involved in endless lawsuits. In 1588 he was one of the chief consultants for the engineering works required to safeguard Dover Harbour. His attempts to stop the corrupt practice of drawing pay for dead soldiers made him so many enemies that he lost his standing with the army commanders after his experiences under Leicester. A will, designed to prevent his wife, Anne, from enjoying his fortune should she remarry, was circumvented by Shakespeare's friend, Thomas Russell (q.v.), who married Digges's widow eight years after his death.

Ibid.
A. L. Rowse, *The Elizabethan Renaissance, the Cultural Achievement* (1972)

DONNE, John (1573–1631), poet: son of John Donne, Master of the Ironmongers' Company and his wife Elizabeth (Heywood), a relation of Sir Thomas More. The family was Roman Catholic and Donne was educated largely by his Jesuit uncle, Jasper Heywood. He entered Hart Hall, Oxford at the age of eleven and after three years there spent another three at Trinity College, Cambridge (c. 1584 to 1590). He is said to have studied Spanish and the Spanish mystics at Oxford. In 1592 Donne became a member of Lincoln's Inn. He abandoned his early religious views and embarked on a passionate pursuit of sex, finishing with an affair with a married woman. To this period belong his earlier

poems, the *Satires*, and many of the *Songs and Sonnets*. Donne was experimenting in verse as well as life. He went with Essex on both his expeditions, to Cadiz (1596) and the Azores (1597); from these voyages came the verse letters, *The Storm* and *The Calm*, addressed to his friend Christopher Brooke (q.v.). On the Cadiz expedition Donne met Sir Thomas Egerton's son, and

John Donne

in 1598 he became secretary to Egerton (q.v.). His personal life was transformed, as he fell in love with Egerton's niece, Anne More, who came to keep house for her uncle in 1600 when she was just sixteen. Next year the couple were secretly married. Anne's father, Sir George More (q.v.) discovered their secret and had Donne dismissed and arrested. After his release Donne and his wife faced fifteen years of poverty. They had eleven children before Anne's death in childbirth in 1617. At first they lived at Mitcham, in a house so damp and unhealthy that Donne headed some of his letters, "from my hospital at Mitcham". But Donne gradually found employment and patronage. In 1607 he was introduced into the Herbert (v. *Edward Herbert*) circle and became especially devoted to Magdalen Herbert. Another influential patron was Lucy, Countess of Bedford (q.v.); and Sir Robert Drury was so impressed with his elegy on his daughter Elizabeth Drury, who died aged fourteen, that from 1610 he let Donne have rooms in his house in Drury Lane. Drury also took Donne abroad with him. Donne tried to obtain preferment through the Court as well, and wrote an *Elegy upon Prince Henry* and a *Marriage Song* for his sister, Princess Elizabeth, in the same year (1613). He repeated the compliment of an epithalamium for the Earl of Somerset's wedding in December. Donne's literary work in this period was mostly elegies, epithalamia, and verse letters directed at friends and patrons. Another influence was beginning to appear, however. In 1609, Donne was seriously ill and his thoughts turned again to religion. He wrote the first of his Divine Poems in that year. From then on, he was writing some religious verse; his friends, and finally James I himself, continually urged him to take holy orders. Donne wrote an anti-papal treatise, the *Pseudo-Martyr*, in 1610 and followed it with an attack on the Jesuits, *Conclave Ignati* (1611). In 1615 Donne was ordained and began a new phase in his life as Curate of Paddington. From 1616 he was Divinity Reader to the Benchers of Lincoln's Inn, and in 1621 he became Dean of St Paul's. Although economic necessity may have been partly responsible for his ordination, Donne's passion for God was as great as his earlier passions, and appears in his poetry and the sermons, upon which he increasingly concentrated. He wrote his last Divine Poem eight days before his death (on 31 March 1631) having had his portrait painted in his shroud.

John Donne, *Poems*, ed., Sir H. J. C. Grierson (Oxford edition, 1945); ed., H. L'A. Fausset (*Everyman* edition, 1947)

DORSET, first Earl of see SACKVILLE, Thomas.

DOVER, Robert (1582–1652), lawyer, organiser of "Cotswold Games": son of John Dover of Great Ellingham, Norfolk, educated at Queen's College, Cambridge (1595) and Gray's Inn (1605). In 1609/10 he married Sibella Sanford, a widow and daughter of William Cole, Dean of Lincoln. Dover decided to practise law in Gloucestershire and bought a house at Saintbury. His brother Richard lived at Evesham, where he eventually became Recorder (1618) and the two may have shared their practice. Richard Dover was a distant connection by marriage of William Combe II (q.v.) of Stratford-upon-Avon and Robert Dover acted as Combe's attorney in the King's Bench in 1616, in an action over tithes. In 1623 Dover was called to be of the Grand Company of Ancients of Gray's Inn, and he left Saintbury for a time; towards the end of his life he went to live with his son John at Barton on the Heath, Warwickshire. During his years in Gloucestershire, Dover's most famous activity was his reorganisation of the "Cotswold Games" probably after 1612. These ancient sports took place on the Thursday and Friday of Whitsun week on Weston Hill, about a mile from Chipping Campden and Saintbury, later known as Dover's Hill. The original games, mentioned by Drayton in *Polyolbion*, consisted of country sports like wrestling, running, and fighting with staves. Dover added chess, cards, dancing, horseracing and coursing, to attract the gentry. The courtier Endymion Porter, who later employed Dover, visited the games and arranged for Dover to wear a suit of James I's cast-offs, so that he might preside with greater dignity. The whole festivity was celebrated in verse by a collaboration of thirty-three poets, including Drayton, Heywood and Jonson, written between 1620 and 1626, and called *Annalia Dubrensia*. The games continued, after an interruption under the Commonwealth, until 1850 when Dover's Hill was enclosed. Attempts have been made to link Shakespeare with the games, because of references in the plays, but there is no evidence he ever attended them, though he may well have known the Dovers.

C. Whitfield, "Robert Dover and William Shakespeare", *Transactions of the Worcestershire Archaeological Society*, 38 (1961)

DOWLAND, John (1563–1626) English lutenist and composer: was possibly born in Dublin, with the family name "Dolan", or perhaps in Westminster. By 1579 he was in the service of Sir Henry Cobham as ambassador in Paris, where Dowland remained for some five years and became a Roman Catholic. By 1588 he was in England, and gained a degree in music at Oxford. His fame as a lutenist grew during a series of journeys on the Continent, 1594–5. He returned to England in 1596 and his *First Book of Songs* was published in 1597 and dedicated to the Lord Chamberlain, Hunsdon (q.v.). This collection was followed by a Second Book (1600) and a Third Book (1603). His songs were harmonised tunes, not madrigals. From 1598 to 1606 he was a royal lutenist in Denmark, a Protestant kingdom where his Catholicism aroused less suspicion than in England. His *Lachrymae* in 1605 contains instrumental music in five parts for dances; it was composed in London while he was on leave from Denmark and was dedicated to Queen Anne, herself a Danish princess. From 1606 until 1626 he lived in Fetter Lane, London, apart from some months spent in Pomerania (1622–

3). His masterpiece, *A Pilgrim's Solace*, was published in 1612, the year in which he was appointed lutenist in the King's Music. With his son Robert, he performed as lutenist for Chapman's masque in honour of the marriage of Princess Elizabeth and the Elector Palatine, February 1613.

Diana Poulton, *John Dowland* (1972)

DRAKE, Francis (?1540–96), seaman: born at Crowndale, near Tavistock, Devon, the son of a fanatically Protestant sailor and farmer. Francis Drake was

Sir Francis Drake

associated with the slave-trading voyages of his kinsman, Hawkins (q.v.). From 1570 onwards Drake concentrated on attacking Spanish treasure vessels making for Nombre de Dios in the Isthmus of Panama. In November 1577 he set out on his famous voyage of circumnavigation aboard the *Pelican*, which he renamed *Golden Hind* after the heraldic device of Hatton (q.v.), a leading shareholder.

Drake sailed through the Straits of Magellan, up to Valparaiso, and northwards to refit in a bay on the coast of California, claiming the territories as an English possession ("New Albion"). He then crossed the Pacific to the Moluccas, called at Java and returned by way of the Cape of Good Hope and Sierra Leone to Plymouth, which he reached in November 1580. He was knighted by the Queen's command at Deptford on 4 April 1581. He sat as M.P. for the Cornish borough of Bosinney from November 1584 until March 1585. He was then appointed Admiral of a royal expedition to raid Spain's West Indian possessions, a voyage lasting from September 1585 until July 1586. In 1587 he "singed the King of Spain's beard" by raiding Armada preparations in Cadiz and he was second in command against the Armada in 1588. With Sir John Norris (q.v.), he led an expedition of 150 ships and 18,000 men to Portugal (April-July 1589), destroying Corunna but failing to take Lisbon and restore the claimant to the Portuguese throne. His lack of success was investigated by a court martial and, although his name was cleared, he remained out of favour with the Queen. After six years of retirement at his home of Buckland Abbey, Devon, he sailed with Hawkins (q.v.) to raid the Isthmus of Panama once again (August 1595). Although he took Nombre de Dios, the expedition found Spanish resistance formidable. He could not capture Panama, as he had wished, and his health gave way. He died at sea off Porto Bello in January 1596.

J. A. Williamson, *Sir Francis Drake* (1951)
G. M. Thomson, *Sir Francis Drake* (1974)

DRAYTON, Michael (1563–1631), poet and dramatist: born at Hartshill, Warwickshire, and brought up as a page in the household of Sir Henry Goodere,

whose daughter, Anne (Rainsford q.v.), married Sir Henry Rainsford of Clifford Chambers, a village two miles south of Stratford-upon-Avon. Drayton had a lifelong admiration for Anne who inspired his poems to "Idea" in 1593–4 and part of the sonnet sequence "Idea" (1619) which includes the famous "Since there's no help,

Michael Drayton

come let us kiss and part". The Rainsfords were among Drayton's patrons, as were many other people of eminence, including the Princes Henry and Charles and the Countess of Bedford (qq.v.). Drayton tried his hand at writing plays for the Admiral's Men between 1597 and 1602, when Francis Meres (q.v.) listed him as among the "best for tragedy" in England. Principally he collaborated with other authors in historical plays like *Sir John Oldcastle* (1599), an answer to Shakespeare's picture of Falstaff in *Henry IV*. Drayton's real fame depends on his poetry, notably his sonnets and *Poems Lyrical and Pastoral* (1605) which contains the *Ballad of Agincourt*. He also wrote highly original historical and topographical poems: *Heroical Epistles* (1597–9) is a collection of love letters in verse between historical characters; *Polyolbion* (1612) is a survey of England in thirty songs, including geographical description, history and legend. Drayton is traditionally reckoned a friend of Shakespeare and reputedly joined Jonson in a drinking party at Stratford which led to Shakespeare's final illness. There is no evidence for this theory; Drayton was, in fact, a notably sober man. He had, however, many literary friends and, as he was treated at Clifford Chambers with "syrup of violets" by Dr Hall (Shakespeare's son-in-law), he may well have known the family. Hall refers to Drayton as *poeta laureatus*. The eccentric Victorian scholar, Frederick Fleay, maintained in 1891 that Drayton was "the rival poet" of Shakespeare's sonnets but could not substantiate his hypothesis.

B. H. Newdigate, *Michael Drayton and his Circle* (1961)

DROESHOUT, Martin (1601–51), engraver: born in London, the grandson of a Flemish painter and joiner, Jan Droeshout, who had emigrated from Brussels to London in 1566 to escape religious persecution. Martin Droeshout was invited to prepare the copper-plate engraving of Shakespeare for the title-page of the First Folio, published on 8 November 1623. It is unlikely Droeshout ever saw Shakespeare in person and probable that the commission to make the engraving came through Gheerart Janssen (q.v.), whose family — like the Droeshouts — appear to have been members of the congregation of the Dutch refugee church in London at Austin Friars. Ben Jonson commended the Droeshout engraving in his verses which preface the First Folio, but critics complain it is a poor piece of work, with head out of

proportion to shoulders and eyes out of alignment.

S. Schoenbaum, *Shakespeare's Lives* (1970)

DRUMMOND, William, of Hawthornden (1585–1649), poet: son of John Drummond, Gentleman Usher to James VI in Scotland. He came to Court with his father in 1603, was educated at Edinburgh University (M.A., 1605) and studied law in Paris and Bourges. When Drummond's father died in 1610, he came back to Hawthornden as laird and never went far from home again. His fiancée, Mary Cunningham, died on the eve of their wedding in 1614/15 and Drummond became something of a recluse, spending his life in poetry and mechanical experiments. He wrote many songs and sonnets to his dead Mary, as well as elegies (including one to Henry, Prince of Wales in 1613), hymns and satires. He also wrote, in prose, *The Cypress Grove* (1623), a meditation on death, and the *History of Scotland* from 1423 to 1524 (1655). Drummond was a friend of Drayton and Jonson and his notes on Jonson's visit to him in 1619 provide most of the material for Jonson's biography. Drummond eventually married Elizabeth Logan (1632) and had nine children. During the Civil War he was at heart a royalist and friend of Montrose, but was forced to sign the Covenant. His death was hastened by grief for the fate of Charles I.

DUDLEY, Robert (1532–88) see LEICESTER, Earl of.

DUDLEY, Robert (1573–1649), navigator, naval engineer: the son of the Earl of Leicester and Lady Douglas Sheffield (qq.v.) Leicester always acknowledged Dudley, who was very like his father, and supervised his upbringing and education. Dudley entered Christ Church

Oxford, registered as a son of an earl (1588) and inherited Kenilworth Castle on the death of his uncle, the Earl of Warwick (1590). He was a friend of Thomas Cavendish, the explorer, whose sister he

Sir Robert Dudley, Earl of Warwick and Duke of Northumberland

may have married; in 1593 he was left two of Cavendish's ships. Next year Dudley went on a voyage of exploration and war to the West Indies. He destroyed some Spanish ships, and visited the Orinoco River and Guyana. In 1596 he went with Essex to Cadiz and was knighted by the Earl. Dudley's first wife had died meanwhile, and he married Alice Leigh. Possibly prompted by his new father-in-law, Dudley decided to reopen the question of his legitimacy. His claim,

supported by his mother, was answered by a bill put forward by Lettice, dowager Countess of Leicester, and the case finally came to Star Chamber in 1605. Dudley lost and was fined £100. Disgusted with England, he deserted his wife and family, and went to Europe with his cousin and mistress, Elizabeth Southwell (q.v.), disguised as his page. The couple became Roman Catholics and were given a papal dispensation to marry as they were related; no mention was made of Dudley's wife. Dudley refused to return to England and his estates were sold, Henry Prince of Wales buying Kenilworth (1611). In 1613 Dudley settled in Florence, became Chamberlain to the Duchess of Tuscany and invented new designs in shipbuilding. The Emperor Ferdinand II, reviving old Dudley titles, created him Earl of Warwick and Duke of Northumberland in the Holy Roman Empire, (1620). Dudley drained the marshes between Pisa and the sea for the Duke of Tuscany, enabling Livorno (Leghorn) to become a great port, and was rewarded with a pension and the Villa Rinieri at Castello. Dudley wrote *Voyage to Trinidad* (1600), a pamphlet advising James I how to rule without Parliament (1612), and his great work, *Dell'Arcano del Mare*, in three volumes dedicated to the Duke of Tuscany (1646–7). This is a treatise on navigation and naval architecture, with many maps and diagrams. Dudley and Elizabeth Southwell had thirteen children most of whom married into the Italian nobility; he died at Castello. His deserted wife, Alice, became Duchess Dudley in her own right in 1645.

J. T. Leader, *Robert Dudley* (1895)

DUTTON, Lawrence (fl. 1571–91), actor: is known to have been with Sir Robert Lane's Men (1571–2), Lincoln's or Clinton's (1572–5), Warwick's (1575–6), Oxford's (1580), Queen's (1589–91).

John Dutton, his brother, was also in three of these companies. Such frequent changes of company prompted the wits to nickname the Duttons "chameleons" (for comedians) and satirical verses were written abut them in 1580.

E. K. C., *E.S.*

DYER, Edward (1543–1607), courtier, poet: son of Thomas Dyer of Weston, Somerset, and educated at Balliol College or, more probably, Broadgates Hall, Oxford, where he began to write poetry and play the lute but took no degree. He travelled abroad, returning to look after the family estates on his father's death in 1565, and became a courtier in Leicester's service. The Queen appointed him Steward of the Royal Manor of Woodstock in 1570 and commended his role in the Woodstock entertainment of 1575 even though he had by then lost some of his privileges to Sir Henry Lee (q.v.). From 1575 to 1586 Dyer shared the fortunes of his close friend, Philip Sidney (q.v.): the two men went on diplomatic missions to the Prince of Orange, left Court in disapproval of the Queen's projected French marriage, and had similar views on politics and literature. Dyer was a member of the "Areopagus" literary circle, but was not with Sidney in his final expedition to the Netherlands. As well as undertaking further diplomatic missions to the Netherlands and Denmark (1588–9), Dyer paid two visits to Prague to examine the claims of Edward Kelly, an erstwhile associate of John Dee (q.v.), to be able to turn other substances into gold. So impressed was Dyer with Kelly that he secured official backing from Burghley to entice Kelly to England. Emperor Rudolf II, who held Kelly in high favour, was incensed by Dyer's activities and kept him under house arrest until he received a personal letter from Queen Elizabeth requesting Dyer's return to England. This failure put an end to Dyer's service abroad. He sat in the Commons for Somerset in the Parliaments of 1589 and 1593, was considered as a possible Secretary of State in 1590 and worked with Robert Cecil, who helped Dyer become Chancellor of the Order of the Garter, with a belated knighthood, in 1596. Dyer was also devoted to Essex's interests, having met the Earl when he was the young step-son of his patron, Leicester. He stood by Essex on his return from Ireland in disgrace and acted as go-between when Lady Essex (Frances Walsingham, q.v.), was being blackmailed for her husband's letters. Dyer secured a reduction of the blackmailer's demands from £3,000 to £1,720, helping Frances Essex meet this sum with a loan, even though he was always short of money. Essex had used Dyer as an intelligence contact with Scotland, but these connections brought Dyer no influence with James I. He lost his Woodstock Stewardship in 1604 and spent his last three years of life in retirement. He is best remembered for his lyrical and melancholy poetry: Meres (q.v.) rated him "famous for elegy" in 1598; but his poems were published rarely and only in anthologies. Most famous are his verses on contentment, which begin "My mind to me a Kingdom is"; the poem was set to music and published by William Byrd in 1588.

R. M. Sargent, *At the Court of Queen Elizabeth* (1935)

E

ECCLESTONE, William (?—?1625), actor: was a member of the King's Men by 1610—11, leaving them for Lady Elizabeth's in 1611, returning in 1613 and appearing regularly in the acting lists of the King's Men until 1622. At this time he performed especially in the plays of Beaumont and Fletcher, but also appears in the First Folio actors List.

EGERTON, Thomas (1540—1617), lawyer and Lord Chancellor: a bastard of Sir Richard Egerton, his mother being Alice Sparke. The father showed much interest in his son's advancement but his illegitimate origin may have hampered Thomas's early career as well as implanting in him a ruthless craving for status and recognition. He was educated at Brasenose College, Oxford, and was at Lincoln's Inn for over ten years before being called to the Bar (1572). Skilful advocacy impressed the Queen who appointed him Solicitor-General in 1581. In this capacity he helped prepare the indictment of Mary, Queen of Scots, in 1586. He sat in the Parliaments of 1584—5 and 1586—7, occasionally ruffling tempers by an arrogance of tongue; he was elected in 1588 but the Commons complained that he absented himself for service in the House of Lords. In 1592 he was promoted Attorney-General and knighted soon afterwards. He became Master of the Rolls in April 1594 and was appointed Lord Keeper of the Great Seal in May 1596. The combination of these offices, never held simultaneously by anyone else, gave him wealth, patronage and influence throughout the last seven years of Elizabeth's reign. He was, at this time, one of the leading literary patrons in London, associated in particular with Lambarde (q.v.), and Donne (q.v.) who was his secretary and married his niece. Sir

Thomas was a friend of Essex, who was entrusted to his keeping by the Queen after returning from Ireland in disgrace. Essex abused the friendship by holding Egerton as a hostage during his abortive revolt (1601). Subsequently Egerton succeeded Essex as High Steward of Oxford, thus adding to his powers of patronage. Sir Thomas was married three times, his third wife being Alice Spencer (q.v.), the widowed Countess of Derby. Her acerbity and temper led to quarrels: "Before I was never acquainted with such tempests and storms", Egerton complained to his son in 1610, after ten years of married life with Alice. But the Egertons entertained Queen Elizabeth at Harefield Place in Middlesex from 31 July to 1 August 1602, on a grand scale: Sir Thomas spent £4000 on the visit; and he accepted some three dozen generous gifts from friends whose concern that he should "the more honourably entertain the Queen's Majesty" matched their desire for advancement. In 1603 he became Lord Chancellor, being created Baron Ellesmere. He helped draft the act of union of England and Scotland, as well as occasionally assisting James over questions of international law, notably the status of ambassadors and matters of trade. In general Ellesmere sympathised with the Puritans and was opposed to the Howard faction, but he was a traditionalist in interpreting the King's prerogative, refusing to believe that such matters as new forms of taxation were fit for Parliamentary debate; and he thus has some responsibility for the failure of the 'Addled Parliament' in 1614. His claim for the paramountcy of the judiciary was expressed with greatest clarity in his speech during the case of Robert Calvin in 1609. He presided with dignity over the trials of the Earl and Countess of Somerset (Robert Carr and

74

Frances Howard, qq.v.) for the murder of Overbury (q.v.). Ill health and domestic frustration soured Ellesmere's last years. He secured a viscountcy (taking the title of Brackley) in 1616, but was denied the earldom which he had expected from James. His health finally gave way in March 1617. Soon afterwards he died — "of conceit, fearing to be displaced", a contemporary declared.

W. J. Jones, *The Elizabethan Court of Chancery* (1967)
H. S. Reinmuth, ed., *Early Stuart Studies* (1970)

ELDE, George (?—1624), printer: son of John Elde, carpenter, of Derbyshire. He was apprenticed to Richard Bolton for eight years from Christmas 1592 and became a freeman of the Stationers' Company in 1600. Elde acquired his business from his wife, who was the widow of two printers already. He printed Shakespeare's *Troilus and Cressida* for Richard Bonian and Henry Walley, and the Sonnets for Thomas Thorpe (both in 1609) Elde's shop was the "Printer's Press", Fleet Lane, in 1615.

ELIZABETH I (1533—1603, reigned from November 1558), Queen of England: born at Greenwich, the daughter of Henry VIII and Anne Boleyn, who was executed when Elizabeth was two years and eight months old. The Princess was highly intelligent and well-educated, notably by the Cambridge humanist, Roger Ascham (1515—68). She was fluent in French and Italian, knew Spanish and showed skill in Latin and Greek as well as having some knowledge of patristic literature. Her life was in peril during the reign of her Roman Catholic half-sister, Mary, and she was for a time imprisoned in the Tower of London and at Woodstock. Her political flair and shrewd understanding of foreign governments enabled her to establish and maintain a compromise settlement in

religious affairs while retaining some freedom of action in war and diplomacy. She relied heavily for advice on William Cecil (Burghley, q.v.) and Walsingham (q.v.) as well as on the Earl of Leicester (q.v.), the favourite who longest stirred her emotions. Her reign was marked by five moments of crisis: the rebellion of the northern earls in 1569; the threat of assassination during the imprisonment of Mary, Queen of Scots, in England, especially in the years 1583—6; the Spanish Armada of 1588; the revived Spanish threat of the 1590s and Spanish encouragement of the revolt of Tyrone (q.v.) in Ireland; and the conspiracy of her fallen

Elizabeth I. Painting attributed to Gheeraerts

favourite, Essex (q.v.) in 1601. Her subjects expected the Queen to marry, but she preferred to use her unwedded state as a diplomatic bargaining counter. The most persistent of her foreign suitors was the French Duke of Alençon, an unprepossessing dwarf whom the queen nicknamed her "frog" and whom she encouraged to woo her intermittently from 1572 until his death in 1584. The Alençon marriage project was far from popular with her courtiers. The Queen possessed the personality to convert her subjects' passive acceptance of the Tudor monarchy into a cult, in which the Sovereign was idolised as "Gloriana" or the "Faerie Queene". She enjoyed music, dancing and singing; she liked masques and plays, allowing the theatrical company associated with Tilney and Tarlton (qq.v.) to be known as the "Queen's Men" from 1583 onwards; she loved dresses and jewellery, and expected lavish entertainments when she moved around the south of her kingdom in a royal "progress". But while she looked on her Court as a cultural haven, she was not prepared to spend money freely on patronage. Her graciousness was marred by hot temper, jealousy and financial meanness; she was often hesitant over great questions of policy and inclined to shift the responsibility for decision-making on to other shoulders. These weaknesses were transcended by her natural gift of eloquence: "Though God hath raised me high, yet this I count the glory of my crown: that I have reigned with your loves", she declared to members of the last Parliament of her reign, in November 1601. She died at Richmond on 24 March 1603, having declined to the last to name her successor.

Modern biographies by J. E. Neale (1934); Elizabeth Jenkins (1958); P. Johnson (1972)

ELIZABETH, Princess (1596–1662), daughter of James VI and I: born at Dunfermline, travelled south to London after her father's accession but spent much of her childhood under the guardianship of Lord Harington at Combe Abbey, Warwickshire. She showed intelligence and was much liked for her graceful spon-

taneity when she came to reside at Court in 1608, and she was a close and welcome companion for her brother, Prince Henry (q.v.). From the winter of 1610–11 the

Princess Elizabeth, Queen of Bohemia. Frederick V, King of Bohemia

"Lady Elizabeth's Men", played before the Princess and her brothers, as well as in the provinces. In May 1612 she was betrothed to the German Protestant Elector Palatine, Frederick V (q.v.). They were married on St Valentine's Day 1613 in the midst of several weeks of festivity, during which "Lady Elizabeth's Men" performed twice while Shakespeare's company presented twenty plays, probably including *Henry IV* Parts 1 and 2, *Julius Caesar, The Tempest, The Winter's Tale* and *Much Ado about Nothing.* Francis Bacon was "chief contriver" of Beaumont's Inner Temple masque for the wedding; his admiration for Elizabeth was so great that he dedicated his *Henry VII* to her in 1622. Donne (q.v.) celebrated the wedding with an Epithalamium. The marriage of Frederick and Elizabeth, though an act of state, became an idyllic romance. Yet, characteristically, Elizabeth never bothered to learn Frederick's native language. Her strong will and frivolity confused her husband's statecraft, notably during the period 1619–20 when they resided in Prague as King and Queen of Bohemia. The first phase of the Thirty Years War deprived them both of Bohemia and of the Palatine Electorate and by the end of 1621 Elizabeth was reconciled to a life of exile at The Hague. She remained a popular figure in England, an idealised Protestant champion; and the poet-diplomat Wotton (q.v.) composed a famous verse tribute to "the Queen of Bohemia". Elizabeth gave birth to thirteen children (including the future Electress Sophia, the mother of King George I). After her husband's death in 1632, she continued to live at The Hague, suffering from poverty after the establishment of the Cromwellian Commonwealth. She returned to London in 1661, dying there at Leicester House in the following February.

C. Oman, *Elizabeth of Bohemia* (1938)
C. V. Wedgwood, *The Thirty Years War* (1938)

ELWES, Gervase (1561–1615), Lieutenant of the Tower: son of John Elwes of Askham, Nottinghamshire, educated at St John's College, Cambridge from 1573. Elwes took no degree, but entered the Middle Temple in 1579. He did not come to prominence until 1603, when he was knighted by James I. Elwes, "somewhat an unknown man" according to the letter writer Chamberlain, was made Lieutenant of the Tower in 1613 by the influence of the Howard family, to whom he paid £2,000 for the privilege. Use was made of Elwes to gain access to Overbury, (then a prisoner in the Tower), by the Earls of Northampton and Somerset (Henry Howard, Robert Carr, qq.v.) who sent letters, and the Countess of Somerset (Frances Howard, q.v.), who sent poison. Elwes, persuaded by Northampton, hurried on the inquest after Overbury's death. When the case was being investigated in 1615 Elwes was the first to confess his part in it, although claiming he had sought to prevent the actual murder. He was tried, convicted and hanged in November 1615.

B. White, *Cast of Ravens* (1965)

ESSEX, Frances, Countess of (1567–1632) see WALSINGHAM, Frances.

ESSEX, Frances, Countess of (1592–1632) see HOWARD, Frances.

ESSEX, Robert Devereux, second Earl of (1566–1601), soldier and royal favourite: born at Netherwood, Hertfordshire, the eldest son of Walter Devereux, first Earl of Essex (1541–76) and Lettice Knollys (v. *Leicester, Lettice, Countess of*). He spent much of his boyhood in Pembrokeshire but was educated at Trinity College, Cambridge, 1579–81. After his father's death, his mother married Leicester (q.v.) and it was as Leicester's step-son that Essex was first presented at Court in 1584. He fought under his stepfather in the Netherlands, showing courage at Zutphen and returning to England with the sword of his cousin, the heroic Sidney (q.v.), whose widow he secretly married in the winter of 1589–90. Despite her disapproval of this marriage, Elizabeth treated Essex with great favour

Robert Devereux, second Earl of Essex

and indulgence from 1587 until 1594. He was created a Knight of the Garter at the age of twenty-two. Quarrels with Ralegh made him unhappy at Court and he joined Drake's expedition which raided Corunna and the Portuguese coast in the summer of 1589. In 1591 and 1592 he commanded forces sent to help Henri IV against the Catholic League in Normandy but he was recalled to serve at Court, as Elizabeth believed he was rashly risking his life. From 1592 to 1596 Essex built up a powerful political faction, much of it as patron of borough elections in Pembrokeshire and Denbighshire, and he became leader of an anti-Cecil faction, with Francis Bacon (q.v.) as an ally. He was made a Privy Councillor in 1593 but

displeased the Queen a year later by the intemperance he showed in hounding her personal physician, Lopez (q.v.), to his death. In June and July 1596 he gained his greatest military success, as General-in-Chief of the expedition which raided the Spanish coast, sacked Cadiz and frustrated Philip II's attempts to fit out a second Armada. Enemies at Court began thereafter to intrigue against Essex, largely through dislike of his arrogance and distrust of his ambitions, and some supporters deserted him, notably Bacon. From July to October 1597 Essex and Ralegh together undertook the so-called "Islands Voyage", an abortive attempt to capture the Spanish treasure fleet and raid the Azores. He was created Earl Marshal in 1597 and Chancellor of Cambridge University in 1598, the year in which his bad manners at Court provoked the famous scene in which the Queen boxed his ears and he drew his sword in anger. After outward reconciliation Essex was given command of an army of 15,000 men and entrusted with wide powers as Lord Lieutenant of Ireland (March 1599) but in a six-month campaign he failed to subdue the rebel Tyrone (q.v.). His military lethargy, and the excessive number of knights whom he created, infuriated the Queen. When he returned precipitately to Court in September 1599, she ordered his arrest. In June 1600 he was charged with disobeying the Queen's orders, with parleying with Tyrone, and with cheapening the dignity of knighthood. A special commission sentenced him to be deprived of his titles. In collaboration with his second stepfather, Christopher Blount (q.v.), and his friend the Earl of Southampton (q.v.), Essex planned to capture the Queen and her Court and dictate political terms to her. This ill-planned coup began with a request to Shakespeare's company for *Richard II* to be played at the Globe Theatre on 7 February 1601, an event given especial significance because of the deposition scene. The Council placed Essex and his friends under house arrest in his residence in the Strand but on 8 February he broke out and tried to raise the City of London against the Queen's counsellors. There was no support. He was arrested, put on trial on 19 February for treason and beheaded six days later. During his heyday as a courtier Essex was a sonneteer and a patron of literature, a company of actors and music, his wealth coming for the most part from a monopoly of the sweet wine tax farm, granted to him by the Queen in 1589 and enjoyed by him until his disgrace in 1600.

G. B. Harrison, *Life and Death of Robert Devereux* (1937)

ESSEX, Robert Devereux, third Earl of (1591–1646), soldier: son of the second Earl and his Countess, born Frances Walsingham (q.v.). The disgrace and execution of the second Earl deprived his son of his rightful titles until the accession of James I, who took the boy under his protection. For some years he was a companion of Prince Henry (q.v.). In 1606 the King encouraged a marriage between the Earl and Frances Howard (q.v.). Essex served overseas from 1607 to 1609, and his wife began a liaison with Robert Carr (q.v.). The marriage was dissolved in 1613 because the Countess complained that her husband was incapable of cohabiting with her. Essex fought for Frederick, Elector Palatine (q.v.) in the Rhineland in 1620 and, emulating his father, served as an army commander in the bungled and abortive raid on Cadiz, October 1625. His sympathies, on his return, were with the government's critics and he supported the Petition of Right. In 1631 he married Elizabeth, daughter of Sir William Paulet; a son was born but died in infancy, and the marriage ended in separation. Resentment

at his treatment by Charles I and opposition to Strafford encouraged him to support the Parliamentarians. He accepted

Robert Devereux, third Earl of Essex

the post of General in the Parliamentarian army, July 1642, opposing the King in the battles of Edgehill and Newbury but being outmanoeuvred in Cornwall. He resigned his command in April 1646 and died five months later.

Vernon F. Snow, *Essex the Rebel 1591–1646* (1970)

EVANS, Henry (fl. 1582–1612), scrivener and theatre manager: born in Wales, but was in London by 1582 when he appears as overseer of the will of Sebastian Westcott (q.v.). In 1583 he took over the lease of the room in Blackfriars where the Children of the Chapel Royal performed (v. *Farrant, Hunnis*). He was intermittently a manager of boys' companies for twenty-five years. At first he managed the Earl of Oxford's Boys, with the dramatist Lyly (q.v.), and later a combined company until 1585. Evans took the new Blackfriars on a twenty-one year lease from Richard Burbage in 1600 and presented the Children of the Chapel there, but he and their master, Nathaniel Giles, were accused in Star Chamber of impressing "gentlemen's sons" and other ineligible boys (February 1602). Henry Evans sought to shift responsibility on to others but was (as he complained) betrayed by these partners and fled the country (May 1602). The new reign, and the appointment of a new Lord Chamberlain, enabled Evans to return before the Christmas festivities of 1603. He presented the boys as "Children of the Queen's Revels" in 1604 and January 1605, although ensuring that his role as impresario was not publicised. The satirical plays which his boys performed frequently caused trouble for both the company and the dramatists. The production *Eastward Ho!* in 1605 cost the company its Royal Patent (v. *Chapman, Jonson, Marston*) and in 1608 Chapman's *The Conspiracy and Tragedy of Charles Duke of Byron* also provoked an outcry. Later that year Evans was glad to arrange the transfer of his lease back to Burbage, but he remained engaged in querulous litigation against his old associates until 1612.

E. K. C., *E.S.*

EVESHAM, Epiphanius (1570–?1634), sculptor: born, on the Feast of the Epiphany, in Hereford, the fourteenth son in a family which seems to have exhausted the commoner Christian names. He came to London where, in the 1590s, he is known to have been a pupil of the Brabant monument-maker, Richard Stevens. At the turn of the century he crossed to France, working in Paris until 1614; it is probable that he was a Roman Catholic. His sculptured figures show a greater variation in posture than was common in earlier English church monuments and, despite his years abroad, he was regarded as

the first representative of a native school of sculptors. Among his earlier work, after his return to England, are tombs at Marsworth in south Buckinghamshire and Felsted in Essex. His most famous, and most naturally expressive, are the grouped family monuments in two churches near Faversham in Kent: the Hawkins monument at Boughton-under-Blean; and the Teynham monument, eight miles to the west, at Lynsted.

F

FARNABY, Giles (?1565–1640), composer: was either the son of an East Anglican immigrant to Truro, Cornwall, or (more likely) son of Thomas Farnaby, joiner, of London and his wife Jane. In this case, Farnaby was born in 1565, married Katherine Roane at St Helen's Bishopsgate in 1587, and left two sons and a daughter. He became a Bachelor of Music of Oxford University in 1592, and in 1598 published his *Canzonets to Four Voices*, a collection of madrigals. Farnaby also wrote tunes for psalms, but his chief fame is as a composer for the virginals, surpassed only by William Byrd (q.v.). Fifty of his pieces are found in the *Fitzwilliam Virginal Book*, the earliest collection of virginal music.

FARRANT, Richard (?–1580), cleric, choirmaster and composer: he became a Gentleman of the Chapel Royal (a chaplain or clerk) about 1553. In 1564 he was appointed Master of the Children of the Chapel at Windsor, and he began producing plays for them at Court. By 1576 he was acting Master of the main choir, the Children of the Chapel Royal in London. He took a lease on some rooms in Blackfriars and converted them into a theatre for performances by the Chapel Boys, the first instance of the use of Blackfriars as a theatre. Farrant is also known to have composed some songs, possibly for use in the plays.

E. K. C., *E.S.*

FAWKES, Guy (1570–1606), conspirator: born in York of Protestant parentage but accepted the Roman Catholic faith of a stepfather and crossed to Flanders in 1593, entering the Spanish army. He returned to England early in 1604 at a time when hopes that James I would relax the penal laws against Roman Catholics were receding. In May he was enlisted in a conspiracy, which originated with Robert Catesby (q.v.), for blowing up the House of Lords when the King, Queen and Prince Henry attended the opening of the new Parliament. Fawkes, as a veteran soldier, was required to guard and to fire a store of gunpowder placed in a cellar under the Palace of Westminster and reached by a short tunnel from the cellar of an adjoining house, rented by the conspirators. Rumours of the conspiracy reached Robert Cecil eleven days before the opening of Parliament, and Fawkes was arrested in the cellar at eleven o'clock at night on 4 November 1605, the eve of the opening of Parliament. He was executed on 31 January 1606. The plot intensified hostility to "Popery". A royal proclamation immediately added to the Anglican Book of Common Prayer a form of annual service commemorating frustration of the plot, and use of this service was authorised until 1859.

J. Hurstfield, *Freedom, Corruption and Government in Elizabethan England* (1973)
H. Garnett, *Portrait of Guy Fawkes* (1962)
H. R. Williamson, *The Gunpowder Plot* (1941)

FENNER, George (fl. 1566–1618), seaman: member of a Sussex family. Nothing is known of his early life. He first appears as a sea captain in association with Sir John Hawkins (q.v.) in 1566, distinguishing himself by the good gunnery of his vessel, *The Castle of Comfort*, in action against Portuguese ships off the Azores. He was a privateer, often in government pay, for the next twelve years, and took part in the Armada engagements, in Essex's "Islands Voyage" of 1597, and unsuccessfully gave chase to the abortive second Armada (November 1597). His cousin, Thomas Fenner, was also a naval commander, closely associated with Drake.

J. Corbett, *The Successors of Drake* (1917)

FERRABOSCO, Alfonso (?1575–1628), Court musician: son of Alfonso Ferrabosco, musician to Queen Elizabeth, who returned to Bologna in 1578, leaving behind two (probably illegitimate) children. Ferrabosco the younger was born at Greenwich and brought up as a Court musician. From 1592 he received a pension, raised to £50 a year under James I. He was music master to Prince Henry, and after his death in 1612 to Prince Charles, and Composer in Ordinary and Composer of the King's Music after Charles's accession. Each of these posts brought him £40 or £50 a year. Ferrabosco is chiefly known as composer of the music for Ben Jonson's (q.v.) Court Masques. He composed for six of them, including the Masques of *Blackness* (1605), *Beauty* (1608) and *Queens* (1609) and also sang a part in *Hymenaei* (1606). He also composed church and instrumental music, writing chiefly for viols; and he is credited with the invention of the lyra-viol, an adaptation of the small bass viol, which became a very popular instrument in the sixteenth century. Ferrabosco published two volumes of music in 1609: *Ayres* (dedicated to Prince Henry), and *Lessons for 1, 2 and 3 Viols*, dedicated to the Earl of Southampton. He died at Greenwich, leaving three sons who all became Court musicians.

FIELD, Nathan (1587–?1620), actor and dramatist: baptised at St Giles's, Cripplegate. He was the son of John Field, a preacher who denounced the stage, and is known to have had two brothers, Nathaniel (who became a printer) and Theophilus, who was Bishop of Llandaff, a strongly Puritan diocese. Nathan was a Scholar of St Paul's School but by 1600 he had been impressed by Nathaniel Giles (q.v.) into the Chapel Royal. Here his education was continued by Ben Jonson,

Nathan Field

who supervised his reading of Horace and Martial and who later praised his gifts as an actor. Field performed in Jonson's plays and remained with the company until 1613 when it was absorbed into Lady Elizabeth's, whose leader he became. In 1615 he joined the King's Men but his name does not appear in their lists, except for the First Folio, after May 1619. During that year he was involved in a scandal with Lady Argyll, of whose daughter he was alleged to be the father; this was not the first scandal attached to his name. His best part was Bussy in Chapman's *The Revenge of Bussy D'Amboise*, a role he played both before and after joining the King's Men. He wrote two comedies himself (*A Woman is a Weathercock*, 1609 and *Amends for Ladies*, ?1611) and a defence of the stage, as well as collaborating with Massinger (q.v.) in *The Fatal Dowry* and probably with other playwrights. Field was ranked with Burbage as "best actor" by Jonson (*Bartholomew Fair*, 1614); his portrait in Dulwich College shows him as dark and handsome.

E. K. C., *E.S.*
W. Peery, *The Plays of Nathan Field* (1950)

FIELD, Richard (1561–1624), bookseller and printer: born in Bridge Street, Stratford-upon-Avon, the son of Henry Field, a tanner and friend of John Shakespeare. Richard was apprenticed to a London printer in 1579. His second master was a Huguenot, Thomas Vautrollier, who had a shop in Blackfriars; when he died, Richard married his widow Jacqueline, and took over the shop. Publications included the *Art of English Poesie* in 1589 (v. *Puttenham*), John Harington's translation of Ariosto's *Orlando Furioso* (1591), Philip Sidney's Arcadia (1598), and the later editions of North's Plutarch. In 1593 he printed his fellow townsman Shakespeare's *Venus and Adonis*, which was distributed by the bookseller, John Harrison (q.v.). After two editions Harrison acquired the copyright of *Venus and Adonis*, together with *The Rape of Lucrece* which Field printed for him in 1594. Both poems were considerably successful and Field must have regretted parting with the copyrights. Field joined other residents of Blackfriars in signing a petition in 1596 against James Burbage's conversion of the Blackfriars Theatre. About a third of Field's output was theology and allied works, and he was therefore sometimes in trouble with the authorities. In 1599 he was one of the printers summoned to Stationers' Hall to hear the stricter censorship rules. By 1615 Field had a new shop, the "Splayed Eagle" in Wood Street, where his widow carried on the business after his death.

S. S.
A. E. M. Kirkwood, "Richard Field, Printer, 1589–1624", *The Library*, Series 4, XII (1931)

FISHER, Thomas (fl. 1600–1602), bookseller: was originally a draper, and transferred from the Drapers' to the Stationers' Company in January 1600. He had his shop at the "White Hart", Fleet Street from 1600 to 1602. Fisher published Shakespeare's *Midsummer Night's Dream* (1600).

FITCH, Ralph (?1550–1611), pioneer traveller: a "leatherseller of London" who accompanied John Newbery (q.v.) on his third journey to the Levant, leaving England in March 1583. Fitch separated from Newbery, near Agra, in September 1584, and travelled down the rivers Jumna and Ganges, later becoming the first Englishman to visit Burma and Thailand (studying the trade from China in 1587). He went south to Malacca early in 1588, Colombo in 1589, and eventually up the Tigris to Mosul and Aleppo, finding an English ship in Tripoli which brought him back to London in April 1591. For the remainder of Queen Elizabeth's reign he was one of the principal members of the Levant Company and Consul at Aleppo, 1596–7. His adventures were "written up" by Hakluyt in 1598–1600 and aroused wide interest, especially in London, where he lived from 1599 until his death in October 1611.

M. Edwardes, *Ralph Fitch, Elizabethan in the Indies* (1972)

FITTON, Mary (1578–1647): came from Gawsworth, Cheshire. In 1595 the influence of her father's friend, Sir William Knollys (q.v.), enabled her to become a maid of honour to Queen Elizabeth. Knollys, although married, fell in love with Mary, but in 1600 there was a considerable scandal at Court when Mary became pregnant by William Herbert (who succeeded as third Earl of Pembroke, q.v., a year later). Mary used to escape from the Court to meet her lover, disguised as a man in a long white cloak, with her skirts tucked up. The baby died soon after birth and Pembroke refused to marry Mary, although the Queen sent him to the Fleet Prison. Mary then became the mistress of Vice-Admiral Sir Richard Leveson. Upon his death in 1605 Mary was at last married, taking as her husband one of his officers, the Cornish captain William Polwhele, by whom she had a son and a daughter. She was twice left a widow: Polwhele died in 1610 and a second husband, Captain Lougher, in 1636. At the turn of the nineteenth-twentieth centuries Mary Fitton was a fashionable candidate to be the "Dark Lady" of Shakespeare's Sonnets, largely on the strength of her relationship with Pembroke; but 1600 is too late a date for the events of the Sonnets; and Mary is known to have had brown hair and grey eyes.

A. L. Rowse, *Discoveries and Reviews* (1975)

FLEMING, Thomas (1544–1613), judge: born at Newport, Isle of Wight, entered Lincoln's Inn in 1567 and was called to the Bar in 1574. He sat in the Commons as M.P. for Winchester in the Parliaments of 1584–5, 1586–7, and 1589. In 1595 he was knighted and appointed Solicitor-General, sitting in the Commons of 1597–8 and 1601 as M.P. for Hampshire and speaking for the Crown in cases concerning monopolies. James I appointed him Chief Baron of the Exchequer in 1604. Fleming gave the historic judgment in the case of John Bate, a merchant who declined to pay customs duty on currants which, he held, was being levied without Parliamentary sanction: Fleming's ruling (1605), that the raising of taxes on foreign commodities was part of the absolute prerogative of the Crown provided the King with the opportunity of establishing new taxes (an unjustifiable extension of the narrowly legalistic reasoning which had influenced Fleming). He finished his career as Chief Justice of the King's Bench, 1607–13.

W. J. Jones, *Politics and the Bench* (1971)

FLETCHER, Giles, I (1546–1611), scholar, diplomat and poet: born in Watford, educated at Eton and King's College, Cambridge, a Fellow of King's 1568–81, University Lecturer in Greek, Doctor of Civil Law, entered Parliament in November 1584. His linguistic skill and connections with the City companies led him to be sent on a trade mission to Tsar Feodor Ivanovich in Moscow. He returned a year later and published an account of what he had observed, entitled *Of the Russe Commonwealth*. In 1593 he published a collection of sonnets, *Licia, or Poems of Love*. He was the brother of Bishop Richard Fletcher, the father of the poets Giles and Phineas Fletcher, and uncle of the dramatist John Fletcher, (qq.v.).

L. E. Berry, *The English Works of Giles Fletcher the Elder* (1964)
G. Fletcher, *Of the Russe Commonwealth*, ed., Pipes and Fine (1966)
A. Cross, *Russia under Western Eyes* (1971)

FLETCHER, Giles, II (?1588–1623), poet and Anglican clergyman: son of Giles and brother of Phineas (qq.v.), educated at Westminster School and Trinity College, Cambridge (1601–6, Fellow, 1608). He was ordained in 1613 but remained at Cambridge as Reader in Greek Grammar (from 1615) and Language (from 1618). Fletcher was also Rector of Helmingham and Alderton in Suffolk. He wrote allegorical religious poems, modelled on the work of Spenser, the most famous being *Christ's*

Victory and Triumph in Heaven and Earth (1610).

FLETCHER, John (1579–1625), dramatist: born at Rye, Sussex, where his father Richard Fletcher (q.v.) was then Vicar. He was a nephew of Giles Fletcher (q.v.) and cousin of the clerical poets Giles and Phineas Fletcher (qq.v.). John Fletcher became an undergraduate at Corpus Christi College, Cambridge, in 1591. His career as a dramatist really began with his collaboration with Beaumont (q.v.) in about 1606, but he had probably written plays for the Queen's Revels before then. Together Beaumont and Fletcher produced up to fifteen plays while Fletcher himself was the author of at least sixteen, from *The Faithful Shepherdess* (1610) to *Rule a Wife and Have a Wife* (1624). Most of these plays were comedies or romances. Fletcher also collaborated with Massinger, Middleton, Rowley and possibly Jonson (qq.v.), mainly in romantic and artificial tragedies and tragicomedies. An exception is *Sir John van Olden Barnavelt* (1619), a dramatic presentation of contemporary Dutch history, probably written in collaboration with Massinger. *The Two Noble Kinsmen*, published in 1634, is thought to be by Fletcher and Shakespeare while Fletcher is also credited with parts of Shakespeare's *Henry VIII*. He died of the plague in August 1625, and is buried at St Saviour's, Southwark.

C. Leech, *The John Fletcher Plays* (1962)

FLETCHER, Lawrence (?–1608), actor: in 1595 and 1599–1601 he toured Scotland as leader of a company and became the favourite actor of King James VI. His company involved James in a dispute with the Kirk in Edinburgh, which sought to suppress the players (November 1599). In that year, and for two years afterwards, Fletcher led an official company for James in Scotland and, presumably for this reason, his name appears first on the 1603 Patent for the King's Men in England. There is, however, no record that he ever acted with them.

E. K. C., *E.S.*

FLETCHER, Phineas (1582–1650), poet and Anglican clergyman: born at Cranbrook, Kent, son of Giles Fletcher (q.v.) and cousin of the dramatist John Fletcher (q.v.). He was educated at Eton and King's College, Cambridge, where he graduated in 1604 and of which he became a Fellow in 1611. From 1616 to 1621 he served as chaplain to Sir Henry Willoughby and was then Rector of Hilgay, Norfolk, for the remaining twenty-nine years of his life. In 1615 he wrote *Sicelides*, a play intended to be presented by King's College before James I to celebrate his visit to Cambridge, but it was not, in fact, performed until afterwards. Fletcher's poetry was of the Spenserian school, his main work being an allegory on the human body and mind, *The Purple Island*, published in 1633.

FLETCHER, Richard (1544–95), bishop: born at Watford, educated at Eton and King's College, Cambridge. He became Vicar of Rye, Sussex and was appointed Almoner to Queen Elizabeth. Fletcher, reputedly the most handsome churchman of his generation, was long in the Queen's favour. He was appointed Bishop of Bristol in 1587 and, after a brief spell as Bishop of Worcester, succeeded Aylmer (q.v.) as Bishop of London in 1593. By then he was a widower and the Queen had let him know that she disapproved of married bishops. Soon after his translation to London, however, the fifty-year-old Fletcher married a young widow whose character was not entirely above reproach. The Queen accordingly banished Bishop Fletcher from Court, deprived him of his remunerative Almonership, and suspended him for several months from the spiritual functions of his episcopate. A partial reconciliation with the Queen was followed by the Bishop's sudden death as he sat "in great jollity with his fair lady . . . taking tobacco in his chair". Among the Bishop's eight children was the dramatist John Fletcher (q.v.).

A. L. Rowse, *The England of Elizabeth* (1950)

FLORIO, John (1545–1625), Lexicographer and translator: born in London, the son of an Italian Protestant refugee, the family originally coming from Siena. He was educated at Magdalen College, Oxford, and appears to have been briefly in the service of Leicester before entering the household of the Earl of Southampton (q.v.) in the early 1590s. It is probable Shakespeare knew him at this time. Several writers have claimed that the character of Holofernes in *Love's Labour's Lost* owes something to Florio; Dr Rowse more plausibly suggests that Don Armado in the same play "owes some strokes" to Florio; and Florio, who appears to have been a ready conversationalist, may have inspired some of the Italian background setting for Shakespeare's plays. In 1598 Florio published *A World of Words*, technically an Italian dictionary but with the meanings of words expressed in unusually vivid English. Five years later his translation of Montaigne's *Essais* introduced a racier and less aphoristic prose style into English essay writing as represented by Francis Bacon (q.v.). "Montaigne speaks now good English", declared Sir William Cornwallis (q.v.), himself an essayist. Shakespeare made use of Florio's translation of Montaigne's essays on cannibals and on cruelty for *The Tempest* and possibly for

some speeches in *Hamlet* and *King Lear*. Florio was Reader in Italian to Queen Anne, with the rank of Groom of the Privy Chamber from 1604 onwards, and was one of Prince Henry's tutors. He died from the plague, in Fulham. Florio's wife was a sister of Samuel Daniel (q.v.).

F. A. Yates, *John Florio* (1934)
A. L. Rowse, *Shakespeare's Southampton* (1965)

FLUDD, Robert (1574–1637), physician and mystic writer: born at Bearsted in Kent, the son of Sir Thomas Fludd, Treasurer of War to Queen Elizabeth. He was educated at St John's College, Oxford from 1592 to 1596, spending five years on the Continent before returning to Christ Church, Oxford, where he took his medical doctorate in 1605 and immediately began to practise in London. For most of his years in London he lived (and eventually died) in Coleman Street, Cripplegate. He was elected a Fellow of the College of Physicians in 1606, becoming one of its most eminent members. From 1616 until 1636 he published a series of studies (written mainly in Latin) which sought to establish a philosophical system based upon the three cosmic elements of the Swiss alchemist, mystic and physician Paracelsus (1493–1541) — God, World, Man. Fludd was also responsible for spreading the so-called Rosicrucian medico-theosophical ideas which are associated, in the first place, with the Lutheran pastor, Johann Andreae (1586–1654). Fludd's first work (1616), *Apologia Compendiaria Fraternitatem de Rosea Cruce Afluens*, excited wide interest by reviving some of the old craving for alchemy. The more serious aspects of his philosophy were critically examined by such eminent figures as the great German astronomer Johann Kepler and the French mathematician and philosopher, Pierre Gassendi, who made nonsense of Fludd's generalisations in 1631. A curious family connection was established in 1618 between Fludd and William Alabaster (q.v.), who in that year married Fludd's widowed mother.

S. Hutin, *Robert Fludd* (1953)

FORD, John (1586–?1640), dramatist: born in Devon and was probably a nephew of the Lord Chief Justice, Sir John Popham (q.v.). Ford matriculated at Exeter College, Oxford, in 1601 and entered the Middle Temple in 1602. He was expelled for non-payment of a buttery bill in 1606 and not reinstated until 1608; poverty remained with him for most of his life. From 1613 he wrote for the stage, at first collaborating with Dekker on comedies. His plays were in the collection of the eighteenth-century antiquarian Sir John Warburton, four of the manuscripts being "unluckily burned" by Warburton's cook. The three chief surviving plays are *'Tis Pity She's a Whore*, *Broken Heart* and *Love's Sacrifice*, all written between 1628 and 1632. These are tragedies, marked by a deeper sense of despair and melancholy resignation than in the era of Shakespeare and Jonson. Ford's *Perkin Warbeck* (1634), although historical in content, is primarily a study in endurance rather than a chronicle in the tradition of the Shakespeare histories.

C. Leech, *John Ford and the Drama of his Time* (1957)

FORMAN, Simon (1552–1611), astrologer and doctor: born near Wilton, educated at grammar school in Salisbury but apprenticed to a grocer on his father's death in 1563. He abandoned his apprenticeship in 1573, going to Oxford in attendance on his cousins, and then served as a schoolmaster until 1579 when he settled near Salisbury to "practise physic and magic". This activity led to a year's imprisonment, but on his release he practised "physic and surgery" in Salisbury and London until 1589, when he settled

Simon Forman

permanently in the capital. The plagues of 1592 and 1594 made his fortune for, while most doctors fled, he stayed in London, cured himself and his family, and acquired a reputation as a physician, publishing in 1595 a *Discourse on the Plague*. His success led him into conflict with the Royal College of Physicians, and he suffered several brief terms of imprisonment until in 1603 he was licensed as a doctor by Cambridge University. Forman had many wealthy clients, some of whom sought love potions from him. His posthumous reputation was damaged by an assertion that he had given Lady Essex a love potion with which she tried to poison Sir Thomas Overbury (q.v.) in 1613. Forman kept a diary describing his practice, and also a *Book of Plays* which contains records of theatrical performances at the Globe in April and May 1611: *Macbeth, Cymbeline,*

The Winter's Tale and a *Richard II* which differs from the accepted version.

A. L. Rowse, *Simon Forman* (1974)

FORTESCUE, John (?1531–1607), courtier and M.P.: step-son of Sir Thomas Parry, Queen Elizabeth's first Controller of the Household and protector during the reigns of her brother and sister. It is possible that Fortescue was one of her tutors when she was a princess. He became Master of the Wardrobe, was knighted, and from 1572 onwards was a leading royal spokesman in the remaining Parliaments of the reign. He became Privy Councillor and Chancellor of the Exchequer in 1589, delivering a succession of judicious and conciliatory speeches on the raising of revenue. He enjoyed much patronage, inside and outside the House of Commons: in 1593, with the aid of his friend Burghley, he found safe seats for three sons; and in 1597 he could count on support from a brother, two sons, a nephew and three kinsmen by distant marriage, including the elder Oliver Cromwell (q.v.). Queen Elizabeth appointed him Chancellor of the Duchy of Lancaster in the autumn of 1601, a post he held until his death. In 1603 James I peremptorily deprived him of the Exchequer, and his election as M.P. for Buckinghamshire in 1604 was challenged and scrutinised. Rather surprisingly, he succeeded in remaining on friendly terms with Ralegh, Francis Bacon and, until his treason, with Essex as well as with the Cecils; but his chief friend was Sir Thomas Bodley (q.v.), and he was benefactor of Bodley's new library at Oxford. He died during the Christmas festivities of 1607. Fortescue's nephew and namesake was a recusant, and, from 1590 to about 1604, tenant of the Blackfriars Gatehouse later bought by Shakespeare. John Fortescue the younger entertained priests, and possibly Gunpowder Plotters, there (v. *Matthew Bacon*).

J. E. Neale, *Elizabeth I and her Parliaments 1584–1601* (1957)

FRAUNCE, Abraham (c. 1558–c. 1633), lawyer and writer: born at Shrewsbury and educated at Shrewsbury School, where he was acquainted with Philip Sidney, who paid for him to receive a university education at St John's College, Cambridge, (1576–80, Fellow, 1581). While at Cambridge Fraunce was a notable actor in Latin plays, himself writing *Victoria*, an Italian play rendered by him into Latin. In 1583 Fraunce became a member of Gray's Inn and over the following nine years wrote both treatises on logic and experimental verses, dedicating his work to various members of the Sidney and Herbert families. He also translated the famous pastoral of Torquato Tasso, *L'Aminta*. Fraunce seems to have abandoned his literary work on receiving a legal administrative post under the Council of Wales.

FREDERICK V of Wittelsbach (1596–1632, Elector Palatine 1610–23, King of Bohemia 1619–20): born at Amberg, Bavaria, succeeded his father, the Calvinist leader, Frederick IV, when he was fourteen and remained much under the influence of his mother (a daughter of William the Silent) and of his father's Chancellor, Prince Christian of Anhalt, who was responsible for negotiating Frederick's marriage to James I's daughter, Elizabeth (q.v.). Frederick was in England from September 1612 until 25 April 1613, the marriage taking place on 14 February. During these seven months he was a prominent figure at Court, taking over patronage of the theatrical company, Prince Henry's Men after the sudden death of Henry (q.v.) in November 1612.

Frederick was encouraged by Christian of Anhalt and by his wife to accept the Crown of Bohemia when anti-Catholic resentment flared up in Prague in 1618. This action exposed Frederick to vigorous counter-measures by the Emperor Ferdinand II, whose troops deprived Frederick of his Rhenish Palatinate and defeated the Bohemian Army at the Battle of the White Mountain, outside Prague, on 8 November 1620. Frederick, an amiable but weak man, spent his remaining years in exile, hoping to achieve diplomatic recognition as the leader of German Protestantism. He died in Mainz from the plague, contracted at Bacharach on the Rhine, where he was campaigning after the battle of Lützen.

C. V. Wedgwood, *The Thirty Years War* (1938)

FREEMAN, Thomas (fl. 1607–14), poet: probably born in Gloucestershire, near Moreton-in-Marsh. He was educated at Magdalen College, Oxford (1610–11) and then went to London, where he became a poet. Two books of his epigrams survive. In the second, *Run and a Great Cast* (1614) is a poem in praise of Shakespeare, as author of *Venus and Adonis* and *Lucrece* as well as comedies.

FRITH, Mary (1570–1650) see CUTPURSE, Moll.

FROBISHER, Martin (?1539–94), seaman: born in the West Riding of Yorkshire, orphaned as an infant and became a ward of his mother's father, Sir John York, a pioneer in the Russia Company. Frobisher went to sea as a boy; he traded in the Mediterranean from Aleppo to the Barbary coast as well as serving on expeditions to Guinea. From 1560 until 1571 he appears to have indulged in piracy. On five occasions he was arrested by English officials but was never put on trial for piracy and may well have been acting as an unofficial agent of the Crown. In 1575 he was authorised by the government to search for a north-west passage. He made three voyages into the northern ice, returning with black pyrites which a London alchemist of Italian origin, Agnello, declared to be gold. Disillusionment with Frobisher's "north-western gold" turned public opinion against him although he remained in the Queen's favour. He may have reverted to piracy, but served under Drake (q.v.) in 1585, enjoying some of the profits from the assault on Cartagena in the Spanish West Indies. Frobisher distinguished himself in command of *Triumph* during the Armada campaign, was knighted at sea by the Lord High Admiral but quarrelled over payment for his services, even threatening to fight Drake. Between 1589 and 1592 he continued to seize Spanish treasure ships as frequently as possible, generally near the Azores. He was mortally wounded while commanding a squadron helping the French Huguenots recapture Brest from the Spaniards in November 1594, dying on returning to Plymouth a few days later.

W. McFee, *Martin Frobisher* (1928)
J. A. Williamson, *The Age of Drake* (1938)
G. Mattingly, *The Defeat of the Spanish Armada* (1959)

FULBECKE, William (1566–1603), jurist: born at Lincoln, educated at St Alban Hall, Oxford, matriculating in 1577 and later becoming a Fellow of Corpus Christi College (1582). He was admitted to Gray's Inn in 1591 but was subsequently ordained, being Vicar of Waldeshore in Kent at the time of his death. Fulbecke is remembered as the author, in 1600, of one of the earliest legal textbooks, *Direction or Preparation to the Study of the Law*, which remained in use for over two hundred years. He contributed two speeches to *The Misfortunes of Arthur* (1588) (v. Hughes).

G

GAGER, William (1560–1621), poet and scholar: educated at Westminster School, entering Christ Church, Oxford in 1574, graduating in 1577 and taking a doctorate in civil law in 1589. His literary reputation was based on his Latin verses and tragedies performed at Christ Church, but his (lost) comedy *Rivales* was also praised. His career as a playwright extended only from 1582 to 1592; he was the first Oxford dramatist to see his work through the University Press, and all the stage directions are therefore authentic. While showing hostility to the professional stage, he defended university acting. His Latin poems include lines praising his contemporary, Peele (q.v.), and *Pyramis* (1608), a long poem on the Gunpowder Plot. In 1606 he became Chancellor of the diocese of Ely.

GARDINER, William (c. 1531–97), Justice of the Peace, property dealer, money-lender: born in Bermondsey, a member of two City companies but did not practise a trade. His considerable wealth was acquired from property deals, the arrangement of mortgages and loans, and from defrauding his relatives by marriage. In 1558 Gardiner married a widow, Frances Wayte (née Luce), and on her death in 1576 Gardiner obtained all her family property, cheating the relations of her first husband as well as her son, William Wayte (q.v.). Twice Gardiner was briefly imprisoned for insulting and violent behaviour. His many frauds included retaining paid bills and demanding money twice, and avoiding the receipt of mortgage payments in order to foreclose. In 1580 he secured possession of the property of his step-daughter-in-law, Wayte's wife, and two years later perpetrated a similar swindle against John Stepkin, his son-in-law.

Stepkin brought a Star Chamber action against Gardiner, also accusing him of irreligious beliefs. After Stepkin's death, which was believed to have been hastened by his father-in-law's behaviour, there were accusations of witchcraft, sorcery and "keeping two toads" against Gardiner. Despite these allegations, Gardiner became so rich that it was inevitable he should acquire office. In 1580 he became a Justice of the Peace, and was the busiest and most energetic magistrate in Surrey. During 1596 Gardiner, as the magistrate responsible for the Bankside, quarrelled with Francis Langley (q.v.) of the Swan Playhouse, and possibly with Shakespeare, too. Dr Leslie Hotson (*Shakespeare versus Shallow*, 1931) has sought to identify Justice Gardiner with the Justice Shallow of *Henry IV*, Part II, and of *The Merry Wives of Windsor*; Hotson noticed, *inter alia*, that the coat of arms of Gardiner's first wife, quartered with Gardiner's own, contained three luces or pike and suggested a reference to the opening scene of the *Merry Wives* (but v. *Lucy*). Gardiner owned a country estate, with an enclosed deer park, at Godstone on the North Downs, and died there on 26 November 1597.

L. Hotson, *Shakespeare versus Shallow* (1931)

GARNET, Henry (1555–1606), Jesuit priest: born at Heanor, Derbyshire, and was converted to Catholicism in his youth, studying theology at the Collegium Romanum under the great Jesuit controversialist, Bellarmine. Father Garnet left Rome in 1586 to work on the English Mission, of which he became the Superior a year later. His zeal, and sympathy for the Spanish cause, made him a leading traitor in the eyes of the English government. He was named (alias Farmer), under torture, by one of the conspirators in the Gunpowder Plot and was arrested shortly afterwards. His trial opened on 28 March 1606, James I personally attending it that day, incognito. Garnet admitted he had "equivocated" in determining not to reveal knowledge of the plot, of which he had information beforehand. He was condemned and executed on 3 May 1606. The remarks of the drunken porter in Act II of *Macbeth* on hearing the knocking at the gate ("Here's a farmer that hanged himself on th'expectation of plenty"... "Faith here's an equivocator..'.") would seem to refer to the trial and fate of Father Garnet.

H. R. Williamson, *The Gunpowder Plot* (1941)

GATES, Thomas (c. 1560–1621), seaman and colonialist: nothing is known about him before 1585–6 when he participated in Drake's privateering raid on Vigo and St Domingo in the Caribbean. From 1591 until 1599 he served in military actions associated with the Earl of Essex: in Normandy; at Cadiz; in Ireland. He seems also to have been an acquaintance of the Earl of Southampton and became a member of Gray's Inn (1598). In 1606 he was one of the original patentees of the Virginia Company and in 1609 was appointed Lieutenant-General of the Virginia expedition, in which Sir George Somers (q.v.) was Admiral. Eight of the nine ships in this expedition safely reached Jamestown, but Gates and Somers were forced to spend ten months as castaways on the Bermudas after the flagship, *Sea Venture*, was wrecked in a storm. This episode, reported to London by Sylvester Jourdain and William Strachey (qq.v.), provided Shakespeare with source material for *The Tempest*. In the spring of 1610 the castaways duly reached Virginia in two cedar pinnaces, made on the island. Gates served as Governor of the colony of Virginia from 1611 until 1614 when he

returned to England and was knighted by James I. He died at The Hague in April 1621 while on a mission to the Netherlands.

A. L. Rowse, *The Elizabethans and America* (1959)

GERARD, John (1564–1637), Jesuit priest: born in Lancashire, educated at Exeter College, Oxford, and at Jesuit colleges at Douai, Rheims and in Rome. He was ordained priest in 1588, secretly coming to England, and was an active Jesuit missionary from 1589 until 1594, when he was arrested. Despite torture in the Tower of London, Gerard succeeded in escaping in 1597 and for nine years continued in his missionary activity, even though government agents were anxious to recapture him. It was considered that he was largely responsible for the Gunpowder Plot and an intensive search was made for him in numerous homes of the Catholic gentry throughout the year 1605. In May 1607 he returned to the Continent after eighteen years of work in England. He helped organise English Jesuit colleges at Louvain, Liège and Ghent from 1609 to 1627, spending the last ten years of his life at the English College in Rome. His works include a Latin autobiography describing, in particular, his experiences in Elizabethan and early Jacobean England.

P. Caraman, *John Gerard, the Autobiography of an Elizabethan* (1951)

GHEERAERTS, Marcus (1561–1635), artist: born in Bruges, the son of Marcus Gheeraerts the Elder (c. 1510–90) who settled in London, probably in 1568. The son — whose name was frequently anglicised as Mark Garret — became a fashionable portrait painter in the last decade of Elizabeth's reign, largely under the patronage of Henry Lee (q.v.), but he reached his peak of achievement and influence in the later years of James I, from about 1618 to 1623. He specialised in full-sized portraits, his subjects standing before heavy curtains and beside a chair or a table. Typical examples of his work are the portraits of Sir Henry Savile and William Camden (qq.v.) in the Bodleian Library's collection at Oxford. One of Gheeraerts's sisters married the miniaturist, Isaac Oliver (q.v.).

GIBBONS, Orlando (1583–1625), composer and musician: born at Oxford into a family of musicians. He became a

Orlando Gibbons

member of King's College Cambridge choir at the age of thirteen and showed such talent that as early as 1604 he was appointed organist of the Chapel Royal. James I showed him numerous favours. Gibbons, the last of the great polyphonic composers, was the heir of Byrd (q.v.). His first collection of madrigals was published in 1612, and he composed for viols and virginals as well as for the organ. His famous anthem 'O Clap your Hands' was composed to celebrate a doctorate in music bestowed on him by Oxford University in 1622. A year later he became organist of Westminster Abbey. He died suddenly at

Canterbury, where the Court awaited the arrival of Charles I's bride, Henrietta Maria.

E. H. Fellowes, *English Cathedral Music* (1941)

GILBARD, William (alias Higgs) (c. 1540–1612), Stratford resident: lived and worked in Stratford-upon-Avon for over fifty years. He was under School-master in 1561–2 and was frequently acting Schoolmaster between 1564 and 1574. By 1576 he was receiving the curate's salary of £10 a year, earning an extra pound for looking after the town clocks. He was highly literate, for he drew up wills for many prominent citizens, including Richard Hathaway (Anne's father) and signed the parish register for the first eight years of James I's reign; during this period there are more Latin words than usual entered on the register. Gilbard was married three times and was father to ten children. In 1604 he was described by the Vicar and eight Aldermen as a person of "a very honest, quiet, sober and good behaviour towards all men". It is possible he may be the original of the Curate, Sir Nathaniel, in *Love's Labour's Lost*.

M. E.

GILBERT, William (1540–1603), physician and physicist: born and died at Colchester, educated at St John's College, Cambridge. Gilbert settled in London in 1573, achieving eminence as a doctor of medicine and becoming personal physician to Queen Elizabeth in 1601, attending her in her last illness. His scientific study *De Magnete* (1600) established that the earth is a magnet, and he conducted the first experiments in electro-magnetism, introducing the term "electricity" into the language. He was also a pioneer in scientific method, building his book up from three hundred experiments. His second work, *De Mundo*, was published posthumously and is concerned primarily with Gilbert's astronomical calculations and in particular with the relationship between the earth and the moon.

A. L. Rowse, *The Elizabethan Renaissance, the Cultural Achievement* (1972)

GILBURNE, Samuel (fl. ante 1605), actor: named in the First Folio list, but otherwise he is known only from the will of Augustine Phillips in 1605, where he is mentioned as Phillips's "late apprentice". He may have given up acting when he reached manhood.

GILES, Nathaniel (?1559–1634), cleric and choirmaster: educated at Magdalen College, Oxford, serving as Master of the Children of the Chapel Royal from 1597 until his death. In 1600 he joined with Henry Evans (q.v.) to present performances by the boys at the Blackfriars and also revived their plays at Court (v. *Farrant*): these are the productions attacked in the exchanges between Rosencrantz and the Prince (*Hamlet*, Act II, Scene 2). In 1602 Giles and Evans were accused of impressing ineligible boys; Evans went into exile, but Giles continued to mount performances by the boys until 1604, when Evans took over again. A new royal commission, presented to Giles in 1606, contained a clause forbidding choristers of the Chapel Royal to perform plays, and thereafter all connections ceased between the boys' companies and the royal choirs. Giles also became known as a composer of church music.

E. K. C., *E.S.*

GILES, Thomas (fl. 1584–90), cleric and choirmaster: Almoner of St Paul's, becoming Master of the Choir School there in

1584. The boys had already appeared in plays at Court and at the Blackfriars in a combined company managed by Henry Evans (q.v.), and Giles continued the tradition, producing the boys at Court in plays by Lyly (q.v.) nine times before 1590.

GOLDING, Arthur (?1536–?1605), translator: came from an Essex family, was a friend of Philip Sidney and brother-in-law of the sixteenth Earl of Oxford. Golding's only original work was a *Discourse upon the Earthquake*, the unusually severe seismic disturbance which shook England in 1580. He is best known for his translations of the classics, including Ovid's *Metamorphoses* (1565–7), a translation familiar to contemporary poets, including Shakespeare. In 1575 Golding translated a tragedy, *Abraham's Sacrifice*, from the French of Theodore Beza, but it was probably never performed.

GOODMAN, Gabriel (?1529–1601), Dean of Westminster: born at Ruthin, Denbighshire, and educated at Christ's College, Cambridge and Jesus College, Cambridge, becoming a Master of Arts in 1553. He was a chaplain to Sir William Cecil and held livings in Rutland and Buckinghamshire before becoming a Canon of Westminster in 1560. For the last forty years of his life he was Dean of Westminster, Burghley's confidant and executor, and also a friend of Camden (q.v.). Goodman founded Christ's Hospital in his native Ruthin and helped establish Sidney Sussex College, Cambridge, but his principal service to education was the protection and patronage which he accorded to Westminster School throughout most of Elizabeth's reign. He was succeeded as Dean of Westminster by Lancelot Andrewes (q.v.).

GOODMAN, Godfrey (1583–1656), bishop: born in London, educated at Westminster School and Trinity College, Cambridge. After serving as Vicar of Stapleford Abbots in Essex, he was appointed chaplain to Queen Anne in 1616, gaining a good knowledge of life at James I's Court, of which he later made use in his entertaining *The Court of King James I*. Goodman was appointed Dean of Rochester in 1621 and consecrated Bishop of Gloucester in 1625. His views on Eucharistic theology, and especially his interpretation of the Doctrine of the Real Presence, caused some consternation in 1626, and he was rebuked by the Privy Council. His attempt to secure election to the see of Hereford in 1633 was condemned by Laud (q.v.), and Archbishop and Bishop remained in conflict for the next seven years. Goodman was forced to resign the Bishopric of Gloucester in the winter of 1643–4 when Parliament sought to root out episcopacy. His last years were spent in some poverty in Westminster.

G. I. Soden, *Godfrey Goodman, Bishop of Gloucester* (1953)

GORGES, Arthur (1557–1625), poet, translator, sailor: son of Sir William Gorges, the Vice-Admiral and Winifred (Budockshead) first cousin of Ralegh (q.v.). He was probably born near Plymouth and was educated at Oxford (B.A., 1574); Gorges went to Court and by 1580 was a Gentleman Pensioner, but his fortunes followed those of Ralegh. He served against the Armada and was four times an M.P. between 1584 and 1601. By 1584, Gorges had met the great love of his life, to whom most of his earlier poems are addressed, Douglas Howard, then aged twelve, the daughter of Henry Howard, second Viscount Bindon. The couple were married in October that year. They had one daughter, Ambrosia, born 1588, and were extremely happy until Douglas's death in 1590; Spenser's *Daphnaida* (1591), in which Gorges appears as Alcyon, was written as an elegy to her. Gorges was involved in litigation with the Howard family over his daughter's inheritance until she, too, died in 1600. He had remarried in 1597, choosing Elizabeth Clinton, daughter of the Earl of Lincoln, a marriage which involved his immediate banishment from Court through the Queen's displeasure, and more quarrelling over property in the future. Gorges was allowed to accompany Ralegh on the Islands Voyage of 1597 and commanded his flagship, *Warspite*. He was knighted by Essex on the expedition and commended for his bravery, but avoided involvement in Essex's disgrace, taking Ralegh's side throughout. Gorges wrote his narrative of the Islands Voyage for Prince Henry in 1607 (published 1625); he pleased the Prince enough to become his Gentleman of the Privy Chamber in 1611. But the Prince's death next year, and Ralegh's disgrace, ended any hope of advancement as Gorges was never in favour with James I. He retired into a comfortable private life, having acquired much property in London, Lancashire and the West Country. Gorges became a J.P., wrote an elegy on Prince Henry and several tracts on naval matters, and was the first translator of Lucan's *Pharsalia* into English (1614).

H. E. Sandison, ed., *Poems of Sir Arthur Gorges* (1953)

GORGES, Ferdinando (1566–1647) soldier, sailor and coloniser: born at Wraxall, a cousin of Sir Arthur Gorges (*supra*). He fought in Normandy under Essex who knighted him at Rouen (1591), and he sailed with Essex on the Islands Voyage as well as serving under him in Ireland. In 1601 he gave evidence against Essex at his trial. While serving as Governor of Plymouth, Devon, he helped organise the Plymouth Company which in 1606 was authorised to explore and plant settlements along the New England coast. Many of Gorges's enterprises were unsuccessful but in 1620 he reformed the company as the Council for New England, which granted land for a colony at New Plymouth and a settlement at Massachusetts Bay, communities which were to thrive under Puritan colonisation. Gorges personally gained extensive rights in what was to become Maine.

C. M. Macinnes, *Ferdinando Gorges and New England* (1965)

GOSSON, Henry (fl. 1601–40), bookseller: son of Thomas Gosson, bookseller, of London, who died in 1600. Henry Gosson was made a freeman of the Stationers' Company in 1601, presented by his widowed mother. He had several shops in London: "The Sun", Paternoster Row (1603–9); on London Bridge (1608–40); in Catherine Wheel Alley (1613); in Pannier Alley (?1615–22). He produced mainly popular literature: ballads, broadsides, news, romances and joke books. In 1609 Gosson published two quartos of Shakespeare's *Pericles*.

GOSSON, Stephen (1554–1624), dramatist, poet, pamphleteer and cleric: born in Kent, educated at Corpus Christi College, Oxford (1572–6). He is known to have been writing poetry and plays in London during the years 1572–6 and he may also have acted in this period. Puritan criticism of plays and acting led him to renounce the stage and become a tutor: in 1579 he published *The School of Abuse* which attacked the theatre and poetry. This work was, without authorisation, dedicated to Sir Philip Sidney who repudiated the dedication. Gosson continued the attack in *Ephemerides of Phialo*. He was answered by Lodge (q.v.) and by

revivals of his own plays. Gosson finally retaliated with *Plays Confuted in Five Actions* (1582). He admits to the authorship of three plays: the tragedy, *Catiline's Conspiracy*; the comedy, *Captain Mario*; and a moral play, *Praise at Parting*. In 1591 Gosson became the Rector of Great Wigborough in Essex and he was appointed Rector of St Botolph's, Bishopsgate, nine years later. Despite his censorious attacks on play-acting he remained a lifelong friend of Edward Alleyn (q.v.).

E. K. C., *E.S.*

GOUGHE (or GOFFE), Robert (?– 1625), actor: appeared with the Admiral's or Strange's Men in 1590–1, but had joined the King's Men by 1603. He was married to the sister of Augustine Phillips (q.v.), and he witnessed Phillips' will in 1604, inheriting his share in the company. Although Goughe appears in the First Folio list, he did not act after 1621 when he became a Court Messenger.

G. E. B.

GREEN, John (fl. 1606–27), actor: little known in England but toured Germany frequently from 1606 onwards. He began as a member of the company of Robert Browne (q.v.), taking over the leadership of these players and going with them to Danzig. Then, in 1608, he entered the service of Archduke Ferdinand at Graz in Styria; few English actors visited Austria. In 1613 Green was at Utrecht (Netherlands) and in 1615 at Danzig again. He returned to Danzig a third time in 1616 travelling by way of Copenhagen, with Robert Reynolds (q.v.), but next year he was once more serving Archduke Ferdinand, both at his coronation as King of Bohemia in Prague, and in Vienna. Green spent the remaining period of his acting career in Germany (possibly with Browne again) and in Utrecht. There is, however, a gap between 1620 and 1626, no doubt attributable to the Thirty Years War.

GREENE, John (c. 1575–1640), lawyer: brother to Thomas Greene (q.v.). He was a member of Clement's Inn and acted as Hamnet Sadler's lawyer in 1599. In 1612 Greene became Town Solicitor for Stratford, serving as Chief Burgess on the Council, 1612–15, and as Deputy Town Clerk to his brother in 1613. He acted as steward for Thomas Russell (q.v.) at Alderminster in 1615, but he failed in an attempt to be elected Town Clerk of Stratford (1617). A remark made to him in September 1615 by Shakespeare "that I was not able to bear the enclosure of Welcombe" was noted in Thomas Greene's diary and has been variously interpreted, the word "bear" probably meaning "bar". John Greene became a trustee of Shakespeare's house in Blackfriars on behalf of Susanna Hall (q.v.), Shakespeare's daughter, in 1618.

M. E.
S. S.

GREENE, Robert (1558–92), dramatist, novelist, and pamphleteer: son of a Norwich saddler and educated at St John's College, Cambridge, from 1575 to 1578. By his own account in later writings he then led a dissolute life in Italy and Spain for about five years before returning to Clare Hall, Cambridge as a reformed character to take a Master of Arts degree in 1583 and to marry. He soon relapsed into vice, leaving wife and child before 1586 and living dissolutely in London among villains of all sorts, his mistress being the sister of a notorious thief, "Cutting" Ball, later hanged at Tyburn. At first Greene earned a living by writing romantic, euphuistic novels. The most widely known

are *Menaphon* (1589), which was republished as *Greene's Arcadia* and contains his best-known lyrics, and *Pandosto* (1588), source for the plot of Shakespeare's *Winter's Tale*. Already, about 1587, Greene had started writing plays, mainly for the Queen's Men, although in 1591 he tried to sell his *Orlando Furioso* to them and to the Admiral's Men at the same time. His plays were romantic mixtures of history and comedy, providing retorts to the atheistic Marlowe; the most successful is *Friar Bacon and Friar Bungay* of which the main plot treats the *Faustus* theme with the light touch of comedy, while the subplot concerns a romance between the young Edward I and a beautiful keeper's daughter. Repentance came to Greene again at the end of his life, and he produced moral pamphlets, partly autobiographical in character, which exposed the villainies of his world. The last of these was *A Groatsworth of Wit bought with a Million of Repentance*, written in his final illness and edited by Henry Chettle (q.v.). The pamphlet contains an attack on Shakespeare as "an upstart crow, beautified with our feathers . . . and in his own conceit the only Shake-scene in a country". At the same time Greene showed that he had also quarrelled with Marlowe, Nashe and Gabriel Harvey, (qq.v.). A surfeit of wine and pickled herrings ruined his health and he died in September 1592 in squalor after a month's illness.

E. K. C., *E.S.; W.S.*
S. S.

GREENE, Thomas (c. 1578–1641), lawyer: a kinsman of Shakespeare, whom he described as his "cousin". Greene entered the Middle Temple in 1595 (his sureties being the dramatist Marston (q.v.) and his father) and was Solicitor for Stratford in 1601 when he helped Richard Quiney support the town rights against Sir

Edward Greville (qq.v.). Next year Greene was called to the Bar. From 1603 until 1617 he was Town Clerk of Stratford and was for many years close to the Shakespeare family circle, his two children being named Anne and William. In 1609 the Greenes were living with the Shakespeares at New Place while waiting to move into St Mary's House, close to the church. Greene joined Shakespeare in the Chancery suit about their tithes in 1611. He spent much of his time in London as Counsel for Stratford, and a memorandum by Greene survives (dated 5 September 1614) in which he recorded a meeting with Shakespeare in London to discuss the threatened enclosure of Welcombe. A year after Shakespeare's death, Greene resigned as Town Clerk, sold his house at Stratford and retired to Bristol for the rest of his life. He was chosen Reader at the Middle Temple in 1621 (the year in which his son William was admitted) and finally became a Master of the Bench and Treasurer. Professor Schoenbaum has pointed out the curious omission of so close an acquaintance from Shakespeare's will. It is possible that Thomas Greene may also have been the poet friend of Drayton (q.v.) and have written a sonnet to him as well as a poem of welcome to James I in the year he became Town Clerk.

S. S.
E. K. C., *W.S.*
M. E.
E. I. Fripp, *Shakespeare's Stratford* (1928)

GRENVILLE, Richard (1542–91), soldier and seaman: born in Devon, the son of Sir Roger Grenville, Commander of Henry VIII's finest warship, *Mary Rose*, who was drowned when she capsized and sank off Portsmouth, 19 July 1545. Richard spent his early years with his stepfather, Thomas Arundell, and entered the Inner Temple in 1559. Three years later he was disgraced when he was involved in an affray in the Strand, in which he killed a companion of the elder Fulke Greville (q.v.). Grenville was pardoned, but in 1566 left the country and for two years served under the Emperor Maximilian II, fighting against the Turks in western Hungary. He was elected M.P. for Cornwall in the eight-week Parliament of 1571 and was Member for Launceston a year later. By now, like his cousin Ralegh (q.v.), he was interested in colonisation and in 1585 he played a leading part in establishing the colony at Roanoke, in what became North Carolina. He commanded the land defences of Cornwall in 1588, and spent two years seeking to settle Munster before joining Sir Thomas Howard as Vice-Admiral of a squadron intended to intercept the Spanish treasure fleet in the Atlantic. Grenville, commanding the *Revenge*, was surprised and trapped at Flores in the Azores by a powerful Spanish fleet under Alonzo de Bazan in August 1591. Grenville sought to escape by sailing *Revenge* through the Spanish line, drawing on himself the fire of some fifteen vessels in a day-long naval engagement. Grenville was mortally wounded and the *Revenge* forced to surrender but, together with sixteen of Bazan's vessels, was soon afterwards sunk in a sudden cyclone. Grenville's heroism, commemorated by his cousin Ralegh in fine prose, rapidly became a legendary epic, still celebrated by Tennyson nearly three hundred years later.

A. L. Rowse, *Sir Richard Grenville of the Revenge* (1937)

GREVILLE, Edward (c. 1565– c. 1621), lord of the manor of Stratford: son of Lodowick Greville (q.v.) of Milcote-on-Avon. Edward inherited his father's estate in 1589, having accidentally killed his elder brother with an arrow while still a boy, and bought the lordship of the manor of Stratford in 1591. He represented Warwickshire in Parliament, 1593 and 1604, and was Sheriff of the county, 1595. In 1596 he held musters in Stratford for Essex's expedition to Cadiz and was knighted by Essex in the Azores, 1597. Greville, as lord of the manor, was often in dispute with Stratford Corporation, especially over market tolls and his attempts to enclose the town commons in 1601. Richard Quiney (q.v.) in particular opposed his efforts and died after a brawl involving Greville's men in the spring of 1602. Greville married Joan Bromley, daughter of Sir Thomas, Lord Chancellor from 1579–87. They had one son and seven daughters, but the son died before his father and the estate was left heavily encumbered by debts as a result of Greville's speculations. By 1610 Greville had been forced to give up his lordship of the manor and in 1622, after his death, the estate was sold to Lionel Cranfield (q.v.), Earl of Middlesex.

M. E.

C. C. Stopes, *Shakespeare's Warwickshire Contemporaries* (1897)

E. I. Fripp, *Master Richard Quyny* (1924)

GREVILLE, Fulke, I (1535–1606), Warwickshire landowner: knighted in 1565, resided at Beauchamp's Court, Alcester. Sir Fulke was Recorder of Stratford from 1591 to 1606 and was succeeded by his son and better-known namesake (*infra*). In 1584, together with Sir Thomas Lucy, he arbitrated in a suit brought by Shakespeare's friend Hamnet Sadler (q.v.). Sir Fulke was a personal friend of Richard Quiney (q.v.) and persuaded his cousin, Edward Greville (*supra*) to accept Quiney as Bailiff of Stratford in 1592. During the Armada invasion threat of 1588 Sir Fulke raised a cavalry troop which he sent to Tilbury Camp. He was presiding at the Great Assize in Warwick when Queen Elizabeth's death was reported, and at once came down from the bench and proclaimed James I King. The circuit judges, more cautious men, refused to do so. Sir Fulke showed his loyalty to James again at the time of the Gunpower Plot when he "raised the country" for the King.

M. E.

GREVILLE, Fulke, II, later Baron Brooke (1554–1628), writer and public servant: only son of his namesake (*supra*). He entered Shrewsbury School on the same day in 1564 as Philip Sidney (q.v.) whose lifelong friend and biographer he became. He matriculated at Jesus College, Cambridge, in 1568 — where his tutor was Legge (q.v.) — but took no degree and went to Court, rapidly winning the Queen's favour. Like Sidney, Greville was a poet and member of the "Areopagus" group; his collected poems, *Caelica*, were published after his death. He wrote love poetry but, despite a probably undeserved reputation as a womaniser, he never married. His principal income came from various offices under the Council for the Welsh Marches; he gained these posts, in the first instance, under the patronage of the Council's president, Sir Henry Sidney, his friend's father. Although Greville was allowed to accompany Philip Sidney to Germany in 1577, the Queen thereafter tried to prevent him from going abroad. She was angered by visits which he made to Holland with Walsingham in 1578 and to Henry of Navarre's headquarters in Poitou in 1587. He served at Tilbury Fort in 1588, subsequently being sent by the Queen to quell an army mutiny at Ostend. Greville entered the Commons in 1580 through a by-election at Southampton, sat for Hayden in Yorkshire in 1584–5, and represented Warwickshire in the remaining Parliaments of Elizabeth's reign and in

1621 also. He was appointed Treasurer of the Navy in 1598 but was unable to reform corrupt practices, not least because of the opposition of Cecil (q.v.). Greville was knighted by James I in 1603 but forced, by Cecil, to resign office a year later. Already he had been responsible for publishing Sidney's *Arcadia* (1590) and now that he was in retirement he wrote his friend's *Life* (published 1652). His hopes of writing a biography of Queen Elizabeth were frustrated by Cecil, who denied him access to official papers. He revised a tragedy, *Mustapha* (1609), a political drama aimed at tyrants and unwelcome to James I. However, with Cecil's death, Greville resumed his career, becoming Chancellor of the Exchequer in 1614 and an active Privy Councillor. The King granted him the ruins of Warwick Castle, which he restored. In 1618 Greville was appointed head of a commission to reform the system of expenditure, following the dismissal of the Lord Treasurer, Suffolk (q.v.) for venal conduct. Failing health prevented Greville from succeeding Suffolk and he finally resigned office in 1621, the King creating him Baron Brooke in the same year. On 1 September 1628 Greville was stabbed by a servant, Ralph Hayward, for no apparent motive. He died four weeks later.

R. A. Rebholz, *Life of Fulke Greville* (1971)

GREVILLE, Lodowick (1538–89), Warwickshire landowner: owned an estate at Milcote-on-Avon, near Stratford, and was cousin to the elder Sir Fulke. Lodowick obtained a licence in 1567 to build a great house, which was to be called Mountgrevell; he began the building but it was never finished. Lodowick was a violent man. He made a joke of his son Edward's shooting his elder brother and, in a fit of temper, he struck down Sir John Conway in a London street, an assault for which he was imprisoned in 1579. In 1588 he raised

as many horsemen as his cousin Fulke to send as cavalry to Tilbury, but in reality his finances were by then so precarious that he had perpetrated an ingenious crime. With the help of two servants he had murdered a wealthy tenant, Thomas Webbe. One of the murderers impersonated Webbe, taking to his bed as though dying and making a will by which all of Webbe's property was left to Lodowick Greville, who then induced one of his accomplices to murder the other, for fear of betrayal. The plot was, however, discovered. Greville declined to plead when brought to trial and was therefore not technically convicted, his refusal to speak saving the estate for his son, Edward. But Greville's silence meant that he was executed by being slowly crushed to death, at Warwick on 14 November 1589.

M. E.

GREY, Thomas, fifteenth Baron Grey of Wilton (c. 1560–1614), soldier: born at Whaddon, Buckinghamshire, succeeding his father as Baron in 1593. His military career followed a familiar pattern: service against the threatened Armada in 1588; participation in the Islands Voyage of 1597; campaigning in Ireland and the Netherlands, 1599–1600. He quarrelled with Southampton (q.v.) who he thought had displaced him as a field commander of yeomanry. With some satisfaction Grey of Wilton acted as General of the Horse against Essex and Southampton in 1601. He was himself implicated in the so-called Bye Plot of George Brooke (q.v.) against James I and was reprieved on the scaffold (November 1603). The last eleven years of his life were spent in the Tower of London.

GRIFFIN, Bartholomew (?–1602), poet: probably from a Northamptonshire family. In 1596 he published a sequence of sixty-two sonnets, *Fidessa, More Chaste* *than Kind*. The third sonnet, beginning "Venus and young Adonis" was included by William Jaggard (q.v.) in his collection *The Passionate Pilgrim* (1599), which he attributed to Shakespeare. It is possible that some of the other poems in this collection may also be by Griffin.

GWINNE, Matthew (c. 1558–1627), doctor and writer: born in London, the son of a Welsh grocer. He was educated at Merchant Taylors' School and St John's College, Oxford (1574–8) becoming a doctor of medicine in 1593. When Queen Elizabeth made her second visit to the University (in 1592) Gwinne was overseer of plays. Five years later he became Professor of Physic at the newly founded Gresham College in London and later still he practised as a doctor in the capital but he retained close links with Oxford, where he had gained a reputation as a dramatist with his two Latin plays *Nero* and *Vertumnus*, a comedy performed by men from St John's at Christ Church before James I during his state visit of August 1605. The comedy sent the King to sleep.

H

HAKLUYT, Richard (?1552–1616), geographer: born in London, a member of a Herefordshire family, educated at Westminster School and Christ Church, Oxford. Although ordained in the Church of England, Hakluyt acquired from a cousin and namesake, who was a lawyer in the Middle Temple, maps and documents of travel; problems of navigation and voyages of discovery became the younger Hakluyt's absorbing interest, and he learned the major foreign languages in order to benefit from the principal books on the Continent concerned with the "New World". He was employed on several occasions by Walsingham as an intelligence agent, serving as chaplain and courier to the English ambassador in Paris, 1583–9. While in Paris he compiled his great work, *The Principal Navigations, Voyages, Traffics and Discoveries of the English Nation*, which was issued in 1589. A much enlarged version, in three folio volumes, appeared in 1598–1600, chronicling for the first time the achievements of the English seamen and navigators of his century. The patriotic pride in Hakluyt's work also stimulated further voyages and colonisation. He was Rector of Wetheringsett in Suffolk, 1590, a prebendary in Westminster Abbey 1602–4, Archdeacon of Westminster and Chaplain of the Savoy 1604–12, and Rector of Gedney in Lincolnshire for the last four years of his life. Hakluyt provided maps and information, not only for English seamen such as Cavendish and Ralegh, but for the Dutchman Willem Barents, who perished on Novaya Zemlya in 1597. He was aware of the need for finding settlements for the rapidly mounting population and his colonising propaganda also stressed the importance of seeking markets for English cloth in a wider world. Towards the end of his life Hakluyt was accumulating new manuscripts for a further work; most of these papers were subsequently used by Samuel Purchas (q.v.).

Richard Hakluyt, *Voyages and Discoveries*, ed., J. Beeching (1972)
G. B. Parks, *Richard Hakluyt and the English Voyages* (1928)

HALL, Elizabeth (1608–70), Shakespeare's granddaughter: baptised at Stratford on 21 February 1608. In his will her grandfather left her his plate. Elizabeth's father, Dr John Hall (*infra*) cured her of fever and convulsions in 1624 and noted that she was then "well for many years". She married Thomas Nash (q.v.) on 22 April 1626 but was left a childless widow in 1647. In June 1649 she married again, her husband being John Bernard, a Northamptonshire squire a year her junior. Charles II created Bernard a baronet in 1661 for his loyalty to the Crown's cause. Lady Bernard inherited Shakespeare's Stratford property but lived and died at Abington Manor, near Northampton. With her death, childless, Shakespeare's direct line became extinct. She left the houses in Stratford to the grandson of Shakespeare's sister, Joan Hart (q.v.).

M. E.
S. S.

HALL, John (1575–1635), medical practitioner and son-in-law to Shakespeare: born in Bedfordshire and was a graduate of Queen's College, Cambridge, where he took his B.A. degree in 1594 and his M.A. three years later. His father, William Hall, was a physician from Acton in Middlesex and he himself studied medicine although there is no record of his taking a medical degree or being licensed. He settled in

Stratford around the turn of the century, and married Shakespeare's elder daughter, Susanna, on 5 June 1607. Their only child, Elizabeth, was born in the following February. Local tradition makes "Hall's Croft", near New Place, the Halls' first home but they are known to have lived at New Place after Shakespeare died. Hall accompanied his father-in-law to London in the autumn of 1614, and was there again two years later to prove Shakespeare's will, of which he and Susanna were executors. He spent his life practising medicine in and around Stratford, keeping Latin case-books. Some details of his methods, translated from the case-books, were published after his death as *Select Observations on English Bodies* (1657), which included 178 of his "cures". Most of these remedies were typical of the age in which he lived although his treatment of scurvy with his own "Scorbutick beer" (specified herbs boiled in sweetened ale) was more advanced. His most notable patients were the poet Drayton and his patron, Lady Rainsford (qq.v.) and the Earl of Northampton. Hall's busy practice, which sometimes took him forty miles on horseback around the countryside, allowed him little time for public affairs. He refused to be knighted in 1626 and managed to stay off the Town Council until 1632. Thereafter his attendances were described as rare and marked by "continual disturbances" and he was expelled from the Council a year later. He was a devoted churchman, inclined to Puritanism, and he was Church warden in 1628–9, donating a pulpit to Holy Trinity Church where his tomb lies in the chancel, near to that of his father-in-law.

M. E.
S. S.

HALL, Joseph (1574–1656), poet, satirist, bishop; born at Ashby-de-la-Zouche,

entering Emmanuel College, Cambridge in 1589. His *Satires Virgidemiarum* ("Three Biting Satires") of 1597 were followed two years later by his "Toothless Biting Satires". Both were condemned as licentious by Archbishop Whitgift (q.v.). Hall was nevertheless ordained priest in December 1600, serving as Vicar of Halstead, Essex, from 1601 to 1608 and writing two works of moral reflections. He became Dean of Worcester (1616), attending the Synod of Dort (1618–19) to discuss the problem of Arminianism. In 1627 he was consecrated Bishop of Exeter. Although Laud regarded him as too indulgent towards Calvinists in his diocese, Hall completed two powerfully written works in defence of episcopacy (1640–1). He was translated to Norwich but briefly imprisoned in the Tower and subsequently ejected from his episcopal palace by the Puritan townsfolk. He spent the last ten years of his life writing poems, meditations and an autobiography (*Hard Measure*) in the Norfolk village of Higham. His collected works fill ten substantial volumes, as he was one of the most prolific and varied writers of his age.

T. F. Kinloch, *Life and Works of Joseph Hall* (1951)

HALL, Susanna (1583–1649), elder daughter of Shakespeare: baptised on 26 May 1583. In May 1606 she was summoned with twenty other defendants before the ecclesiastical court of Stratford for not receiving communion at Easter. She did not appear but the case was dismissed before the second hearing. Many of the defendants were known "papists", but if Susanna had Catholic scruples she soon overcame them for on 5 June 1607 she married her doctor, John Hall, whose views were Protestant and Puritan. Her only child, Elizabeth, was born eight and a half months later. On 15 July 1613 Susanna brought an action for defamation in the consistory court at Worcester Cathedral against John Lane (q.v.) for saying she had committed adultery with Ralph Smith (q.v.) and that she suffered from gonorrhoea. Lane did not appear in court, a witness testified for Susanna, the case was quashed and Lane formally excommunicated. Susanna and her husband inherited the main part of Shakespeare's estate and were executors of his will, living for the rest of their lives in New Place. During the Civil War the widowed Susanna sold some of her husband's case-books to James Cooke, a surgeon with the Parliamentarian army and he later published a translated selection from them (cf. *John Hall*). Susanna is buried with her husband in the chancel of Holy Trinity, Stratford-upon-Avon. Her epitaph describes her as "witty above her sex"; she could at least write her name.

M. E.
S. S.

HALL, William (fl. 1577–1620), printer: son of William Hall, clerk, of Shropshire. Hall was apprenticed to John Allde for seven years from January 1577 and admitted freeman of the Stationers' Company in 1584. He was in partnership with Thomas Haviland, with whom he printed commercial papers, and later with John Beale who took over Hall's copyrights in 1614. Hall is thought to have bought his business from Robert Robinson. In 1608 the Company allowed him to print one edition of the works of Justin in Latin. Sidney Lee and others made him a candidate for "Mr W. H." of Shakespeare's Sonnets on the grounds of his initials; the entire name "W. Hall" can be read into the dedication of the Sonnets if the full stop after "W. H." is omitted. There is no evidence for Hall's connection with the work otherwise.

HARDWICK, Elizabeth (?1527–1608), 'Bess of Hardwick': daughter of John Hardwick of Hardwick Hall, Derbyshire. She was married and widowed four times: to Robert Barley from 1543 to

Elizabeth Hardwick. Portrait possibly by Rowland Lockey

1544; to Sir William Cavendish, by whom she had six children, from 1547 to 1557; to Sir William St Loe from 1559 to 1565; and to George Talbot, sixth Earl of Shrewsbury (q.v.) from 1567 to 1590. After her first marriage she became lady-in-waiting to the Duchess of Suffolk and a friend of the then Princess Elizabeth. From her second and third husbands she inherited wealth and lands, including Chatsworth which she helped Sir William Cavendish to buy. She completed the building of Chatsworth House with her third husband's money in 1564. It was her chief purpose to further the interests of her Cavendish children, an object which led to quarrels over money with her fourth husband, although they had arranged a double marriage between their children (Gilbert Talbot to Mary

103

Cavendish, and Henry Cavendish to Grace Talbot). As Bess and her family grew richer, so Shrewsbury became poorer. His troubles were not helped by serving for sixteen years from 1569 as guardian of the imprisoned Mary, Queen of Scots; she was an expensive guest and a mischief-maker. In 1583 Bess separated from Shrewsbury, thereafter living at Chatsworth or Hardwick Hall with her orphaned granddaughter, Arbella Stuart (q.v.), fruit of the dynastic marriage she had arranged for her daughter Elizabeth and Charles Stuart, Earl of Lennox. Bess spent the last twenty-five years of her life quarrelling with Shrewsbury or, after his death, with her step-son Gilbert Talbot, and trying to control the wayward Arbella. But she retained sufficient energy to supervise between 1590 and 1600 the complete rebuilding of Hardwick Hall into its present magnificence. (v. *Mary Talbot*.)

D. N. Durant, *Bess of Hardwick* (1977)

Hardwick Hall

HARINGTON, John (1561–1612), courtier and translator: born at Kelston Park, near Bath, and educated at Winchester and Christ's College, Cambridge. His parents had been imprisoned in the Tower with Queen Elizabeth (q.v.) before her accession. She willingly agreed to become Harington's godmother and treated him with indulgence throughout her reign. It was at the Queen's suggestion that Harington translated the long Italian poem by Ariosto, *Orlando Furioso* (which may have been one of Shakespeare's sources for *Much Ado about Nothing*). Harington was a man of ingenuity and wit: he invented, and installed at Kelston, the first water closet; but his somewhat bawdy satires — notably his *Metamorphosis of Ajax*, 1596 — strained the sense of decency in even a broad-minded court and he was briefly banished from the Queen's presence. He served in Ireland under Essex (q.v.) and was knighted by him on the field, much to the Queen's displeasure. Harington avoided entanglement in the Essex conspiracy, surviving to record a vivid description of Essex's behaviour, the Queen's anger, the last years of her life, and of how he found James I's conversation aridly concerned with learning — he "showed me his own (learning) in such sort as made me remember my examiner at Cambridge". Most of Harington's literary remains were published in *Nugae Antiquae*, edited by one of his descendants in 1769.

I. Grimble, *The Harington Family* (1958)
D. W. Willson, *King James VI & I* (1956)

HARIOT, Thomas (1560–1621), mathematician: born in Oxford and educated there, at Oriel College. He served as mathematical instructor, cartographer and scientific adviser to Ralegh (q.v.), visiting Roanoke as early as 1585–6 with Grenville (q.v.). His *Brief and True Report of the new found land of Virginia* was published in 1588, translated into German, French and Latin within two years. It is the earliest book on English colonisation in what was to become the U.S.A. Hariot prepared a manual of navigation for Ralegh, and charts and maps for his voyage to Guiana. From 1607 until his death Hariot lived and worked in Sion House, a pensionary of Henry Percy, Earl of Northumberland (q.v.). Hariot was briefly imprisoned after the Gunpowder Plot for having cast the

King's horoscope for his patron, the suspect Northumberland. Hariot was using an astronomical telescope almost as powerful as that of Galileo by 1610 and was observing sunspots and other unusual phenomena. He invented navigational instruments of his own and spent his last years seeking to perfect theories of algebraic equations. Scholarly reluctance to publish his discoveries meant that his most important work, *Artis Analyticae Praxis*, did not appear until 1631, ten years after his death. He is, reputedly, the first Englishman to have smoked pipe tobacco and is known to have died from cancer of the nose.

H. Stevens, *Thomas Hariot* (1900)

HARRISON, John (? — 1617), bookseller: was a member of the Stationers' Company at the time of its incorporation (1557) having been a freeman of the original guild. He was admitted to the Livery of the Company in 1564 and was three times Warden and three times Master. Harrison's shops were the "White Greyhound", St Paul's Churchyard, and the "Greyhound", Paternoster Row. He sold Shakespeare's *Venus and Adonis* printed by Richard Field (q.v.) in 1593, then acquired the copyright of the poem together with *The Rape of Lucrece*, printed by Field for him in 1594. Harrison passed his copyrights in the poems to other publishers, *Lucrece* going first to his half-brother, John Harrison the younger. (v. *Barrett, Jackson, Leake*).

HARRISON, William (1534–93), chronicler, Anglican clergyman: born in London and had degrees from both Oxford and Cambridge (Christ Church, Oxford, B.A., 1556; B.D., Cambridge, 1569). He was Rector of Radwinter, Essex, and several other parishes, and chaplain to William Brooke, Lord Cobham. Harrison

contributed the *Descriptions* of England and Scotland which are the preface to the *Chronicles* of Holinshed (q.v.) in both the 1577 and 1587 editions. *England* was largely copied from Leland's *Itinerary*, with original additions on contemporary society. *Scotland* was translated from Boece's Scottish history. Harrison, now a Canon of Windsor, enlarged his work for the 1587 edition and emphasised his favourite theory, that giants once lived in England. From 1577 till his death, he was also engaged on a "Great Chronology" of the world, which was left unfinished. Another work, on weights and measures, remained in manuscript.

A. L. Rowse, *The England of Elizabeth* (1950)
S. Booth, *The Book Called Holinshed's Chronicles* (1968)

HARSNET, Samuel (1561–1631), archbishop: born in Colchester, the son of a baker. He was educated at Pembroke College, Cambridge, taking his B.A. in 1581 and becoming a Fellow in 1583. From 1587 to 1588 he was Master of Colchester Grammar School and he held several livings in Essex: Vicar of Chigwell, 1597–1605; Rector of Shenfield 1604; Vicar of Hutton 1606–9; and Archdeacon of Essex from 1603 to 1609. He was also Prebendary of St Paul's (1598) and Rector of St Margaret, Fish Street, from 1599 to 1604, serving as chaplain to Bishop Bancroft (q.v.). In this capacity he had to license books for the press, and he was in serious trouble with Coke and the Star Chamber authorities for having allowed the printing of a history of the early years of Henry IV's reign by his college friend Hayward (q.v.) which was dedicated to the Earl of Essex and which seemed to justify rebellion. Harsnet's assurances that he did not perceive the political implications of a historical narrative were accepted by Coke. In 1603 Harsnet published *A Declaration of Egregious Popish Impostures*, a work which shows that he had some knowledge of plays and the theatre, and which was printed by James Roberts, who was to produce the second quarto of *Hamlet* soon afterwards. Shakespeare evidently read Harsnet's book for he makes extensive use of it in *King Lear*, notably when Edgar names the devils in his feigned lunacy. Harsnet was consecrated Bishop of Chichester in 1609, translated to Norwich in 1619 and spent the last two years of his life as Archbishop of York. His *Considerations for the better founding of Church Government* was commended by Charles I in 1629. Archbishop Harsnet was founder of Chigwell School and is buried at Chigwell.

Kenneth Muir, "Samuel Harsnet and King Lear", *Review of English Studies*, N.S., no.2, (1951)

HART, Joan (1569–1646), Shakespeare's sister: was the fourth of the eight children in the family, and the only girl to survive childhood. She married a hatter, William Hart, some time before 1600, when her first son, William, was born. Of her four children only the boys, William and Thomas, reached manhood. Shakespeare left his sister £20, all his clothes, and the life tenancy of the western house in Stratford ("the Birthplace"), where the Harts were already living. In 1670 Shakespeare's granddaughter, Lady Bernard (Elizabeth Hall, q.v.) bequeathed all the Shakespeare property to Joan's grandson, Thomas, son of Thomas.

E. K. C., *W.S.*
M. E.

HARVARD, Catherine (1584–?): daughter of Thomas Rogers, a butcher and Alderman of Stratford-upon-Avon, who rebuilt his house in High Street after the fire of 1594 with fine carved wood. In 1605 Catherine married Robert Harvard of Southwark; their son John, baptised at St

Mary Overbury, Southwark, in 1607, settled in Massachusetts and became the founder of Harvard University (1638). The Rogers' great house in Stratford was presented to the University in 1909 and is now known as "Harvard House". The initials of Catherine's parents, TR and AR, may still be seen on the façade of the house.

E. I. Fripp, *Shakespeare Studies* (1930)

HARVEY, Gabriel (?1550–1630), university lecturer, critic: son of a ropemaker, of Saffron Walden, Essex. He was educated at Cambridge, matriculating at Christ's College (1566) and moving to a Fellowship at Pembroke Hall (1570). At Pembroke he began the quarrels with his professional colleagues that were to hamper his career and the other Fellows opposed his M.A., but he also made a friend among the undergraduates, Edmund Spenser (q.v.). Harvey appears as "Hobbinol" in Spenser's *Shepheardes Calendar*. In 1574 Harvey was appointed Professor of Rhetoric. His lectures, embodying his belief that content is more important than form, were published in 1577. His practical approach to teaching appears in his advice to students on how to study, contained in the lectures. Harvey, who called himself "father of the English hexameter", tried to write quantitative verse in English, on the classical model, although in one of his letters to Spenser he declares that a standard phonetic spelling must be established first. He used such a spelling in his *Marginalia*, marginal notes on the books he read. Harvey began the practice of annotating his library at Cambridge when he was sixteen. His notes are of three kinds: symbols, to enable him to identify passages; critical comments; and reflections unconnected with the text. In 1578 Harvey moved to a Fellowship at Trinity Hall but his career received another check in 1579 with the publication of his correspondence with Spenser, thought to contain an attack on the Earl of Oxford (q.v.) as the supreme example of "euphuism" (a word invented by Harvey). Cambridge and the Court took offence. Harvey failed to become Public Orator, and in 1585 his election as Master of Trinity Hall was blocked by the government. Nothing deterred Harvey from controversy. His long feud with the poets Robert Greene and Thomas Nashe (qq.v.) began with his *Four Letters* in 1592, directed against Greene, and pamphlets flew back and forth between Nashe and Harvey, who were opposed because of Harvey's Puritanism as well as on literary grounds. By 1593 Harvey was tired of the literary fashions of the day and urged young men to leave poetry for studies of more "effectual use". His own interest in navigation and the sciences led him to exalt the "expert artisan". However, some writers pleased him still. In 1601 Harvey gave his judgment on Shakespeare; the "younger sort" liked *Venus and Adonis*, but *Lucrece* and *Hamlet* pleased the "wiser sort". Finally Harvey and Nashe were banned from printing polemics and their existing works were confiscated. Harvey published nothing more. He made one further attempt, in a letter to Robert Cecil (q.v.) of 1598, to obtain the Mastership of Trinity Hall. When this failed he retired to Saffron Walden, where he spent the last thirty-three years of his life in the study of science and medicine.

G. C. Moore Smith, ed., *Harvey's Marginalia* (1913)
A. L. Rowse, *Elizabethan Renaissance, The Cultural Achievement* (1972)
Virginia F. Stern, *Gabriel Harvey, His Life, Marginalia and Library* (1979)

HARVEY, William (1578–1657), physician and anatomist: born at Folkestone and educated at King's School, Canterbury and Caius College, Cambridge, graduating in 1597. From 1598 to 1602 he studied medicine at Padua, before returning to Cambridge for further study of the blood. By 1609, when he became House Physician at St Bartholomew's Hospital, he had settled in London and married Elizabeth, the daughter of Sir Lancelot Browne, physician to Queen Elizabeth I and James I. In 1615 he propounded his theory of the course followed by the blood through the body, developing his ideas

William Harvey

further before publishing his conclusions on the circulation of the blood in *Exercitatio Anatomica de Motu Cordis et Sanguinis* (1628). He was physician both to James I and Charles I (until 1646). For some years Harvey was also Francis Bacon's doctor: "I *cured* him", he later remarked lightheartedly to Aubrey. He was present at the Battle of Edgehill in 1642, took up residence in Oxford and served as Warden of Merton College during the Civil War, before returning to London to complete his studies in embryology. His *Exercitationes de Generatione Animalium* was published in 1651, but thereafter he was partly paralysed by gout and settled in Essex, where he died. He is buried at Hempstead, near Saffron Walden.

A. Malloch, *Sir William Harvey* (1929)
O. L. Dick, ed., *Aubrey's Brief Lives* (1949)

HATCLIFFE, William (1568–1631), gentleman: born in Lincolnshire, matriculated at Jesus College, Cambridge, in 1582 and became a friend of the poet, Thomas Campion. In 1586 he entered Gray's Inn and was elected "Prince of Purpoole" for the Christmas Revels of 1587. Although Hatcliffe inherited his father's estate in 1612, nearly all of it was squandered by 1630; he spent most of his adult life in debt. Dr Leslie Hotson has suggested that Shakespeare knew Hatcliffe when he was at Gray's Inn but the evidence is internal and cryptographic and depends on Hotson's own dating of the Sonnets, which assigns them to this period, far earlier than is generally accepted. Hatcliffe is Dr Hotson's candidate for the "Mr W. H." to whom the printed edition of the Shakespeare Sonnets was dedicated in 1609.

L. Hotson, *Mr W.H.* (1964)

HATHAWAY, Anne (?1556–1623) see SHAKESPEARE, Anne.

HATHAWAY, Bartholomew (ante 1560–1624), Shakespeare's brother-in-law: was a farmer in Shottery, succeeding to the tenancy of his father (Richard Hathaway, q.v.) after the death of his father's widow, Joan, in 1599. Bartholomew was in charge of Hewlands Farm from the time of his father's death in 1581, finally buying the property in 1610 for £200. The farmhouse, popularly known as "Anne Hathaway's Cottage" remained in the family by the male line until 1746 and by the female line until 1892 when it was purchased by the Shakespeare Birthplace Trust. Bartholomew was Churchwarden of the parish from 1605 to 1609; he was married with four children, one of whom, named Richard after his grandfather, was Bailiff of Stratford in 1626.

M. E.

HATHAWAY, John (1586–?), nephew of Shakespeare's wife, a second son of her brother Bartholomew. At Easter 1616 he became Churchwarden of Holy Trinity and was thus in office for Shakespeare's funeral. All the Hathaway property at Shottery passed into his hands.

HATHAWAY, Richard (d. 1581), Shakespeare's father-in-law. Richard Hathaway (alias Gardner) farmed in Shottery, a mile from Stratford and was tenant (copyholder) of land called Hewlands Farm, of which the farmhouse survives as "Anne Hathaway's Cottage". The property had been held by his father, John, at least since 1543. Richard Hathaway's personal fortunes seem to have fluctuated considerably and he was probably married twice. In 1566 he was in debt, and there is evidence that his family were already friendly with the Shakespeares, for John Shakespeare (q.v.) was his surety and paid off some of his debts. His daughter Anne (or "Agnes", as he called her) did not marry William Shakespeare until a year after her father's death. In his will Richard Hathaway appointed his wife, Joan, executrix and residuary legatee, with the use of some land for his eldest son, Bartholomew (q.v.), who was to serve Joan as a guide over farming matters as a whole. Richard left money to his remaining children: £10 to his son, William, and ten marks to Thomas, John, "Agnes" and Catherine which they would receive on their marriage, while their sister Margaret would inherit ten marks when she was seventeen.

E. K. C., *W.S.*
M. E.

HATHWAY, Richard (fl. 1598–1603), dramatist: is known to have been part-author of plays for the Admiral's Men, 1598–1602, and for Worcester's Men, 1602–3. His only surviving work is in Part One of the *Life of Sir John Oldcastle* of 1599, the Admiral's company's answer to the Falstaff of *Henry IV*. This Richard Hathway had no kinship with Shakespeare's wife nor with her father, his namesake (*supra*).

HATTON, Christopher (1540–91), courtier and Lord Chancellor: born at Holdenby, Northamptonshire, educated

Sir Christopher Hatton

at St Mary Hall, Oxford before entering the Inner Temple where he had a prominent part in the Christmas masque of 1561. His fine dancing attracted the attention of the Queen. He became a member of the Corps of Gentlemen Pensioners — the Queen's bodyguard — and was appointed their Captain in 1572. He sat as Member of Parliament for Higham Ferrars in 1571 and for his native county in the Parliaments of 1572–86. To some extent he was spokesman for the Queen in the Commons, and he enjoyed the electoral patronage of a party leader. Extravagantly worded letters of devotion to the Queen helped keep him in favour: Elizabeth forced the Bishop of Ely to hand over his London home, Ely Place in Holborn, to Hatton in 1576. She knighted him in 1577 and appointed him a Privy Councillor a year later. In 1581 he was temporarily out of favour because of his opposition to the Queen's encouragement of her French suitor, the Duke of Alençon, and also because of her liking for the newcomer to Court, Ralegh (q.v.), whose presence Hatton deeply resented. At Holdenby Sir Christopher spent money freely on building an ornate country house, dedicated as a shrine to the Queen, who lent him many thousands of pounds for its construction. His patronage of the voyages of Drake (q.v.), Frobisher and others brought him prestige but little monetary reward. He was Lord Chancellor from 1587 until his death, and his speech for the opening of Parliament in February 1589 anticipates in style the patriotic oratory of Chatham and Churchill. From 1588 to 1591 he was Chancellor of Oxford University as well as being High Steward of Cambridge. His patronage of literature included support for his friends Spenser and Thomas Churchyard (qq.v.) and he also encouraged the music of Byrd (q.v.).

E. St John Brooks, *Sir Christopher Hatton* (1946)

HATTON, Lady Elizabeth (1577–1646, née Cecil): daughter of Lord Burghley's elder son, Thomas, Earl of Exeter. She was married very young to Sir

William Hatton, nephew and heir of Queen Elizabeth's favourite, Christopher Hatton (*supra*). Sir William died in 1597, the same year in which his stepbrother, William Underhill (q.v.) sold New Place to Shakespeare; this extremely tenuous connection has made Elizabeth a possible "Dark Lady" in some eyes. Elizabeth was left a wealthy widow, her property including the Isle of Purbeck (with Corfe Castle) and Hatton House, Holborn, the subject of dispute with successive bishops of Ely, whose London residence it had been. She was courted by Francis Bacon and Edward Coke (qq.v.). The Cecil family preferred Coke, the Attorney-General, and Elizabeth married him in November 1598. She refused, however, to use his name or to live with him after the birth of their daughters, Elizabeth and Frances. After the accession of James I she became a popular figure at Court, sharing Queen Anne's amusements. She continued to quarrel with Coke over his mis-appropriations of her property and his refusal to maintain her until 1616 when he fell into disgrace and was dismissed from his post as Chief Justice. Elizabeth then stood by her husband, even going to live with him at Stoke Poges, but in the following year a dispute over their daughter Frances's marriage led to their last and bitterest quarrel. Coke wished her to marry Buckingham's elder brother; Elizabeth went to great lengths to prevent this, stealing Frances away and forging a proposal to her from the Earl of Oxford. Frances was kidnapped back by her father. At first Elizabeth received help from Bacon, but he changed sides on hearing that James I favoured the marriage; Elizabeth was placed under house arrest, and Frances whipped into submission. After the marriage (November 1617), Elizabeth submitted to the King and was released, but she was never reconciled to her husband. She continued to live at

Hatton House until Coke's death, giving parties to which Coke was not admitted. When in 1623 Frances left her (now insane) husband for a lover, Elizabeth was involved in her daughter's disgrace. She supported the Parliamentarian cause in the Civil War, and survived her daughter Frances by some six months.

L. L. Norsworthy, *The Lady of Bleeding Heart Yard* (1953)
D. Du Maurier, *The Winding Stair* (1976)

HAUGHTON, William (c. 1575–1605), dramatist: wrote plays for the Admiral's Men from 1597 to 1602, mainly in collaboration with Chettle, Day and Dekker. The only extant play of which he was sole author is a comedy, *Englishmen For My Money* (1598). Haughton is known to have borrowed frequently from Henslowe and was in the Clink for debt in 1600.

HAWKINS, John (1532–95), seaman: second son of William Hawkins (c. 1495–1554) who, as Mayor and M.P. for Plymouth intermittently from 1532 to 1553, was responsible for making the city the chief port for trade with the Americas. After acquiring much wealth from trade with the Canary Islands, John Hawkins, backed by a syndicate, made the first slave-trading voyage from the Guinea coast to the Spanish Indies. In further voyages in 1564 and 1567 Queen Elizabeth was a shareholder while Cecil (Burghley, q.v.) was, in effect, Chairman of the joint-stock company which managed the third of the slave-trading voyages. The Earls of Leicester and Pembroke were also heavy investors. Most of the ships and booty on the third voyage were seized by the Spaniards at San Juan de Ullao (September 1568). Three months later Hawkins's brother, William (1519–89), as Mayor of Plymouth impounded three Spanish treasure ships forced to seek refuge in Plymouth

Sound from gales in the Channel. These two acts, at San Juan and Plymouth, marked the start of an undeclared naval war between England and Spain which was to continue until 1604. John Hawkins sat as M.P. for Plymouth in the Parliament elected in 1572. As Treasurer of the Navy he improved ship design but is known to have made a comfortable profit from management of the navy yard. In 1588 he commanded *Victory* against the Armada and was one of the naval captains knighted at sea by the Lord High Admiral. He founded an almshouse at Chatham in 1592, spending most of his last years in London. In 1595 he was appointed joint commander with Drake (q.v.) of a joint-stock company expedition, partly financed by the Queen, intended to incommode the Spanish on the isthmus of Panama and in the Caribbean. The two commanders were at variance over tactics, objectives and even rationing of victuals. Both Hawkins and Drake were sick and tired men. Neither survived the voyage, Hawkins succumbing first, off Puerto Rico in the second week of November.

J. A. Williamson, *Hawkins of Plymouth* (2nd edition, 1969)
Rayner Unwin, *The Defeat of John Hawkins* (1960)

HAWKINS, Richard (1560–1622), seaman: only child of Sir John Hawkins (*supra*) and his first wife, Katherine Gonson, daughter of a former Treasurer of the Navy. He was in command of a ship at the age of twenty-two, appears to have accompanied Drake (q.v.) in 1585–6 and probably in the Cadiz raid of 1587. He commanded *Swallow* against the Armada. In June 1593 he sailed from Plymouth in a vessel which his Puritan stepmother christened *Repentance* but the Queen renamed *Dainty*. His attempt to plunder the treasure towns of Peru proved disastrous, as Spanish defences had improved in the

preceding ten years. *Dainty* was sunk after a three-day running fight with a Spanish squadron north of Valparaiso in June 1594. For three years the wounded Hawkins was held captive in Peru. He was shipped to Spain in 1597 and imprisoned in Madrid but offered freedom for a ransom of £3,000. His widowed stepmother refused to allow any of the family funds to be handed over to Catholic Spain and he languished in Madrid until the money was raised from other sources, apparently by Cecil (q.v.). His misadventures made a considerable impression on his contemporaries. After returning home for the first time in ten years, he wrote some memoirs, *Observations*, which were published soon after his death. James I knighted him and appointed him Vice-Admiral of Devon but, apart from a confused expedition against the Barbary pirates in the last year of his life, he remained in Plymouth or London until his death. Like his father and grandfather he sat as M.P. for Plymouth.

J. A. Williamson, *Hawkins of Plymouth* (2nd edition, 1969)

HAY, James, later first Earl of Carlisle (?1580–1636), favourite: son of Sir James Hay, born at Pitcorthie, Fife. Hay was educated in France, and became Gentleman of the Bedchamber to James I from 1603 to 1615. He was a great favourite with James: Hay, who was a Privy Councillor from 1617, was created Viscount Doncaster (1618), Earl of Carlisle (1622), and a Knight of the Garter (1625). He was frequently employed on embassies, to Paris (1616, 1622, 1623) Madrid (1616, 1623) Germany (1619–20) and Venice (1628). On the German embassy Hay took 150 people at a cost of £30,000 in an unsuccessful attempt to mediate in the Bohemian conflict. In all he was the most extravagant of James I's favourites; he spent more than £400,000 in his lifetime and left nothing to his heirs. Hay was twice married. His first wife, Honora Denny, daughter of the Earl of Norwich, died of a miscarriage after being violently robbed on Ludgate Hill. His second wife was the beautiful Lucy Percy, (Countess of Carlisle, q.v.) whom he married against the wishes of her father, the Earl of Northumberland (q.v.) in 1617. The King attended their wedding. Hay was equally favoured by Charles I who made him Governor of the "Caribee" Islands. He died in Whitehall and was buried in St Paul's Cathedral.

HAYES, Thomas (?–?1604), bookseller: was first apprenticed to John Sheppard, but transferred in January 1580 to William Lownes by order of the Stationers' Company. He became a freeman in 1584 and was admitted to the Livery of the Company in 1602. Hayes had his shop at the "Green Dragon", St Paul's Churchyard (1600–3). He was one of the publishers of *England's Parnassus* (1600), a verse anthology, and in the same year published Shakespeare's *Merchant of Venice*. The copyright of this play was claimed in 1619 by his son Lawrence, who produced an edition of it in 1637.

HAYWARD, John (?1564–1627), historian: born near Felixstowe, Suffolk, and educated at Pembroke College, Cambridge (B.A., 1581), where he was a friend of the later Archbishop Harsnet (q.v.). He came to London to practise law but began to write history. His *First Part of the Life and Reign of Henry IV*, published in 1599, contained a fulsome dedication to Essex (q.v.) and an apparent justification of Richard II's overthrow, as well as passages which (as Coke maintained) "suggested that deposers of kings had had good success". Hayward was imprisoned, but defended by Francis Bacon (q.v.) before

Star Chamber with the plea that Hayward should be accused of theft rather than treason since he had stolen so much from Tacitus. He may have remained in prison until 1603; but he pleased James I by pamphlets justifying, on historical grounds, the King's accession and the union of England and Scotland. Hayward was one of two "Doctors in History" (Camden being his colleague) appointed by the King when he attempted to found a new university, Chelsea College, in 1610. Hayward was encouraged by Prince Henry to publish his *Lives of the Norman Kings* (1613), but he combined a law practice with the writing of both history and devotional works, and was engaged intermittently from 1605 onwards in a study justifying the predominance of the State in Church affairs, *Ecclesiastical Supremacy* (published 1624). Hayward became Chancellor of Lichfield and was Master in Chancery in 1616, being knighted three years later. He was M.P. for Bridgnorth in 1621 and for Saltash in 1626, accumulating much land and property around Tottenham and Wood Green, to the north of London. Hayward's *Life and Reign of Edward VI* was published three years after his death and reprinted, with his *Beginning of the Reign of Queen Elizabeth*, in 1636. He was a good pioneer professional historian, using original sources such as the *Anglo-Saxon Chronicle* and a diary of Edward VI, both of which he could see in manuscript in the collection of Cotton (q.v.).

H. S. Bennet, *English Books and Readers, 1603–40* (1970)

J. Hayward, *Annals of the First Four Years of Queen Elizabeth*, ed., J. Bruce (1840)

HEICROFT, Henry (?1549–1600), Vicar of Stratford-upon-Avon: came from Hampshire, graduated from St John's College, Cambridge, 1566–7, becoming a Fellow of the college. He served as Vicar of

Stratford from 1569 until 1584, marrying Emme Careless two years after his arrival. Five children were born to the Heicrofts in Stratford, three of them dying in infancy. Heicroft is recorded as having preached special Lent sermons in 1583 and on Trinity Sunday that year he baptised Shakespeare's daughter, Susanna. In 1584 Heicroft moved to the richer living of Rowington, ten miles away.

M. E.

HELME, John (?–?1616), bookseller: son of John Helme, tailor, of Smithfield, London. He was apprenticed to Nicholas Ling (q.v.) for nine years from 1599 and became a freeman of the Stationers' Company in 1607. His shop was in St Dunstan's Churchyard. Helme published plays, including Chapman's *Bussy d'Amboise*. In 1611 he produced an edition of the *Troublesome Reign of King John* described as "written by William Sh----". Anne Helme, his widow, succeeded to the business.

HEMINGES, John (?–1630), actor: his family came from Droitwich, Worcestershire. His name is first mentioned in March 1588, when he married Rebecca, the widow of Knell (q.v.), an actor with the Queen's Men, murdered in 1587. Presumably Heminges started with the same company, but by May 1593 he was with Strange's, soon joining the Chamberlain's Men and appearing in all their lists until 1629, including the Royal Patent of 1603 and the First Folio. From 1596 he was payee for Court performances of the Chamberlain's Men. After Burbage's death, he heads the company's list (1619–29), but he does not seem to have acted after 1611, concentrating on the business side of the enterprise. A poem on the burning of the Globe in 1613 already refers to him as "old, stuttering Heminges", and Jonson also calls him old in 1616. He was trustee and overseer for the wills of many members of the company, most of whom — including Shakespeare — left him legacies. Heminges served as trustee for Shakespeare for the dramatist's Blackfriars house, and was co-editor with Condell (q.v.) of the First Folio. There is no supporting evidence for the statement by Malone, in the late eighteenth century, that Heminges was the original Falstaff. Heminges is known to have attended St Mary's, Aldermanbury, from 1590 until his wife's death in 1619, and he was buried there, although not a resident of the parish at the time of his death. He had eight daughters and five sons: four of his children are known to have predeceased him. In a will prepared on his death-bed he is described as "citizen and grocer of London". He died wealthy, owning a quarter of the shares in each of the company's theatres, Globe and Blackfriars. It is probable that these shares included the portion previously owned by his son-in-law, William Ostler (q.v.), although Heminges's daughter (Thomasine Ostler) sued her father for the value of the shares which he had insisted on retaining when she was widowed in December 1614.

E. K. C., *E.S.*, *W.S.*
G. E. B.
S. S.

HENEAGE, Thomas (c. 1534–95), courtier: born at Lincoln, entering Queen's College, Cambridge, in 1549. He appears to have made his first impact at Court under the patronage of Burghley, who found him a succession of constituencies in his native Lincolnshire in the Parliaments of 1563 to 1572. By 1566 he was favoured at Court by the Queen, who used him as a witty foil to Leicester (q.v.). Lucrative rewards came to him, as well as a knighthood in 1577. He was able to build a fine house in Essex, Copt Hall, and to shift his interests away from Lincolnshire to his new home county, while living in state in London in what had once been the town house of the Abbots of Edmundsbury. Sir Thomas was M.P. for Essex from 1584 to 1593, carrying much patronage as a Privy Councillor and from 1590 as Chancellor of the Duchy of Lancaster. He was also Treasurer of the Chamber and in 1587 succeeded Hatton (q.v.) in the politically important post of Vice-Chamberlain. As leading spokesman for the Crown in 1593 he was frequently short-tempered with the Commons, partly because he was troubled by the gout. On 2 May 1594, long a widower, he married Mary, dowager Countess of Southampton (q.v.), a celebration which Dr Rowse, and others, have suggested as the occasion of the first performance of *A Midsummer Night's Dream*. Sir Thomas died less than eighteen months later, bequeathing a jewel to the Queen "who, above all other earthly creatures, I have thought most worthy of all my heart's love and reverence".

J. E. Neale, *Elizabeth 1 and her Parliaments 1584–1601* (1957)
A. L. Rowse, *William Shakespeare* (1963)
C. C. Stopes, *Life of ... Southampton* (1922)

HENRY, Prince of Wales from June 1610 (1594–1612): born at Stirling, the eldest son of James VI and I. With his mother he settled in England in the summer of 1603. His sharp intelligence made him a good listener, even as a child, his wealth promised welcome literary patronage, and his independence of will made him a likely champion of dissidents of whom his father did not approve. He was a patron of George Chapman and Ben Jonson, a friend and vigorous defender of Ralegh (q.v.), and the first public figure to employ Inigo Jones (q.v.), whom he appointed his Surveyor of Works in May 1610. The Admiral's Men, led by Alleyn (q.v.), were taken into his service as a company of actors in 1603 and known as the Prince's Men until his death. Henry's investiture as Prince of Wales on 4 June 1610 was marked by a week of elaborate festivities in London, including a water pageant, masques and jousting. Henry died at St James's Palace on 6 November 1612, apparently from typhoid fever after swimming in the Thames at Windsor. "Numberless were the elegiac offerings to his memory, and sufficient might now be collected to fill a bulky volume" wrote a near-contemporary biographer during Charles I's reign.

C. Hill, *Intellectual Origins of the English Revolution* (1965)
A. Palmer, *Princes of Wales* (1979)

HENSLOWE, Philip (?–1616), theatre manager: came from Lindfield, Sussex, and started life as servant to Lord Montagu's bailiff. By 1577 Henslowe is known to have settled in London, in the Liberty of the Clink at Southwark, and married his master's widow, Agnes Woodward. With the property which this marriage brought him, Henslowe was able to go into business, probably in the first instance as a dyer, later becoming a dealer in real estate, especially theatres. Henslowe bought the site of the Rose on Bankside in 1584–5 and by 1588 had built a theatre there, in which Strange's Men appeared. From 1594 until 1600 Henslowe managed the Rose for the Admiral's Company, led by Edward Alleyn (q.v.). In October 1592 Henslowe's stepdaughter, Joan Woodward, married Alleyn, who thereafter remained his close business associate. By 1594 Henslowe was also managing the theatre at Newington Butts, and he and Alleyn obtained an interest in the Bear Garden on Bankside.

The two associates built a new theatre in 1600, the Fortune in Golden Lane, which copied the Globe in many respects and was constructed by the same carpenter (Peter Street, q.v.). Henslowe's record of his transactions with the Admiral's Men ends with a final accounting in 1604: he kept a half share in the Fortune, but left the running of it to Alleyn while he concentrated on new ventures. From 1602 to 1604 he was promoting Worcester's Men at the Rose and in 1604 became joint Master, with Alleyn, of the "Royal Game of Bears, Bulls and Mastiff Dogs". This "sport", profitable in itself, also gave Henslowe the opportunity to pull down and redevelop the Bear Garden; and, with a new partner (Jacob Meade, "Keeper of Bears", q.v.) he built the Hope on the site, a building which could be used for bear and bull baiting as well as for a theatre. Henslowe presented Lady Elizabeth's Men here in combination with the Queen's Revels Company but the association led to a law suit in 1615. Henslowe's accounts show he acted as banker for the theatrical companies, buying plays for them and providing costumes as well as lending money outright. While his relations with theatrical associates were for the most part good he acquired a reputation as a hard business man, especially over property dealings with his tenants. During the 1615 lawsuit he was alleged to have remarked "Should these fellows come out of my debt, I should have no rule with them", a comment which suggests that he was as much interested in power over people as in monetary gain.

E. K. C., *E.S.*
R. A. Foakes and R. T. Rickert, eds., *Henslowe's Diary* (1961)

HERBERT, Edward, later Baron Herbert of Cherbury (1583–1648): oldest son of Sir Richard Herbert of Montgomery

Castle and his wife Magdalen. The poet, George Herbert (1593–1633), was their fifth son; the family was distantly related to the Earls of Pembroke. Herbert entered University College, Oxford, in 1596, shortly before his father's death. His mother arranged his marriage (about 1599) with a cousin, Mary Herbert, heiress to her

Edward Herbert, later Baron Herbert of Cherbury

father's estates provided she married a man named Herbert. Magdalen Herbert leased a house in Oxford for herself, her son and daughter-in-law, entertaining her son's friends and becoming a patron of literature. She moved her salon to London in 1600. Herbert learnt French, Italian, Spanish and music to supplement his classical studies. He was dark and handsome, and his brief appearance at Elizabeth's Court made the Queen remark "It is a pity he was married so young." He was knighted at James I's coronation. After some years of study at Montgomery he travelled abroad in 1608, together with his college friend Thomas Lucy III (q.v.). He became friendly with Henri IV and leading figures at the French Court, subsequently campaigning under Edward Cecil (1610) and the Prince of Orange (1614), as well as travelling in Germany and Italy. Herbert kept up an old friendship with Ben Jonson and John Donne and was himself the author of metaphysical verses. He was popular at Court, especially with Queen Anne. He was appointed to command the Duke of Savoy's army in 1614 but was imprisoned in Lyons while travelling to Piedmont and was forced to return to England with a recurring ague. Friendship with Buckingham (q.v.) brought him an embassy to Paris; he was ambassador from 1619 to 1624, although absenting himself briefly in 1621 after a quarrel with King Louis XIII's favourite. While in Paris he published his treatise *De Veritate*, a pioneer attempt to study comparative religion. His Paris mission ended when he disagreed with James I's terms for a marriage between his son Charles and Princess Henrietta Maria, a match of which Herbert himself was the originator. He returned home in debt, settled once more at Montgomery Castle and began to write a biography of Henry VIII. Charles I created him a peer in 1629 (Baron Herbert of Cherbury), but the Crown would not subsidise his historical studies. His sons fought as Royalists in the Civil War, but Herbert had to yield Montgomery Castle to a Parliamentary garrison in order to save his papers and library in London, and he accepted a pension from Parliament. He completed *Henry VIII*, a standard work for two centuries, and was writing an autobiography when he died, in London (August 1648). The autobiography was eventually published in 1763–4 by Horace Walpole.

M. H. Carré, ed., *Lord Herbert of Cherbury, De Veritate* (1937)
G. C. More Smith, ed., *Poems of Edward, Lord Herbert of Cherbury* (1923)

HERBERT, Henry (1534–1601), **Mary** (née Sidney, 1561–1621), **Philip** (1584–1650), **William** (1580–1630) see PEMBROKE.

HERBERT, Henry Somerset, Lord Herbert of Chepstow, later fifth Earl and first Marquess of Worcester (1577–1653): son of Edward Somerset, fourth Earl of Worcester (q.v.). Lord Herbert was educated at Magdalen College, Oxford from 1591. In 1600 he married Anne Russell, daughter of Lady Russell (q.v.). The wedding was a splendid one, in the presence of the Queen, and was once thought a likely occasion for the first performance of Shakespeare's *Midsummer Night's Dream*, but is now considered too late a date. The couple had nine sons and four daughters. Herbert joined his father on the Council for the Welsh Marches in 1601, and was Lord Lieutenant of Glamorgan and Monmouth with him from 1626 to 1628, continuing on his own after his father's death. He sat in the Parliament of 1604 as Lord Herbert. As Earl of Worcester he is said to have done "secret service" for Charles I in Wales, and lent the King so much money that he made him a Marquess (1643). His Castle at Raglan was one of the last to hold out against the Parliamentary forces. He died in custody in London and is buried at St George's, Windsor.

HERTFORD, Edward Seymour, Earl of (1537–1621): son of Edward Seymour, Duke of Somerset and Lord Protector. Seymour was born on the same day (12 October) as his cousin Edward VI, and was knighted at his coronation. He was restored from the attainder on his estates after his father's execution, but did not come into prominence until the reign of Elizabeth. In 1559 he was created Baron Beauchamp and Earl of Hertford, but dissipated the Queen's goodwill by secretly marrying Lady Catherine Grey, great-niece of Henry VIII, sister of Lady Jane and claimant to the throne. After discovery of the marriage husband and wife were imprisoned in the Tower (1561). He was released, but not forgiven by the Queen until Catherine's death in 1568. She left him two sons, born in the Tower. In 1582 he married Frances Howard, sister of Lord High Admiral Charles Howard and Lady Sheffield (qq.v.). From that year Hertford became patron of a company of actors who toured the provinces until 1591 and again from 1596 to 1607. In January 1592 they appeared at Court, possibly because the Queen had paid a reconciliatory visit to the Hertford house at Elvetham, Hampshire the summer before. However, in 1596 Hertford was in the Tower again for trying to legitimise his son by Lady Catherine. His second wife died two years later and he married Frances Pranell, a widow, originally another Frances Howard, daughter of the first Viscount Bindon. In 1602 Hertford avoided another visit to the Tower by disclosing to the government the attempt of Arbella Stuart (q.v.), a claimant to the throne, to marry his older grandson Edward; she eventually succeeded in marrying the younger, William Seymour (q.v.). In the reign of James I Hertford enjoyed a quieter life, being employed only once, on an embassy to the Archduke in Brussels in 1605. He was Lord Lieutenant of Somerset and Wiltshire in 1602 and 1608, and is buried in Salisbury Cathedral in a large and ornate tomb.

HERVEY, William (c. 1565–1642), soldier: a younger son of Henry Hervey of Ickworth in Suffolk by a Welsh wife, his grandfather having been a Gentleman of the Privy Chamber to Henry VIII. He distinguished himself in service against the Armada, was knighted for his enterprise in the Cadiz raid of 1596 and served under Southampton (q.v.) in the Islands Voyage. He wished to marry the dowager Countess of Southampton (q.v.) in May 1598, but her son disapproved of the match and it was postponed until the following year. After the former Countess's death, Sir William

took as his second wife, Cordell Annesley (q.v.), by whom he was father to three sons and three daughters. Intermittent service in Ireland was rewarded by James I with an Irish baronage in 1620. Eight years later Hervey received an English peerage, "Baron Hervey of Kidbrooke" in Kent. Hervey's initials and his kinship to Southampton have led to suggestions that he was "Mr W. H.", the "only begetter" of Shakespeare's Sonnets. Dr Rowse states that the dedication was by the publisher (Thorpe, q.v.) and not Shakespeare, that "begetter" in Elizabethan usage implied "one who obtained" rather than an inspirer, and that Thorpe was thanking W. H. for providing him with the manuscripts.

A. L. Rowse, *Shakespeare's Southampton* (1965)

HETON, Martin (1552–1609), bishop: son of George Heton of Dean, Lancashire. He was educated at Westminster School and Christ Church, Oxford (1571–4), becoming a Canon of Christ Church in 1582, Vice-Chancellor in 1588 and Dean of Winchester a year later. He was consecrated Bishop of Ely in 1599, pleasing Queen Elizabeth by allowing the Crown to have many of the wealthiest Ely manors and pleasing James I by his style of preaching. He died at Mildenhall in Suffolk at a time when he was considered likely for further preferment.

HEYWOOD, Thomas (?1574–1641), dramatist: his family came from Lincolnshire and he claimed, probably correctly, to have been educated at Cambridge University. He was an actor, as well as a dramatist, appearing with the Admiral's Men in 1598–9 and then for Worcester's Company (later Queen Anne's) from 1602 to 1619. Many of his plays are lost, for he is known to have been a prolific writer. The most famous surviving plays are *Four*

Prentices of London (1600), *A Woman Killed with Kindness* (1603), a domestic tragedy, and *If You Know Not Me, You Know Nobody* (1605), with scenes of Gresham building the Royal Exchange. Heywood also produced non-dramatic works, especially his *Apology for Actors* (1612) and an unfinished and lost *Lives of All the Poets* (c. 1614). His cycle of four plays *Golden Age, Silver Age, Brazen Age* and *Iron Age* (1611–13) was concerned with the lives of the gods and the Trojan War. After 1619 he gave up acting and wrote little until he reappeared as a dramatist in the 1630s. There were then many revivals of earlier plays, and two successful new ones, *The Fair Maid of the West* (printed 1631), a romantic melodrama about the Spanish Main and *The English Traveller* (printed 1633), a tragedy with a comic underplot. Heywood also wrote prologues for Marlowe's *Jew of Malta* and a series of Lord Mayor's pageants. It was his boast to have had "an entire hand, or at least a main finger" in two hundred and twenty plays.

F. S. Boas, *Thomas Heywood* (1950)

HICKES, Sir Michael (1543–1612), Burghley's secretary: son of Robert Hickes, a prosperous mercer with a shop in London who died in 1557. Hickes went to Trinity College, Cambridge in 1559, but took no degree, and entered Lincoln's Inn in 1565. He helped his mother in their shop until 1573, when he obtained a post in the household of Burghley (q.v.). By 1580 he was promoted to the secretariat, where he was in charge of domestic patronage. This proved most profitable, especially the disposal of wardships of minors, as successful applicants usually showed their gratitude to the Patronage Secretary. Hickes bought land, and also lent money as an investment. He performed general secretarial duties as well, including the difficult task of looking after Burghley's papers. He was M.P. for Truro (1584), Shaftesbury (1588, 1593) and Gatton, Surrey, (1597–8), a pocket borough. In 1592 his mother died and he inherited her estates in the West Country. Two years later he married a widow, Elizabeth Parvish, who brought him nine stepchildren but also money and a house at Ruckholt, Essex. The couple had three more children; Burghley was godfather to the oldest son, William. Hickes had sufficient standing to entertain the Queen at Ruckholt in 1597. Meanwhile, he had become a close friend of Robert Cecil (q.v.), Burghley's son and eventual successor. Although they intrigued together for appointments, (including Cecil's as Secretary of State), Cecil did not keep Hickes on as secretary after 1598 when Burghley died. Hickes remained his friend and unofficial assistant, but the friendship grew less intimate after 1608 and Cecil refused him many requests for patronage. Hickes spent much time from 1598 until his death acting as a financial official of the local government in Essex, Hertfordshire and Middlesex. James I visited him at Ruckholt in 1604. Hickes was with Cecil in his last illness in May 1612 and died himself three months later. He was buried in Leyton Parish Church, near Ruckholt.

Alan G. R. Smith, *Servant of the Cecils* (1977)

HILLIARD, Nicholas (1547–1619), artist: born in Exeter, the son of a goldsmith, Hilliard was painting miniature portraits by the age of thirteen and came to London in the mid-1560s, apprenticed to a goldsmith whose daughter he married in 1576. By 1572 he was recognised as official "limner" (miniaturist) to the Queen. He spent the years 1576–8 at the French Court, perfecting a tightly disciplined art form in which miniature portraits are represented almost as jewels to be held in the hand. He settled in Gutter Lane, off Fleet Street, reaching his peak of fashionable success in the closing decade of the century. Although Hilliard remained limner to James I, his

Nicholas Hilliard

pupil Isaac Oliver (q.v.) rivalled him in popularity and became official limner to James's consort, Anne of Denmark. Hilliard defended his own style in a treatise, *The Art of Limning*, written about 1600 although never completed. Hilliard's graceful economy of style, "plain lines without shadowing", delighted Elizabeth, her courtiers and some later poets, notably John Donne.

E. Auerbach, *Nicholas Hilliard* (1961)

HOBSON, Thomas (?1544–1631), Cambridge carrier: born at Buntingford, moved to Cambridge in 1561. From his father he inherited a small carrier business which he expanded until he was running the first of the regular transport services between London and a distant town. His service operated between Cambridge and the Black Bull in Bishopsgate. Hobson's strictures over the hire of his horses were intended to prevent members of the University from exhausting already tired animals, but his injunction, "This one, or none" as he stood at the stable doors has survived in the phrase "Hobson's choice". He was benefactor of lands to both the University and the town and was responsible for the first conduit in the market place at Cambridge.

C. H. Cooper, *Annals of Cambridge*, III (1842)

HOBY, Edward (1560–1617), diplomat: elder son of the ambassador, Sir Thomas Hoby and through his mother (v. *Elizabeth Russell*), a cousin of the Bacons and Robert Cecil. He was educated at Eton and Trinity College, Oxford, (1574–6) afterwards travelling on the Continent for two years. In 1584 he accompanied Henry, Lord Hunsdon, on a mission to James VI in Scotland. Hoby married Hunsdon's daughter and became Constable of Queenborough Castle in Kent. He spent most of his time at Queenborough or at Court, rather than on his ancestral estate at Bisham until after his mother's death in 1609. He accompanied Essex on the Cadiz expedition of 1596. Hoby, to whom James took a great liking at their first meeting, remained a favourite after the King's arrival from Scotland, and the King paid several visits to Bisham. Hoby was a patron of actors, an author of theological pamphlets, and produced several translations. He sat in the Parliaments of 1589, 1593 and 1601, gaining a reputation as a hot-tempered critic of the councillors and being rebuked by the Queen in 1593 for insulting Heneage (q.v.) in the House.

J. E. Neale, *Elizabeth I and her Parliaments, 1584–1601* (1957)
A. L. Rowse, "Bisham and the Hobys", *The English Past* (1951)

HOBY, Margaret (1571–1633, née Dakins), diarist: the daughter of a wealthy

Derbyshire immigrant to Yorkshire. She was brought up in the household of the Countess of Huntingdon (Leicester's sister) who fostered several girls. The Huntingdons were also guardians of the Devereux family, children of the first Earl of Essex, and of the Countess's nephew, Thomas Sidney, brother of Sir Philip Sidney. To keep Margaret's wealth under control, she was married before she was seventeen to Walter Devereux, who was killed at the siege of Rouen in 1592. She then married Thomas Sidney who died in 1595. In her first widowhood the Cecil family had urged the suit of their candidate for Margaret's hand, Thomas Hoby (*infra*). The death of the Earl of Huntingdon in 1595 threatened Margaret's inheritance of Hackness Manor, near Scarborough, unless she took a third husband. In 1596 she accordingly accepted Thomas Hoby and spent the rest of her life looking after their Yorkshire home. Lady Margaret Hoby is best known for the diary which she kept from 1599 to 1605; it is mainly a daily record of the religious exercises of a Puritan lady, together with details of the management of house and household.

D. M. Meads, ed., *Margaret Hoby's Diary* (1930)

HOBY, Thomas Posthumous (1566–1640), landowner: younger son of Sir Thomas Hoby and brother of Edward (q.v.). He was born after his father had died in Paris but his mother (Elizabeth Russell q.v.) took care to be back in England for the birth in case of problems of inheritance. As a boy he was skinny, undersized and, as some contemporaries say, hunchbacked. His mother wished him to become a lawyer but he ran away from home rather than obey her. In 1592 her brother-in-law, Burghley, collaborated with Lady Russell in a plan to marry him to a Yorkshire Heiress (Margaret Hoby, *supra*). They succeeded at the second attempt, the wedding taking place in Blackfriars in August 1596, immediately after Sir Thomas's return from the Cadiz expedition. Sir Thomas settled down as squire of Lady Margaret's estate at Hackness. The Yorkshire voters, regarding him as an interloper, refused to return him to Parliament in the 1597 election, but a safe seat was found for him in Scarborough, only six miles from Hackness. He acted as Protestant agent in the strongly Catholic North Riding, where his enthusiasm for catching recusants, and the puritanism of his household, made him unpopular. In 1600 he was plaintiff in a Star Chamber case against some neighbours, who had come uninvited to his home. They drank, played cards, jeered at his daily prayers and threatened to seduce Lady Margaret, who was ill in bed. The antagonism shown by Sir Toby Belch for Malvolio in Shakespeare's *Twelfth Night* may show some echoes of this well-known Star Chamber case (but cf. *William Knollys*). Hoby appears to have won his suit.

Ibid.
J. E. Neale, *The Elizabethan House of Commons* (1950)

HOLINSHED, Raphael (?– dead by 1582),chronicler: said to have come from either Cheshire or Warwickshire and studied at Christ's College, Cambridge in 1544–5. By 1560 he was working in London for the Queen's Printer, Reginald Wolfe, a translator. Wolfe had a grandiose idea, for which he had the backing of Burghley, of producing a "cosmography of the whole world" with the "histories of every known nation". Two books were actually printed, Saxton's *Atlas* and Holinshed's *Chronicles*, (1577). Holinshed himself wrote the *History of England*, the *Description of England* was contributed by William Harrison (q.v.) and that of Ireland by Edmund Campion in a version edited by his pupil, Richard Stanyhurst.

The work was dedicated to Burghley. Holinshed did not survive his book for long. In 1578 he was steward to Thomas Burdet of Bramcote, Warwickshire and there he died, traditionally in 1580, although his will was not proved until 1582. The popularity of the book was such that a second edition was prepared in 1587, under the supervision of John Hooker, Antiquarian Chamberlain of the City of Exeter and uncle of Richard Hooker (q.v.). The *History of Scotland* was extended and the whole brought down to 1586. There were two new contributors, Abraham Fleming and Francis Thynne, and Hooker himself wrote about Devon and added to the Irish section: Campion's work was allowed to stand, though he had been executed four years before. The censors removed several passages from both editions, the sections on Irish, Scottish and recent history giving most offence. This 1587 edition of Holinshed was the main source book for Shakespeare's history plays and those of his contemporaries.

A. L. Rowse, *The England of Elizabeth* (1950)
S. Booth, *The Book Called Holinshed's Chronicles* (1968)

HOLLAND, Hugh (?1574–1633), poet: son of Robert Holland of Denbigh. He was educated at Westminster School under Camden and was a Scholar of Trinity College, Cambridge (1590–4) where he was known as Roberts, being a Welshman, the son of Robert. After Cambridge he travelled through Europe and the Middle East, visiting Rome, Jerusalem and Constantinople. For a time he became a Roman Catholic during his travels and was reprimanded by an English ambassador to the Sultan for speaking ill of Queen Elizabeth. On his return Holland lived in Oxford, supposedly in Balliol College, for the sake of the libraries but he was also a frequent guest of his school friend, Cotton (q.v.), in London, and he referred to the

meetings of scholars at Cotton's house as "a kind of universitie". He was a friend, too, of Ben Jonson, of Coryat (q.v.) and of some members of the "Mermaid Club". Holland wrote poems in English, Greek, Italian and Welsh; many were commendatory verses for other men's work, including a sonnet for the First Folio of Shakespeare's plays (1623). He wrote two longer poems, one of which, *Pancharis* (1603), is the story of Owen Tudor's love for Queen Catherine. His lament for James I, *Cypress Garland* (1625), shows that Buckingham had become his patron.

B. H. Newdigate, *Michael Drayton and his Circle* (1961)
K. Sharpe, *Sir Robert Cotton* (1979)

HOLLAND, Philemon (1522–1637), translator: born at Chelmsford, son of a clergyman, John Holland, educated at Chelmsford School and Trinity College, Cambridge (1566–71, Fellow, 1573, M.D., 1579). He intended to be a doctor and practised medicine at Coventry from 1595 onwards. In 1600 he published his first classical translation, of Livy's *History*, and this was followed by Pliny's *Natural History* (1601), Plutarch's *Morals* (1603), Suetonius (1606), Ammianus Marcellinus (1609) and the first English version of a contemporary work, Camden's *Britannia* (1610). By 1608 he had given up medicine and was an usher at Coventry Grammar School, where he was briefly Headmaster in 1628. His last great translation was Xenophon's *Education of Cyrus* (1632). In the same year he received a pension from the City of Coventry. Holland was called the "translator-general in his age", by the historian Thomas Fuller (1608–61).

HOME, George (?–1611), Lord High Treasurer of Scotland: son of Sir Alexander Home, he came early to the Scottish Court and was soon a favourite of James VI.

Home went with James to fetch his bride, Princess Anne, from Norway in 1589 and was knighted the next year. By 1601 he was Treasurer and Master of the Wardrobe, posts he kept when James succeeded to the English throne in 1603. Home became an English Privy Councillor, but his main services to the King were in Scotland and on the Borders. In 1605, now Earl of Dunbar, he presided at the trial in Linlithgow of the rebellious ministers of the Scottish Church and secured their conviction and exile. He was Commissioner to the General Assembly of the Church in 1610 and forced episcopacy back in Scotland, apparently by a combination of bribery and bullying. As Commissioner for the Borders in 1606 Dunbar hanged over 140 notable thieves. He was made a Knight of the Garter in 1608. Dunbar had extensive estates in Scotland and the Borders. He married Elizabeth Gordon and had two daughters. The older, Anne, married her kinsman Sir James Home, from whom the present Earls of Home descend. Dunbar's last service to James I was to recommend his ex-chaplain, George Abbott (q.v.) as Archbishop of Canterbury in 1611.

HOOD, Thomas (?1557–98), mathematician: born in London, the son of a merchant tailor. Hood went to Merchant Taylors' School, under Mulcaster (q.v.), in 1567 and then to Trinity College, Cambridge (1577–81). In 1587 Hood lectured privately in London on mathematics and in the following year he gave the first public lecture on mathematics, an enterprise promoted by the Privy Council and held in Leadenhall. It was hoped that the lecture would be attended by seamen so that their navigation might be improved in Armada year. Hood made this purpose clear in his published version of the lecture: "We have seen them on our coasts and heard the thunder of their shot", he wrote. His first

speciality was geometry and the use of the celestial and terrestrial globes, a subject on which he published treatises in 1590 and 1592. This work, however, was surpassed by Robert Hues's *Tractatus* in 1594. Hood's most original contribution to mathematics was his invention of the "Sector", an instrument anticipating the slide-rule. He published a book on the making and use of the sector in 1598, the year that Galileo invented the same instrument. Hood also produced a "cross-staff" for taking sightings; he explained the value and use of this invention in a treatise published in 1596. His other works were a new edition of William Bourne's *Regiment of the Sea*, printed with Hood's own *Mariner's Guide* in 1592, and the *Elements of Arithmetic* (1596).

D. W. Waters, *The Art of Navigation in Elizabethan and Early Stuart Times* (1958)

HOOKER, Richard (c. 1554–1600), theologian: born at Heavitree, Exeter, educated at Corpus Christi College, Oxford, of which he beame a Fellow in 1577, and was ordained in 1581. He moved from Oxford to London in 1584, living for seven years in Watling Street at the home of a prominent member of the Merchant Taylors Company, John Churchman, whose daughter he married in 1588. From 1585 to 1591 Hooker was Master of the Temple, his sermons seeking intellectually to refute Puritan pretensions. This task he accomplished more effectively as Rector of Boscombe, near Salisbury (1591–5) by using the library of Salisbury Cathedral to write the first four books of *The Laws of Ecclesiastical Polity*, published in 1593. Hooker's great work, notable for a vigorous but temperate prose style, justified the basic political and theological tenets of the Elizabethan Church Settlement. He reconciled English ecclesiastical practice with the form of mediaeval thought, seeing in Anglicanism a national church based upon tradition and the law of reason. His judicious pragmatism denied the validity, not only of Roman Catholic and Presbyterian theories, but of Royalist doctrines of monarchical divine right as well. He became Rector of Bishopsbourne near Canterbury in 1595, completing Book V of the *Laws* two years later, leaving three further books unrevised for posthumous publication. He died and is buried at Bishopsbourne.

A. P. d'Entreves, *The Mediaeval Contribution to Political Thought* (1939)

P. Munz, *The Place of Hooker in the History of Thought* (1952)

HOOKER, Thomas (1586–1647), Puritan divine and colonialist: born near Leicester and educated at Emmanuel College, Cambridge from 1604 to 1608, remaining there as a Fellow until 1618. He was Rector of Esher in Surrey, residing as a domestic chaplain in the household of Drake's widow. From 1626 to 1630 he was a Puritan lecturer in Chelmsford, fleeing to Amsterdam and Delft to escape Laud's attempt to improve Church discipline. In 1633 he crossed to New England, accompanied by many members of his Chelmsford congregation. He became pastor of a church at Hartford in 1636 and for the last eleven years of his life was virtually the theocratic dictator of Connecticut. His principal work, *A Survey of the Summe of Church Discipline*, was published a year after his death: it provided American Congregationalism with a rational basis of political and ecclesiastical theory, adapting the doctrines of the Church as expressed by Browne (q.v.) to the needs of civil society in New England.

W. S. Archibald, *Thomas Hooker* (1933)

HOWARD, Catherine, Lady (?–1603): born Catherine Carey, daughter of Henry Carey, first Lord Hunsdon (q.v.), Queen Elizabeth's cousin. She was maid of honour to the Queen from the beginning of her reign and married Charles Howard, later Earl of Nottingham (q.v.), the Lord High Admiral. Catherine Howard was the supposed recipient of the ring which the Queen had given to the Earl of Essex, and which he tried to send back to her as a plea for mercy just before his execution. Catherine consulted her husband, who advised her to suppress the ring, but she confessed on her death-bed what she had done. There is no evidence for this story.

V. A. Wilson, *Society Women of Shakespeare's Time* (1925)

HOWARD, Catherine, Countess of Suffolk (post 1563–post 1638): born Catherine Knyvett, daughter of Sir Henry Knyvett of Charlton, Wiltshire. A beautiful, ambitious woman, she was married first to Richard Rich, secondly (1583) to Thomas Howard (q.v.) who became Earl of Suffolk and Lord Treasurer under James I. The couple had seven sons and three daughters, of whom Frances (q.v.) was the notorious Court beauty of the Essex divorce and Overbury murder cases; her mother encouraged both her marriages. Another daughter, Elizabeth, married William Knollys (q.v.) in his old age. In 1619 the Countess was tried with her husband in Star Chamber for embezzling public funds. She dominated the Earl and was said to run the Treasury like a shop, as well as being a pensioner of Spain. Coke (q.v.) prosecuted, and the couple were convicted. They were imprisoned in the Tower until their fine of £30,000 was paid.

HOWARD, Charles, Lord Howard of Effingham (1536–1624), created Earl of Nottingham 1597, Lord Admiral of England: a grandson of the second Duke of Norfolk and therefore a first cousin to

Elizabeth's mother, Anne Boleyn. Howard gained the rudiments of seamanship under his father (William Howard of Effingham, Lord Admiral 1553–8) but subsequently served on diplomatic missions and as a soldier. He was prominent at Court from 1573 to 1585 when he was Lord Chamberlain of the Household and married one of the Queen's favourite ladies in waiting, Catherine Carey, daughter of Lord

Charles, Lord Howard of Effingham

Hunsdon. Howard was made Lord Admiral in 1585, retaining the office for thirty-four years. He was appointed Commander-in-Chief against the Spaniards and their allies in 1587, flying his flag in *Ark Royal* during the Armada campaign, and was largely responsible for the cautious tactics of stand-off fighting rather than the action at close quarters, alleged to have been favoured by Drake. In 1596 Howard shared command of the raid on Cadiz with Essex, but distrusted him and was responsible for the swift suppression of Essex's attempted rising in London (February 1601). Howard was patron of the company of actors known from 1576 as Lord Howard's Men, later as the Lord Admiral's Men. This company performed most of Marlowe's

plays for the first time and became prominent under Edward Alleyn (q.v.). Howard was peace commissioner for the treaty with Spain in 1605 and continued to take an active interest in the fleet until the Duke of Buckingham persuaded him, in 1619, to transfer the office of Lord Admiral to him. He retired with a pension of £1000 a year.

Robert Kenny, *Elizabeth's Admiral* (1970)

HOWARD, Frances (1592–1632): daughter of the Earl and Countess of Suffolk (Thomas and Catherine Howard, qq.v.). At thirteen she married the fourteen-year-old third Earl of Essex (q.v.). He immediately went abroad and Frances remained at Court with her parents. After a reputed romance with Prince Henry, Frances began an affair with

Frances Howard, Countess of Somerset

the King's favourite, Robert Carr (q.v.). The liaison was encouraged by her family, especially her uncle, Henry Howard, Earl of Northampton (*infra*) at whose house the lovers first met. In 1610, Essex returned to

England and tried to remove his wife to the country once the celebrations for the investiture of the Prince of Wales were over, but she brought an action for annulment against him. Meanwhile Carr's secretary, Sir Thomas Overbury, was trying to dissuade Carr from marrying Frances, and opposed the nullity suit. Carr and the Howards contrived to have Overbury sent to the Tower for contempt; he died there of poison on 14 September 1613, just before Frances's marriage was ended. She married Carr, now Earl of Somerset, on 26 December. In 1615 an enquiry into Overbury's death was begun by Coke; the Earl and Countess of Somerset were both arrested, along with Sir Gervase Elwes (q.v.), Lieutenant of the Tower, and some employees and associates of the astrologer, Simon Forman (q.v.). Forman himself was dead, but he had certainly supplied Frances with a love potion to give to Carr and possibly drugs to make Essex impotent. At her trial in 1616 the Countess confessed to Overbury's murder and was condemned to death as was her husband. Neither sentence was carried out, but they were detained in the Tower until 1622, and lived quietly at Chiswick until Frances' death. They had one daughter, Anne, born 1616, who married the Earl of Bedford's heir.

B. White, *Cast of Ravens* (1965)

HOWARD, Henry, later Earl of Northampton (1540–1614): son of Henry, the poet Earl of Surrey executed under Henry VIII (1547), and younger brother of Thomas, Duke of Norfolk (executed 1572). Queen Elizabeth reversed the family attainder on her accession and paid for Howard's education at King's College, Cambridge (M.A., 1564), where he was a brilliant scholar. He came to Court in 1570, but advancement was impossible after Norfolk's execution, and his own

brief imprisonment, in 1572, so he retired to bring up his brother's children at Audley End, Essex; the Queen allowed him a pension. Howard was a Roman Catholic and homosexual all his life, and a devious intriguer, mostly by letter. He corresponded with Mary, Queen of Scots, but, although arrested again in 1582, kept out of serious involvement in her end. In the 1590s he attached himself to the Essex

Henry Howard, Earl of Northampton

faction, and became a particular friend of the Bacon brothers (qq.v.). After 1600 he returned to Court through the influence of Robert Cecil and took part in Cecil's secret correspondence with James VI in Scotland. James spoke of Howard's "ample, Asiatic, and endless" letters, which warned the King against his own Queen as well as against Cecil's English rivals. With James' arrival in England, Howard was soon promoted. He became Earl of Northampton and Lord Warden of the Cinque Ports (1604), Lord Privy Seal (1608), High Steward of Oxford (1609) and Chancellor of Cambridge University (1612). He also sought influence through his nephew

(Thomas Howard, *infra*) and encouraged his great-niece Frances (*supra*) in her liaison and marriage with the King's favourite, Carr (q.v.). After Overbury (q.v.), who opposed the match, was imprisoned in 1613, Northampton organised the appointment of Elwes (q.v.) as Lieutenant of the Tower, so that he and Carr, now Earl of Somerset, might bombard the prisoner with letters. Although not involved in the actual murder, Northampton arranged the hasty inquest and burial of Overbury. His letters from Somerset were removed from his study and burnt after his death. By 1613, Northampton was an acknowledged pensioner of Spain and urged on James I a pro-Spanish policy that estranged him from the House of Commons. In spite of age and illness, he engineered the dissolution of Parliament in 1614 and made a quasi-royal progress through London the next day. It was his last intrigue; within a week he was dead of gangrene.

Ibid.

HOWARD, Thomas, later Earl of Suffolk, (1561–1626), Admiral, Lord Treasurer: son of Thomas, Duke of Norfolk (executed 1572). He was educated at St John's College, Cambridge, and married as his second wife Catherine, daughter of Sir Henry Knyvet (Catherine Howard, q.v.) in 1583. Howard was dominated in later life by his wife and his uncle, Henry Howard (*supra*) who had brought him up. He volunteered to command a ship against the Armada (1588) and was knighted at sea by his distant cousin, Lord High Admiral Howard (q.v.). He had a successful naval career during the rest of Elizabeth's reign, commanding a squadron in the Azores, with Grenville (q.v.) as his Vice-Admiral, in 1591, and having similar commands under Essex (q.v.) in 1596–7. Ralegh and his friends were critical of Howard for coming off safe from the Azores after

Grenville's death, but he became Admiral of the Fleet in 1599, and was made a Knight of the Garter and Baron Howard de Walden. In 1601 he was Constable of the Tower, besieged Essex House for the government and sat as a peer at Essex's trial. Like the rest of his family Howard prospered after the accession of James I. In 1603 he became Earl of Suffolk, Lord Chamberlain, and a Privy Councillor, and began his fine new house at Audley End. James later remarked it was "too big for a king, but might do for a Lord Treasurer". On 4 November, 1605, Suffolk, as Lord Chamberlain, searched the room below the House of Lords for gunpowder and, according to the King's account, saw and challenged Guy Fawkes whom he described as a "tall and desperate fellow" (v. *Thomas Knyvet*). In 1614 he was appointed Lord Treasurer. He did not share in his daughter's disgrace from the Overbury murder trials of 1615–16, though he had encouraged her marriage and was involved in destroying his uncle Northampton's incriminating correspondence. However, in 1618, this "plain honest gentleman", as the King called him, was dismissed from the Treasury for fraud, largely through the activities of his wife. He was detained for ten days in the Tower in 1619 and fined £30,000. Suffolk held no other public office except High Steward of Exeter (from 1621) but he was received by the King again after 1620.

HOWARD, Thomas, Earl of Arundel, later Earl of Norfolk (1586–1646): son of Philip Howard, Earl of Arundel, who died in the Tower after eleven years in captivity (1595) and grandson of the Duke of Norfolk executed in 1572. Arundel, who was educated at Westminster School and Trinity College, Cambridge, was brought up by a devoutly Roman Catholic mother, the dowager Countess Anne. He was a consumptive and unattractive youth:

Queen Elizabeth's favourite, Essex, called him a "winter pear". James I restored Arundel to his inheritance in 1604, but his great-uncle and uncle had appropriated most of it (Henry Howard, Thomas Howard, qq.v., *supra*). His mother arranged a wealthy marriage for him with Alathea Talbot, heiress of the Earl of Shrewsbury, in 1606, and his estates returned as his relatives died. He was made a Knight of the Garter (1611) and began his extensive travels abroad by escorting the Princess Elizabeth and her husband to Heidelberg in 1613. Arundel went on to Italy, taking with him Inigo Jones (q.v.) the architect, and began his great collection of Latin and Greek antiquities, statues and inscriptions. On his return he gave up his not very profound Romanism and received Anglican communion with James I at Christmas 1615. From then his career prospered. He rebuilt his house in the Strand in Italian style, became a Privy Councillor (1616) and Earl Marshal for life (1621). Arundel suffered two spells of imprisonment, however, in 1621 for insulting Baron Spencer (q.v.) and in 1627 because of his heir's secret marriage to Elizabeth Stuart, a distant relative of the King. By 1627 the Howard estates were all officially restored. Arundel went as ambassador to Elizabeth of Bohemia (1632) and Holland (1636), and in 1642 escorted Princess Mary to her marriage in Orange. He never returned to England, though he was made Earl of Norfolk in 1644, but died in Padua. He is buried at Arundel, Sussex. His grandson gave his classical inscriptions to Oxford University and his library and manuscripts to the Royal Society.

D. Mathew, *The Jacobean Age* (1971)

HUDSON, Henry (fl. 1607–11), navigator: nothing is known of Hudson's origins. The Muscovy Company employed him in 1607 to find a north-west or north-east passage to China. His first two expeditions took him to Greenland. A third expedition, undertaken for the Dutch East India Company, led him to follow the Virginia coast northwards until he reached the mouth of the river which had been discovered by Verrazzano in 1524 but left unnamed and unexplored. Hudson thought this river might provide a water route to Cathay. Accordingly, in his vessel *Half-Moon*, he sailed up the river, to which he gave his name, and reached the site of the present city of Albany. In April 1610 he set out on a fourth expedition, financed by the English, which took him north-westwards by way of Greenland through the Hudson Strait, and in the spring of 1611 discovered the huge bay which bears his name. He wished to winter in the bay but his crew, believing that food was running short, mutinied and on 23 June 1611 cast him adrift with eight other seamen. Although the mutineers returned to England, nothing more was heard of Hudson and his companions.

C. H. L. Ewen, *The North-West Passage* (1938)
L. Powys, *Henry Hudson* (1927)

HUGHES, Thomas (c. 1557–?1623), barrister, writer: born in Cheshire and educated at Queen's College, Cambridge (1571–6, Fellow, 1576). In 1579 he was admitted to Gray's Inn, where he was called to the Bar in 1585. On 28 February 1588 Gray's Inn performed an entertainment for the Court at Greenwich, *The Misfortunes of Arthur*, a tragedy. The major part was written by Hughes; two speeches were contributed by William Fulbecke (q.v.) and among the devisers of dumb shows was Francis Bacon. *Arthur* has been seen as a political allegory, with the Queen as Arthur and Mary, Queen of Scots, as his enemy, Mordred. Much of the play is borrowed from Seneca and Lucan. Little more is known of Hughes. In 1590 he was sued for keeping the belongings of a fellow-member of Gray's Inn who died, but the outcome of the case is not revealed. Hughes was knighted in 1619 and was committed to the Fleet Prison briefly for a technical offence in the Court of Star Chamber. The last certain mention of him is in 1623 when he was Reader of Gray's Inn and his son was called to the Bar.

E. K.C., *E.S.*
J. Ramel, in *Notes and Queries*, 14, (1967)

HUNNIS, William (?–1597), poet and choirmaster: was a Gentleman of the Chapel Royal in 1553 but was sent to the Tower in 1556 for plotting against Queen Mary. Elizabeth restored him at her accession and he became Master of the Children of the Chapel in 1566, presenting the boys in plays at Court. In 1576 Hunnis handed over the dramatic work to Farrant (q.v.), who was acting Master and who set up the first Blackfriars theatre. From 1580 Hunnis resumed direction of the boys although he transferred the Blackfriars interest to Henry Evans (q.v.). Hunnis also held several other lucrative posts. He was Keeper of the Orchard and Garden at Greenwich in 1562, supplying produce for the Court banquets. From 1567 he was a member of the Grocers' Company, having married a grocer's widow and acquired a shop. He still, however, complained of the cost of looking after the Children of the Chapel, and was given a grant of Crown lands in 1585 to meet his expenses. His poems were mainly of a religious character (*Handful of Honnisuckles*, 1578; *Seven Sobbes of a Sorrowful Soule for Sinne*, 1583), but he also contributed to Leicester's (q.v.) great entertainment at Kenilworth, 1575.

E. K. C., *E.S.*

HUNSDON, Lord see Carey, Henry (?1524–90) or Carey, George (1547–1603).

HUNTINGDON, Earl of (Henry Hastings, 1535–95), courtier and administrator: son of Francis, the second Earl, and of his wife Catherine (Pole). Francis was a direct descendant through six generations of Edward III's son, Thomas of Woodstock; while Catherine was a great-great-niece of the Yorkist Edward IV. These family connections made Henry — always a sound Protestant — a possible alternative for a throne threatened by the succession of the Catholic Queen of Scots. As a child, Henry had been a companion of Edward VI (two years his junior) who knighted him in 1548. Henry married Catherine Dudley, sister of Leicester (q.v.) in 1553 and succeeded his father as third Earl in 1561. He assisted Shrewsbury (q.v.) as custodian of Mary, Queen of Scots, and was Lord President of the North from 1572 until 1595. Although vigilant against "papist treason" and tending to encourage Puritan ministers to settle in the towns, Huntingdon was a just and moderate administrator. He was also Lord Lieutenant of Leicestershire, undertaking numerous charitable works in Leicester itself while expecting to exercise great patronage locally over Church and national affairs. The Huntingdons, husband and wife, were guardians of the Devereux daughters, sisters of Essex, who became Penelope Rich and Dorothy Percy (q.v.); and they also brought up the later Margaret Hoby (q.v.). Despite an innate Puritanism, Huntingdon lived in some style at Ashby-de-la-Zouch. Queen Elizabeth invariably treated the Huntingdons as trusted friends. He died, however, owing the crown £20,000, having incurred the debts in his long service in the north. There followed a four months wrangle between the Queen and his family before she agreed to pay the expenses of his funeral, but she declined to waive his accumulated debts. He is buried, impressively, at Ashby-de-la-Zouch. A Protestant grammar school at Ashby and fellowships and scholarships endowed at Emmanuel College, Cambridge, ensured that his zeal for moderate Puritanism outlived him.

L. Stone, *The Crisis of the Aristocracy* (1965)

J

JACKSON, John (?1574–?1625), London friend of Shakespeare: came from Kingston-upon-Hull, where he purchased property in 1601. He was overseer of the will of Thomas Savage (q.v.) in 1611 and two years later served, with John Heminges and William Johnson (qq.v.), as a trustee for Shakespeare's purchase of the Blackfriars Gatehouse. Soon afterwards Jackson married the widowed sister-in-law of Elias James (q.v.), the brewer, whom Shakespeare may have known. He may well have been the Jackson who frequented the Mermaid Tavern and contributed *Jackson's Egg*, a poem written in the shape of an egg, to the *Crudities* of Thomas Coryat (q.v.). These various activities were attributed by Dr Leslie Hotson to the same John Jackson, but there is no certainty the references apply to the one man.

L. Hotson, *Shakespeare's Sonnets Dated and Other Essays* (1949)

JACKSON, Roger (?–1625), bookseller: son of Martin Jackson, yeoman, of Yorkshire. He was apprenticed for eight years from 1591 to Ralph Newbery, stationer, and became a freeman of the Stationers' Company in 1599. His shops were in Fleet Street. In 1614 Jackson acquired the copyright of Shakespeare's *Rape of Lucrece* which he published in 1616 and 1624.

JAGGARD, Isaac (1597–1627), printer: from 1616 onwards assisted his father William Jaggard (*infra*) in his London printing house. Although William began the printing of the First Folio of Shakespeare's plays, it was Isaac who completed the task and it is his name which appears in it as copyright holder, together with Edward Blount (q.v.).

JAGGARD, William (c. 1568–1623), bookseller, printer: born in Aldersgate London, son of John Jaggard, printer. His brother, John Jaggard, was also a bookseller. Jaggard was apprenticed to Henry Denham for eight years from 1584 and became a freeman of the Stationers' Company in 1591. His first shop was in St Dunstan's Churchyard, Fleet Street, but in 1608 he took over the business of James Roberts (q.v.) and moved to the Half Eagle and Key, Barbican. Here he became printer to the City of London. In 1599 Jaggard published the *Passionate Pilgrim*, ascribed to Shakespeare and containing two Shakespearean sonnets, with verse from *Love's Labour's Lost* and the works of other poets. The collection was reprinted in 1612, with the addition of two poems by Thomas Heywood. When Heywood protested for himself and Shakespeare, Jaggard removed the author's name from the title-page. In 1619 he repeated his activities, producing an edition of ten plays all attributed to Shakespeare: they included *A Yorkshire Tragedy* and *Sir John Oldcastle*, part 1, as well as the genuine plays. Before publication was complete the Lord Chamberlain tried to protect his company's rights by banning further printing without authority, but Jaggard backdated the remaining imprints to the dates of the original editions of the plays (1600 and 1608) to circumvent the ruling. Jaggard refused to print "errata" or "corrigenda", blaming all mistakes on bad proof-reading by authors. Rapidly failing eyesight led him to rely increasingly on his son Isaac (*supra*) from 1613. Despite their failings and sharp practices the Jaggards had a good press and were associated in the publication of the First Folio of Shakespeare's plays in 1623.

E. C. Willoughby, *A Printer of Shakespeare* (1934)

JAMES I (1566–1625, reigned as James VI of Scotland from 1567, coming to the English throne in 1603), King: born in Edinburgh Castle, the only son of Mary, Queen of Scots, and Henry, Lord Darnley, from both of whom he inherited claims to the English throne. Mother and son were separated for ever when he was eleven months old. The Scottish Protestant nobility forced her abdication in July 1567. A succession of Regents restrained James's authority, nominally until 1578 and in practice until 1583. From 1586 he received an English annual subsidy. The chief object of his policy was peaceful succession to the English throne if Queen Elizabeth died childless. When his mother was executed in 1587 James made purely formal protests to London. Two years later he married Anne of Denmark (q.v.). Although his inclinations were homosexual, seven children were born of the marriage: only the Princes Henry and Charles and the Princess Elizabeth (qq.v.) survived infancy. In Scotland James was frequently in conflict with the Kirk; he maintained that Scottish Presbyterianism agreed "as well with monarchy as God and the Devil". He much enjoyed theatrical entertainment, encouraging English actors to visit Scotland from 1594 onwards (v. *Lawrence Fletcher*) and probably had a company of his own in Scotland, 1599–1601. He took over patronage of the Chamberlain's Men (Shakespeare's company) by Royal Patent on his accession in 1603 and they played more frequently at Court than in Elizabeth's reign. James was well received on arrival in England but he lost popularity rapidly, despite general condemnation of Fawkes (q.v.) and the Gunpowder Plot (1605). The "sale" of titles was felt to degrade royal prerogatives. Attempts to levy "impositions" and to sell commercial monopolies to favourites angered the Commons. His subjects resented their sovereign's tendency to behave as "schoolmaster of the realm" (v. *Harington*). His works, *True Law of Free Monarchies* (1598 and 1603) and the precepts on Government, *Basilikon Doron* (1599) asserted a modernised doctrine of the divine right of kings; his *Counterblast to Tobacco* (1604) denounced the evils of smoking. His partiality for favourites at Court (v. *Buckingham, Carr, Hay*) prevented him from judging dispassionately the ability of his ablest servants, men like Francis Bacon, Robert Cecil and Lionel Cranfield (qq.v.). Parliament frequently complained that his foreign policy was too well-disposed towards Spain and too lukewarm in defence of Protestantism. The King's assertion that foreign affairs and religion were no business of the House of Commons threatened conflict between Crown and Parliament. He died on 27 March 1625 at Theobalds in Hertfordshire, the estate he acquired from Cecil in exchange for Hatfield.

D. H. Willson, *King James VI & I* (1956)

JAMES, Elias (c. 1579–1610), London brewer: grandson of a Dutch immigrant, his father establishing a brewery at Puddle Wharf, Blackfriars, which Elias inherited in 1590 when it was worth £800. He was possibly connected by marriage with John Jackson (q.v.). Elias was buried in St Andrew by the Wardrobe, across the street from Shakespeare's Blackfriars property, and an epitaph on him was ascribed to Shakespeare in a seventeenth-century manuscript.

L. Hotson, *Shakespeare's Sonnets Dated and Other Essays* (1949)

JANSSEN, Cornelis (1593–1661, also known as Cornelius Johnson), portrait painter: born in London, his parents being refugees from the Netherlands. It is probable he received some of his artistic training in the Netherlands. He was the most fashionable portrait painter in England from 1618 until the arrival of van Dyck in 1632, specialising in bust portraits set in an oval. He remained in England until 1643 when he emigrated to the Netherlands, spending the last eighteen years of his life painting worthy and wealthy burghers and their wives. He is known to have painted Ben Jonson, John Milton in 1618 (when he was ten), the family of Sir Thomas Lucy (q.v.) at Charlecote, and the daughter of the Earl of Southampton (q.v.). An extremely elegant portrait of a Jacobean gentleman, in silken doublet with white lace collar, hangs in the Folger Library, Washington, D.C.; it is said to be Janssen's portrait of Shakespeare and carries the inscription "Aet. 46, 1610"; doubts remain.

S. Schoenbaum, *Shakespeare's Lives* (1970)

JANSSEN, Gheerart (fl. 1600–23, also known as Gerard Johnson), stonemason: responsible for the bust of Shakespeare placed in Holy Trinity Church, Stratford-upon-Avon, soon after Shakespeare's death. Janssen was one of four sons of a refugee from Amsterdam (also called Gheerart Janssen) who settled in Southwark in the late 1560s. The father, who died in 1611, established a stonemason's business, with a largely aristocratic clientele. It was flourishing close to the Globe theatre, during the years Shakespeare was in London. Shakespeare's friend, John Combe (q.v.) who died in 1614, set aside £60 in his will for a monument in Holy Trinity Church which was fashioned by the younger Janssen and known to the Shakespeare family before they commissioned the famous bust.

Ibid.

JEFFES, Abel (fl. 1584–99), printer: was apprenticed to Henry Bynneman (q.v.) and became a freeman of the Stationers' Company in 1580. He had shops at the "Bell", Fore Street, near Grub Street (1584–8), the "Bell" London Wall (1589–90), St Paul's Churchyard (1591) and Puddle Wharf, Blackfriars (1594–9). Jeffes printed the works of several famous authors, including Greene, Kyd, Lodge and Nashe, but in 1595 his press was seized for printing the *Most strange prophecies of Doctor Cipriano* and other "lewd ballads and things very offensive". He was imprisoned and lost his press for ever, but continued to sell books. Jeffes became very poor and was supported by loans from the Stationers' Company.

JENKINS, Thomas c. 1548–?), schoolmaster: came from a poor London family, his father being an "old servant" of Sir Thomas White, the founder of St John's College, Oxford. Jenkins himself was a Fellow of St John's from 1566 to 1572 (B.A., 1566). The college gave him leave "to teach children" from 1566 to 1568 and in 1572 leased him "Chaucer's House" in Woodstock, Oxfordshire. Three years later he arrived in Stratford-upon-Avon as a schoolmaster, from Warwick. He was Master of Stratford school from 1575 until 1579 when he found his own replacement, John Cottam (q.v.) who, as Jenkins recorded, gave him £6 "in consideration of my departure". Jenkins is known to have had two children. If anyone taught Shakespeare at Stratford school, it must have been Jenkins; and his Welsh name led to a belief that he was the original of Sir Hugh Evans in *The Merry Wives of Windsor*, although Jenkins was a Londoner.

M. E.

JENKINSON, Anthony (c. 1530–1611), merchant and traveller: nothing is known of his childhood, although he was probably born in Northamptonshire. He spent the years 1546–56 in the Mediterranean, principally in the Levant, and obtained a personal guarantee of free trading rights from Sultan Suleiman the Magnificent at Aleppo in November 1553. In 1555 Jenkinson returned to London, respected as "a man well travelled". He was admitted to the Mercers' Company and two years later appointed principal agent of the Muscovy Company. He undertook four journeys to Russia: 1557–60; 1561–4; 1565–6; 1571–2. In 1558 he became the first western European to travel down the Volga to Astrakhan and cross the Caspian Sea; and during his second visit he penetrated as far as Kazvin, where he was received by the Shah of Persia. Jenkinson was also used by Queen Elizabeth as an assessor of the value of the voyages of Frobisher (q.v.) and as commander of anti-piracy patrols in English home waters. His greatest importance is as a geographer, describing in greater detail than any of his English predecessors the full extent of Muscovy, and the lands to the east.

M. S. Anderson, *Britain's Discovery of Russia* (1958)

JOHNSON, Arthur (?–1631), bookseller: son of Thomas Johnson, husbandman, of Derbyshire. He was apprenticed for two years to William Young, draper and bookseller, then to Robert Dexter, stationer, for seven years from 1594. In 1601 Johnson became a freeman of the Stationers' Company and had his shop at the "Flower de Luce and Crown" in St Paul's Churchyard (1602–21). He published all kinds of literature, including several plays, one being Shakespeare's *Merry Wives of Windsor* (1602): this was an edition pirated for John Busby who passed the copyright to Johnson. In 1624 Johnson began assigning his copyrights to other

publishers. He set up as a stationer in Dublin and died there.

JOHNSON, Cornelius see JANSSEN, Cornelis.

JOHNSON, Gerard see JANSSEN, Gheerart.

JOHNSON, William (fl. 1591–1616), vintner: landlord of the Mermaid Tavern, at the corner of Bread Street and Friday Street in the City of London. He served an apprenticeship to the previous landlord from 1591 to 1600, when there was a notable riot outside the Mermaid (v. *Baynham*). By 1603 he was landlord in his own right. Shakespeare and Johnson were acquainted, for he was trustee for the purchase by Shakespeare of a house in Blackfriars on 10 March 1613. Shortly afterwards Johnson was in trouble for selling meat on Fridays — an imprudence so close to Billingsgate fish market — but the case may not have come to court. Johnson was still landlord of the Mermaid when Shakespeare died. The letters of Coryat (q.v.) show that, from 1611 onwards, poets, politicians and scholars met socially at the Mermaid. Although he mentions, among others, Cotton, Donne, Holland, Inigo Jones and Jonson (qq.v.), there is no evidence that Shakespeare belonged to this fraternity.

JONES, Davy (fl. 1577–83), resident of Stratford: married Elizabeth Quiney, daughter of John Shakespeare's friend, in 1577, taking Frances Hathway as a second wife in 1579. In 1583 Jones organised a Whitsun "pastime", for which the town paid him 13s 4d, the only recorded contribution made by Stratford Corporation for local acting talent. It has been suggested by Professor Eccles that Jones was known to Shakespeare, who may have been one of the young participants acting in the "pastime".

M. E.

JONES, Inigo (1573–1652), architect: born in Smithfield, London. With the backing of the Earl of Arundel (q.v.) he travelled to Italy to study landscape painting but became fascinated by the Palladian style of architecture, especially in Venice. He first exercised his skills as an architect in Denmark, on the palaces of Rosenborg and Frederiksborg, receiving an introduction to the English Court from James I's brother-in-law, the Danish king, Frederick IV. Inigo Jones helped arrange the masques of Ben Jonson (q.v.) beginning with the Masque of Blackness (January 1605), until 1613. He was responsible for mounting plays at Christ Church, Oxford, in August 1605 for the visit of James I to the University: and on this occasion first used revolving screens in the Italian theatrical style, so as to change the scenery. Jones also introduced the proscenium arch, framing a picture-stage. In May 1610 he became Surveyor of Works to Prince Henry, upon whose death Jones again travelled to Italy for further study of the work of Palladio. Coryat (q.v.) has shown he belonged to the "Mermaid" fraternity. In 1615 he became Surveyor-General of the royal buildings, designing a year later the Queen's House at Greenwich (first stage finished 1618, work completed 1629–35). From 1619 to 1622 he was engaged on the Banqueting House, Whitehall, working subsequently on the Queen's Chapel at St James's Palace (1623–7), St Paul's Church and piazza at Covent Garden (1625), the planning of Lincoln's Inn Fields and many English country houses. His studies and designs influenced a school of architects throughout the first half of the century. No one in England before Jones had separated the comprehensive and creative aspects of architecture from the practical task of surveying the work of a builder-contractor. Jones, who suffered badly from dyspepsia for all his adult life, remained a royalist. As late as Christmas, 1640, he designed the décor for a masque at Whitehall (on the theme of a king who loved his people) with words by Davenant (q.v.). Jones was captured by the parliamentarians after Cromwell's siege of Basing House (1645), heavily fined for "popish practices" and badly treated; but he survived until within a fortnight of his seventy-eighth birthday.

John Summerson, *Inigo Jones* (1965)

JONES, Richard (fl. 1583–1624), actor: is known to have been with Worcester's company in 1583, leaving it to join Robert Browne (q.v.) for a tour in Germany, 1592. Jones already had connections with the Admiral's Men and it was to them he returned, 1594 and 1596, remaining in the company until 1602, apart from a brief venture with Pembroke's Men at the Swan in 1597 (v. *Langley*). In 1610 Jones was again associated with Browne and Rosseter (q.v.) as a manager of the Children of the Revels under their new Royal Patent. He went back to Germany, probably in 1615, either with Browne, or in advance of him; for this trip he borrowed money from Alleyn. By 1620 Jones was in Danzig, and his recorded career ended as a musician in the service of the Duke of Wolgast in Pomerania, 1622–4. His wife, Harris Jones, toured with her husband although she had inherited the Leopard's Head Inn, Shoreditch, from her father in 1620, and corresponded with Alleyn about the property.

E. K. C., *E.S.*

JONES, Robert (c. 1575–1615), lutenist

and composer: for many years a lutenist enjoying the patronage of Robert Cecil. His *First Book of Songs and Aires* (1600) contained "Farewell, dear heart" parodied by Shakespeare for Sir Toby Belch in *Twelfth Night*. Jones's *Muses' Garden of Delights* was published in 1610.

JONSON, Ben (1572–1637), poet and dramatist: born in Westminster, the son of a clergyman, possibly of Scottish origin. He was educated at Westminster School under William Camden (q.v.) who

Ben Jonson

inspired him with enthusiasm for classical learning but Jonson's stepfather, a bricklayer, apprenticed him to his own trade. Jonson hated bricklaying and after military service in the Netherlands became an actor, though not a good one. By July 1597 he was one of Pembroke's Men and part-author with Nashe (q.v.) of the *Isle of Dogs*, performed at the Swan. Allegations of sedition in the play led to closure of the theatres and the imprisonment of some actors, including Jonson, in the Mar-

shalsea; he was not released until October. He wrote for the Admiral's Men intermittently until 1602 but none of these plays survive; his major work was done for other companies. Jonson quarrelled with one of the leading actors of the company, Gabriel Spencer (q.v.), and killed him in a duel on 22 September 1598. Jonson escaped execution by pleading benefit of clergy and while imprisoned in Newgate he was converted to Roman Catholicism. The first of his great comedies, *Every Man in His Humour* was performed by the Lord Chamberlain's Men in 1598 with Shakespeare's name in the cast list, and tradition maintains that Shakespeare was already a friend of Jonson, recommending his work to the company. *Every Man Out of His Humour* (1599) also went to the Lord Chamberlain's Men, now established at the Globe. Jonson's devotion to classicism led him to stress the observance of the unities and to cut out romance and farce, his comedies having a strong vein of critical satire. His attacks on writers of a different kind led to the so-called "War of the Theatres" (1600–2). Already Jonson had begun writing for the more sophisticated audience at the Blackfriars theatre, where the Children of the Chapel performed his *Cynthia's Revels* in 1601. He took a special interest in two boy actors, Pavey, whose epitaph he wrote and Field (qq.v.), who became his pupil. In 1602 the children played his *Poetaster*, which attacked adult actors in general and satirised Marston and Dekker (qq.v.), provoking Dekker to write *Satiromastix* in reply. (There is a reference to this feud between the boys' and men's companies in *Hamlet*, when the prince is in conversation with Rosencrantz, Act II Scene 2.) However, Jonson's next play, *Sejanus* (1603), the first of two classical tragedies, was acted by the King's Men, with Shakespeare in the cast. *Sejanus* caused Jonson to be summoned before the Council on suspicion of "treason and popery". The King's Men played his other tragedy, *Catiline* (1611) and most of his remaining comedies (*Volpone*, 1606; *Alchemist*, 1610; *Bartholomew Fair*, 1614; *The Devil is an Ass*, 1616; *Staple of News*, 1625, etc.). Exceptions are *Eastward Ho!* (1605) and *Epicoene* (1609), both performed by the Children of the Revels. *Eastward Ho!*, written in collaboration with Chapman and Marston (qq.v.), landed Jonson in prison again, chiefly for ridiculing the Scots. As Jonson was still a Roman Catholic and had been questioned about the Gunpowder Plot, his position was serious; his old mother later said she had been prepared to give her son poison and take it herself. Jonson was released, and subsequently abandoned his Catholicism.

As well as writing plays, Jonson was author of eight out of the ten Court masques, Queen Anne's favourite amusement, performed between 1605 and 1612. In collaboration with Inigo Jones, Ferrabosco and (later) Nicholas Lanier (qq.v.), he produced the nearest English equivalent to opera at that time. Jonson continued to write masques and other royal entertainments until 1631, when he quarrelled with Inigo Jones. In 1616 he published all his poems, plays and masques (except those for the Admiral's Men) in a collected edition, which included two groups of poems: "Epigrammes", containing the epitaphs on Pavey and his own son; and "The Forrest", which includes "Drink to me only with thine eyes". That same year Jonson was unofficially recognised as Poet Laureate. Four years after his death a commonplace book was published in which Jonson discussed his theories of literature. All that is known of his life comes from conversations he held with William Drummond (q.v.) of Hawthornden during a visit paid to him by Jonson in 1619, with Drummond taking notes of what he said. The friendship with Shakespeare has been the subject of much legend, near-contemporaries relating anecdotes of genial rivalry, for tales of drinking parties at the Mermaid and just before Shakespeare's death tended to include the presence of Jonson as a matter of course. The facts are that Jonson, by nature a quarrelsome man, did not quarrel with Shakespeare, that he genuinely — though critically — admired him as a writer, and that he was author of the chief eulogy of Shakespeare in the First Folio of 1623.

E. K. C., *E.S.*; *W. S.*
S. S.

JORDAN, Edward (1569–1632), physician: born at High Halden, near Tenterden in Kent, and probably educated at Hart Hall, Oxford, although he took no degree. Jordan travelled in Europe and took his doctorate of medicine at the University of Padua. In 1595 he was licensed by the Royal College of Physicians, of which he was elected a Fellow two years later. Jordan specialised in the study of hysteria, particularly as manifested in women. His book, *A Brief Discourse of a Disease called the Suffocation of the Mother* (a disease of both mind and body — "mother" meaning womb) was published in 1603; it advocated a light diet, moderate religious practice and apparent sympathy from the doctor who, Jordan said, "should politicly confirm them in their fantasies". Jordan's linking of hysteria with supposed possession by evil spirits led James I to employ him in order to investigate and expose a girl subject to "demoniac" possession. He settled in the city of Bath and, not surprisingly, became interested in spa treatments; Jordan's *A Discourse of Natural Baths and Mineral Waters* was published in the year before he died.

A. L. Rowse, *Elizabethan England; the Cultural Achievement* (1972)

JOURDAIN, Sylvester (c. 1580–1650), merchant and colonialist: born at Lyme Regis, Dorset, into a Puritan family with strong links with Devonshire (his brother, Ignatius Jourdain, was a much respected Mayor of Exeter and represented the city in the House of Commons, 1621, 1625 and 1626). Sylvester is known to have been a merchant, trading from Poole from 1603 onwards. He accompanied Sir George Somers (q.v.), who also came from Lyme Regis, on his voyage in *Sea Venture* to Virginia, 1609, and was therefore one of the castaways in Bermuda (v. *Gates* and *William Strachey*). After returning to London in 1610 Jourdain wrote an account of the storm and shipwreck, printed and published as *A Discovery of the Bermudas*, which is believed to have provided Shakespeare with source material for *The Tempest*. Jourdain probably settled in London as a merchant adventurer, dying unmarried in the parish of St Sepulchre-beyond-Newgate in the first year of the Commonwealth.

J. Q. Adams, ed., *Jourdain's Discovery of the Bermudas* (1940)
W. T. MacCaffrey, *Exeter 1540–1640* (1975)

K

KEELING, William (?1578–1620), master mariner: nothing is known of his life until 1604 when he was sufficiently experienced to receive command of the *Susan* on the East India Company's second Java venture. With Henry Middleton in the flagship *Dragon* and two other vessels, Keeling visited the trading post at Bantam which Lancaster (q.v.) had established in 1601. He then began a homeward voyage, having transferred to command of *Hector* and carrying cargoes of pepper and spices. *Susan* sank in the Indian Ocean and, of *Hector*'s crew, only Keeling and thirteen others survived. Keeling was appointed commander of the third East India Company's expedition in March 1607, sailing in the flagship *Dragon*, with William Hawkins as his deputy in *Hector*, and charged with a mission to the Great Mogul in Agra. According to Keeling's journal of the voyage, he had his ship's company perform *Hamlet* (5 September) and *Richard II* (30 September) while lying off Sierra Leone. *Hamlet* was repeated at Socotra, in the Indian Ocean, on 31 March 1608, "to keep my people from idleness and unlawful games, or sleep", as Keeling put it. These are the first recorded amateur performances of Shakespeare. Sidney Lee in his life of Shakespeare (1898) doubted the authenticity of the journal, as the original has disappeared, but F.S.Boas and other later authorities have accepted it. Keeling left Hawkins in Surat and successfully completed the voyage to Sumatra and Java. He sent *Dragon* home, transferred to *Hector* and spent several months in the eastern end of the Indonesian archipelago before returning to Java in order to avoid friction with Dutch traders. In October 1609 he sailed for England, discovering the Cocos-Keeling Islands during the voyage and reaching home waters in May 1610.

He undertook his last East Indian expedition from 1615 to 1617, again aboard *Dragon*, and vainly hoping until the eve of departure that the company would allow his wife to accompany him. At Surat he landed Sir Thomas Roe as resident ambassador to the Mogul, proceeding to attack Portuguese shipping along the western Indian coast from Goa to Calicut (Kozhikode). There, and at Achin (Ajteh), Keeling negotiated trading concessions with the local kings. Despite a serious bout of dysentery in Sumatra, Keeling hoped to remain in Java as commander of the Company's affairs but was summoned home in September 1616, only a month after landing in Java. He reached England in May 1617, broken in health and having lost sixty-two of *Dragon's* crew on the expedition. James I rewarded Keeling by appointing him a Groom of the Chamber and Captain of Cowes Castle on the Isle of Wight. Keeling lived at Park Place near Carisbrooke and was friendly with the island's Governor, the Earl of Southampton (q.v.), to whom he sent Javanese gifts in 1618. He died a wealthy man, leaving gold and silver plate, jewels and East India Company stock; and he is buried in Carisbrooke Church.

F. S. Boas, *Shakespeare and the Universities* (1923)
M. Strachan and B. Penrose, eds., *The East India Company Journals of Captain Keeling and Master Bonner, 1615–17* (1971)

KEMPE, William (?–?1608/9), comic actor: a member of Leicester's Men when they accompanied their patron to the Low Countries (1585–6). He then toured in Denmark but, by 1590, was already known as a "most comicall and conceited" actor in London (Nashe, q.v.). In 1592 he was with Strange's Men, most conspicuously in *A Knack to Know a Knave*; to this anonymous play he contributed a "merriment", in the scene of the Men of Gotham. Kempe became famous for these merriments — short passages of repartee in which Kempe invariably came off best. He was also well known for his "jigs" — sketches with song and dance, which were often obscene. The titles of several jigs are listed in the Stationers' Register for 1595, e.g. *Kempe's New Jigge betwixt a Soldier and a Miser and Sym the Clown*. "Whores, bedles,

William Kempe

bawdes and sergeants filthily chaunt Kemp's Jigge", declared a Puritan pamphleteer in 1598. At this time Kempe was with the Chamberlain's Men, whom he had joined in 1594–5, staying with the company until 1599 and playing Peter in *Romeo and Juliet* and Dogberry in *Much Ado*. He was one of the original seven shareholders in the new Globe theatre, but sold his share soon after the lease was signed in 1599. It is possible he wished to free himself from the company for his next enterprise, his famous morris dance from London to Norwich. Kempe left the capital on 11 February 1600, arriving in Norwich on 11 March: nine days were spent in actual dancing but there was no limit on rest periods. An overseer, George Sprat, accompanied Kempe to ensure that he did, indeed, dance every mile. Kempe made a good deal of money from bets and gifts during the dance, including an annuity of forty shillings from the Mayor of Norwich. He also produced a book about the exploit, *Kempe's Nine Daies Wonder* in which (with a pun on the Globe theatre) he declares, "I have daunst myself out of the world." It is unlikely that he returned to the Chamberlain's Men; he visited Italy and Germany, came back poorer than when he set out, and joined Worcester's Men, 1602–3. In 1602, however, he is still called a fellow of Burbage and Shakespeare (in *Return from Parnassus* 1606) and his name appears in the First Folio list, although there is little doubt he was dead by 1609.

E. K. C., *E.S.*
A. Dyce, *Kempe's Nine Days Wonder* (1840)
C. R. Baskervill, *The Elizabethan Jig* (1929)

KEYSAR, Robert (fl. 1606–13), goldsmith and theatre manager: acquired an interest in the Blackfriars theatre in 1606, presenting the Children of the Revels who had lost their Royal Patent in the previous year after the *Eastward Ho!* affair (v. *Chapman, Jonson, Marston*). Under Keysar they became known as the Children of the Blackfriars. In 1608 Keysar left the Blackfriars (which reverted to the Burbages), bought out the share of his partner, Marston (q.v.) and managed to present the company at Court again. With a new partner, Rosseter (q.v.), he succeeded in acquiring a Royal Patent and the old name of "Queen's Revels" was restored to the company, which from 1609 onwards operated at the Whitefriars theatre. In 1610 a three-cornered legal case began, involving Keysar, Henry Evans (q.v.) and the King's Men concerning the lease of the Blackfriars. The King's Men eventually won the suit, and no more was heard of Keysar as a theatre manager.

E. K. C., *E.S.*

KILDARE, Frances, Lady (ante 1572–1628): daughter of Lord High Admiral Howard and his wife Catherine (qq.v.). Frances was first married to Henry Fitzgerald, Earl of Kildare, before 1590. He died in 1597, and Frances was given an annuity of £200 from the Crown. In May 1601 she married Henry Brooke, Lord Cobham (q.v.) but preferred to be known still as Lady Kildare. Cobham, with Ralegh and Northumberland, (qq.v.) was opposed to James I's succession. Lady Kildare was a supporter of James and eventually became governess to his daughter, Princess Elizabeth. In 1603 Cobham was sent to the Tower for conspiracy. Lady Kildare had nothing more to do with him, but lived on her own at Cobham Hall, Kent which she was granted for life with part of her husband's estate. She was buried in Westminster Abbey.

V. A. Wilson, *Society Women of Shakespeare's Time* (1925)

KING, John (?1559–1621), Bishop of London: born in Buckinghamshire and educated at Westminster School and Christ Church, Oxford. He became chaplain to Egerton (q.v.) in 1594 and a royal chaplain in 1601, preaching a tactful sermon of welcome to James I in 1603. To contemporaries he gave an impression of grave profundity in the pulpit, but he was also highly articulate. James I, trying as ever to be almost witty, described him as "a king of preachers" and summoned him to the Hampton Court Conference, where he preached to the Presbyterians on the errors of their ways. He became Dean of Christ Church in 1605 and Vice-Chancellor of Oxford University from 1607 to 1610. He served with Archbishop Abbot (q.v.) on the special commission to hear the divorce suit of Lady Essex (Frances Howard, q.v.) in 1613, sharing the Archbishop's disinclination to annul the marriage. The bishop's son, Henry King (1592–1669), was a friend and executor of Donne (q.v.) and was himself the author of elegiacs and a work of *Poems and Psalms*, published in 1624; he was Bishop of Chichester in 1642–3 and from 1660 to 1669.

M. Crum, *The poems of Henry King* (1965)

KIRBYE, George (c. 1565–1634), composer: probably born at Bury St Edmunds in Suffolk, where he spent virtually all of his life. He was house musician to Sir Robert Jermyn at Rushbrooke Hall, only six miles from Hengrave where Wilbye (q.v.) held a similar position in the Kytson household. Kirbye composed church music and viol pieces but his reputation rests on his set of twenty-four English madrigals for four, five and six voices, published in 1597 and dedicated to the daughters of the Jermyn household. His madrigals show an apt and effective use of discordant harmonies, technically in advance of some of his more prolific contemporaries. He contributed a madrigal for six voices to *The Triumphs of Oriana* which Morley (q.v.) edited in 1601.

KNELL, William (?–1587), actor: was one of the Queen's Men and played Prince Hal in the anonymous *Famous Victories of Henry V*. On 13 June 1587, while the company was playing at Thame in Oxfordshire, Knell assaulted a colleague and was killed by him. Knell's widow married Heminges (q.v.). The Queen's Men are known to have visited Stratford-upon-Avon in September 1587; they were unexpectedly short of one actor and could have recruited Shakespeare. There is no evidence for this speculation, first suggested by Professor Eccles in 1961.

S. S.

KNOLLYS, Francis (?1514–1596), statesman: son of Robert Knollys, Gentleman Usher to Henry VII and Henry VIII. In 1538 Henry VIII renewed to Knollys the grant made to his father of the manor of Rotherfield Greys, Oxfordshire. Knollys was a strong Puritan and popular with Edward VI, but thought it wise to go to Europe in Mary's reign. By 1546 he had married Catherine Carey, first cousin to Princess Elizabeth, and so was in a position of influence from 1558, when Elizabeth succeeded as Queen. Knollys at once became Privy Councillor, a position he held until his death, and Vice-Chamberlain of the Household. From 1562 he was frequently M.P. for Oxfordshire and spoke often in the House, especially when the Puritan cause needed support. Later his Puritanism brought him particularly into conflict with Archbishop Whitgift (q.v.). Knollys was in charge of Mary Queen of Scots from 1568 to 1569, and suggested that she should marry his wife's nephew, George Carey (q.v.). When his own daughter, Lettice, married the Earl of Leicester (qq.v.) in 1578 Knollys's distrust of Leicester was so great that he insisted on a second ceremony at which he could be present himself as witness. From 1572 until his death Knollys was Treasurer of the Household; his second son William (q.v.) eventually succeeded to this post. Knollys had seven sons, of whom six sat in the House of Commons, mainly for Berkshire or Oxfordshire seats, and four daughters. He was made a Knight of the Garter in 1593.

J. E. Neale, *Elizabeth I and her Parliaments 1584–1601* (1957)

KNOLLYS, Lettice (1540–1634), daughter of Sir Francis Knollys see LEICESTER, Lettice, Countess of.

KNOLLYS, William, later Viscount Wallingford, Earl of Banbury (?1547–1632), Comptroller and Treasurer of the Royal Household: son of Sir Francis Knollys of Rotherfield Greys, Oxfordshire, and Catherine (Carey) the Queen's cousin, and brother of Lettice, later Countess of Leicester. Knollys was educated by a Puritan tutor and at Magdalen College, Oxford, but took no degree. He served as a captain against the northern rebels (1569), in the Low Countries under Leicester, who knighted him (1586), and at Tilbury against the Armada (1588). He was M.P. for Tregony, Cornwall (1572–83) and for Oxfordshire frequently between 1584 and 1601, and Lord Lieutenant of Berkshire and Oxfordshire from 1596. In that year his father died and Knollys succeeded him in the Queen's Council. He also, like his father, became Comptroller and subsequently Treasurer (1602) of the Household. In the former capacity, Knollys was able to use his influence to obtain a position for a friend's daughter, Mary Fitton (q.v.). Although he had married Dorothy Brydges, Lady Chandos, he fell in love with Mary and made himself laughable in his pursuit of her, even dyeing his beard. His elderly wife died in 1605, but by this time Mary Fitton had left Court in disgrace. Knollys, now sixty-eight, promptly married Elizabeth Howard, aged nineteen, daughter of the Earl of Suffolk, and sister of Frances, Countess of Essex (qq.v.). Knollys had retained his position at Court under James I, who made him a baron (1603), Master of the Wards (1614) and a Knight of the Garter (1615). The Howard influence began to decline after the Overbury murder trials of 1615–16 (v. *Carr, Frances Howard, Overbury*). By 1618 Knollys had resigned his Court offices, but was not disgraced; he became Viscount Wallingford (1616) and Earl of Banbury (1626), and was High Steward of Oxfordshire from 1620. He was still active in the

Lords, where he took a leading part in the case against Bacon (q.v.) in 1621. He continued to hawk and ride to hounds well into his eighties. Knollys's second wife had two sons (born in 1627 and 1631) but he did not acknowledge them; his will left his estate to his wife for life, with no mention of children. After his death, his widow began litigation on the boys' behalf and they were eventually reinstated as heirs. Dr Hotson has seen Knollys as the model for Shakespeare's Malvolio, because of his position at Court and hopeless love for Mary Fitton.

L. Hotson, *The First Night of Twelfth Night* (1954)

KNYVETT, Thomas (c. 1548–1622), courtier and M.P.: born at Charlton in Wiltshire and educated at Jesus College, Cambridge, coming to Court in his early twenties. He was eventually appointed a Gentleman of the Privy Chamber. He represented Westmorland in the Commons, 1572, 1576 and 1581 and was one of the two Members for Westminster in 1584–5, 1586–7, 1589, 1597–8, 1601 and from 1604 to 1607. In 1582 he fought a duel with the Earl of Oxford (q.v.) who had taken as his mistress Knyvett's cousin, Anne Vavasour, and made her pregnant. The duel was followed by scuffles between supporters of Oxford and Knyvett, some of whom were killed. As an M.P. he showed himself to be an ardent Protestant, fiercely critical of Mary, Queen of Scots, in November 1586. On 24 February 1587 Knyvett was one of four Puritan M.P.s authorised by the Commons "to search certain houses in Westminster suspected of receiving and harbouring of Jesuits, seminaries, or of seditious and Popish books and trumperies of superstition". Subsequently Knyvett, who was knighted in 1595, became principal Justice of the Peace in Westminster. In this capacity he was ordered on 4 November 1605 to search

the rooms beneath the House of Lords where, shortly before midnight, he found and arrested Guy Fawkes (q.v.). Knyvett already stood high in favour with James I, who granted him the manor of Stanwell in 1603. His part in defeating the Gunpowder Plotters brought him further rewards: more land in Stanwell, admission to the Privy Council, and a barony. He became Lord Knyvett of Escrick in 1607. He spent most of his last years in retirement at Stanwell. Knyvett's estates passed to his niece, the Countess of Suffolk (Catherine Howard, q.v.).

J. E. Neale, *Elizabeth 1 and her Parliaments, 1584–1601* (1957)

KYD, Thomas (1558–94), dramatist: born in London and educated at Merchant Taylors' School. He may have worked as a translator before becoming a dramatist. His famous *Spanish Tragedy* was written about 1589 and performed in 1592. It was a tremendous popular success, coupled in public esteem with *Titus Andronicus*; it was also the first English tragedy on the popular theme of revenge, and contains all the devices associated with later Elizabethan plays: soliloquy, supernatural appearances, dumb-shows and discovery scenes. The hero, Hieronymo, was a great actor's part, and the play was revived, as well as revised, later. A blank verse Senecan tragedy, *Pompey the Great, his fair Cornelia's Tragedy* was published in 1595, a sustained exercise in lamentation. None of Kyd's other plays has survived; he may have been the author of an earlier version of *Hamlet* and *The Taming of a Shrew*, both lost plays allegedly used by Shakespeare. It is also possible that Kyd was author of a tragedy, *Solyman and Perseda*, published in 1599. Kyd died in disgrace; he was arrested on 12 May 1593 on suspicion of "lewd and mutinous libels". His papers had become mixed up with those of his friend Marlowe (q.v.), as both authors were under similar patronage at that time. When these papers were discovered, Marlowe too was arrested; Kyd was released, repudiating both the charges and his friendship with Marlowe, but he never recovered his position, and he died within a year.

KYFFIN, Maurice (?1555–99), poet, translator: probably the son of Thomas Kyffin who lived near Oswestry. From 1578 to 1580 Kyffin was in London as a pupil of John Dee (q.v.). He left Dee to become a tutor, but remained friendly with him. By 1587 he was tutor to the sons of Lord Buckhurst (Thomas Sackville, q.v.) and translated Terence's *Andria* into English prose. In the same year he published a poem in praise of Queen Elizabeth, *The Blessedness of Britain*. He wrote poems in Welsh as well as English but they were not printed. Kyffin then embarked on a new career, as a financial officer in the army: Surveyor of Muster Rolls in the Netherlands (1588), Deputy Treasurer of the Normandy expedition (1591), and Controller of Muster Rolls in Ireland (from 1596 until his death). In 1594 he published a Welsh translation of Bishop Jewel's *Apologia*. Kyffin died in Dublin and was buried there.

KYTSON, (Sir) Thomas (1540–1602), patron of the arts: a posthumous son of his namesake, a London mercer and Suffolk landowner who had acquired the manor of Hengrave, some 3 miles north-west of Bury St Edmunds, in Henry VIII's reign. The son devoted his life to the patronage of art and music, mostly at Hengrave. In this pursuit he was assisted by his wife, a member of the Norfolk gentry family of Cornwallis. They had as household musicians two of the contributors to Morley's *The Triumphs of Oriana*, the little-known Edward Johnson and the fine madrigal composer, John Wilby (q.v.). An inventory made in 1603 shows that Kytson had at Hengrave a collection of 50 song books and 42 musical instruments. He also had 28 pictures in his galleries as well as 10 decorative maps, an ornate chessboard and "one billiard board, with two staves to it of bone and two of wood and four balls". Lady Kytson outlived her husband by twenty-four years, seeking to maintain at Hengrave Hall the standard of cultured elegance attained by her husband.

M. St Clare Byrne, *Elizabethan Life in Town and Country* (rev. ed., 1961)

L

LAKE, Thomas (c. 1567–1630), government servant: born at Southport, served for a time as personal secretary to Francis Walsingham and became Latin secretary to James I, who knighted him soon after his accession. He was M.P. for Launceston in 1604 and for Middlesex in 1614, when he was sworn of the Privy Council. He is said to have introduced George Villiers (Buckingham, q.v.) to James I at Apethorpe in Northamptonshire while the King was on progress through the Midlands in August 1614. From January 1616 until February 1619 he was Secretary of State. He was deprived of office and imprisoned in 1619 for defaming the character of Lady Exeter, gaining his release in a widespread amnesty in July 1621.

LAMBARDE, William (1536–1601), antiquary and jurist: born in London, entered Lincoln's Inn in 1556 becoming a barrister in 1567 and holding a succession of minor legal posts, eventually becoming Deputy Keeper of the Rolls in 1597. He compiled three legal handbooks: *Eirenarcha* (1582) for Justices of the Peace, *The Duties of Constables* (1583), and a study of the High Courts of Justice, *Archeion*, which was presented to Robert Cecil in 1591 but not published until 1630. Lambarde's fame rests on his pioneer antiquarian county history, *A Perambulation of Kent* (completed by 1570 and published in 1576) and on his account of an audience with Queen Elizabeth in August 1601 soon after the Essex conspiracy. On this occasion Lambarde presented the Queen with a catalogue of the records within his keeping at the Tower of London. When her eye noticed the documents surviving from Richard II's reign, she said to him, "I am Richard II, know ye not that?" After Lambarde made a tactful reference to the wickedness of Essex as "the most adorned creature that ever your Majesty made", the Queen concluded, "He that will forget God will also forget his benefactors. This tragedy was played forty times in open streets and houses." Lambarde died a fortnight after this audience.

M. Warnicke, *William Lambarde, Elizabethan Antiquary* (1973)

LAMBERT, Edmund (c. 1525–87), relative by marriage to Shakespeare: known to have married Joan Arden, Shakespeare's aunt, by 1550 and to have lived at Barton-on-the-Heath, fifteen miles south of Stratford, a name echoed in Sly's reference to "Burton-heath" in *The Taming of the Shrew*. Lambert was probably godfather to John Shakespeare's youngest son, Edmund, in 1580. In 1578 John Shakespeare mortgaged a house and fifty-six acres at Wilmcote, which were part of his wife's inheritance, to Lambert for £40. The money was to be repaid by Michaelmas 1580, but this was not done, the property remaining Edmund Lambert's until his death, when it passed to his son John (*infra*).

E. K. C., *W.S.*
M. E.

LAMBERT, John (fl. 1587–1602), first cousin of Shakespeare: the son of Edmund Lambert (*supra*). His uncle, John Shakespeare, sued him in Queen's Bench in the Armada year for recovery of the Wilmcote property mortgaged to his father, or alternatively for another £20 that John Lambert had allegedly agreed to pay for the title to the land. Lambert denied any such obligation and won his case. In 1597 the Shakespeares again sued him, in Chancery, but were once more the losers. The Wilmcote land was never recovered by the Shakespeare family.

LANCASTER, James (?1554–1618), seaman and explorer: born in Basingstoke and became a member of the Skinners' Company before going to sea and qualifying as a mariner. His vessel, the *Edward Bonaventure*, was part of the fleet which shadowed the Armada up the Channel in 1588. Three years later he commanded the ship on a voyage to the East Indies where he raided Portuguese settlements without conspicuous success. Adverse winds and a mutinous crew deprived him of his ship and his meagre takings; he did not arrive home until May 1594, having been rescued from near starvation by a French vessel. The following autumn he commanded the *Consent*, one of three vessels raiding the Portuguese settlements along the coast of Brazil. He gained great wealth from the seizure of the town and warehouses of Pernambuco (April 1595) but was fortunate to escape from a strategic trap set by superior Portuguese and Spanish vessels. In April 1601 he led the first expedition commissioned by the newly established East India Company, five vessels with crews totalling in all almost 500 men, of whom more than a third perished in the two and a half year voyage to present-day Indonesia. Lancaster reached Sumatra in June 1602, gaining trade concessions from the local ruler at Atjeh, and then sailed for Java, where the first East India Company "factory" was established at Bantam on the Sunda Strait. On his return to England in September 1603 Lancaster, by now a rich man, was knighted. He spent the last years of his life helping to establish the East India Company, while encouraging other voyages of discovery, putting some of his money into

one of the quests for a north-west passage (1618).

W. Foster, *The Voyages of Sir James Lancaster* (1940)

LANE, John (1590–1640), resident of Stratford: grandson of Nicholas Lane, a wealthy Stratford man who had sued Shakespeare's father in 1587, and a nephew of Richard Lane (*infra*). John Lane was the defendant in a slander suit brought by Shakespeare's daughter, Susanna Hall (q.v.) in July 1613. He did not appear, and was excommunicated. Six years later he was sued in Star Chamber for riot and for libelling the Vicar and Aldermen; he was also presented by the Churchwardens of Stratford to the Church Court as a drunkard. His sister Margaret married John Greene (q.v.), Shakespeare's kinsman.

M. E.
E. I. Fripp, *Shakespeare's Haunts near Stratford* (1929)

LANE, Richard (c. 1556–1613), Warwickshire landowner: son of the wealthy Nicholas Lane, who lent money to Shakespeare's uncle and sued his father for its recovery (v. *Shakespeare, Henry* and *John*). Richard Lane helped John Shakespeare in his litigation over Wilmcote and joined William Shakespeare and Thomas Greene (q.v.) in the tithes dispute of 1611. He married Joan Whitney from Surrey and in 1603 bought Alveston Manor, on the left bank of the Avon. Lane appointed Shakespeare's son-in-law, Hall, trustee for his children on 9 July 1613, six days before his nephew John Lane (*supra*), was sued by Hall's wife, Susanna, for defamation.

Ibid.
M. E.

LANGLEY, Francis (?–1601), goldsmith and theatre owner: brother-in-law to Sir Anthony Ashley, Clerk of the Privy

Council, and in 1582 became Inspector of Cloth (Alnager) for the City of London. Langley bought the manor of Paris Garden at the west of Bankside in 1589, and five years later his intention to build a theatre on his land induced the Lord Mayor to protest to Burghley against his activities. By 1595, however, Langley had built the Swan in the north-east corner of his land; this playhouse was described and drawn by the Dutch priest, Johannes de Witt, in the following year, thus providing the main source of information on the appearance and nature of an Elizabethan theatre. During 1596 Langley quarrelled with the Surrey Justice of the Peace, William Gardiner (q.v.), calling him a "false perjured knave". For these words Gardiner brought three suits for slander against Langley, but none of the actions came to court and Langley petitioned against Gardiner and his stepson Wayte (q.v.) to keep the peace. Wayte retaliated in November 1596, by bringing a similar petition against Langley, two women, and William Shakespeare. No other evidence connects Shakespeare's company, the Chamberlain's Men, with the Swan playhouse. In 1597, Langley was presenting Pembroke's Men, whose performance of *The Isle of Dogs* by Jonson and Nashe (qq.v.) at the Swan in the summer of 1597 offended authority. The play contained so much "very seditious and slanderous matter" that all theatres were closed on 28 July. By the time the ban was lifted, most of Pembroke's Men had joined the Admiral's Company and were not available to Langley, who tried litigation but failed to get them back. Langley succeeded in keeping plays going at the Swan, with a small company of actors, until 1598 when the playhouse was used for other forms of entertainment (acrobats, fencers, etc.) culminating in the great fiasco of *England's Joy* in 1602 (v. *Vennar*). By then, however, Langley was dead. In January 1602 his

property on Bankside was sold to Hugh Browker, a lawyer, and the Swan never again flourished.

E. K. C., *E.S.*
L. Hotson, *Shakespeare versus Shallow* (1931)

LANIER, Emilia (1570–1654), possible "Dark Lady" of the Sonnets; the illegitimate daughter of Baptiste Bassano, one of a family of Venetian musicians who had served the English monarchs from Henry VIII's reign. Emilia's father died when she was young and left her £100, which she may never have received. She was brought up in the household of the Countess of Kent, but in her late teens became the mistress of the first Lord Hunsdon (Henry Carey, q.v.). In 1593 Emilia was pregnant, presumably by Hunsdon, and was married off to Alphonse Lanier, also a Court musician and one of a family of musicians from Rouen. She received jewels and a pension of £40 per annum, but Lanier's extravagance was such that the family was very poor by 1597. Lanier decided to take service under the Earl of Essex in his expedition to the Azores and in Ireland. The Laniers consulted the astrologer Simon Forman (q.v.) about Alphonse's prospects and Emilia had some kind of physical relationship with Forman which teased him considerably. He recorded his doubts that she might be an "incuba" rather than a woman. Emilia reformed during the latter part of her husband's life, and in 1611 published a long religious poem *Salve Deus Rex Judaeorum*, basically a vindication of the women of the Bible, from Eve to the Virgin Mary and the women of Jerusalem at the time of Christ's Passion. It shows a good deal of learning and was preceded by dedicatory poems to Queen Anne, Princess Elizabeth, Lady Arbella Stuart and six Countesses, not all of whom were known to the author. The book was not widely distributed, and after Lanier's death (1613) Emilia was poor again. In 1617 she tried a new venture, keeping a school for gentlemen's children in London, but fell foul of her landlord over repairs and rent, and was finally arrested (1619). Her son Henry (presumed to be Hunsdon's) may have kept her till his death in 1633; he was musician to Charles I. From 1633 Emilia was suing for maintenance from her brother-in-law for herself and her two orphaned grandchildren. By the time of her death she had succeeded in acquiring some kind of pension from the Crown. Emilia has been suggested as Shakespeare's "Dark Lady" chiefly by Dr Rowse, on the grounds of her connection with Hunsdon, who as Lord Chamberlain was patron of Shakespeare's company, her musicality, and her character as described by Forman.

A. L. Rowse, *Shakespeare's Sonnets* (1973); *The Poems of Shakespeare's Dark Lady* (1978)

LANIER, Nicholas (1588–1666), composer: born at Greenwich, the son of John Lanier, a court musician to Elizabeth I. Many other members of the family were musicians. Nicholas rose rapidly to eminence in the household of Prince Henry from 1604 onwards as a singer, player of the flute and composer. At the age of twenty-five he composed music for the masque held in honour of Robert Carr's marriage to Frances Howard and he introduced recitative into England for the masque written by Ben Jonson and presented at Lord Hay's house on 22 February 1617. On this occasion Lanier not only sang but also painted the scenery. He became Master of the King's Music to Charles I, holding the post throughout his reign and being reinstated by Charles II at the Restoration of 1660. Lanier was an artist of taste, too; he was employed by Charles I in the early years of his reign to travel in Europe and make purchases of paintings for the royal collection.

LANMAN, Henry (1536–?92), theatre owner: a tenant of Curtain Close, part of the district of London known as the Liberty of Holywell, in Finsbury Fields. The second London playhouse, the Curtain, was built on this land before the end of 1577. It is probable that the Curtain was built by Lanman, and he certainly shared the profits from the playhouse with the Burbages from 1585 to 1592, when it was used as an "easer" to the theatre. The Chamberlain's Men are believed to have played at the Curtain from October 1597 until the opening of the new Globe in 1599: they presented *Romeo and Juliet* there, John Marston (q.v.) speaking of "Curtain plaudities" in connection with the play.

E. K. C., *E.S.*

LAUD, William (1573–1645), archbishop: born at Reading, the son of a master tailor, educated at St John's College, Oxford, becoming a Fellow in 1593 and serving as President of the college 1611–21. He was ordained in 1601 and acted as chaplain to the Earl of Mountjoy (Charles Blount, q.v.). In this capacity he was responsible for marrying Mountjoy and the divorced Penelope Rich (q.v.), an act which later preyed on Laud's conscience. Laud was a vigorous opponent of Calvinist influence in the Church of England, first as Dean of Gloucester (1616–21) and later as Bishop, at St David's (1621–6), at Bath and Wells (1626–8) and at London (1628–33). In 1629 he became Chancellor of Oxford, his reforming statutes shaping the character of the University for over two hundred years. As Archbishop of Canterbury, effectively from 1633 to 1641, he tried to enforce liturgical uniformity on the Church, combating the prevalent leaning towards Puritanism by strict discipline. His association with Thomas Wentworth (q.v.) in an authoritarian policy of "thorough" government led to his impeachment by the Long Parliament. He was imprisoned in the Tower from 1641 until his execution on 10 January 1645.

H. R. Trevor-Roper, *Archbishop Laud* (1940)

LAW, Matthew (?–1629), bookseller: was originally a member of the Drapers' Company, but in 1595 published a volume of sonnets and transferred to the Stationers' Company in 1600. Law's shops were in St Paul's Churchyard, first near Watling Street (1601), then at the sign of the "Fox". The Stationers fined him several times for disobedience, opening his shop on Sunday, and selling pirated editions. In 1603 Law took over the copyrights of Shakespeare's *Richard II, Richard III*, and *Henry IV*, part 1 from Andrew Wise. He issued quartos of *Henry IV*, part 1 (1604, 1608, 1613, 1622), *Richard III* (1605, 1612, 1622) and *Richard II* (1608, 1615). Law published poems on the death of Elizabeth I and the coronation of James I. He left his business to his wife Joyce at his death.

LEAKE, William (?–1633), bookseller: origins unknown, he was apprenticed to Francis Coldock and became a freeman of the Stationers' Company in 1584. He was admitted to the Livery of the Company in 1598 and had several shops in St Paul's Churchyard: "The Crane" (1593), "White Greyhound" (1596), John Harrison's (q.v.) old shop, and the "Holy Ghost" (1602–18). He was fined in 1586 for opening his shop on holydays. Along with Harrison's shop Leake acquired the copyright of Shakespeare's *Venus and Adonis* in 1596 and published six more editions of the poem from 1599 onwards. He also sold the pseudo-Shakespearian *Passionate Pilgrim* (1599). Leake was Junior Warden (1604, 1606) and Senior Warden (1610,

1616) of the Stationers' Company and held shares in the Company's stock of Irish and Latin books. His share in the Irish stock involved his heirs in a Chancery suit. In 1617 Leake assigned nearly all his copyrights to William Barrett (q.v.); next year he was Master of the Stationers and retired in 1619 to Hereford. Leake was married four times and left the remainder of his business to his eldest son, William.

LEE, Henry (1533–1611), courtier and landed gentleman: the family came from Cheshire, but acquired the manor of Quarrendon, Buckinghamshire from Henry VIII. Lee's parents were Sir Anthony and Lady Margaret, a sister of Sir Thomas Wyatt. Later gossip made Henry VIII Lee's father. He was knighted in 1553, served in the Scottish border fighting of 1558 and sat as Member for Buckinghamshire in the Parliaments of 1558 and 1572. Lee was a favourite with Queen Elizabeth, who appointed him Lieutenant of the Royal Manor of Woodstock, Oxfordshire, in 1571. In that year he made his first appearance as "Queen's Champion" at the Accession Tilt, an annual event which he may have instituted in 1570, for he was a great expert in tilting and delighted in its accompanying pageantry. Lee entertained the Queen at Woodstock in 1575 and there, or at Ditchley, in 1592; on each occasion he produced a masque, some of which he may have written himself. In 1573 he had his final experience of soldiering with English volunteers besieging Edinburgh Castle. For the last thirty-three years of his life he was Master of the Armoury at the Tower of London, in charge of the army equipment as well as armour for ceremonies of state. At some time between 1581 and 1592 he purchased Ditchley, one of four manors he owned. He was a great builder of houses, an encloser and sheep farmer on his Oxfordshire lands. He spent the remaining years of his life at High Lodge in Woodstock Park, at "Lee's Rest" in Charlbury, or at the rebuilt manor house of Ditchley, homes within a few miles of each other, between Oxford and Stratford-upon-Avon. Lee continued to appear at the Accession Tilt until 1590 when there was an elaborate pageant in honour of his retirement, to which he may have contributed a song (v. *Peele*). His wife, Anne Paget by birth, died in that same year, their three children having predeceased her. Sir Henry lived thereafter with his mistress, Anne Vavasour, a former Gentlewoman of the Bedchamber to the Queen and (in 1581) mistress to the Earl of Oxford (q.v.). Lee's retreat was disturbed by the treasonable activities of his cousin (v. *Thomas Lee*) and, he was placed under formal restraint in 1601 but allowed to visit Bath for his gout. Two years later he was well enough to attend the coronation of James I, and was soon in favour with his new sovereign who loved the hunting at Woodstock; the Court was there in 1603, 1604 and 1605, and Queen Anne visited Sir Henry and Anne Vavasour at Charlbury in 1608. In 1601 Lee received permission to make a park at Ditchley. He died there in the autumn of 1611, rich in lands but not in money.

E. K. Chambers, *Sir Henry Lee* (1936)

LEE, Richard (ante 1549–1608), diplomat and trader: the illegitimate younger half-brother of Sir Henry Lee, left £100 by their father. He married a widow, acquiring her Oxfordshire estate. In about 1582 he went on his first foreign mission which appears to have been a trade venture to Russia. In 1588 he served as a volunteer during the Armada invasion scare, and was member for Woodstock in the Parliaments of 1589, 1593 and 1598. Lee's personal fortunes prospered when, in 1589, he was able for a second time to marry a rich

widow. He was knighted in 1600 and entrusted with a government mission to Boris Godunov, Tsar of Russia, to discuss a marriage alliance between the Tsar's son and an English bride. Lee was also employed by the Muscovy Company. He returned through Livonia and Germany, representing Queen Elizabeth at the baptism of the Duke of Sweden's son, but was the poorer for the expedition, as he could not get his expenses from the Queen or from the Company. Lee brought presents, including manuscripts, from Russia for the new Bodleian Library at Oxford (v. *Bodley*). In 1604 he again sat in the Commons for Woodstock, but trouble over his lands and the burden of poverty over-taxed his health. Upon his death the Crown confiscated his estates. To the Bodleian Sir Richard left a rare cloak of "Tartar lamb", presented to him by Boris Godunov. The cloak was seen, infrequently, until the 1640s but disappeared during the Civil War.

Ibid.

LEE, Thomas (1552/3–1601), soldier, "Captain Lee": cousin of Henry and Richard Lee (*supra*). Most of his military experience was gained in Ireland; he probably served there originally in 1573–6 under the first Earl of Essex, his kinsman. Lee saved most of Kildare from the rebels in 1581, married a widow with land there and settled in Ireland, acquiring a reputation for brawling and looting, and falling foul of Ormonde (q.v.). This feud embroiled him with the government for the rest of his life. Lee, often in debt, was helped by his cousin, Sir Henry. After serving briefly in the Netherlands, he was employed again in Ireland in 1593, primarily to mediate with his old friend, Tyrone (q.v.). Lee's attitude towards Tyrone aroused suspicion in London: he published a book in England urging his fellow Englishmen to treat Tyrone and other Ulster landowners more wisely. In 1598 Lee was imprisoned in Dublin Castle on a charge of treason but his appeals to the Privy Council postponed action until his friend, the second Earl of Essex (q.v.), became Lord Deputy in April 1599, when Lee was released to negotiate again with Tyrone. Lee, still suspected of treason, returned to England with the disgraced Essex, found shelter with his cousin Henry at Woodstock, and tried to clear his name, Sir Henry standing surety for him and pleading for his pardon. Thomas Lee spent the winter of 1599–1600 writing another book, *The Discovery and Recovery of Ireland* (unpublished), tactfully dedicated to Robert Cecil. Lee might have been saved but for his desperate role in Essex's rebellion (1601). Having first offered to kill Essex for the government, he joined the other rebels attending the performance of *Richard II* at the Globe on 7 February. Five days later he was again prepared to betray the plot, although in the late afternoon he was proposing to kidnap the Queen as hostage for Essex's life. That evening (12th February) he went to the Privy Chamber but nobody accompanied him and he was easily arrested. After a speedy trial, he was executed on 17th February.

Ibid.

LEGGE, Thomas (1535–1607), dramatist and academic: came from a Norwich family, entering Corpus Christi College, Cambridge, in 1552. Five years later he became a Bachelor of Arts and Fellow of Trinity, in 1568 a Fellow of Jesus, and Master of Caius College in 1573, taking his doctorate of laws two years later. As Master of Caius he was accused of encouraging Catholicism and the Fellows called him "an horrible papist". This did not prevent his election as Vice-Chancellor in 1593. Meres (q.v.), writing in 1597–8, included Legge among the "best for tragedy". Legge's reputation rests on *Richardus Tertius* (1580), a tragedy in Latin played at St John's College, Cambridge, before the Earl of Essex, and the *The Destruction of Jerusalem*, a play said to have been plagiarised before performance and no longer extant. *Ricardus Tertius* influenced Greene and Marlowe, and perhaps Shakespeare.

F. S. Boas, *University Drama in the Tudor Age* (1914)

LEICESTER, Lettice, Countess of (1540–1634): born Lettice Knollys, daughter of Sir Francis Knollys, Treasurer of the Household to Queen Elizabeth, and his wife Catherine (Carey) the Queen's cousin. Lettice was born at Rotherfield Greys, Oxfordshire. She married Walter Devereux, later first Earl of Essex, between 1560 and 1565. He obtained his earldom by favour of Leicester, but when Essex, then Earl Marshal of Ireland, died there in 1576 it was rumoured Leicester had poisoned him to marry Lettice. Leicester and Lettice were in fact married in 1578. Her four children by Essex were mainly brought up by the Earl and Countess of Huntingdon; the second son, Walter was killed at the siege of Rouen in 1591, but the other three lived to greater notoriety (v. *Robert, 2nd Earl of Essex, Dorothy Percy, Penelope Rich*). Her marriage to Leicester produced one son, who died by the age of four. After Leicester's death in September 1588, Lettice married Sir Christopher Blount (q.v.) before the end of the year. He was a friend of her elder son. Christopher Blount was involved in Essex's conspiracy of 1601 and executed with his leader. After this final tragedy Lettice lived a retired life, mostly at Drayton Bassett in Staffordshire; she is buried in St Mary's

Church, Warwick, near Leicester's tomb.

E. W. Dormer, "Lettice Knollys", *Berks, Archaeological Journal*, Vol. 39, No. 1 (1935)

LEICESTER, Robert Dudley, Earl of (1532–88), soldier and courtier: born in London, the fifth son of the Duke of Northumberland (executed in 1553). As Lord Robert Dudley he married, in June 1550, Amy Robsart from Norfolk, the county for which he was returned as M.P.

Robert Dudley, Earl of Leicester

in 1553. He was sentenced to death and imprisoned in the Tower at the start of Mary's reign, as he was held to have been an accomplice of his father in seeking to put Lady Jane Grey on the throne. In October 1554 he was freed and served in the army against the French. Upon Elizabeth's accession he was appointed Master of the Horse, created a Knight of the Garter and a Privy Councillor. By 1559 the Spanish ambassador and other observers believed the Queen infatuated with Robert Dudley. The death of his wife in a fall at Cumnor in September 1560 started wild rumours that she had been murdered so that her husband "might be King", but there is no evidence her death was anything but accidental. The Queen was generous to Leicester (as he became in 1564) and he frequently entertained her, most notably at Kenilworth in July 1575. From 1569 onwards he intrigued against Burghley and the Cecil faction, and he identified himself with the Puritans against the established clergy. This religious attitude of Leicester was out of character, for he was a considerable patron of actors, Lord Leicester's Men (with James Burbage, q.v., among them) receiving a Royal Patent as early as May 1574. Marriage to Lettice, the widowed Countess of Essex, in 1578 temporarily offended the Queen, and there was widespread prejudice against him, not least because of his management of county elections so as to secure a party of his own in the Commons. In 1585–6 he commanded the English forces in the Netherlands without great success, although the heroic death of his nephew, Philip Sidney (q.v.) at Zutphen made the campaign memorable. A second spell of warfare in the Netherlands in 1587 was equally ineffectual, perhaps because his health was beginning to fail. In 1588 he commanded the camp at Tilbury, as "Captain-General of the Queen's armies and companies" awaiting a Spanish invasion. At the end of August he set out for Buxton to take the waters but, at his house at Cornbury in Oxfordshire, he developed a sudden fever and died there on 4 September. He is buried in the Beauchamp Chapel of St Mary's Church, Warwick.

E. Jenkins, *Elizabeth and Leicester* (1961)
E. Rosenberg, *Leicester, Patron of Letters* (1955)
R. B. Wernham, "Elizabethan War Aims and Strategy", J. Hurstfield, ed., *Elizabethan Government and Society* (1961)

LEVESON, William (fl. 1580–1612), merchant: a member of the Mercers'

Company from about 1580, later becoming a Merchant Adventurer and shareholder in the Muscovy Company. He was out of favour in 1595, when he was briefly imprisoned for insulting behaviour, but two years later he was lending money to the Queen to help finance military operations in France and by 1599 he was a churchwarden of St Mary's, Aldermanbury (a church in which one of the other churchwardens was Condell (q.v.) and Heminges (q.v.) was a sidesman). Leveson became one of the nominal trustees of the Globe in February 1599. Two years later he received royal backing in support of his application to acquire the lease of a Cheapside tavern, the Queen commending his loyalty when Essex (q.v.) and his supporters were seeking to win the support of the City of London in January 1601. Under James I Leveson was especially identified with the plantation of Virginia, seeking to raise money for the Virginia Company in 1607 and in June 1612 supervising the running of a City lottery, under royal patronage, for the Virginian enterprise. In the winter of 1611–12 Leveson became a founder-member of the North-West Passage Company.

L. Hotson, *I, William Shakespeare* (1937)

LINCOLN, Elizabeth, Countess of (?1570–?): born Elizabeth Knyvett, one of the daughters of Sir Henry Knyvett of Wiltshire (v. *Catherine Howard, Countess of Suffolk*). She married Thomas Clinton, heir to the Earl of Lincoln, in 1584. He died in 1619, having been Earl himself for only three years. Elizabeth survived him long enough to write *The Countess of Lincoln's Nursery* (1622) a treatise advocating breast-feeding instead of the employment of wet nurses by ladies of quality. Her arguments were mainly religious ones.

LINCOLN, Henry Clinton, second Earl of (?1541–1616), patron of actors: son of Edward Clinton, first Earl, and his second wife. He was knighted at Queen Mary's coronation (1553), was M.P. for Lincolnshire (1571) and went with his father on his mission to conclude the Treaty of Blois with France (1572). Clinton became Earl of Lincoln in 1585. He was known as a spendthrift and a tyrant to the gentry of Lincolnshire. He was one of the lords presiding at the trials of Mary, Queen of Scots (1586), Arundel (1589) and Essex (1601). In 1596 he was sent on an abortive diplomatic mission to Hesse. Lincoln was married twice: before 1557 to Catherine Hastings, daughter of the second Earl of Huntingdon, and after 1586 to Elizabeth, widow of the Honourable William Norreys. He continued to patronise the company of actors, Lord Clinton's or the Earl of Lincoln's Men, started by his father. From 1572 to 1575 they were led by Lawrence Dutton (q.v.) and played at Court, but appeared in the provinces after 1599.

LING, Nicholas (?–?1610), printer, bookseller: son of John Lyng, parchment-maker, of Norwich. He was apprenticed to Henry Bynneman (q.v.), printer, for eight years from 1570 and became a freeman of the Stationers' Company in 1579. He had several shops in London: "The Mermaid", St Paul's Churchyard (1580–3), at different doors of St Paul's (1584–97), and in St Dunstan's Churchyard, Fleet Street (1600–7). Ling published very little until 1590, then joined with other printers in various ventures, including *England's Parnassus* (1600). In 1597 he edited another anthology, *Politeuphuia, Wits Commonwealth* and wrote the Dedication and Preface to it himself. Ling and John Trundell together were responsible for the First Quarto *Hamlet* (1603) and Ling for the Second Quarto (1604). In 1607 he acquired more Shakespeare copyrights from Cuthbert Burby, *Loves' Labour Lost, Romeo and Juliet* and the old *Taming of a Shrew*. Of these Ling published only *Shrew* and assigned the other copyrights to John Smethwick (w.v.).

LOBEL, Mathias de (1538–1616), naturalist: born at Lille, travelling widely as a young man and not entering the University of Montpellier until he was twenty-seven. He made many visits to England, the earliest being in 1565. His principal work, a detailed collection of botanical observations, was published in 1576. From 1579 to 1584 he was one of William the Silent's physicians. He became a friend of Lord Zouche (q.v.) whom he accompanied on a visit to Denmark in 1598, subsequently spending most of his later years in England; Lobel — who gave his name to the genus of plants known as "Lobelia" — directed the planting of Zouche's "physick garden" at Hackney as well as serving James I both as a botanist and a physician. The King formally appointed him "Botanicus Regius" in 1607, and he was honoured by the College of Physicians in 1614. His son, Paul, was brother-in-law to the principal royal physician, Mayerne, and practised as an apothecary in Lime Street, London, during James I's reign, often preparing medicines prescribed by Mayerne for the celebrities imprisoned in the Tower (including Overbury, q.v.); but there was no suggestion that Paul de Lobel ever substituted poison for the prescribed drugs. Mathias de Lobel himself died while staying at Highgate.

LODGE, Thomas (1558–1625), dramatist, novelist, explorer, physician: son of Sir Thomas Lodge, a Lord Mayor of London, educated at Merchant Taylors' School and Trinity College, Oxford (1573–7) entering Lincoln's Inn a year later. Although he wrote his *Defence of Plays* (1581) in reply to

Gosson (q.v.), Lodge's principal literary works were novels, euphuistic in style. Best known of them were *Rosalynde* (1590), source for the plot of *As You Like It*, and *A Margarite of America* (1596). He wrote the earliest romantic poem on a classical subject, *Scylla's Metamorphosis* (1589) and a tragedy on the lives of Marius and Sulla, *Wounds of Civil War* (c. 1588), which was played by the Admiral's Men. With Robert Greene (q.v.), he collaborated on *A Looking Glass for London*, a kind of morality play exposing the vices of the town. This satirical vein Lodge expressed in verse satires and epistles in Horatian style, *A Fig for Momus* (1595), and a tract, *Wit's Misery and the World's Madness* (1596). He also translated Josephus and Seneca, wrote a *Treatise on the Plague* (1603) and published a collection of lyric poems, songs and sonnets, *Phillis* (1593). This literary versatility was matched by the varied character of his life. Early in his career his free mode of expression made him suspect to the Privy Council and in 1581 he was ordered to report regularly to the Council. In 1588 he went on a voyage to the Canaries and in 1591 to South America. His conversion to Roman Catholicism led to exile; he took a medical degree at Avignon and, from 1602, practised as a doctor. In 1610 he returned to England. Later he practised medicine in the Netherlands, but died in London.

E. K. C., *E.S.*
C. J. Sisson, ed., *Thomas Lodge and Other Elizabethans* (1966)

LOK, Michael (?1532–1615?), trader, translator: youngest son of Sir William Lok, merchant and Alderman of London. Lok left school at thirteen and travelled in France and Flanders. In 1552 he was in Spain and by 1576 had visited most of Europe and the Middle East, captaining his own ship. He was an excellent linguist, and a student of history. On returning to

England he was the main instigator of Frobisher's (q.v.) expedition to find the North-West Passage in 1576. Next year he became a governor of the Cathay Company but Frobisher's failure to reach China led to Lok's financial ruin. He claimed to have spent £7,500 in supplies and equipment for the expedition and in 1579 petitioned the Privy Council for relief. Lok, who had fifteen children to support, was sued for debt and spent part of 1581 in the Fleet Prison; he was still being pursued by the liabilities of the Cathay Company in 1614. Lok obtained a position with the Levant Company, as consul in Aleppo in 1592. The contract was for four years, but the company cancelled it after two. In 1613 Lok published his translation of part of Peter Martyr's *De Orbe Novo* as *The History of the West Indies*.

LOPEZ, Roderigo (fl. 1559–d. 1594), physician: born in Portugal, a member of a Jewish family. He fled from Portugal in 1579 to escape the Inquisition and settled in London, practising as a doctor and serving as house physician at St Bartholomew's Hospital until 1580. By then he had acquired a good reputation as a dietician and a wise counsellor, who included Walsingham and Leicester among his patients. In 1586 he was appointed chief physician to Queen Elizabeth. At Court he championed the cause of the Portuguese pretender, Antonio Perez, but subsequently broke with him and quarrelled with Perez's powerful champion, Essex (q.v.), against whose policy and conduct he rashly spoke out. In January 1594 Essex claimed to have discovered a conspiracy in which Lopez was to poison the Queen. Lopez was examined by Burghley, Robert Cecil and Essex, but no incriminating evidence was found. Under torture some of Antonio Perez's servants claimed that Lopez had sought to involve them in a plot to kill both the Portuguese claimant and the Queen. Essex alleged that Lopez received money from Philip II, and the doctor was tried and condemned to death. For three months the Queen remained unconvinced of his guilt, but he was hanged, drawn and quartered at Tyburn on 7 June 1594. There is little doubt Lopez suffered from the latent anti-Jewish feeling in Elizabethan England which was brought into the open by the alleged conspiracy. Shakespeare may have drawn Shylock in *The Merchant of Venice* (entered in the Stationers' Register 1598) from Lopez.

S. Lee, "The Original of Shylock", *Gentleman's Magazine*, CCXLVI (1880)
G. B. Harrison, *Life and Death of Robert Devereux* (1937)

LOWIN, John (1576–1653), actor: a London carpenter's son, apprenticed to a goldsmith 1593–1601. He turned actor as

John Lowin

soon as he was free, playing with Worcester's Men in 1602. By June 1603 he was one of the King's Men, becoming the most famous member of the company in the post-Shakespeare period. Lowin was of enormous stature and played mainly hearty heroes or bluff and gruff villains. He was the original Bosola in *The Duchess of Malfi*, and may have been Shakespeare's Henry VIII: the pioneer theatrical historian, John Downes (writing in 1708) said that his contemporary Betterton learnt the part of Henry VIII from Davenant "who had it from old Mr Lowin, that had his instructions from Mr Shakespeare himself". Lowin's name is in all the actors' lists for the King's Men until the closing of theatres in 1642, including the First Folio list. By 1628 Lowin and Joseph Taylor (q.v.) were joint payees for the company with John Heminges (q.v.). They succeeded Heminges as managers after his death (1630) and purchased his Globe and Blackfriars shares (each having one-eighth of either theatre). After spending most of his life in Southwark, Lowin retired to keep the Three Pigeons Inn at Brentford in old age.

G. E. B.

LUCAS, Thomas (fl. 1604–19), lawyer resident in Stratford: admitted to Gray's Inn in June 1604. He became unpopular in Stratford, with a reputation for belligerency, and in 1609 he made an affidavit in a case of complaint against the haberdasher, Gilbert Shakespeare (q.v.). In 1617 his fellow lawyer, Francis Collins (q.v.), alleged in his will that Lucas had combined with the Vicar, John Rogers (q.v.), to defraud the poor of Stratford of two houses. Scurrilous verses current after Rogers' replacement as Vicar in 1619 accused Lucas of having betrayed him. Shakespeare and Thomas Greene (q.v.) employed Lucas as their lawyer over the Welcombe enclosure suits of 1614.

M. E.

LUCY, Thomas I (1532–1600), Warwickshire landowner: the Lucy family seat was at Charlecote, four miles east of Stratford, the legendary scene of Shakespeare's deer poaching episode. Thomas Lucy was an ardent Protestant, who had John Foxe as his tutor for a year. At the age of fourteen his father arranged for him to marry the thirteen-year-old heiress, Joyce Acton, and her wealth enabled him in 1558 to pull down his house at Charlecote and build there the earliest Elizabethan mansion in the county. Here he was knighted by Leicester in 1565 and here, too, Queen Elizabeth stayed in 1572. Sir Thomas, who had served as a Member of Parliament for Warwickshire in 1571, was Deputy Lieutenant in the county and a Justice of the Peace. He lived in some style, keeping forty servants, including for a time Abraham Sturley (q.v.). In 1583 he was particularly active in raiding local Roman Catholic houses and making arrests, after the affair of John Somerville (q.v.), but he found time next year to arbitrate with Sir Fulke Greville in a lawsuit between one of his servants and Shakespeare's close friend, Hamnet Sadler. Sir Thomas died in 1600 at a time of scandal in his household, for his granddaughter Elizabeth Aston had eloped with a man-servant. His funeral was a grand affair, testimony to his eminence; it was arranged by the Clarenceux King of Arms (William Camden, q.v.) and attended by Lancaster and Windsor Heralds.

The legend of Shakespeare's deer poaching from Charlecote has persisted from the early eighteenth century, and was thought to be the reason for his leaving Stratford. Charlecote was, in fact, not emparked until after 1618, but Stratford poachers took rabbits and small game from the "warren" there and Sir Thomas employed keepers. From 1584 onwards he also had use of Fulbrook Park, across the Avon,

155

although the family did not buy it until 1615. Significantly, in 1584 Sir Thomas tried to secure the passage of a bill through Parliament which would have made poaching a felony. Justice Shallow in *The Merry Wives of Windsor* may owe something to Sir Thomas Lucy, at least to his pride in the "luces" embodied in his coat of arms (but v. *William Gardiner*).

M. E.
S. S.
A. Fairfax-Lucy, *Charlecote and the Lucys* (1958)

LUCY, Thomas II (1551—1605), Warwickshire landowner, son of the first Sir Thomas. Until he inherited Charlecote in 1600, he lived mainly in Gloucestershire and London. From 1574 to 1580 he was married to Dorothy Arnold, who owned considerable estates in Gloucestershire and Monmouthshire over which he spent much time in litigation. On her death he married Constance Kingsmill, heiress to £50,000 and a ward of Sir Francis Walsingham. He was knighted in 1592 and served as Deputy Lieutenant and Sheriff of Warwickshire, 1601—5. The second Sir Thomas was generally reckoned a bad landlord, greatly reducing the value of the Arnold property in Gloucestershire.

Ibid.

LUCY, Thomas III (1585—1640), landowner: son of the second Sir Thomas, inheriting Charlecote in 1605 and spending most of his later life there. He matriculated at Magdalen College, Oxford in 1601 and there became friendly with Edward Herbert (q.v.). Lucy entered Lincoln's Inn in 1602 and frequented the Herberts' circle in London, meeting John Donne and his own future wife, Alice Spencer, who was niece by marriage to Lord Ellesmere, the Lord Chancellor (Thomas Egerton, q.v.). Lucy and Herbert

toured France together in 1608—9, being shipwrecked on their way home. Soon afterwards Lucy married Alice Spencer, by whom he had fourteen children, and settled down at Charlecote. He was a Justice of the Peace, Member of Parliament for Warwickshire in 1614, 1621 and possibly 1628—9, County Sheriff and (from 1632) Recorder of Stratford. Sir Thomas — he was knighted in 1609 — brought a Star Chamber action against deer poachers in his park at Sutton, Worcestershire in 1610, bought the estate and park of Fulbrooke near Stratford in 1615, and was granted a licence to empark Charlecote in 1618. These activities, perhaps wrongly attributed to his grandfather, helped associate the Lucy family with the legend of Shakespeare's poaching. Another tradition makes this third Sir Thomas a friend of Shakespeare in his later years at Stratford. Sir Thomas was a cultured man; he entertained players in 1633, and his tomb in Charlecote Church (reputedly by a pupil of Bernini) depicts shelves of his favourite books.

M. E.
A. Fairfax-Lucy, *Charlecote and the Lucys* (1958)

LUMLEY, John (c. 1534—1609), patron of learning and artistic connoisseur: born at Thwing in Yorkshire and educated at Queen's College, Cambridge, where he matriculated in 1549, two years after becoming the second Baron Lumley. Much of his considerable wealth came from coal; there were half a dozen small pits in the Lumley parkland around Chester-le-Street and other pits were leased elsewhere on his Durham properties. Although he spent freely on embellishing Lumley Castle, in Durham, he came south each year to London and Surrey and in 1593 interested himself in the Chichester election. In general, however, Lumley avoided political entanglement, especially after a term of imprisonment in 1569 when he was suspected of involvement in the Ridolfi Plot. He inherited the former royal palace at Nonsuch from his father-in-law, the 12th Earl of Arundel, but in 1592 he tactfully presented the palace to the Queen, who had long coveted it. Elizabeth complimented Lumley on having "garnished and replenished" the most ornate of her father's palaces. Lumley duly received property elsewhere. From 1559 until his death he was High Steward of Oxford University. In 1583 he established the Lumleian lectures at the College of Physicians and he was a sponsor of the lectures on mathematics given by Hood (q.v.) in Leadenhall. Lumley had a collection of over 250 pictures and a remarkable library, almost entirely in Latin. In 1603 he entertained James I at Lumley Castle on the king's journey south from Edinburgh and he subsequently became one of the many tutors of Prince Henry (q.v.), who on Lumley's death purchased his library out of the privy purse. Lumley was an active member of the original Elizabethan Society of Antiquaries.

LYLY, John (?1554–1606), novelist and dramatist: his family came originally from Hampshire, his grandfather being a High Master of St Paul's School and his father a diocesan official in Canterbury. Lyly was educated at Magdalen College, Oxford, (1571–3) and, through Burghley's influence, hoped to gain a Fellowship. When he failed to do so he went to London, living in the Savoy and writing *Euphues, the Anatomy of Wit* in 1578. His ornate, antithetical style proved most influential, and the book became the first in a line of romantic "euphuistic" novels. By 1580 Lyly was serving the Earl of Oxford (q.v.), later managing a company of boy actors under Oxford's name, really a combination of Paul's Boys and the

Children of the Chapel Royal. From 1583 to 1584 Lyly leased the Blackfriars theatre, and there the boys began to play his sophisticated and witty comedies which, although they included lyrics, were the first to be written in prose. As Lyly was in prison for debt in July 1584, this venture probably failed, but he continued to turn out plays for Paul's Boys. Between 1583 and 1590 he wrote six comedies: *Campaspe* and *Sappho and Phao* for the combined company; and for Paul's *Galathea, Endymion, Midas, Love's Metamorphosis*, and an interlude, *Mother Bombie*. His last play, *The Woman in the Moon*, was possibly for a new company. Together with Thomas Nashe (q.v.) Lyly wrote some of the retorts to the Martin Marprelate pamphlets of 1589–90. He sat in the Parliaments of 1589, 1593, 1598 and 1601, but he was really waiting for preferment at Court, hoping for the Mastership of the Revels. When in 1597 the reversion of that office went to George Buck (q.v.), Lyly wrote complaining to the Queen and Robert Cecil. He may have acquired some reward after Essex's disgrace in 1601, when many offices at Court became vacant.

G. K. Hunter, *John Lyly, the Humorist as Courtier* (1962)

M

MABBE, James (1572–?1642), poet, translator: born in Surrey, son of James Mabbe and grandson of a jeweller, according to Anthony à Wood. Mabbe was educated at Magdalen College, Oxford (1588–94) and remained a Fellow from 1594 to 1633. He was University Proctor in 1606 and Bursar of Magdalen six times before 1630. From 1611 to 1613 he was secretary to Sir John Digby, ambassador to Spain. On his return Mabbe became a lay prebendary of Wells Cathedral, Somerset. He eventually left Oxford to live with his friend Sir John Strangeways of Abbotsbury, Dorset, and is presumed to have died there. His most famous works were translations from Spanish, *Celestina or the Spanish Bawd* (1631) by Ferdinando de Rojas being the most popular. He also translated some Cervantes. At Oxford Mabbe became friendly with another Spanish expert, Leonard Digges (q.v.). This fact supports the generally accepted identification of Mabbe as "I.M." who, like Digges, contributed laudatory verses to the First Folio of Shakespeare's plays. Most of Mabbe's original verse was of this kind. His first printed poem was in Latin, a preface to the Italian dictionary of John Florio (q.v.) containing the anagram "ori fons alieno" (source for foreign speech) a transposition of "Ioannes Florio".

J. Mabbe, *Celestina*, ed., J. Fitzmaurice Kelly (1894)

MAINWARING, Arthur (fl. 1614–15), steward to Lord Ellesmere: the son of Sir George Mannering of Ightfield, Shropshire, and Anne More, whose sister Elizabeth became second wife to the Lord Chancellor, Lord Ellesmere (Thomas Egerton, q.v.). Mainwaring had bought land in Welcombe, Stratford-upon-Avon, and with his cousin by marriage, Replingham

(q.v.), was trying in 1614 to enclose it. This activity brought him into conflict with Shakespeare and the Town Council. Mainwaring, through Replingham, made an agreement on 28 October 1614 to compensate Shakespeare, giving up the enclosure scheme altogether in 1615, when Chief Justice Coke ruled against it.

MANNERS, Francis (1578–1632), sixth Earl of Rutland;
MANNERS, Roger (1576–1612), fifth Earl of Rutland; see RUTLAND, Earls of.

MANNINGHAM, John (?1576–1622), diarist: son of Robert Manningham of Fen Drayton, Cambridgeshire, but adopted by a wealthy relation, Richard Manningham of East Malling, Kent. He was educated at Magdalen College, Oxford (B.A., 1596), entered the Middle Temple in 1598 and was called to the Bar in 1605. His room mate at the Middle Temple was Edward Curle, son of Robert Cecil's servant, who had sufficient influence to obtain a minor official post for Manningham. In 1607 Manningham married his friend's sister, Anne Curle, by whom he had three sons and three daughters. From 1612, when he inherited the Kentish estate of his "father in love" (as he called him), he spent the rest of his life as a country gentleman. Manningham kept a diary while a law student, from 1602 to 1603. On 2 February 1602 he saw Shakespeare's *Twelfth Night* performed at the Middle Temple and was much struck by the joke played on Malvolio. A few weeks later (13 March) he entered a scurrilous anecdote, current earlier, about Shakespeare and Richard Burbage (q.v.): after a performance of *Richard III*, Shakespeare anticipated his friend in the embraces of one of Burbage's female fans, saying

"William the Conqueror was before Richard III." Manningham's diary also has an account of the death of Queen Elizabeth for, thanks to a friendship with one of her chaplains, Manningham was at Richmond on 23 March 1603, where he gathered news of the Queen's condition on the day before she died. The diary ends soon after his account of James I's accession. It was discovered among the Harleian manuscripts at the British Museum by J. Payne Collier in 1831. Collier's penchant for forgery led to doubts about the authenticity of the Shakespearian parts of the diary, but they are now generally accepted.

J. Bruce, ed., *Diary of John Manningham* (1868)
S. Race, "Manningham's Diary", *Notes and Queries*, 199 (1954)

MARKHAM, Gervase (1568–1637), soldier and writer: the third son of Robert Markham, from Nottinghamshire. He was a soldier and horseman, said to have imported the first Arab horse into England. After his military career, Markham wrote mainly on horses and horsemanship. He also produced *A Way to Get Wealth* (1631–8), containing separate treatises on animal husbandry, country sports, agriculture, horticulture and housewifery. Markham wrote religious poetry and sonnets, and at least one play, *The Dumb Knight* (1607–8), for the Children of the Revels; he may have written plays as early as 1596–7 for the Admiral's Men. Markham has been identified as the original of Armado in Shakespeare's *Love's Labour's Lost*. He has also been considered a possible candidate for the "rival poet" of the Sonnets, largely because his poem on the sinking of the *Revenge* included in the introduction a sonnet to the Earl of Southampton. It has been argued by the American scholar, Dr C.W. Wallace, that there were at least two Markhams, the dramatist, if not the poet, being distinct from the Nottinghamshire writer on horses.

G. E. B.

MARKHAM, Mary (1570–1650) see CUTPURSE, Moll

MARLOWE, Christopher (1564–93), poet and dramatist; son of a Canterbury cobbler who was head of a feckless and turbulent family, often involved with the law. Marlowe was educated at King's School, Canterbury, from 1578/9 to 1580, at the cost of £1 a quarter. He matriculated at Corpus Christi College, Cambridge in December 1580, being elected to a Matthew Parker Scholarship. In 1587 he left Cambridge. The University authorities at first refused to allow him to take his Master of Arts degree on the grounds that, as he spent some time in Rheims, he had not kept the necessary terms of residence, but the Privy Council intervened, declaring Marlowe had been employed "in matters touching the benefit of his country". Marlowe's later connections with the Walsingham family have prompted suggestions that he was engaged in espionage at the English seminary in Rheims. From 1587 until his death Marlowe's known profession was a dramatist's, his plays being performed by the Lord Admiral's company (*Tamburlaine*, 1587/8, *Jew of Malta*, 1592, *Faustus* and *Edward II*, 1593). He also wrote poems and translated Ovid and Lucan. In 1589 he was arrested after a street fight (v. *Thomas Watson*), and three years later bound over to keep the peace following a fracas in Canterbury. This rowdy private life culminated in a visit to a tavern in Deptford on 30 May 1593 when he was accompanied by Nicholas Skeres, Robert Poley and Ingram Frizer. After supper there was a dispute over the bill: Marlowe attacked Frizer, and in the struggle was killed, stabbed above the right eye according to the report of the inquest. Marlowe was at the time a guest of Thomas Walsingham (q.v.) in Chiselhurst, Frizer was one of Walsingham's servants and Poley a spy in Francis Walsingham's pay. Shortly before his death Marlowe had appeared before the *Privy Council (v. Kyd)*, and was accused posthumously by various writers of atheism and blasphemy. Since the middle of the nineteenth century he has also been regarded as a possible "rival poet" in Shakespeare's Sonnets. There has been some support for the theory that Marlowe was not killed in the tavern brawl, but survived at least until the end of the year, and died of natural causes. He has also been credited with the authorship of Shakespeare's plays.

L. Hotson, *The Death of Christopher Marlowe* (1925)
A. L. Rowse, *Christopher Marlowe* (1964)
"Marlowe and Canterbury", *Times Literary Supplement* (13 February 1964)

MARSTON, John (1575/6–1634), satirist and dramatist: son of a Shropshire lawyer, living in Coventry, and an Italian mother. He was educated at Brasenose College, Oxford (1592–4), entering the Middle Temple in order to become a lawyer as his father wished. Soon, however, he began writing: his erotic and satirical poems *The Metamorphosis of Pygmalion's Image* and *The Scourge of Villainy* were both published in 1598 under the pseudonym W. Kinsayder. He also wrote plays for the Admiral's Men until 1599, and after that date for Paul's Boys. Marston participated in the "War of Theatres" against Jonson (q.v.) and his circle, attacking Jonson in *Jack Drum's Entertainment* (now lost) and *What You Will* (1601), as well as collaborating with Dekker in *Satiromastix* (1601). Jonson hit back in *The Poetaster* of 1601 when Marston is portrayed as "Crispinus", a character

ridiculed for his writing and appearance — red hair and little legs. By 1604 Marston was one of the managers of the Children of the Revels, for whom he wrote his remaining plays, and he was reconciled to Jonson. The two dramatists, with Chapman (q.v.) were in trouble for their allegedly anti-Scottish comedy *Eastward Ho!* of 1605 but Marston escaped the imprisonment imposed on his colleagues. By 1608 he was, however, in Newgate Prison, having probably offended James I with a play now lost. He abandoned the stage, leaving a last tragedy, *The Insatiate Countess*, unfinished. His plays were mainly satirical comedies, but he also wrote tragedies of the popular "revenge" type and in his *The Malcontent* of 1604 he succeeded in combining the revenge theme with satire. His style is rough and energetic, his work moral in purpose and obscene at the same time. He married Mary Wilkes, daughter of a chaplain to the King. Jonson once declared that Marston wrote Wilkes's sermons, while Wilkes wrote his son-in-law's comedies. In his late thirties Marston himself was ordained, for by 1616 he was incumbent of the parish of Christchurch, Hampshire, where he remained until he resigned the living in 1631. He then returned to London, dying in the parish of Aldermanbury.

E. K. C., *E.S.*

MASSINGER, Philip (1583–1640), dramatist: born in Salisbury, the son of Arthur Massinger, confidential servant to Henry Herbert, second Earl of Pembroke (q.v.). He entered St Alban Hall, Oxford, but left in 1606 without a degree, becoming a Roman Catholic and thereby losing the interest of the Herbert family until the time of the fourth Earl, who was his patron in the 1630s. Massinger may not have written plays before 1616, but is thought to have contributed to Shakespeare's *Henry VIII* and *The Two Noble Kinsmen* (v. *Fletcher*). He is known to have collaborated with Dekker, Fletcher and Nathan Field (qq.v.); his own unaided work begins with the tragedy *Duke of Milan* (1623) and was mostly romantic drama or tragedy. His most famous play, however, is the comedy *A New Way to Pay old Debts* (published 1633), in which the character of "Sir Giles Overreach" was modelled on the unpopular monopolist, Mompesson (q.v.). Massinger's plays contain attacks on the foreign policy of Buckingham (q.v.) and a certain nostalgia for the Tudor age.

MATHEW, Tobias (1546–1628), Archbishop of York: of Welsh descent, son of John Mathew of Herefordshire. He went to school at Wells, entered University College, Oxford in 1559, but transferred to Christ Church for his B.A. (1564). At the age of twenty, he disputed before Queen Elizabeth in St Mary's Church, Oxford, and, although he took the side of elective monarchy, his wit and slender good looks so impressed her that his advancement was rapid. He was Public Orator at twenty-three, President of St John's College at twenty-six, Dean of Christ Church at thirty and Vice-Chancellor at thirty-three (1579). Mathew's wife, although more inclined to Puritanism than himself, must have helped his rise in the Church. She was Frances Parker, widowed daughter-in-law of Archbishop Parker, and one of five daughters of the Bishop of Chichester, all of whom married bishops. Mathew was chaplain to the Queen and held various livings and cathedral canonries along with his University posts before becoming successively Dean (1583) and Bishop (1595) of Durham. He took a severe line against recusants in the north, but was generous to "Church papists" (those who attended without receiving communion). Mathew kept up his preaching along with

other episcopal duties. He is said to have preached 1,992 sermons in his life, and sometimes confirmed over 500 candidates at once and had to take to his bed afterwards. His contemporaries described him as always cheerful, without loss of dignity. Mathew became Archbishop of York in 1606. His later life was less happy, as a result of his son's recusancy (*infra*). His letter refuting the views of Edmund Campion was published posthumously (1638). He is buried in York Minster.

D. Mathew, *Sir Tobie Mathew* (1950)

MATHEW, Tobie (1577–1655), translator and diplomat: born in Oxford, the son of Dean Tobias Mathew (*supra*). He studied at Christ Church (1590–4), showing brilliance as a disputant and orator, but did not enter Gray's Inn until 1599. There he met Francis Bacon (q.v.), who became a great friend, trying to advance Mathew's career by securing his election as M.P. for Newport, Cornwall, in 1601 and for St Albans in 1604. Mathew, however, was uninterested in public affairs and their friendship was more concerned with literary matters, Bacon often consulting him over his writings. He was permitted to travel abroad (1604–7) and visited Florence and Rome where he met Parsons (q.v.) and other Jesuits. Conversion to Roman Catholicism was followed, either then or later, by ordination as a priest. On returning to England he was imprisoned for refusing to take the oath of allegiance to James I. Attempts by his father (now Archbishop of York), by Archbishop Bancroft (q.v.) and by Bacon to persuade him to recant were unsuccessful. Robert Cecil and Donne (q.v.) also visited Mathew in prison. By Cecil's kindness he was released and went into exile in 1608. He crossed to Brussels, where he met Rubens and helped him sell his paintings to Englishmen, and later went to Madrid,

Germany and Italy. Buckingham (q.v.) pleaded Mathew's case before James I and he was allowed to live in England from 1617 to 1619, mainly at Bacon's country home, Gorhambury. There he completed the first English translation of the *Confessions of St Augustine* (1620) as well as rendering Bacon's essays into Italian. Pamphlet allegations of pro-Spanish sympathies and too frequent visits to the Spanish ambassador, forced him abroad again (1619–21) but when the King sought a Spanish marriage for Prince Charles (q.v.), Mathew was restored to favour, knighted and sent to Madrid in 1623 to assist and safeguard Charles and Buckingham. He was not popular with Charles I — who once called him "little, pretty Tobie Mathew" — but he retained some influence with the King's ministers until 1635, largely through his friendship with the Countess of Carlisle (q.v.). When she began to cultivate Pym, Mathew retired to write the account of his conversion, finishing his work in 1640 shortly before Parliament called for his banishment. He died in the English college in Ghent. His *Character of the Countess of Carlisle*, edited by Donne's son, was published posthumously, with his letters (1660).

Ibid.

MATTHEWS, Augustine (fl. 1619–53), printer:

became a freeman of the Stationers' Company in 1615. His shops were the "Parsonage House", St Bride's Lane (1620) and Cow Lane, Holborn, where he was in partnership with the son of William White (q.v.). Matthews printed Shakespeare's *King John* for Thomas Dewe (1622). Although he mainly printed plays, he was caught reprinting a banned book, Dr Cole's *Holy Table*, and lost his press. He must have recovered it later, as he was still printing up to 1653.

MAYERNE, Theodore Turquet de (1573–1655), physician:

born at Mayerne, near Geneva, the son of a French Protestant antiquarian. He was educated at the University of Montpellier, where he took his medical doctorate in 1597. From

Sir Theodore Turquet de Mayerne

1600 to 1603 he was physician to King Henri IV in Paris, but his use of chemical remedies was considered too advanced by the Paris College of Physicians and he settled in England in 1606, being appointed Chief Physician to King James I in 1611. He was elected a Fellow of the College of Physicians in 1616 and knighted in 1624. His treatise on Prince Henry's typhoid in 1612 was a medical document of great value, as also were his practical precautions against the plague which he developed into a basic study, eventually published in 1644. Mayerne was one of the first physicians to make considerable use of chemical remedies, notably mercury. His activities aroused widespread interest among contemporary physicians.

MEADE, Jacob (?−1624), keeper of bears and theatre manager: lived in St Saviour's parish, Southwark. Meade was originally a waterman, but by 1599 he was Keeper of Bears in the Bear Garden on Bankside. In this capacity he became associated with Henslowe (q.v.), the two men contracting with a carpenter, Gilbert Katherens, to convert the Bear Garden into the Hope theatre in 1613. After Henslowe's death Meade and Alleyn (q.v.) kept the play-house going and made an agreement with Prince Charles's Men to play there (1616). Meade's "intemperate action" led to quarrels and the Prince's Men left the Hope in 1617, because Meade took their share of the profits. Two years of legal disputes led the Hope theatre to decline as a playhouse, Meade preferring bull and bear baiting. Technically, however, he remained Alleyn's deputy for the administration of the theatre and the animals.

E. K. C., *E.S.*
G. E. B.

MERES, Francis (1565−1647), author: born in Kesteven, Lincolnshire, educated at Pembroke College, Cambridge and (according to the title-page of his devotional work, *God's Arithmetic*) at Oxford too. He lived in Botolph Lane, London, during the late 1590s and is remembered as a pioneer literary critic through his *Palladis Tamia, Wit's Treasury* (1598), an anthology of quotations and maxims from many writers, together with a critical assessment of 125 English writers, musicians and painters, comparing "our English poets, with the Greek, Latin and Italian poets". Meres praises Shakespeare as "excellent" for comedy and tragedy, commends his gifts for bedecking the English language "in rare ornaments and resplendent habiliments", and mentions his poems, especially "sugared sonnets among his private friends". Meres regarded Sidney (q.v.) as "our rarest poet" and rated the "golden-mouthed" Drayton (q.v.) almost as high as Shakespeare as a tragedian. For most of his life Meres was resident Schoolmaster and Rector at Wing, Rutland.

MEYRICK, Gelly (?1556−1601), Essex's steward: oldest son of Rowland Meyrick, Bishop of Bangor. The Bishop died in 1565 and Meyrick was brought up on his mother's estate in Pembrokeshire. Here he entered the service of the local great landowner, Sir George Devereux, uncle of the second Earl of Essex. Like his kinsman, Roger Williams (q.v.), Meyrick joined Essex in his foreign campaigns, serving with him in Leicester's army in the Netherlands (1583−5), and accompanying him to Portugal (1589) and Normandy (1591). From about 1587 Meyrick was also steward of the Essex household, and in 1588 (and probably 1597) M.P. for Carmarthenshire. After Williams died (1592) Meyrick became Essex's most trusted Welsh servant, and was rewarded with lands, including Wigmore Castle, Herefordshire, which he made his main seat. He accompanied Essex to Cadiz, where he was knighted as Sir "William", and the Azores (1596−7), and served under him in Ireland (1599−1600). In January 1601 it was Meyrick's task to rally the Welsh soldiers for Essex's coup. As well as the Devereux clients Meyrick had his own following in Radnorshire (his wife's county) and Carmarthenshire. He billeted his Welshmen in London and on Saturday afternoon, 7 February 1601, went with other Essex supporters to see the Lord Chamberlain's Men play Shakespeare's *Richard II* at the Globe. Meyrick was chiefly responsible for procuring the performance, hoping to stir up the mob (v. *Augustine Phillips*). After the abortive rising on 8 February he organised the defence of Essex House. Meyrick was convicted and executed at Tyburn. His son was restored by James I, but his nephew, John Meyrick, followed the third Earl of Essex (q.v.) on to the Parliamentary side.

MIDDLETON, Hugh (?1560–1631), Member of Parliament, financier and entrepreneur: born at Galch Hill near Denbigh, where his father was Constable of the castle. He was apprenticed to a goldsmith, became a banker and was one of the backers of Ralegh (q.v.). From 1604 to 1629 he represented Denbigh in the House of Commons. His fame rests on his construction of the New River, a canal bringing water from springs near Ware in Hertfordshire to augment the supply of the growing population of London. Work on the thirty-nine mile long canal began in 1609 and was completed in 1613, the year in which Middleton's brother, Thomas, became Lord Mayor of London. Hugh Middleton was knighted as soon as the work was completed and created a baronet in 1622. In later years he retired to Denbigh, continuing to enjoy a comfortable profit from developing land and silver mines in Cardiganshire.

A. H. Dodd, "Mr Myddelton, the Merchant of Tower Street", *Elizabethan Government and Society*, eds., S. Bindoff and J. Hurstfield (1961)

MIDDLETON, Thomas (1580–1627), dramatist: came from a wealthy London family and was not "a bricklayer's son", as popular legend maintains. He matriculated at Queen's College, Oxford, in 1598, having already completed his first literary work, *The Wisdom of Solomon Paraphrased* (1597), and he may be the "T.M." of various verses and prose pamphlets. Possibly as early as 1599 (and certainly from 1602) he was writing plays for the Admiral's Men, later for Paul's Boys and other companies. His earliest plays, some of which were written in col-

laboration with Dekker, Drayton, Munday and Webster, are all lost. His most famous surviving plays are the comedies *A Chaste Maid in Cheapside* (1611), *A Fair Quarrel* (1617), written with William Rowley (q.v.), and the tragedies *The Changeling* (also with Rowley and published in 1623) and *The Witch* (written before 1627, but not published until 1778). The highly successful Middleton-Rowley partnership began about 1617 and wrote mainly for Prince Charles's Men. Middleton was sole author of the popular *A Game at Chess* (1624), a satire showing the English people's dislike of a Spanish marriage for Prince Charles (v. *Buckingham*). The political content of the play caused author and actors to be summoned before the Privy Council who imposed a ban on its further performance. In both his comedies and tragedies Middleton showed greater realism than some of his contemporary dramatists. *The Witch*, which may well have been performed by the King's Men, provides an interesting comparison with *Macbeth*; and the Hecate scenes in Macbeth are generally thought to be interpolations by Middleton. His other main activity was writing pageants for the City companies and in 1620 he was appointed Chronologer to the City of London. He lived and died at Newington Butts.

E. K. C., *E.S.*

MILDMAY, Sir Walter (?1520–89), Chancellor of the Exchequer: youngest son of Thomas Mildmay of Chelmsford, educated at Christ's College, Cambridge, but took no degree, and entered Gray's Inn in 1546. As a fervent Protestant, Mildmay prospered under Edward VI. He was knighted and made a Commissioner for the Revenue in 1547, and was a member of several other financial commissions. Such was his ability that his religion was no bar to continued service during Mary's reign, when he was Treasurer to the forces at Calais, but his most rapid advancement was under Elizabeth. He was made Treasurer of the Royal Household (1558), appointed to supervise the new coinage (1560) and in 1566 became Chancellor of the Exchequer. This post, subordinate to Burghley as Lord Treasurer, was as high as ill health and Calvinism would allow Mildmay to climb. In the Commons he represented Lostwithiel (1545), Lewes (1547), Maldon (1552), Peterborough (1553), and Northamptonshire (1557–89). Mildmay was the messenger who told Mary, Queen of Scots of her approaching trial and sat on the commission which tried her in 1586. His name was suggested as ambassador to Scotland, but his health was not good enough for the journey. Mildmay was a benefactor and refounder of Chelmsford School, and endowed scholarships at his old college, Christ's. In 1584 he founded Emmanuel College, Cambridge, to preserve Puritanism and provide learned preachers. Emmanuel kept its own customs in religion, with an unconsecrated chapel and seated communion. Mildmay added an unusual statute: no member was allowed to remain at the college for more than ten years after taking his Mastership. Emmanuel's preachers went further abroad than even their founder could have hoped; they provided much of the ministry of New England. Mildmay was a close friend of Burghley and Sir Francis Walsingham (q.v.), whose sister Mary he married.

MILLINGTON, Thomas (fl. 1583–1603), bookseller: son of William Millington, husbandman, of Oxfordshire. He was apprenticed to Henry Carre, stationer, for eight years from 1583 and became a freeman of the Stationers' Company in 1591. His shop was under St Peter's Cornhill (1593–1603). Millington published *The Contention of the Two Famous Houses of York and Lancaster* (1594, 1600)

and *The True Tragedy of Richard, Duke of York* (1595, 1600) the original versions of Shakespeare's *Henry VI*, parts 2 and 3. He also joined with Edward White to sell the first quarto of *Titus Andronicus* (1594) and with John Busby for *Henry V* (1600). At other times he was in partnership with Henry Gosson and Nicholas Ling. In 1602 he assigned his copyrights in *Titus* and *Henry VI* to Thomas Pavier (q.v.).

MILTON, John (c. 1563–1647), musical composer: probably born at Stanton St John, Oxfordshire. He came from a Roman Catholic family but was disinherited by his father for accepting Protestant beliefs and singing in the choir of Christ Church, Oxford. Subsequently Milton worked as a scrivener in Bread Street, Cheapside, modifying the spread-eagle device on the family coat-of-arms so as to provide a shop-sign. He was awarded a gold chain in recognition of his virtuosity in composing an *In nomine Domini* of forty parts. He is known to have composed fantasies for viols, four motets and a madrigal for six voices, "Fair Orian in the morn", included in the collection *The Triumphs of Oriana* which Morley (q.v.) edited in 1601. Milton's more famous son and namesake was born in Bread Street seven years later, inheriting his father's love for music.

E. H. Fellowes, *The English Madrigal Composers* (1948)

MOFFET (or MOUFET), Thomas (1553–1604), physician, entomologist, writer: son of Thomas Moffet, a London haberdasher, although Scottish in origin. He was educated for five years at Merchant Taylors' School, where he was a contemporary of Edmund Spenser, and entered Trinity College, Cambridge in 1569. He moved to Caius College, took his B.A. there (1573) but was expelled by Thomas Legge (q.v.), the Master, probably for Puritan views. After returning to Trinity for his M.A. (1576), Moffet graduated in medicine at Basle University and observed the habits of the silkworm in Italy and Spain (1578–9). At some stage in his career he also learnt chemistry from John Dee (q.v.), together with Philip Sidney, who became Moffet's friend. By 1580 he was back in England and, after accompanying Lord Willoughby on a mission to Denmark, he settled down to practise medicine. He was one of the first doctors in England to use chemical medicine, which he had learnt in Germany. Among his patients were the Duchess of Somerset, widow of the Protector, and Sir Francis Walsingham. In 1583 he wrote an essay on his medical principles and by 1588 was Fellow and Censor of the College of Physicians. His *Insectorum Theatrum*, an entomological study, was finished by 1590 but not published until 1634. Dr Moffet accompanied Essex as a physician during the Normandy campaign of 1591. Soon afterwards he settled at Wilton, under the patronage of the Countess of Pembroke (q.v.), in whose laboratory at Wilton House he continued his studies. He sat as M.P. for Wilton, 1597–8, and found time to produce *Nobilis*, a Latin biography of his friend Philip Sidney, in which he deplores the "blind art" of surgery as practised on Sidney at Zutphen. Moffet's other works are a poem on the silkworm (1599) and a treatise on diet and personal hygiene, *Health's Improvement* (published 1655). It has been suggested that the nursery rhyme, *Little Miss Muffet* is about Moffet's daughter Patience. This seems unlikely: the familiar version first appeared in the nineteenth century; the rhyme in other forms is very much older than the entomologist of Wilton.

Thomas Moufet, *Nobilis*, eds., V. B. Heltzel and
  H. H. Hudson (1940)

MOMPESSON, Giles (1584–?1651), M.P., monopolist: born at Bathampton, Wiltshire, and entered Hart Hall, Oxford in 1600, but took no degree. In 1612 he married the daughter of Sir John St John, and so became connected with Buckingham (q.v.) who advanced Mompesson's career. In 1614 he was elected M.P. for Great Bedwyn, Wiltshire and was knighted two years later. From 1617 onwards Mompesson enjoyed rights as commissioner or licence-holder, which brought him considerable wealth. Most profitable was the licensing of inns and alehouses. Mompesson had been responsible for pushing this measure through the Commons, and was able to exploit his position by extracting heavy fees and fines from landlords. He was also surveyor of the profits of the New River Company, which brought him £200 a year. His extortions were so notorious that he was satirised in several plays, notably by Philip Massinger (q.v.) in *A New Way to Pay Old Debts*. He was returned to Parliament again in 1620–1 but was at once impeached as a monopolist, stripped of his knighthood, fined £10,000 and imprisoned, after being marched down the Strand in disgrace. On his release, Mompesson was supposedly banished for life, but returned to England often until his property was finally confiscated by Parliament because of his Royalist sympathies. He is not mentioned after 1651.

R. Zaller, *The Parliament of 1621* (1971)

MONTAGU, Richard (1577–1641), bishop: educated at Eton and King's College, Cambridge. After holding two rural benefices he was appointed Dean of Hereford in 1616 and Canon of Windsor a year later. He was a vigorous champion of the High Anglican tradition which, in his *Appello Caesarem* (1625), he saw as a safeguard against both popery and Puritanism. Laud encouraged the King to appoint him Bishop of Chichester in 1628 and he served as Bishop of Norwich for the last three years of his life.

MONTEAGLE, Lord (1576–1622), political dissident: born William Parker but was always known as Lord Monteagle, a courtesy title taken from his mother's family. Monteagle was a recusant, with properties in Warwickshire, Worcester and Essex. He fought in Ireland under the Earl of Essex, by whom he was knighted, and he supported the Essex rebellion of January 1601, being one of the Essex partisans who attended the performance of *Richard II*, the day before (v. *Meyrick, Phillips*). For these activities Monteagle was imprisoned in the Tower for eight months and fined £8,000. On his release he was contacted by the Catholic fanatic, Catesby (q.v.), with whom he maintained close relations until the accession of James I. In the winter of 1604–5 Monteagle informed the King that he was prepared to abjure his Catholicism; he was duly accorded the title Monteagle as of right and was authorised to take his seat in the House of Lords when Parliament assembled in November 1605. While at supper in his house at Hoxton on 26 October 1605 he received a secret message which he interpreted as evidence of a conspiracy to blow up Parliament, and he passed on this news to Cecil (q.v.) and other members of the Council. For his action in exposing the Gunpowder Plot (v. *Fawkes*) Monteagle was given landed property by the King and an annual pension of £500. He invested substantially in the Virginia Company (becoming a member of the Council in 1609) and in the East India Company. When he died at his home in Great Hallingbury, Essex, his family complained that his annual pension was several years in arrears.

MORE, George (1553–1632), M.P., Lieutenant of the Tower: son of Sir William More of Loseley, Surrey. More was educated at Corpus Christi College, Oxford, probably from 1570, and at the Inner Temple from 1574. He sat in eleven Parliaments between 1584 and 1626, representing Guildford or Surrey, and on four occasions accompanied his father, whose experience of the Commons went back to Edward VI's reign. Under both Elizabeth and James I More spoke frequently in debate, championing the traditional liberties of Parliament. He was knighted in 1597, succeeded to his father's estates in 1600, and added the manor of Godalming to them. In 1601 his third daughter, Anne, secretly married the poet Donne (q.v.). More's fury resulted in Donne's imprisonment; not until 1608 did he relent sufficiently to make Donne a small allowance. Although More held a minor Exchequer post from 1600, his career really advanced under James I, who visited him at Loseley in 1603 and 1606. More was treasurer to Prince Henry, Chancellor of the Order of the Garter (1611) and in 1615 became Lieutenant of the Tower, his predecessor being arrested for complicity in the murder of Overbury (q.v.). While Somerset (Carr, q.v.) was in the Tower More, acting for the King, had to persuade him to stand trial for the murder without making too many "aspersions" (as James wrote in his increasingly panicky letters to More). After 1617, when he sold his Lieutenancy for £2,400, More seems to have lost the royal favour, although Prince Charles visited him at Loseley in 1621. More made efforts to get back into Court circles and kept his influence in Surrey, where five of the fourteen M.P.s of 1624 were his connections.

J. E. Neale, *Elizabeth I and her Parliaments 1584–1601* (1957)

R. E. Ruigh, *The Parliament of 1624* (1971)

MORGAN, Lucy (alias Parker) (fl. 1579–1600), possible "Dark Lady" of the Sonnets: one of Queen Elizabeth's gentlewomen from March 1579 to January 1582. She was three times given dresses by the Queen and was well liked among the Court ladies. By 1595 Lucy Morgan, or Parker, also known as "Lucy Negro" was a brothel keeper in St John Street, Clerkenwell. That "Lucy Negro" 's real name was Morgan is confirmed by her appearance in the Queen's Bench in 1596, and in January 1600 she was sentenced to Bridewell under the name of Morgan or Parker. She was a notorious character in London, figuring in the Gray's Inn entertainment of 1595, and having her epitaph published in *Wit and Drollery* (1656). G. B. Harrison first suggested "Lucy Negro" as the "Dark Lady", but it was Leslie Hotson who identified her with the Queen's gentlewoman; the identification depends on supposed cryptic references to "Lucy" and "Morgan" in the Sonnets.

L. Hotson, *Mr W. H.* (1964)

MORGAN, William (1541–1604), bishop: born at Gwybrnant, Penmachno, Caernarfonshire, educated at St John's College, Cambridge, where he gained a high reputation as a Hebrew scholar. As Vicar of the Denbighshire parish of Llanrhaeadr ym Mochnant he collaborated with one of his Cambridge friends, Archdeacon Edmund Prys (a gifted poet) to produce in 1588 the first translation into Welsh of the whole Bible. Archbishop Whitgift (q.v.), who had gained experience of Welsh affairs when he was Bishop of Worcester, warmly supported Morgan's efforts, recommending the Privy Council to order a copy of the translation to be placed in every church in Wales before the end of the year. The translation had a double importance: it provided the Welsh

people with a high standard of prose, disciplining a language rapidly sinking into mere spoken patois; and it identified the Anglican church in Wales with the vernacular, thus lessening the appeal of Latin Catholicism. Morgan became Bishop of Llandaff in 1595 and Bishop of St Asaph in 1601.

MORLEY, Thomas (1558–1603), organist and composer: believed to have been born in Lincolnshire and to have been a pupil of Byrd (q.v.) at Lincoln Cathedral. He took the degree of Bachelor of Music at Oxford in 1588, by which time he was already organist of St Giles, Cripplegate. He became organist of St Paul's Cathedral in 1591, a post he held together with an appointment as a Gentleman of the Chapel Royal, 1592–1602. A book of short songs for three voices in 1593 was followed a year later by his *First Book of Madrigals*, the earliest work in England to use the word "madrigal" on its title-page to describe the contrapuntal compositions which Byrd had begun to popularise, on the Italian and Flemish models, in 1588–89. In all, Morley published five collections of his own part-songs, for anything from two to six voices and 125 of his madrigals survive. An instruction manual, written in the form of a dialogue (often light-hearted in character), was published as *A Plain and Easy Introduction to Practical Music* in 1597 and Morley followed it with *The First Book of Consort Lessons* in 1599. He also wrote Church music, solo songs with the lute and compositions for viols and the keyboard. In 1601 he edited the famous collection of twenty-five madrigals published in honour of Queen Elizabeth and known as *The Triumphs of Oriana*. Morley contributed "Arise, awake, awake" for five voices and "Hard by a crystal fountain" for six voices; and among the other composers were Robert Jones, Kirbye, Milton, Tomkins, Weelkes and Wilby (qq.v.). It is probable that Morley was consumptive: he hints at ill-health in the dialogue of *A Plain and Easy Introduction* and he was forced to resign from the Chapel Royal in the autumn before his death. He is best remembered for "Now is the month of maying" (1595), but he also wrote settings for "It was a lover and a lass" in *As You Like It* and for "O Mistress Mine" in *Twelfth Night*. For several years Morley appears to have been a near neighbour of Shakespeare in the parish of St Helen's, Bishopsgate.

E. H. Fellowes, *The English Madrigal Composers* (1948)

MORYSON, Fynes (1566–1630), traveller, writer: son of Thomas Moryson of Lincolnshire, four times M.P. for Grimsby; probably named Fynes after Edward Fiennes Clinton, later Earl of Lincoln, and was educated at Peterhouse, Cambridge (1580–4). He was Bursar of the college in 1589–90, and a Fellow by royal mandate from 1586 until 1600. In May 1591, he was granted a licence to travel abroad. After escaping pirates from Dunkirk, Moryson landed safely and spent the next four years visiting Germany, the Netherlands, Denmark, Switzerland, Austria, Italy and Poland. He entered the Universities of Basle and Leyden (1592 and 1594) and returned to London in May 1595. Moryson found his brother Henry preparing for a journey to Jerusalem and Constantinople, so decided to accompany him. The brothers left in November, 1595, went overland to Venice, took ship to Palestine and Lebanon and reached Antioch by land. Here Henry died of dysentery, and Fynes was very ill. He recovered, sailed back by Crete and Constantinople to Venice, and reached London in July 1597. Moryson spent some time visiting Edinburgh, then began to sort out his notes on his travels. He interrupted his work to be secretary to Lord Mountjoy (q.v.) in Ireland, from 1600 to 1606. Moryson spent the years 1609–17 writing his *Itinerary* first in Latin, then translating it. Most of it was printed in 1617; Part II, his history of Tyrone's rebellion, and Part III, a general discussion of the countries, remained in manuscript in Corpus Christi College, Oxford, although approved for publication in 1626. He introduced his work with a valuable account of exchange rates for the currencies of all the countries described. His plan to provide an abstract of their histories (taken from other books) was abandoned when the material grew too long. Part II of the *Itinerary* was not published until 1735 (in Dublin) and Part III appeared in an edited version only in 1903.

Fynes Moryson, *Itinerary* (1907)
C. Hughes, ed., *Shakespeare's Europe* (1903)

MOUNTJOY, Charles, Lord (1563–1606), soldier and administrator: born Charles Blount, eldest son of the sixth Baron Mountjoy, whom he succeeded in 1594. He was educated briefly at Oxford and admitted to the Middle Temple before deciding in 1583 to seek his fortune at Court. He was a good-looking and graciously mannered courtier, always prepared to be a patron of poetry, while personally achieving some success in the tilt yard. The favours shown towards him by the Queen aroused the jealousy of Essex (q.v.) who challenged Blount to a duel. Although Essex was slightly wounded he bore Blount no malice and the two men became close friends. From 1586 until 1594 Blount was engaged in campaigns in the Netherlands and Normandy, subsequently accompanying Essex to Cadiz and to the Azores on the "Islands Voyage" of 1597. He was appointed to succeed Essex as Lord Lieutenant in Ireland (October 1599). Essex wrongly believed he could count on military support from Mountjoy in his abortive revolt in London (January 1601), and Mountjoy appears at this time to have been involved in devious political intrigues, notably to ensure the

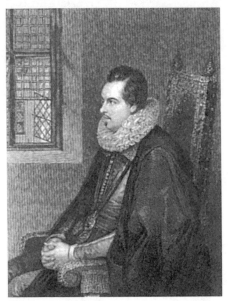

Charles Blount, Baron Mountjoy, Earl of Devonshire

succession of James VI of Scotland. From March 1601 until March 1604, however, Mountjoy waged a patient and thorough campaign to crush the Irish rebellion of Tyrone (q.v.), keeping him out of Ulster by a ring of improvised forts and gradually destroying his power in Munster. In October 1601 Mountjoy gained a notable triumph in cutting off a force of some 4,000 Spanish who had landed at Kinsale to assist Tyrone; they surrendered to Mountjoy on 2 January 1602 after Kinsale was besieged for nine weeks. James rewarded Mountjoy for his past support by creating him Earl of Devonshire but the King publicly rebuked him, soon after his accession, for smoking "filthy stinking" tobacco. The King was also scandalised by Mountjoy's marriage in 1605 to Essex's

sister, the divorced Penelope Rich (q.v.), who had been Mountjoy's mistress for nearly twenty years and borne him six children.

Cyril Falls, *Mountjoy, Elizabethan General* (1955)
F. M. Jones, *Mountjoy, 1563–1606* (1958)

MOUNTJOY, Christopher (fl. 1598–1613), London tiremaker: a French Huguenot, who had settled in London as a "tiremaker", one who made ladies' ornamental headgear. Shakespeare lodged in his house, on the corner of Monkswell and Silver Street near St Olave's Church in Cripplegate ward, certainly in 1604 and probably earlier, as he knew the family from 1602 onwards. Shakespeare was matchmaker in the marriage of Mountjoy's daughter Marie and his former apprentice, Belott (q.v.). Mountjoy was alleged to have promised £60 as his daughter's portion. After Mrs Mountjoy died in 1606, the widower led a dissipated life, quarrelled with the Belotts, and was likely to cut them off entirely. In 1612 Belott sued his father-in-law for the rest of the marriage settlement, and Shakespeare was called to London from Stratford as a witness to the original arrangement. On 11 May 1612 he gave evidence in the Court of Requests, declaring he could not remember the exact details; he did not testify at a second hearing. The case was referred to the Elders of the French Reformed Church, who censured both parties for their debauched way of life and awarded Belott only twenty nobles. A year later, Mountjoy had neither paid up nor abandoned his licentious habits.

S. S.

MOUNTJOY, Marie (?–1606), resident of Cripplegate, London: wife of Christopher Mountjoy (*supra*). During 1604, the year in which Shakespeare lodged with the

Mountjoys and in which her daughter was married, Marie Mountjoy was having an affair with a mercer, Henry Wood. She consulted the astrologer, Simon Forman (q.v.) about a possible pregnancy and whether she should leave her husband's business and set up shop with Mrs Wood. In fact she stayed with Mountjoy, urging him to be more generous toward their daughter and son-in-law, Stephen Belott (q.v.).

S. S.

MULCASTER, Richard (c. 1530–1611), scholar and schoolmaster: born in Cumberland, educated at Eton, King's College, Cambridge, and Christ Church, Oxford, where he graduated as a Master of Arts in 1556. He became Headmaster of Merchant Taylors' School in the City of London in 1561, teaching the classics, and encouraging music and drama so that the boys were able to present plays at court from 1574 to 1583. Mulcaster wrote an important study of education, *Positions*, which he presented to the Queen in 1581. A year later a second study, *The First Part of the Elementary*, was dedicated to the Earl of Leicester. Mulcaster strongly championed the use of the vernacular and was insistent that children should be taught how to write good English as well as to study Latin, Greek and Hebrew. He also favoured the proper education of girls, in schools and not merely under private tutors. Mulcaster retired from Merchant Taylors' in 1586 but he returned to teaching ten years later as High Master of St Paul's, where he served until 1608. No other schoolmaster had such influence in the late sixteenth century. Among Mulcaster's pupils were Lancelot Andrewes, Thomas Hood, Thomas Lodge, Edwin Sandys and Edmund Spenser (qq.v.).

A. L. Rowse, *The England of Elizabeth* (1950)

MUNDAY, Anthony (1560–1633), actor and dramatist: son of a London draper, Christopher Munday, who died in 1571. The orphaned Anthony was apprenticed in 1576 to a stationer who went out of business in 1582 before Munday finished his apprenticeship. Through his father, however, he was entitled to membership of the Drapers' Company, which gave him standing. He achieved some notoriety as an actor for extemporising, possibly with the Earl of Oxford's company, and was hissed off the stage, wisely turning his attention to writing and producing translations, ballads, lyrics and possibly plays. Already in 1578–9 he had been to Rome, to get material for a series of attacks on the Jesuits, and from 1581 he was working for Richard Topcliffe (q.v.), hunting down recusants. By 1588 he was a Messenger of the Chamber and employed to execute the Archbishop of Canterbury's warrants against the Martin Marprelate authors. From 1594 to 1602 he was writing plays for the Admiral's Men, of which three survive: *John à Kent and John à Cumber* (1594), about a conflict between wizards, and two tragedies on the life and death of Robin Hood (1598). Meres (q.v.), in 1598, included Munday among the "best for comedy", calling him "our best plotter", but he was the frequent butt of other writers, both for his style and his quasi-official functions. From 1605 onwards he devised Lord Mayors' pageants for the City companies, the most notable being his pageant of 1618 for the Ironmongers, in which a real gun was fired. Munday also produced the Corporation of London's formal welcome to Henry, Prince of Wales in 1610. Munday wrote many plays in collaboration, mainly for the Admiral's company: the best known is *Sir John Oldcastle* (1599), on which he worked with Drayton, Hathway and Wilson (qq.v.). He must certainly have written some of *Sir Thomas More* (c.

1595–6) as the manuscript of the play was originally in his handwriting, subsequent additions coming from five different hands, and Shakespeare being held to have served as one reviser. Munday was a friend of Stow (q.v.) and produced a posthumous edition of his *Survey of London* (1618).

E. K. C., *E.S.*
G. E. B.

MYDDELTON see MIDDLETON.

MYTENS, Daniel (c. 1590–c. 1642), portrait painter: born and trained in The Hague, coming to England in about 1618, receiving Court patronage soon thereafter. Charles I gave him the official standing of Royal Painter in 1625 and he competed in popularity with Janssen (q.v.) until eclipsed by the arrival of van Dyck in 1632. Mytens appears to have returned to the Netherlands in 1635. He specialised in full-length portraits, of which the painting of the third Earl of Essex (q.v.) in the National Portrait Gallery is a fine example.

N

NAPIER, John (1550–1617), mathematician: son of Archibald, Baron Napier. He was educated at St Andrew's University from about 1563, but took no degree. From 1574 he lived at Gartnes, County Stirling, moving to Merchiston Castle in 1608 when he succeeded to his father's title and status as Laird of Merchiston. While still at Gartnes Napier produced the earliest Scottish book on the interpretation of Scripture, *A Plain Discovery of the Whole Revelation of St John* (1593), reflecting his staunch Presbyterianism. The work was dedicated to James VI (with whom Napier often differed), warning him against papist schemers at Court. Napier possessed much mechanical ingenuity; he drew up plans for several instruments of war, including an armoured fighting vehicle, a seventeenth-century tank. He is best remembered, however, for devising logarithms, which he explained in his earliest mathematical work *Mirifici Logarithmorum Canonis Descriptio* (1614) and set out in his *Constructio* five years later, leaving their further development to Henry Briggs (q.v.). Napier was also the first mathematician to use the decimal point as it is still used today. In *Rabdologia* (1617) he described his manually operated calculator, later known as "Napier's Bones": these were sets of rods and metal plates for multiplying and dividing. His son, Robert, prepared the *Constructio* for publication two years after his father's death.

NASH, Anthony (d. 1622), of Welcombe, Stratford: a friend of Shakespeare, witnessing agreements made by him in 1602, 1603 and 1614. He also managed Shakespeare's tithes for him and was left two marks to buy a ring in Shakespeare's will. Nash died wealthy, leaving property and more than £1,000 to his son Thomas (q.v.) who married Shakespeare's granddaughter.

M. E.

NASH, John (d. 1623), of Stratford-upon-Avon: the brother of Anthony Nash (*supra*) and, like him, was remembered by Shakespeare in his will, receiving two marks to buy a ring. His second wife, Dorothy, was the widow of the vintner who kept the Bear Inn in Bridge Street, which therefore passed into Nash's ownership. In 1619 Nash was sued in Star Chamber for leading a riot against the new vicar, the rioters having allegedly threatened to flay the vicar alive in his church.

M. E.

NASH, Thomas (1593–1647), lawyer: son of Shakespeare's friend, Anthony Nash (q.v.). Although he was admitted a member of Lincoln's Inn on 15 May 1616, his father's death seven years later left him so comfortably off that he did not need to practise law. He also inherited the Bear Inn from his uncle John (*supra*). In 1626 he married Shakespeare's granddaughter Elizabeth Hall (q.v.), and it is probable that they lived in Nash House, next to New Place. He is buried in the chancel of Holy Trinity Church, near Shakespeare.

M. E.
S. S.

NASHE, Thomas (1567–1601), dramatist and satirist: the son of William Nashe, a clergyman from Herefordshire living in Lowestoft, Suffolk. Thomas Nashe was educated at St John's College, Cambridge, from 1582 until about 1588, (B.A., 1586). His first published work (1589) was a preface to *Menaphon* by Robert Greene (q.v.). The preface, in the form of a letter "to the Gentlemen Students of Both Universities", criticises actors and illiterate dramatists, like Kyd, while praising Peele. Nashe lived by his writing, serving various patrons including Lord Strange, Sir George Carey (Lord Hunsdon) and Archbishop Whitgift. He wrote satirical pamphlets like *Pierce Penniless* (1592) and was employed by Whitgift to write tracts against Martin Marprelate. In this activity he was associated with Lyly and as a result quarrelled with Gabriel Harvey (q.v.). He answered Harvey's charge of plagiarism in *Have With You to Saffron Walden* (1596). The pamphlet war between Nashe and Harvey became so scurrilous that in 1599 they were banned from writing further polemics. Nashe's prose works include the first English novel of adventure, *The Unfortunate Traveller* (1594). He wrote a comedy, *Summer's Last Will and Testament* (1592) which mixes allegory, topical satire and clowning; it also contains his two famous poems, "Spring, the sweet spring" and "Adieu, farewell earth's bliss". Nashe's only other extant dramatic work is his share — whatever it may be — in Marlowe's *Dido, Queen of Carthage* (?1593). In 1596 he was still writing, or collaborating in, plays and in the following year he was part-author with Jonson (q.v.) of the satirical comedy *Isle of Dogs* which appears to have contained attacks on Russia and Poland that were reckoned bad for trade. Nashe escaped imprisonment but discreetly withdrew to Great Yarmouth where he found the hospitality so generous that he wrote *Lenten Style* (1599), a burlesque in praise of red herring. This was his last known work.

G. R. Hibberd, *Thomas Nashe* (1962)

NEVILLE, Alexander (1544–1614), secretary to three Archbishops, son of Richard Neville of South Leverton, Nottinghamshire. He was educated at St John's College, Cambridge from 1559, then studied law in London, where he became a friend of Gascoigne. Neville may have been an M.P., for Christchurch, Hampshire (1584–6) and Saltash (1601), but his main career was as secretary to successive Archbishops of Canterbury, serving Parker until his death (1575), Grindal (1575–83) and Whitgift (q.v.). He wrote an elegy on Archbishop Parker. His main work was a Latin account of Kett's rebellion of 1549, together with a description of Norwich (published 1575). Neville so disparaged the Welsh soldiers sent against the rebels that he was forced to write an apology to the gentlemen of Wales. He also translated Seneca's *Oedipus*. He died in London, but is buried in Canterbury Cathedral.

NEVILLE, Henry (?1564–1615): son of Sir Henry Neville of Berkshire, whose father Edward Neville had the unlikely reputation of being the illegitimate son of Henry VIII. Neville was educated at Merton College, Oxford, from 1577 and introduced to the Court by Burghley. In 1599 he was appointed ambassador in Paris and knighted, subsequently easing Anglo-French relations which had become strained when France made peace with Spain (May 1598). He spent £4,000 on his mission, and complained of his treatment by the French. In February 1600 he asked to be recalled on the grounds of increasing deafness. Southampton and Essex confided in him and he was confined to the Tower after the failure of their plot in 1601, although it was never suggested that he approved of it. Neville was fined £5,000 besides, a fine which he had begun to pay in yearly instalments of £1,000 when the accession of James I restored him to freedom. From 1604 he sat in Parliament as M.P. for Berkshire, and advised the King to conciliate the Commons. In 1612 he was one of the candidates for Secretary of State and was considered most likely to succeed as he had the support of the King's favourite, Carr (q.v.), as well as Southampton. In the same year he drew up a memorial for James I embodying his suggested concessions to Parliament. Neville was passed over for Secretary in 1614 in favour of Winwood (q.v.). The King followed a version of his advice in the "Addled Parliament" that year, but it was too late. Neville has been confused with another Sir Henry Neville, of Sussex, who sat in the last six Parliaments of Elizabeth's reign (from 1584).

NEWBERY, John (c. 1550–85), pioneer traveller: a London merchant, who may have had trading connections with the Netherlands. He travelled in the Levant in 1579. A year later he went down the Euphrates and the Tigris to the Portuguese trading port of Hormuz on the Persian Gulf, then overland through southern Persia to Constantinople, into the Black Sea and through the Ukraine and Poland to Danzig. No Englishman had ventured into these regions of Asia Minor or the far hinterland of Eastern Europe before. In 1583 Newbery set out for the Far East in a party of six (including Ralph Fitch, q.v.). Newbery reached Hormuz again, was taken under Portuguese escort to Goa and travelled through southern India to Bijapur and eventually to Agra, presenting a letter from Elizabeth to the Mogul Emperor, Akbar (September 1584). Newbery then set out overland for England, but was never heard of again. His adventures were recorded by Hakluyt (q.v.) and published in the enlarged edition of his *Principal Navigations* (1598–1600).

W. Foster, *England's Quest of Eastern Trade* (1933)

NORDEN, John (1548–1625), cartographer and writer: probably born in Middlesex. His fame rests upon his pioneering efforts to compile, by map and word, a survey of the English counties, the *Speculum Britanniae*. He was authorised by a Privy Council order in January 1593 to travel through the kingdom to make "perfect descriptions, charts and maps", of the counties. His first volume, on Middlesex, appeared later that year. Poverty limited his output: his *Description of Cornwall* is comprehensive, and he also produced a *Chorography of Norfolk* and material on Essex, Hertfordshire and Northampton. His maps clearly showed roads, were often pictorial in detail, and included triangular distance scales. He was also the author of a manual of surveying, *The Surveyor's Dialogue* (1607), *An Intended Guide for English Travellers* (1625), and a simple book of Protestant devotions, *The Pensive Man's Practise* which reached its fortieth printing two years after his death.

A. L. Rowse, *The England of Elizabeth* (1950)

NORRIS, John (?1547–97), soldier: born near Thame in Oxfordshire. He spent some terms at Hart Hall, Oxford, leaving in 1571 to serve for the following thirteen years as a soldier in France, Ireland and the Netherlands. For some nine months in 1584–5 he was Lord President of Munster, but he returned to the Netherlands in the spring of 1585 and was wounded in winning the Battle of Grave, 1586. He much resented the appointment of Leicester (q.v.) as his commander; he had himself fought in every major action over the preceding five years and knew the terrain and the fighting qualities of the opposing armies. Nevertheless, he accepted a knighthood from Leicester and became his deputy at Tilbury Camp when invasion threatened in 1588, his special responsibility being defence of the Kentish shore.

In April 1589 he shared with Drake (q.v.) command of the largely abortive raid on Corunna and Lisbon. He fought for Henri IV in France (1591–3) and, in collaboration with Frobisher, gained a decisive victory against Spanish forces defending the fort of Crozon in Brittany (November 1593). In 1595 he returned to Munster to put down Tyrone's rebellion. But "Black John", as Norris was called, found the Irish problem intractable. His temper always made him a difficult colleague and he was exasperated by the wrangling inseparable from politics or fighting in Elizabethan Ireland. He died suddenly in Munster in July 1597.

C. Falls, *Elizabeth's Irish Wars* (1950)

NORTH, Roger, second Baron North (1530–1600), diplomat and soldier: son of Edward, first Baron. He may have been educated at Peterhouse, Cambridge, but came early to Court and in 1555 married Winifred Dudley, widowed daughter-in-law of Lord Protector Northumberland and sister-in-law of Leicester, who became North's lifelong friend. Until he inherited the barony in 1564, North represented Cambridgeshire in Parliament. He went on the Garter mission to Emperor Maximilian in Vienna (1568), sat as commissioner in Norfolk's trial (1572) and was ambassador extraordinary at the French Court in 1574. On his return North spent most of his time at Kirtling, his country estate east of Cambridge, and here he entertained the Queen in 1578. In the same year he witnessed Leicester's secret marriage to Lettice Knollys. His quiet country life gave way to action when he distinguished himself under Leicester in the Netherlands (1585–7), serving subsequently under Willoughby (q.v.) until summoned home in 1588 to muster the Cambridgeshire militia and lead them to Tilbury Camp to await the threatened invasion. He held no more military posts but was on the commission to try the Earl of Arundel (1589). In 1596 he became a Privy Councillor and Treasurer of the Royal Household, being made Keeper of the Royal Parks at Eltham and Horne a year later. As Lord Lieutenant of Cambridgeshire (from 1569) he found himself in conflict during the last years of his life with the University, jealous of its jurisdiction over the town of Cambridge. He was a royal favourite, the Queen naming a horse "Grey North" after him. By 1598 North was completely deaf and the Queen sent him a recipe for a cure: it consisted of putting half a hot loaf, made with bitter almonds, on each ear; and it is said to have worked. He died in his London home in Charterhouse Yard.

Lady Frances Bushby, *Three Men of Tudor Times* (1911)

NORTH, Thomas (?1535–?1603), translator: youngest son of Edward, first Baron North. North is said to have been educated at Peterhouse, Cambridge, before entering Lincoln's Inn in 1556. He was made a freeman of Cambridge in 1568. By 1570 North had produced his first translation, *Moral Philosophy* from the Italian of Doni, a collection of fables and Oriental stories. In 1574 North accompanied his older brother Roger (*supra*) on an embassy to France, and on his return settled in Cambridgeshire, where Roger provided him with a house. He probably needed financial support from his brother as well; he was married twice and had three children by his first wife. He produced a translation from Guevara's Spanish and French edition of Marcus Aurelius' *The Dial of Princes* (1577) and then his best-known work, the English version of Plutarch's *Lives of the Noble Grecians and Romans* (1579), dedicated to Queen Elizabeth. North translated his Plutarch from the French of Jacques Amyot, Bishop of Auxerre, but his interpolations show his own knowledge of Greek. The book was immensely popular and a major source for the Roman and Greek plays of Shakespeare and other dramatists; it went eventually into eight editions. In the fourth edition North introduced fifteen new lives, translated from Probus. Meanwhile he had become a soldier. He fought with his brother under Leicester in the Low Countries (1585–7) and trained the militia at Ely in Armada year. He also had two campaigns in Ireland, in 1582 and 1596–7; on the second he was accompanied by his son Edward, who remained for five or six years with the army. North's conduct in this second Irish campaign was unscrupulous; he seems to have drawn more money than he had soldiers or equipment. Nevertheless he held one more military post, Officer of the Watch at the Tower in 1601, and helped put down the Essex rebellion in London. He had been knighted in 1591 and was J.P. for Cambridgeshire a year later. After his last active service in 1601 the Queen granted him a pension; he probably did not survive her death.

Ibid.
H. H. Davis, "The Military Career of Thomas North", *Huntington Library Quarterly* XII (1949)

NORTHUMBERLAND, Dorothy Percy, Countess of (1564/5–1619) see PERCY, Dorothy.

NORTHUMBERLAND, Henry Percy, ninth Earl of (1564–1631):

born at Tynemouth, but was not allowed to live in the north, or to visit it, after the execution of his uncle, the seventh Earl, in 1572. He succeeded to the title in 1585 when his father, the eighth Earl, died in the Tower, allegedly having shot himself through the heart. Henry fought in the Netherlands in 1585–6, against the Armada in 1588, and in the Netherlands again in 1599–1600. When not campaigning he lived principally at Petworth in Sussex, where he began to indulge those interests in science which won him the sobriquet, "The Wizard Earl". In 1594 he leased the remains of Syon Palace, Isleworth, from the Crown. The estate was given to him by James I in 1604 as a reward for North-

Henry Percy, ninth Earl of Northumberland

umberland's services in ensuring his peaceful accession. Northumberland duly built a new Syon House on the site; and he was allowed to use Essex House as his London headquarters. A visit by his kinsman and agent, Thomas Percy (q.v.), on 4 November 1605 heavily implicated Northumberland in the Gunpowder Plot. He was sent to the Tower and charged in Star Chamber on 27 June 1606, with misprision of treason. He was sentenced to life imprisonment and fined £30,000. In fact, he was confined in the Tower until 1621 and paid little more than a third of the fine. Within three months he was attended by servants in the Tower, and soon began to live there in some state, hiring additional quarters on Tower Hill for his personal suite. He continued to take an interest in scientific experiment, had some 200 books brought to him from his personal library, and was allowed to smoke tobacco and entertain his guests. When he was released in July 1621 he travelled to Bath to take the waters in a coach with six horses, deliberately showing greater ostentation than the four horses used by the royal favourite, Buckingham. Northumberland spent the last eleven years of his life in retirement at Petworth, still officially forbidden to travel more than thirty miles from his home. He died on 5 November 1631, insisting that he had never shared the faith of Fawkes and his conspirators: "The world knows that I am no Papist", he declared.

G. R. Batho, ed., *Household Papers of Henry Percy, Ninth Earl of Northumberland* (1962)

NOWELL, Alexander (c. 1507–1602), Dean of St Paul's: born in Whalley, Lancashire, educated at Brasenose College, Oxford, subsequently becoming Master of Westminster School and, in 1551, a prebendary of Westminster Abbey. He was elected M.P. for Looe in the Parliament of 1553 but was not allowed to sit in the Commons because he was a member of Convocation. After Elizabeth's accession he enjoyed, at first, the Queen's favour and, at her suggestion, was elected Dean of St Paul's in November 1560, an office he held for forty-two years, holding in plurality a living at Much Hadham, Hertfordshire. Dean Nowell's decision, made soon after his arrival at St Paul's, to take a wife offended the Queen who preferred the clergy to remain celibate. At times there was friction between Dean and Sovereign. When, in 1564, Nowell was speaking of the crucifix in a Lenten sermon, the Queen called out sharply to him, "To your text, Mr Dean; leave that; we have heard enough of that." Nowell more than once criticised the Queen publicly for failing to marry and provide an heir to the throne. He wrote three Catechisms ('Large', 'Middle' and 'Small'), of which the definitive versions were settled in 1572, and he was also partly responsible for the Catechism authorised for the Book of Common Prayer of 1604, work on which was completed by his successor at St Paul's, Dean Overall (q.v.).

NOY, William (1577–1634), lawyer: born at Mawgan, Cornwall, educated at Exeter College, Oxford and called to the Bar of Lincoln's Inn in 1602, sitting for a succession of Cornish boroughs (Grampound, Helston, Fowey, St Ives) in the Parliaments of James I and Charles I. He was much respected by contemporaries as "a man very learned in the law". In 1610 and 1621 he spoke at length and with vigour against monopolies and patents and was known as "a good Commons man". In October 1631, however, he became Attorney-General and (like Thomas Wentworth, q.v.) was subsequently regarded as a turncoat by the Parliamentarians. His persecution of Prynne was vindictive, and he incurred great unpopularity through his legal ingenuity in justifying new sources of revenue for the Crown. He died suddenly in August 1634.

W. J. Jones, *Politics and the Bench* (1971)

O

OKES, Nicholas (fl. 1596–1639), printer: son of John Okes, horner, of London. He was apprenticed to William King for eight years from March 1596, and became a freeman of the Stationers' Company in 1603 and a master printer in 1606. Okes printed Shakespeare's *Rape of Lucrece* for John Morrison the Younger (1607) and *Othello* for Thomas Walkley (1622). He was twice in trouble with the authorities, for printing George Withers' *Motto* (1621) and Sir Robert Cotton's life of Henry III (1627). On the second occasion his son, who was then his partner, was also accused.

OLIVER, Isaac (c. 1562–1617), artist: probably born in Paris, the son of a Huguenot goldsmith who settled in London when the boy was about six years old. Isaac Oliver spent most of his life in London, formally adopting English nationality in 1606. He was a pupil of Hilliard (q.v.), but Oliver's miniatures were more realistic likenesses than those of his tutor and he tended to use more complex and darker colours, completing small-scale portraits rather than the aesthetically unique "jewels" of Hilliard's craftsmanship. Oliver's earliest work – "A Man Aged 59" – was painted in the Armada year. Some of his best miniatures were painted between 1590 and 1596. On the accession of James I he became limner to Queen Anne and one of his most satisfying portraits is the miniature of her companion in the Court masques, Lucy, Countess of Bedford (q.v.).

O NEILL, Hugh (c. 1540–1616) see TYRONE, Earl of.

ORMONDE, Thomas Butler, Earl of (1532–1614), spent most of his childhood at Henry VIII's Court, succeeding to his title when his father, ninth Earl, was poisoned in 1546. Throughout the reigns of Elizabeth and James I the Earl of Ormonde was the most consistently loyal of the Irish territorial magnates. From 1554 to 1562 he helped keep the peace in Ireland but intensive rivalry with his cousin, the Earl of Desmond, led to fighting in the 1560s. After helping to suppress risings in Munster (1570 and 1571) Ormonde resumed the long conflict with Desmond in 1573, finally crushing him in 1583. The zeal shown by Ormonde in murdering Spaniards wrecked on the Irish coast after the defeat of the Armada was recognised in 1589 when he was created a Knight of the Garter. He was appointed Lieutenant-General of the Army in Ireland in October 1597 and over the following two years tried to put down the rebellion of Tyrone (q.v.). "The Black Earl", as Ormonde was called (apparently because of his swarthy looks) was at times a difficult companion in arms for Essex (q.v.) and other Englishmen seeking to restore order in Ireland. His loyalty was rewarded by the cession of extensive lands in Munster in 1603 and by his appointment as Vice-Admiral of Ireland two years before his death.

C. Falls, *Elizabeth's Irish Wars* (1950)

ORSINI, Virginio, Duke of Bracciano (1574–?): son of the Duke Paolo Orsini and his wife Isabella (de Medici). Orsini's own family history was the basis for Webster's play *The White Devil*. Between 1581 and 1585 his father had his mother strangled, murdered the nephew of Pope Sixtus V in order to marry his widow Vittoria and died himself. Vittoria was murdered soon after. Orsini was brought up by his uncle, Ferdinand I, Grand Duke of Tuscany, along with his cousin Maria de Medici. In 1589 he married Pope Sixtus' niece Flavia Peretti. He fought against the Turks in Hungary, and commanded a naval expedition which failed to free Chios from them (1599). The new Pope Clement VIII was hostile to the Medici, and Orsini quarrelled with the Pope's nephew and representative at his cousin Maria de Medici's wedding to Henri IV of France in 1600. As he had recently met William Cecil, Lord Burghley's grandson and British envoy to Florence, he decided to prolong his journey to France in the new Queen's train by visiting England as well. This excursion would irritate the Pope and King of Spain, but please Queen Elizabeth, who hoped to find Tuscany an ally. She entertained Orsini, together with the Russian ambassador, to a state banquet in Whitehall on Twelfth Night (6 January) 1601, and actually danced at a ball in his honour, as well as having a private conversation with him. Orsini's visit was thought in Europe to be of some significance, probably a secret mission from the French King. After the banquet at Whitehall, he saw a play. Dr Hotson argues for *Twelfth Night* being the play, with one of the leading characters renamed Orsino to flatter the guest of honour, but his dating is not generally accepted.

L. Hotson, *The First Night of Twelfth Night* (1954)

OSTLER, William (c. 1588–1614), actor: began his career as a boy with the Children of the Chapel Royal at Blackfriars, appearing in Jonson's *The Poetaster*, 1601. He was taken into the King's Men as an adult, playing in the first production of *The Alchemist* (1610), as well as other plays by Jonson and by Beaumont and Fletcher. He was the original Antonio in Webster's *The Duchess of Malfi*, (1613–14). In 1611 John Davies (q.v.) called Ostler "sole King of Actors" in *The Scourge of Folly*: the poem also suggests he had been involved in a brawl. Ostler married Thomasine, daughter of John Heminges (q.v.), in 1611, and acquired a share in the Blackfriars, also gaining a share in the Globe a year later. He died on 16 December 1614; his name appears in the First Folio list of actors.

E. K. C., *E.S.*

OVERALL, John (1560–1619), Dean of St Paul's and Bishop: born in London, educated at Cambridge, where he was a Fellow of Trinity College, 1581 98, and Regius Professor of Theology, 1595–1607. In 1602 he became Dean of St Paul's. He was one of the translators of the Authorised Version of the Bible, and he wrote the section on the Sacraments in the Prayer-Book Catechism in response to Puritan requests for definition made at the Hampton Court Conference (1604). After the Gunpowder Plot the King invited Overall to prepare a definitive statement of canon law on the relations of the Church and State but James refused to publish Overall's canons, since he felt the Dean was justifying the possible institution of "new forms of government". Nevertheless the King approved Overall's consecration as Bishop of Coventry and Lichfield in 1614 and his translation to Norwich in 1618. Dr Overall rarely preached a sermon, on the grounds that because he had spoken Latin so long he found a continuous oration in English "troublesome". His wife was reputedly the "greatest beauty of her time in England"; her name and obliging disposition lent themselves to bawdy verses which were remembered (and quoted by John Aubrey) more than half a century after her husband had ceased to be Dean of St Paul's.

O. L. Dick, ed., *Aubrey's Brief Lives* (1949)

180

OVERBURY, Thomas (1581–1613), writer, murder victim: son of Sir Nicholas Overbury of Gloucestershire, later a judge in South Wales. Overbury was educated at Queen's College, Oxford (1596–8) and the Middle Temple (from 1597). He went to Edinburgh in 1601 and met Robert Carr (q.v.); then, or later, the two were great friends. When Carr became a favourite of James I in 1607, Overbury decided to

Sir Thomas Overbury. Portrait dated 1613 and painted in the manner of Cornelis Janssen

renew the friendship. He acted as Carr's secretary and guide in political affairs, and was rewarded with possessions and a knighthood in 1608. At first he steered his "precious chief", as he later called him, away from involvement with the powerful Howard family, but from 1609 countenanced Carr's liaison with Frances Howard (q.v.), even writing his master's love letters. He was bitterly opposed to the idea that Frances should divorce her husband, the third Earl of Essex and marry Carr, however. By 1612 Overbury's arrogance had made many enemies and not only among the Howard faction. Neither the King nor Queen could stand him (he may

have been briefly imprisoned in 1611 for insulting the Queen) and he relied on his power over Carr to keep him out of the trouble his insolence caused. But Carr had quarrelled publicly with Overbury about his projected marriage and was partly responsible for Overbury's being sent to the Tower in April 1613; the excuse was that Overbury had refused the King's offer of a foreign embassy. Two separate plots were directed at Overbury with the connivance of the Lieutenant of the Tower, Elwes (q.v.). Frances Howard's greatuncle, Northampton (Henry Howard) (q.v.) and Carr confused his mind with lying letters, apparently smuggled in. Frances Howard arranged for him to be poisoned. By September Overbury was dead. Northampton arranged a hasty inquest (whose verdict was suppressed) and burial. An enquiry into the death began in 1615 and resulted in the conviction of all the principal opponents of Overbury who were still alive (v. *Carr, Elwes, Frances Howard*). Overbury's works, *The Wife* (a treatise on ideal marriage), a paraphrase of Ovid's *Remedia Amoris*, and the very popular *Characters* were all published after his death.

B. White, *Cast of Ravens* (1965)

OXFORD, Edward de Vere, 17th Earl of (1550–1604), courtier: son of John de Vere, sixteenth Earl. Oxford succeeded his father in 1562 and was a ward of Lord Burghley until he came of age. He was educated at St John's College, Cambridge (M.A., 1564), added an Oxford M.A. in 1566, and entered Gray's Inn the next year. He was an excellent musician, poet and dancer (beginning each day with a dancing lesson at seven o'clock) as well as an expert jouster. However, he was temperamental, quarrelsome and cruel; an early scandal involving the death of one of Burghley's servants was hushed up in

1567. Oxford served in the campaign against the Northern Earls' rebellion and came to Court in 1571. His accomplishments, especially dancing, brought him into the Queen's favour, but neither she nor Burghley were pleased by his marriage to Burghley's favourite daughter, Anne, in December. Almost immediately, Oxford tried to escape abroad, possibly after an attempt to rescue his condemned cousin, the Duke of Norfolk. He was

Edward de Vere, seventeenth Earl of Oxford

brought back, then allowed to travel in Europe, mainly Italy, from 1574 to 1576. He returned a Roman Catholic, more extravagant than ever, and estranged from his wife and father-in-law. The Queen received him back at Court, although his debts were by now enormous, and endured his violent quarrel with Philip Sidney in the tennis court at Whitehall in 1579 (as Oxford, unlike Sidney, supported her proposed French marriage). Next year, however, Oxford made one of the Queen's ladies, Anne Vavasour, pregnant and he was sent to the Tower after the baby's birth in March 1581. He was released on

condition he returned to his wife. This he did, to the extent that four children were born to them before her death in 1588, Burghley providing a home and support for the family. The Vavasour affair involved Oxford in gang warfare with his mistress' cousin and protector Thomas Knyvett (q.v.). The two men fought a duel in 1582, and several of their followers were killed. Oxford's bellicosity had a new outlet during the war in Flanders in 1585, where he commanded troops under John Norris (q.v.). From 1580 onwards Oxford had interested himself in the drama. Lyly (q.v.) was his secretary and wrote plays for the company known as Oxford's Boys, at Court and the Blackfriars theatre in 1583 to 1584 (v. *Henry Evans*). Oxford also supported an adult company, taken over from Warwick (q.v.) in 1580. They played mainly in the provinces and were combined with the actors of the fourth Earl of Worcester in 1602. Oxford wrote plays, though none have survived, and was included by Meres (q.v.) among the "best for comedy" in 1598. This connection with the drama has produced considerable support since 1920 for the theory that Oxford was the real author of Shakespeare's plays, despite the obvious drawback of his being dead when the later plays were written. His theatrical activities combined with general extravagance to put Oxford's finances in a worse state than ever by the 1590s, and he begged the Queen to grant him a monopoly. This she refused, but did eventually allow him a pension. In 1591 he married again, one of the Queen's maids of honour, Elizabeth Trentham, and had a son Henry who succeeded him. Oxford was hereditary Lord Great Chamberlain of England. He had performed this office at the Armada celebration; his last Court appearance was as Chamberlain at James I's coronation.

E. K. C., *E.S.*

P

PADDY, William (1554–1634), physician: born in London, educated at Merchant Taylors' School and St John's College, Oxford (B.A., 1573), subsequently becoming a Fellow. In 1589 he qualified as a doctor of medicine at Leyden. James I knighted him in 1603, appointing him royal physician. Paddy was in attendance on the King during his visit to Oxford in August 1605 where, although admitting he was "a great drinker of tobacco", he argued forcibly in public debate that the practice was injurious to the health. From 1609 to 1611 he was President of the Royal College of Surgeons. He was a friend of Laud (q.v.) and a benefactor of St John's College, where he is buried.

D. H. Willson, *King James VI and I* (1956)

PALAVICINO, Horatio (c. 1540–1600, knighted 1587), financier, ambassador and secret agent: born at Genoa, a member of a north Italian aristocratic family with international banking connections. In 1578 he negotiated a profitable deal with Elizabeth by which she underwrote a loan he had made to the Dutch rebels against Spain. From 1579 onwards Palavicino was the principal financier of English enterprises, becoming a naturalised Englishman in November 1585, serving as ambassador to the Protestant princes in Denmark and Germany, as well as handling intelligence work. The enormous profits made by Sir Horatio, his unscrupulous speculation in corn, and his attempt to establish a world monopoly in pepper lost him Queen Elizabeth's support in 1592–3, and he spent the last six years of his life in retirement on his estates at Babraham, Cambridgeshire, where he experimented with large-scale sheep farming and pioneered irrigation projects. He remained on good terms with Robert Cecil, organising his private espionage system in the contest for supremacy with the Earl of Essex. Palavicino was the wealthiest commoner in Elizabethan England, an unattractive figure because of his ruthless pursuit of wealth; but he was a loyal servant to his adopted country, enlisting as a "gentleman volunteer" in the fleet which met the Armada (and, characteristically, taking charge of the ransom of Spanish prisoners after its defeat). Palavicino's widow, born Anne Hooftman of Dutch parentage, married Sir Oliver Cromwell (q.v.) uncle of the Lord Protector.

L. Stone, *Sir Horatio Palavicino* (1956)

PALLANT, Robert, the older (?–1619), actor: was with Strange's Men, 1590–1. He then joined Worcester's company, which later became Queen Anne's Men, and played for them most of the time between 1602 and 1619. Pallant was a friend of Thomas Heywood (q.v.), for whose *Apology for Actors* (published 1612) he wrote commendatory verses, and he visited Henslowe on his death-bed, 6 January 1616.

PALLANT, Robert, the younger (?1605–?), actor: son of Robert Pallant the older (*supra*), with whom he has been sometimes confused. Robert the younger was with the King's Men from his youth until 1624; he played in *The Duchess of Malfi* (Cariola in 1614, the Doctor, 1619–23).

PARKER, John (?–1648), bookseller: son of George Parker, yeoman, of Warwickshire. He became a freeman of the ·

Stationers' Company in 1617 and had shops in St Paul's Churchyard, "The Ball" (1618) and "Three Pigeons" (1620–48). In 1620 he acquired William Barrett's copyrights, including Shakespeare's *Venus and Adonis* which he continued to publish. Parker was Warden (1641, 1644, 1645) and Master (1647, 1648) of the Stationers' Company.

PARRY, Blanche (1508–90), Lady-in-waiting to Queen Elizabeth: born at Newcourt, Bacton, Herefordshire, the daughter of Henry Parry. She was distantly related to the Cecil family and was probably brought to Court by her aunt, Lady Herbert of Troy, wife of the bastard son of the first Earl of Pembroke. Blanche was appointed to attend on the Princess Elizabeth in 1536 but she may have been in the Princess's household before this, as she herself said she saw Elizabeth rocked in her cradle. She became second gentlewoman on the Queen's accession (1558) and first gentlewoman when Katherine Astley, once the Queen's governess, died (1565). Blanche retained this position until her death, although she was blind in her last years and had to hand over the task of keeping the royal jewels to Mary Ratcliffe in 1587. In 1562 Blanche was granted considerable estates in Herefordshire and Shropshire which involved her in litigation. She was always in close attendance on the Queen and often acted as go-between for courtiers in disgrace or passed on letters to the Queen in private. Burghley drew up her will and was its chief executor. Blanche had prepared a tomb in Bacton Church, with verses probably written by herself, but changed her mind and was buried in St Margaret's Westminster with the rank of Baroness; the Queen paid for the funeral. Blanche Parry was not connected with Sir Thomas Parry, Queen Elizabeth's old Steward, nor did she introduce her "cousin" John Dee to the Queen, as has often been said. There is no traceable relationship between her and Dee at all, although she was godmother to his son.

C. A. Bradford, *Blanche Parry, Queen Elizabeth's Gentlewoman* (1935)

PARSONS, Robert (1546–1610), Jesuit priest: born at Nether Stowey, Somerset, educated at St Mary's Hall and Balliol College, Oxford. He remained at Balliol as a Fellow from 1568 to 1574, when he left England and was received into the Roman Catholic Church at Louvain, becoming a Jesuit in 1575. Three years later he was ordained priest. He was sent to England, landing at Dover on 16 June 1580 disguised as a captain returning from the wars in the Netherlands. A month later he was joined secretly in London by his fellow Jesuit, the distinguished Oxford scholar and natural orator Edmund Campion (1540–81). The two Jesuits spent a year travelling separately through the south Midlands in an arc from Northampton to Gloucester, including the countryside between Warwick and Worcester. Campion was arrested in July 1581 and executed at Tyburn some four months later. Parsons fled to Normandy at news of Campion's arrest. There, at Eu near Dieppe, he founded a Jesuit school for English boys which was re-established at St Omer in 1592, eventually in 1794 becoming Stonyhurst College in Lancashire, the principal Roman Catholic boys school in England. For the last twenty-five years of his life Parsons was chief director of Roman Catholic missionary activity in England. Under the name of Doleman he published *The Conference about the Next Succession to the Crown of England* (1594). In this work he argued that subjects had a religious obligation to set aside the claims of a heretical heir to a throne, that the Pope's power to depose secular sovereigns was an article of faith, and that the natural and true claimant to the Crowns of both France and England was Philip II of Spain's daughter, the Infanta Isabel (1566–1633). Possession of a copy of this extremist work was regarded in England as proof of high treason. Parsons, who lived for nine years in Spain, was Rector of the English College in Rome in succession to Cardinal Allen (q.v.). He was a shrewd long-distance conspirator, a subtle manipulator of political intrigues. There is evidence that he favoured and promoted the abortive marriage project between Rainutio Farnese and Arbella Stuart (q.v.) but no proof he was implicated in the Gunpowder Plot, as many of his Protestant contemporaries believed.

P. Hughes, *The Reformation in England, III* (1959)

PAVIER, Thomas (?–1625), bookseller: was apprenticed to William Barley, draper, transferred from the Drapers' to the Stationers' Company in 1600, and admitted to the Livery of the Company (1604). Pavier's shops in London were at the entrance to the Exchange (1604–11) the "Cat and Parrot", near the Royal Exchange (1612), and in Ivy Lane (1623). In 1600 Edward White (q.v.) as Warden of the Stationers' Company assigned him several copyrights, including Shakespeare's *Henry V* and Kyd's *Spanish Tragedy*. Pavier published an edition of *Henry V* in 1602. In the same year Thomas Millington (q.v.) gave Pavier the copyrights of *Henry VI*, parts 2 and 3, and *Titus Andronicus*: Pavier published *Henry VI* and *Pericles* (1619) but *Titus* was still produced by Millington's colleague in the original edition, Edward White. In 1622 Pavier was elected Junior Warden of the Stationers' Company.

PAVY, Solomon (1590–1603), actor, also known as Salathiel Pavey: best known of the Children of the Chapel Royal who played at Blackfriars. Although pressed into the service, he was for the last three years of Elizabeth's reign "the stage's jewel", in Jonson's phrase. He acted in Jonson's *Cynthia's Revels*, 1600, and *Poetaster*, 1601, and was particularly gifted at playing the role of an old man. He is commemorated in an epitaph by Jonson included in the *Epigrammes*, printed in 1616.

PEACHAM, Henry (?1576–?1643), writer, artist: born at North Mimms, Hertfordshire, son of Henry Peacham, author of *A Garden of Eloquence* (1577) and Rector of North Mimms. He was educated at Trinity College, Cambridge (1593–5) and was for a time Master of Wymondham School, Norfolk. In 1606 Peacham produced the first English instruction book for artists, *The Art of Drawing with the Pen and Limning in Water Colours*; drawing was his favourite activity, and schoolmasters had unsuccessfully tried to beat it out of him, as he said himself. The book went into many editions, after 1612 as *Graphice, or the Gentleman's Exercise*. Peacham's interest in the visual arts continued with his illustrations for James I's *Basilikon Doron* rendered into Latin verse for presentation to Henry, Prince of Wales (1610) and his great work *Minerva Britanna* (1612). This is a survey of contemporary English architecture and interior decoration. After Prince Henry's death in 1612, Peacham duly wrote an elegy for him and turned to verse and prose writing rather more than drawing. He travelled in Europe in 1613 and 1614, visiting France, Germany, Holland, and Italy where he studied music. After his return Peacham produced several more elegies and some epigrams and satire. His most famous work was *The Complete Gentleman* (1622). This was not just a book of etiquette, although it included all a gentleman needed to know about heraldry and arms as well as manners. Peacham recommended history, geography, travel, poetry, music and the study of antiquities to his students. He went on to write Anglican and Royalist political pamphlets, a collection of essays, *The Truth of Our Times* (1638), and his most popular book *The Worth of a Penny* (1641), explaining how to save money. His last work, *The Art of Living in London*, was published in 1642.

Henry Peacham, *The Complete Gentleman*, ed., V.B. Heltzel (1962)

PEARCE, Edward (fl. 1589—1609), choirmaster: became a Gentleman of the Chapel Royal in 1589, resigning on 15 August 1600 when he was appointed Master of St Paul's Choir School. Pearce gave great impetus to the dramatic activities of the Paul's Boys, for whom the practice of producing plays had already been revived, probably in 1599 (v. *Thomas Giles*). Between 1600 and 1606 Pearce produced plays by Chapman, Dekker, Marston, Middleton and Webster, both in Paul's theatre and at Court. So great was the success of the boys that the managers of the Children of the Revels, Keysar and Rosseter (qq.v.), made a bargain with Pearce during the winter of 1608-9 by which they would pay him a "dead rent" of £20 a year not to put on any more plays. The Paul's plays were published, and often taken over by adult companies.

E. K. C., *E.S.*

PEELE, George (c. 1557—96) dramatist and poet: son of James Peele, salter and pageant maker, whose house was within the precinct of Christ's Hospital, London. From 1565 Peele was educated at this school, entering Broadgates Hall, Oxford, in 1571, moving to Christ Church three

years later, (B.A., 1577). The Court of Christ's Hospital refused to allow Peele to live in his father's house after he became an M.A. (1579) and it is possible that this was the reason why he remained in Oxford until 1581, when he came to London and was married. He was back in Oxford in 1583, apparently attending to his wife's business affairs, but also producing plays with William Gager (q.v.) at Christ Church. Gager wrote Latin verses praising Peele's wit and poetry; the wit was recorded after Peele's death in the *Merry Conceited Jests of George Peele* (1605), a work leavened with traditional joke-book material. The poetry found expression in the lyrics of his plays and a long poem, *Polyhymnia* (1590) written for the retirement of Sir Henry Lee (q.v.) as Queen's Champion. *Polyhymnia* concludes with the song "His golden locks time hath to silver turned", the most famous of Peele's lyrics, though possibly written by Lee himself. Nashe (q.v.) reckoned him "primus verborum artifex" (champion word-master) as a dramatist. His extant plays were written for the Children of the Chapel Royal and the Admiral's Men. They include pastorals and historical drama, *Battle of Alcazar* (c. 1589) and *Edward I* (c. 1593). He also wrote the first satire on the romantic drama, *The Old Wife's Tale* (c. 1591—4). As producer of pageants for the Lord Mayors of London, Peele introduced classical features of drama for the first time. Reputedly he was an actor as well as a dramatist, but there is no evidence for this. By 1596 he was a sick man and impoverished, sending a begging letter to Lord Burghley. According to Meres (q.v.) he died soon afterwards of the pox.

E. K. C., *E.S.*

PEMBROKE, Henry Herbert, second Earl of (?1538—1601): son of William Herbert, first Earl, and his wife Anne

(Parr, sister of Queen Catherine Parr). His father at first supported Lady Jane Grey's claim to the throne in 1553 and married his son to her sister Catherine; the family soon reverted to allegiance to Queen Mary and Henry Herbert's marriage was dissolved. His second wife was Catherine Talbot, daughter of the Earl of Shrewsbury (1563). She died childless and Herbert, who had succeeded his father as Earl of Pembroke (1570), married Mary Sidney (*infra*) in 1577. Affairs of state, rather than the literary interests of his wife, occupied the Earl. He played a great part in several treason trials, including that of Mary, Queen of Scots, and in 1586 succeeded his father-in-law, Sir Henry Sidney, as President of Wales. He offered to raise an army in Wales at his own cost in Armada year and again in 1599, and fortified Milford Haven. However, Pembroke also found time to improve his house at Wilton and to maintain a company of actors. Pembroke's Men began their existence about 1592; they were forced to tour in the plague year of 1593, apparently without much success, as Philip Henslowe had to pawn their costumes for them. The company performed *Henry VI* and *Titus Andronicus*, so Shakespeare may have acted with them. Their fortunes took another downward turn in 1597, when the reconstituted company was involved in the *Isle of Dogs* scandal at the Swan theatre (v. *Francis Langley*), and Pembroke's Men are last heard of in 1600. From 1598 the Earl of Pembroke's health began to fail, and he asked to be excused from his Welsh duties. After serious illnesses in 1599 and 1600, he died in January 1601.

T. Lever, *The Herberts of Wilton* (1967)

PEMBROKE, Mary Herbert, Countess of (1561–1621): born Mary Sidney, daughter of Sir Henry Sidney, sister of Sir Philip Sidney and niece of the Earl of Leicester. In 1577 she married Henry Herbert, second Earl of Pembroke (*supra*) and was the mother of William, third Earl, and Philip, fourth Earl (qq.v. *infra*). Mary Herbert was patron of many poets who found refuge at Wilton House, the Pembroke seat near Salisbury. Among them were Nicholas Breton, William Browne, Samuel Daniel and John Davies of Hereford (qq.v.), and Spenser (q.v.) addressed one of the dedicatory sonnets of the *Faerie Queene* to her. She encouraged Daniel to begin writing poetry, inspired her brother Philip's romance *Arcadia* and supervised the completion and second edition of this work in 1593. Her translations include the Psalms and *Antonius*, a tragedy from the French (1590); and she produced a dialogue *Astraea* which was intended to entertain Queen Elizabeth on a projected visit to Wilton during a royal Progress, subsequently re-routed. In October 1603 she was hostess to James I and Queen Anne at Wilton. On this occasion the King's Men were summoned to perform a play. A nineteenth-century tradition makes the play Shakespeare's *As You Like It*, preceded by a letter from Mary Herbert to her son William asking him to bring James I to Wilton as "we have the man Shakespeare with us". Nobody has ever seen this letter, and its existence is mentioned only by William Cory, who came to Wilton from Eton as tutor in 1865. Mary Herbert survived her husband by twenty years and retired eventually to the manor of Houghton Conquest, Bedfordshire, granted her by James I (1615), where she employed Italian architects to build Houghton House. She is buried in the Pembroke family vault in Salisbury Cathedral; her most famous epitaph is that by William Browne (q.v.).

Ibid.
J. Buxton, *Sir Philip Sidney and the English Renaissance* (1964)

187

PEMBROKE, Philip Herbert, Earl of Montgomery, later fourth Earl of Pembroke (1584–1650): younger son of the second Earl of Pembroke and his wife Mary (née Sidney), and brother of the third Earl, William. He was educated at home and, for a few months at the age of nine, at New College, Oxford. Although like his brother

Philip Herbert, Earl of Montgomery, later fourth Earl of Pembroke. Portrait by Daniel Mytens

in his good looks and love of jousting, he was different in all other respects. Philip was violent and quarrelsome, had no intellectual interests, but loved sport and gambling. He was at Court from the age of fifteen or sixteen and became the favourite of James I from 1603 to 1611. After a secret engagement he married the Earl of Oxford's daughter, Susan Vere, at Christmas 1604 in Whitehall. The couple spent their wedding night in the council chamber and the festivities included a good

deal of the King's brand of coarse practical joking. A few months later Philip was created Earl of Montgomery. James rescued him from frequent debts and quarrels. When Philip and Southampton met at tennis in 1609 "their rackets flew about their ears", and on several other occasions Philip's violent temper nearly led to bloodshed. He took an interest in overseas enterprises, belonging to the East India Company as well as supporting the American ventures in which his brother (*infra*) participated. The dedication of the First Folio of Shakespeare's plays was addressed to both the Herbert brothers, Philip and William. In 1626 William gave up his office of Lord Chamberlain to Philip, who succeeded as Earl of Pembroke and married the widowed Lady Dorset (*Anne Clifford*, q.v.) in 1630. His first wife had died in 1629, leaving six surviving children; the second marriage was not a success. From 1632 onwards Pembroke devoted much time and money to rebuilding Wilton and improving the gardens there. He resented the election of Laud (q.v.) as Chancellor of Oxford University in succession to his brother, and his hostility to the Royalist cause increased until he supported Parliament in the Civil War. In April 1649 he was elected M.P. for Berkshire to fill a vacancy in the Long Parliament, a "descent" which provoked much satirical comment, but he was already a sick man and died the following January.

Ibid.

PEMBROKE, William Herbert, third Earl of (1580–1630): elder son of the second Earl, Henry Herbert, and his wife Mary (Sidney). He was educated at home, where Samuel Daniel (q.v.) was his tutor from 1590, and at New College, Oxford (1593–5). He went to Court in 1597, living in London from 1598 onwards.

During this period Herbert wrote verse, for private circulation among his friends. He never began to reach the eminence of his uncle, Philip Sidney, as a poet. He declined two proposed marriages: to Elizabeth Carey (q.v.) in 1595, and to Bridget Vere, Burghley's granddaughter, in 1597. Instead he became the lover of Mary Fitton (q.v.), a maid of honour, but refused to marry her when she was found to be pregnant in 1601. For this offence he was sent to the Fleet Prison and released only to travel abroad. William, now Earl of Pembroke, had dissipated his early popularity at Elizabeth's Court, but he and his brother Philip (*supra*) came into favour under James I. James created him a Knight of the Garter in 1603, appointing him Warden of the Stanneries and Lord Lieutenant of Cornwall a year later. He finally married the plain but wealthy Mary Talbot (the Earl of Shrewsbury's daughter) in 1604. Both at Court and at his country seat at Wilton, Pembroke kept great state. He was generous to the poets he patronised, especially Ben Jonson and his own kinsman, George Herbert. Pembroke was an expert jouster, took part in the masques which were so popular with Queen Anne, and he was a favourite with both the Queen and Prince Henry. He was active in all the companies formed for overseas expansion and was either on the council or a member of the Virginia Company, the North-West Passage Company (both in 1609), the Bermuda Company (1615) and the Guiana Company (1626), as well as receiving a grant of land in Barbados (1629). From 1617 until his death he was Chancellor of Oxford University and one of its great benefactors. Broadgates Hall was transformed into Pembroke College (1624), taking his name. He gave numerous books and manuscripts to Bodley's Library, outside which his bronze statue by Hubert le Sueur still stands. From 1615 to 1626 he was Lord Chamberlain and so responsible

for overseeing the production and publishing of plays: and it was therefore natural for Heminges and Condell in 1623 to dedicate the First Folio of Shakespeare's plays "to the most noble and incomparable pair of brethren", Pembroke and his

William Herbert, third Earl of Pembroke. Portrait by Daniel Mythns

brother Philip. This connection with Shakespeare and his early reluctance to marry (together with his initials) have made Pembroke a candidate for the "Mr W.H." of the Sonnets, but his affair with Mary Fitton is too late for her to be the "Dark Lady". Although Pembroke opposed the King over his treatment of Ralegh and Francis Bacon, he remained on good terms with James I and his successor. He criticised Buckingham's policy but was prepared to arrange a marriage between his nephew and heir and Buckingham's daughter. Illness prevented his taking much part in public life after 1626. Indeed he never had the impact on national affairs that his position and natural gifts warranted, probably because he lacked forcefulness and political ambition; as Bacon said of him, "He was not effectual."

Ibid.

PERCY, Dorothy, Countess of Northumberland (1564/5–1619, née Devereux): younger daughter of the first Earl of Essex and sister of Robert, second Earl, and of Penelope Rich (qq.v.). On their father's death in 1576 Dorothy and Penelope, both "golden-haired beauties", were placed under the guardianship of the Earl of Huntingdon. In 1583 Dorothy escaped from Huntingdon's protection and eloped with Sir Thomas Perrot. The couple took possession of the parish church at Broxbourne, Hertfordshire, bringing two armed men to guard the door and a clergyman to conduct a marriage service. The Queen was so angered by this episode that she still refused to speak to Dorothy four years later, even quarrelling with Essex on her account. After Perrot's death Dorothy married, in 1595, Henry Percy, the "wizard" ninth Earl of Northumberland (q.v.). Incompatible tempers strained their married life, Dorothy spending much time at Essex House, away from her husband. She was an ardent supporter of King James's claims to succeed Elizabeth, on one occasion declaring herself ready to "eat the hearts" of his opponents "in salt". Despite the conflicts with her husband Dorothy pleaded with James I for Northumberland's release from the Tower, where he was imprisoned after the Gunpowder Plot, but she was unsuccessful. Relations between husband and wife were strained again over the marriage of their daughter Lucy, later Countess of Carlisle (q.v.). Dorothy died before her husband's final release from the Tower.

M. S. Rawson, *Penelope Rich and Her Cicle* (1911)

PERCY, Henry, Earl of Northumberland (1564–1631) see NORTHUMBERLAND.

PERCY, Lucy (1599–1660) see CARLISLE, Lucy, Countess of.

PERCY, Thomas (c. 1560–1605), conspirator: a distant kinsman of the Earl of Northumberland (q.v.). He lived for most of his life at Scotton, near Knaresborough in Yorkshire, where it is probable he met Guy Fawkes (q.v.) as a young man, since Fawkes's stepfather was a near neighbour of Percy. During part of his life Percy accepted Anglicanism, but he was by 1604 an aggressively flamboyant Roman Catholic. He served his kinsman as chief agent for his estates in the north and had been Constable of Alnwick since 1596. Percy's role in the Fawkes-Catesby conspiracy is not clear. He appears to have embezzled a considerable sum from Northumberland to finance a rising of the Catholic gentry, and he used his kinship with the Earl to rent premises near the House of Lords for the Gunpowder Plotters. He visited Northumberland at Syon House, Isleworth, shortly before midday on 4 November 1605, but he also appears to have had contact with Robert Cecil less than a fortnight previously; it is possible he was a double agent. When Fawkes was arrested Percy left London for the Midlands and was mortally wounded on 8 November in the attack on Holbeach House, Staffordshire, in which Catesby (q.v.) was killed. Percy's activities implicated his kinsman and appear to have been the chief reason for Cecil's sustained attempt to prove that Northumberland was leader of the plotters.

G. R. Batho, "The Wizard Earl in the Tower", *History Today*, VI no.5 (1956)

H. Garnett, *Portrait of Guy Fawkes* (1962)

PERCY, William (1575–1648), poet and dramatist: born in County Durham, the third son of the eighth Earl of Northumberland. He went to Gloucester Hall, Oxford, in 1589, was a friend of the poet, Barnabe Barnes (q.v.) and published his own *Sonnets to the fairest Celia* (1594). By the end of Elizabeth's reign he had written five comedies and *The Fairy Pastoral* for Paul's Boys or adult actors. The novelty of Percy's plays lies in the provision of different prologues and final scenes as well as different stage directions and properties for companies of boys or men. An instruction in *The Aphrodysial*, for example, insists it should be played with beards "for Actors; for Paul's, without". It is not known how otherwise Percy spent his life: he is said to have been imprisoned in the Tower of London on a murder charge, but by 1638 he was living in retirement at Oxford, "drinking nothing but ale". He died "an aged bachelor", and was buried in Christ Church, Oxford.

E. K. C., *E.S.*

PERKINS, William (1558–1602), Puritan theologian: son of Thomas Perkins, of Marston Jabbet, Warwickshire, educated at Christ's College, Cambridge from 1577. Perkins spent all his life at Cambridge, as Fellow of Christ's until 1595 and lecturer at Great St Andrew's Church until 1602. He wrote an immense number of works of Calvinist theology which were translated into Dutch, Spanish, Welsh and Irish. His right hand was crippled early in life, so he wrote entirely with his left. Apart from *The Reformed Catholic* (1597) he was not a doctrinal controversialist, but more interested in expounding his own faith in predestination and his social philosophy.

The practical nature of his theology appears in the *Direction for the Government of the Tongue* (1592) which includes an admonition to students not to swear in Latin, as God listens in all languages. The *Treatise of the Vocations* (published 1603) is an uncompromising statement of the Protestant work ethic. Perhaps most famous is the *Discourse of the Damned Art of Witchcraft* (published 1609), the Bible of witch hunters in New England as well as at home. Perkins also wrote practical advice for preachers. He was a notable preacher himself, and gave a famous sermon at Stourbridge Fair in 1592. After his death his executors appointed editors to prepare his remaining works for the press and produce an edition for the benefit of his widow and children. The collected *Works* went into eleven editions by 1635 and the influence of Perkins lasted until the Civil War. He is buried in Great St Andrew's, Cambridge.

Lewis B. Wright, "William Perkins", *Huntington Library Quarterly*, III, no.2 (1940)

W. Haller, *The Rise of Puritanism* (1938)

C. Hill, *Puritanism and Revolution* (1958); *Society and Puritanism in Pre-Revolutionary England* (1964)

PERYAM, William (1534–1604), judge: born in Exeter, the son of John Peryam, a prominent merchant in the city who was Mayor in 1563 and 1572, and through his mother a first cousin of Sir Thomas Bodley (q.v.). He was educated at Exeter College, Oxford (B.A., 1551), represented Plymouth in the Commons in 1563 and 1567, was called to the Bar of the Middle Temple in 1565, became a sergeant at law in 1579 and a judge of common pleas in 1581. He married into the Bacon family and in 1593 he was knighted and appointed Chief Baron of the Exchequer. His brother John was one of the M.P.s for Exeter in 1589 and 1593 and a prominent merchant-adventurer. The two brothers were useful representatives of their native town in the capital, typical of so many other rising merchant families from prosperous provincial cities during the later years of the sixteenth century. Sir William died at his country home, Little Fulford, near Crediton.

Wallace T. MacCaffrey, *Exeter 1540-1640* (1975)

PHILLIPS, Augustine (fl. 1590 – d. 1605), actor: is known to have been with the Admiral's or Strange's company 1590–1, then Strange's in 1593, probably joining the Chamberlain's Men when they were founded in 1594. His name is in their acting lists from 1598, the Royal Patent of 1603 and the First Folio list. He was also one of the original sharers in the Globe, 1599. On 18 February 1601 Phillips was examined by Chief Justice Popham about the performance of *Richard II*, given by the company on the eve of Essex's rising at the suggestion of Lord Monteagle, Sir Gelly Meyrick, (qq.v.) and other friends of the Earl. In his deposition Phillips said that the company had intended to stage another play because "that play of King Richard" was so "out of use as that thay should have small or no company at it", but they were persuaded to play *Richard II* for forty shillings. This deposition satisfied the authorities, and no action was taken against the players. Phillips was a versatile performer: he could dance and sing, and his "jig of the slippers" is in the Stationers' Register of 1595. Most of Phillips's life was spent at Southwark but he bought an estate at Mortlake, and died there a comparatively wealthy man. In his will he left 30s each to Shakespeare, Condell and Beeston, 20s to other "fellows", and £5 among the "hired men of the company". Further legacies included 40s cash to his apprentices Gilburne and Sands, together with much clothing and musical instruments, and silver bowls to Heminges and Richard Burbage. His widow, Anne, was to lose her "portion" should she marry again, a stipulation which did not deter her from marrying John Witter within a couple of years. Phillips's share in the Globe became a matter for litigation.

PLATTER, Thomas (1574–1628), tourist: born and educated in Basle, Switzerland, qualifying as a doctor of medicine in 1600 and becoming Professor of Anatomy at Basle in 1614. Platter travelled extensively in France, Spain, the Netherlands and England between 1595 and 1600, writing detailed accounts of his travels soon afterwards. His visit to England in the autumn of 1599 is of particular interest for his information about the University of Oxford, the appearance of the Queen (whom he saw at Nonsuch and at Richmond), and visits to a theatre in Bishopsgate and to the Globe on Bankside. He writes, under the date of 21 September 1599, "After dinner, at about two o'clock, I went with my party across the water; in the straw-thatched house we saw the tragedy of the Emperor Julius Caesar, very pleasantly performed . . ."

C. Williams, ed., *Thomas Platter's travels in England 1599* (1937)
M. Helmer, ed., *Thomas Platter Autobiographie* (1964)

POCAHONTAS (or MATOAKA) (1593/7 – 1617), Indian princess: daughter of Powhatan, Chief of the confederacy of Algonkian speaking tribes in Virginia. She was Powhatan's favourite daughter; Matoaka was her secret Indian name, but she was generally known as Pocahontas, meaning "playful". Her first contact with white men was during the winter of 1607/8 when she is reputed to have rescued Captain John Smith (q.v.) from being sacrificed in her father's camp. Pocahontas enjoyed a special relationship with John Smith and the English colonists in Virginia thereafter. She visited the settlement at Jamestown often during the winter, bringing the supplies her father had agreed to send and turning cartwheels in the streets. By January 1609, the Indians had become hostile. Pocahontas saved Smith again from her father's treachery, but there was no more food for the colony, which suffered greatly; that winter was known as the "Starving Time". Pocahontas left her father's land and went to live among the Patawamake (Potomac) tribe on the banks of their river. Her English sympathies and

Pocahontas

rescue of another hostage, Henry Spelman, may have estranged her from Powhatan, or she may have married into the Patawamake. She seems to have believed that her particular friend, John Smith, who returned to England in September 1609, was dead. In 1613 a trading expedition from Jamestown discovered the whereabouts of Pocahontas and kidnapped her as hostage for her father's good behaviour. She was not ransomed, but was converted to Christianity, baptised "Rebecca" and married a colonist, John

Rolfe (q.v.) in April, 1614. Powhatan sent his brother and two sons as witnesses and made the "Peace of Pocahontas" with the settlers. In the spring of 1615 Pocahontas' son Thomas (q.v.) was born. The Virginia Company decided to fetch the Rolfe family back to England as an advertisement for the success of the colony. They arrived in England in 1616, accompanied by Pocahontas' sister and brother-in-law and about a dozen other Indians, staying first at an inn on Ludgate Hill then at Brentford when Pocahontas' health began to deteriorate in the London smog. Her brother-in-law Uttamatamakin, a priest, defended his religion strongly in debate against English clergy; Pocahontas and he were received at Court, though John Rolfe was not, and in January 1617 had seats of honour at Jonson's Twelfth Night masque *Vision of Delight*. Pocahontas eventually had an emotional encounter with John Smith, which at first deprived her of speech. Although she was very ill, Rolfe decided to return to Virginia. The family started to sail down the Thames but Pocahontas was taken ashore at Gravesend and died there. She was buried in St George's Church on 21 March 1617 but her grave has never been found. Uttamatamakin, disgusted with the English, stirred up trouble for the settlers in Virginia after Powhatan's death, and the Peace of Pocahontas ended with the Indians attacking Jamestown on 22 March, 1622.

P. Barbour, *Pocahontas and her World* (1971)
F. Mossiker, *Pocahontas, the life and the legend* (1977)

POLLARD, Thomas (fl. 1617–42), actor: an apprentice to John Shank (q.v.), probably before Shank joined the King's Men. Pollard first appears in the King's Men acting list of 1617 and continued with the company until 1642, specialising in comic roles. In 1635 he was one of the actors who petitioned for a share in the theatres. He is known to have been dead by 1655.

POPE, Thomas (?–1604), actor: toured Denmark and Germany in 1586 and 1587. He was then with Strange's or the Admiral's Men (1590–1), Strange's in 1593 and probably joined the Chamberlain's Men at their foundation in 1594. Pope was joint payee with Heminges for the company, 1597–9, and one of the original sharers in the Globe, 1599. Rowlands in *Letting of Humour's Blood* (1600) refers to "Pope, the clown" and it is assumed he played comic roles. Pope's name appears in the First Folio list, but he must have retired before 1603 as he was never in the King's Men. He lived and died in Southwark, leaving his share in the Globe and Curtain to Mary Clark and Thomas Bromley. These shares were, however, eventually bought for Ostler (q.v.) and so remained within the company.

POPHAM, John (1531–1607), lawyer and Speaker of the Commons: born at Huntworth, Somerset, and educated at Balliol College, Oxford. He sat as member for Bristol in the Parliaments of 1571, 1572, 1576 and 1581, and first became a Privy Councillor in 1581. He was responsible for drafting the bill which checked idleness by setting the poor to work (1572). He became Speaker of the Commons in January 1581, but held office for only a few months as it harmed his lucrative legal practice. Shortly after Parliament was prorogued in mid-March 1581, he was asked by the Queen what had passed in the House of Commons and is alleged to have replied, "If it please your Majesty, seven weeks." He was thereafter appointed Attorney-General, becoming a Lord Chief Justice (and a knight) in 1592. Together with Anderson (q.v.) he presided over the trials of Essex and Ralegh, and was responsible for sentencing the Gunpowder Plotters of 1605. He made a wealthy marriage to one of the Harvey family and lived, in some estate, both in London and at Wellington in Somerset. According to John Aubrey, Sir John and Lady Popham "both died by excess, and by luxury, and by cosonage by their servants".

PORTER, Henry (fl. 1596–9), dramatist: is first mentioned in Henslowe's diary as writer of plays for the Admiral's Men in December 1596. Three years later Meres (q.v.) counted him as one of the "best for comedy among us". He wrote six plays for the Admiral's Men, either alone or with Chettle and Jonson, but only one is extant, *The Two Angry Women of Abingdon* (c. 1598). One of his lost plays is a sequel to it. Apart from the fact that he frequently borrowed money from Henslowe or the company and that he is described as "Gent" on the title-page of his play, nothing is known of his life. Clearly he was familiar with the Oxford neighbourhood; he could be any one of five Henry Porters who matriculated at Oxford University in or soon after 1589.

E. K., *E.S.*

PORY, John (1572–1636), colonial official, newswriter: born at Thompson, Norfolk, son of William Pory of an old Norfolk family, and educated at Gonville and Caius College, Cambridge (1588–92). After a short period teaching Greek at Cambridge, Pory studied under Hakluyt (q.v.) who saw him as a possible literary heir and encouraged him to translate *A Geographical History of Africa* from the Arabic and Italian of the Moor John Leo. In this work, published 1600, Pory was the first to use many now-familiar names, like Angola and Sahara. His only other geographical publication was the *Epitome of*

Ortelius, (1602–3), an abridgement of the Belgian's great atlas of the world. Pory was predominantly a writer of letters, mostly regular newsletters which he was commisioned to send to his subscribers. He had a regular day for writing to a client, and could earn as much as £20 a year for his services. From 1605 to 1611 while he was M.P. for Bridgwater, his letters gave news of London and the Court; he also sold copies of speeches. Between 1612 and 1617 he travelled in Ireland and Paris (as agent of Lord Carew) and visited northern Italy, where he met Dudley Carleton (q.v.) with whom he corresponded. Pory was in Constantinople until 1617, working for the Levant Company's ambassador there, and returned with Chinese and Persian books. Carleton considered him as a possible secretary, but Pory was by now a drunkard. However, he had been a member of the Virginia Company from its new charter in 1609, and in 1619 was appointed secretary to the Governor, Yardley (q.v.), a connection by marriage. Pory sobered up in Virginia, as there was no wine there. He was on the council governing the colony, and on 30 July 1619 presided as Speaker over the first session of the Assembly of Burgesses, the first such assembly in the New World. He explored the Eastern seaboard of Virginia, and in 1622 visited the newer settlement at Plymouth, Massachusetts, sending a report on its achievements. Pory returned home in 1623, a poor man, after suffering a shipwreck and imprisonment in the Azores. He went back and forth to Virginia for the next two years as a commissioner for the Privy Council investigating the government of the colony. When James I took the administration into his own hands in 1624, Pory was paid £150. Until 1633 he wrote his newsletters from London again, but eventually retired to Sutton St Edmund's, Lincolnshire, where he is buried.

W. S. Powell, *John Pory, the Life and Letters of a Man of Many Parts* (1977)

POUND, Thomas (?1538–?1616), writer: son of William Pound of Belmont (or Beaumonds) in Hampshire, educated at Winchester College, entering Lincoln's Inn in 1560. He contributed to two of the Lincoln's Inn masques, the first celebrating the marriage of his cousin Henry, Earl of Southampton (father of Shakespeare's patron, the third Earl of Southampton, q.v.). Pound became a courtier, noted for writing and performing in masques, until his sudden conversion — or reconversion — to Roman Catholicism, about 1570. It is said that he fell while dancing, an accident so ridiculed by the Queen and Court that Pound realised the vanity of worldly success. He was imprisoned for the first time in 1574, spending most of the next thirty years in prison. By 1579 he seems to have joined the Society of Jesus, though he was never ordained priest. In 1580 he was able to leave the Marshalsea Prison to meet Campion and Parsons (q.v.); he suggested to Campion that he should write a letter stating the non-political nature of their mission, and he was responsible for making their presence in England more widely known. Pound was finally released from prison in 1604 and spent the rest of his life in his old home, reputedly dying in the room in which he was born. His later works — all of them religious in character — include poems and tracts on penance, death, and the authority of the Church as opposed to the authority of Scripture.

E. K. C., *E.S.*
J. Gillow, ed., *Bibliographical Dictionary of English Catholics* (1885)

PURCHAS, Samuel (1575–1626), travel propagandist: born at Thaxted, Essex, educated at St John's College,

195

Cambridge, ordained in the Church of England, serving for the last twelve years of his life as Rector of St Martin's, Ludgate, in the City of London. He appears to have acquired the papers of Hakluyt (q.v.) and his fame rests on three strangely diffuse books which were in part observations of man in his environment, but were principally narratives of voyages: to the Far East and India, in search of a north-west passage, to Africa, and to the West Indies. *Purchas his Pilgrimage, or Relations of the World and the Religions observed in all Ages and Places* was published in 1612; *Purchas his Pilgrim, Microcosmus or the History of Man* in 1619; and *Hakluytus Posthumus, or Purchas his Pilgrimes, containing a History of the World in Sea Voyages and Land Travels* in 1625. Purchas received a grant of £100 from the East India Company for interesting the general public in travel and exploration.

PURFOOT, Thomas (?–1640), printer: son of Thomas Purfoot, printer, of London. He was apprenticed to Richard Collins for seven years from 1584 and became a freeman of the Stationers' Company in 1590 and a master printer in 1591. Purfoot was in partnership with his father until 1615; he had shops near Newgate, first the "Lucrece" and then by St Sepulcre's Church. In 1615 Purfoot had two presses and was employed by most of the important publishers. He printed Shakespeare's *Richard III* and *Henry IV*, part 1 for Matthew Law (1622). Purfoot was Junior (1629) and Senior (1634) Warden of the Stationers' Company.

PUTTENHAM, George (c. 1529–90) and **PUTTENHAM, Richard** (c. 1520–1601). One of these two brothers was author of *The Art of English Poesie*, the first important critical work on the subject of poetry in English. Field (q.v.), Shakespeare's printer friend, published the book anonymously in February 1589, after it was originally licensed to another printer. Field himself wrote the dedication of the book to Burghley, claiming not to know the author, but by 1590 his name was said to be Puttenham, an attribution never successfully disputed. The author indicated that he had also written three plays, prose treatises and at the age of eighteen an eclogue to King Edward VI, although it is not clear if at the time Edward had come to the throne. He also claims to have been at Oxford or Cambridge, to have visited France, Spain, Italy and the Holy Roman Empire, as well as seeing the Courts of China and Tartary. At first it was believed Richard Puttenham was the author: he is known to have accompanied his uncle, the diplomat Sir Thomas Elyot, to the Court of the Emperor Charles V, and he was forced to live out of England from 1563 until about 1570 because of a conviction for rape. Lately George Puttenham has been preferred as the author. Although there is no evidence that he travelled much abroad, George was at Christ's College, Cambridge in the late 1540s and was admitted to the Middle Temple in 1556. He wrote, in his own name, a defence of Queen Elizabeth; Richard is not known to have written anything. Both Puttenhams spent some time in prison, George in 1578 and Richard in 1588; George later received the considerable sum of £1,000 compensation from the government for the injustice of his treatment. The importance of *The Art of English Poesie* lies in the conviction of its author that the English language, like the classical tongues, lends itself naturally and not artificially to poetry. The author shows a sound sense of continuity, from Greek and Latin literature through the English mediaeval tradition to the verbal skills of the Renaissance writers.

G. D. Willcook and A. Walker, eds., *George Puttenham, The Art of English Poesy* (1936)

PYM, John (1584–1643), Parliamentarian: born near Bridgwater, Somerset, entered Pembroke College, Oxford in 1599 but did not graduate. He was admitted to the Middle Temple in 1603. In 1614 he was elected Member of Parliament for Calne, sitting for Tavistock in the Parliaments of 1625 and 1628, as well as in the Short Parliament and the Long Parliament. Pym attacked the sale of monopolies, the projected Spanish marriage for the future Charles I, the predominance of Buckingham, and the alleged "papism" of Laud. He was, in effect, Leader of the Commons in opposition to Charles I in 1640. He helped draw up the Petition of Right and played a prominent part in the impeachment of Strafford and in preparing the Grand Remonstrance. In January 1642 he was one of the "five members" whose arrest Charles I sought in vain. But Pym's outstanding characteristics were his skill in marshalling facts for the presentation of an indictment and his consistent calm. He presented the case for revolution with judicious moderation and his strength lay in his abhorrence of demagogy.

J. H. Hexter, *The Reign of King Pym* (1941)

Q

QUINEY, Adrian (?−1607), mercer in Stratford: until 1557 he lived in Henley Street, Stratford, and was a friend of Shakespeare's father. His son Richard Quiney (q.v.) and two daughters were born there, to his first wife. When he married a widow in 1557 he moved to her house in the High Street. Quiney's name appears among the original Aldermen of the town, in the charter of 1553, and he was Town Bailiff in 1559, 1571 and 1582. In October 1598, he wrote to his son Richard, then in London, to suggest that he might borrow money from Shakespeare.

E. K. C., *W.S.*
M. E.

QUINEY, George (1600−24), Stratford resident: son of Shakespeare's friend Richard Quiney. He was a graduate of Balliol College, Oxford (B.A., 1620), returning to his native Stratford as Curate and assistant at the school. He died of tuberculosis, despite the ministrations of Dr Hall (q.v.), who described him as "of a good wit and expert in languages".

E. R. C. Brinkworth, *Shakespeare and the Bawdy Court of Stratford* (1972)

QUINEY, Judith (1585−1662, née Shakespeare), Shakespeare's daughter: was baptised with her twin brother, Hamnet, on 2 February 1585. The twins were named after Shakespeare's friends, Hamnet and Judith Sadler. She married Thomas Quiney (q.v.) on 10 February 1616. Both were summoned before the Consistory Court at Worcester for marrying in the forbidden season before Easter. Thomas was, for a time, excommunicated but the Court may not have imposed such a penalty on Judith. They were reinstated before November that year when their son, Shakespeare Quiney, was baptised; he lived only until the following May. Judith's father died shortly after her marriage; he left her £100 as a marriage portion, together with £50 if she gave up any claim to his Chapel Lane cottage. A further £150 was to go to Judith or her children three years later, but she would only receive the interest during her marriage. Should she die, this second sum would revert to Shakespeare's granddaughter and sister and not to Judith's husband, unless he had by then settled land on his wife and children. Shakespeare evidently distrusted Quiney's character and ability as a provider, and he was justified. Judith was mother to two more sons: Richard, born in 1618, and Thomas in 1620; both died in 1639, unmarried. Judith is presumably buried in Holy Trinity churchyard but no grave is marked.

M. E.

QUINEY, Richard (ante 1557−1602), Shakespeare's friend: son of Adrian Quiney (q.v.). He became an Alderman of Stratford in 1588 and Bailiff in 1592. Quiney went to London on town business in 1593, 1595 and every year from 1597 to 1601. Much of his work was concerned with collecting relief money for the two serious fires which ravaged Stratford in September 1594 and September 1595, and in this cause he visited Suffolk and Norfolk as well as the capital. He wrote many letters home to Abraham Sturley (q.v.). A letter to Shakespeare (extant, because never delivered) sent on 25 October 1598, asks Shakespeare for a loan of £30 to pay off debts incurred while in London petitioning for a new charter which would have relieved Stratford from taxes. The remission of taxes was granted in January 1599, and Quiney's expenses paid by the Exchequer; he had spent at least £20, and they gave him £44. Quiney also received some belated help from Sir Edward Greville (q.v.). Subsequently, friction developed between Quiney and Greville, who tried to enclose the town commons at Stratford. Quiney and others were charged with riot after flattening Greville's hedges in January 1601. Greville also sued Quiney for asserting the town's right to take toll of grain in the market. With Thomas Greene (q.v.) Quiney travelled to London in February 1601 to consult Attorney-General Coke about this suit, but Coke could not see them because the Essex rebellion was keeping him busy. Despite Greville's opposition Quiney was again elected Bailiff in September 1601, but early in the following May he was wounded by a drunken band of Greville's men, dying by the end of the month. His widow, Elizabeth, was left with nine children under the age of twenty.

M. E.

E. I. Fripp, *Master Richard Quyny* (1924)

QUINEY, Thomas (1589–?1662), vintner and son-in-law to Shakespeare: second surviving son of Richard Quiney (*supra*). As soon as he was old enough he helped run his widowed mother's business, and by 1608 was selling wine to the Stratford Corporation. In 1611 he took the lease of a small house, adjoining that of his mother in Stratford High Street, and ran it as a tavern. Thomas married Shakespeare's youngest daughter, Judith, on 10 February 1616 but was temporarily excommunicated for marrying in the forbidden Lenten season. Immediately after his marriage, Quiney was in worse trouble. On 26 March 1616, he was charged before the Church Court at Stratford with getting Margaret Wheeler (q.v.) pregnant and was sentenced to do penance in a white sheet for three Sundays in the parish church, a penalty subsequently remitted for a fine of 5s and private penance before the Minister of Bishopton chapel. This disgrace may have hastened Shakespeare's death; he certainly took pains to safeguard Judith's interests in his will (v. *Judith Quiney*). In July 1616 Quiney set up his vintry and tobacco shop in "The Cage" on the corner of High Street and Bridge Street, but this venture did not make him rich. The lease of "The Cage" was assigned to a trust in 1633 and eventually made over to his elder brother (a prosperous grocer in Bucklersbury, London) who allowed Thomas £12 a year; he was still selling wine there during the Cromwellian Commonwealth and Protectorate. Despite his disgrace in 1616, Quiney was chosen Burgess and Constable at Stratford in 1617 and Chamberlain in 1621 and 1622. At first his accounts for 1622-3 were voted imperfect by the Council, but passed later. Quiney never became an Alderman. He survived three sons, but probably not his wife. His burial date is unrecorded.

M. E.

S. S.

E. R. C. Brinkworth, *Shakespeare and the Bawdy Court of Stratford* (1972)

R

RAINSFORD, Anne, Lady (1570/1– post 1633): daughter of Sir Henry Goodere of Polesworth, Warwickshire. The poet Drayton (q.v.) was brought up in the Goodere household and became especially devoted to Anne, the younger daughter. As "Idea" she inspired his early poems. In 1595 Anne's father died and she married Henry Rainsford, squire of Clifford Chambers near Stratford-upon-Avon, who was knighted at James I's coronation (1603). Drayton spent most of his summers at Clifford Chambers, although Anne Rainsford was no longer the sole inspiration of his sonnets. The Rainsfords had connections with Stratford also; Shakespeare's son-in-law, John Hall (q.v.) was their doctor, treating Lady Rainsford in her old age (1633) and Sir Henry was named executor in the will of John Combe (q.v.) in 1613. There is even an old legend that Shakespeare was born at Clifford Chambers, his parents having fled the plague in Stratford, but there is no basis for this story. A John Shakespeare, probably a relation of the poets' family, was a tenant of the Rainsfords. Anne continued to live in the Manor House after Sir Henry's death in 1621. The last mention of her is in 1633; the space for her death date in the monument in Clifford Chambers was never filled in.

E. Buckland, *The Rainsford Family* (1932)
B. H. Newdigate, *Drayton and his Circle* (1961)

RALEGH, Elizabeth, Lady (1565– 1647): youngest child and only daughter of Sir Nicholas Throckmorton. Elizabeth's father died in 1571 and she lived with her mother until 1584, when she went to Court as maid of honour to the Queen. She was not a great heiress: her father left her a portion of £500 which the Earl of Huntingdon borrowed and never repaid, and she eventually inherited furnishing, clothes and jewels from her mother and stepfather. Nevertheless, in 1590 Sir Walter Ralegh (*infra*), began to court her and by November 1591 they had been married secretly and Elizabeth was pregnant. In March 1592 her son was born at her brother Arthur's house in Mile End, London. He was baptised Damerei (with the Earl of Essex as godfather), put out to nurse and presumably died in infancy. Elizabeth went back to Court, but by August the secret was out and Sir Walter and Lady Ralegh both in the Tower; they were released by December. The Queen never really forgave Lady Ralegh's deceit and an attempt to reinstate her at Court in 1601 failed. She remained at Sherborne, the Raleghs' house in Dorset, with occasional visits to London. Her second son Walter was born in 1593. From 1603 until 1616 Ralegh was confined to the Tower for his alleged conspiracy against James I. Lady Ralegh seems to have lived with him there most of the time until 1610, when she was ordered to stay in her own house on Tower Hill. Their youngest son Carew was born in 1605, either in the Tower or nearby. In 1609 James confiscated Sherborne to give his favourite Robert Carr (q.v.) although Ralegh fought a long action to prove that he had already conveyed the estate to his son Walter. Lady Ralegh was granted £8,000 as compensation and a pension of £400 for life. She had pleaded unsuccessfully with Sir Robert Cecil and James himself for her husband's freedom and for Sherborne. Lady Ralegh supported her husband through his last fatal expedition in 1618, met him at Plymouth on his return and spent some time in the Tower again with him in the autumn. After his execution on 29 October she was allowed to take only his head, which she had embalmed and kept by her all her life.

A. L. Rowse, *Ralegh and the Throckmortons* (1962)

RALEGH, Walter (?1552—1618), seaman, explorer, courtier, poet and historian: born at Hayes Barton in south-east Devon, educated at Oriel College, Oxford, fought with a contingent of Devonshire volunteers helping the French Huguenots, 1569—74. Subsequently, he fought with great ruthlessness in Ireland, and helped

Sir Walter Ralegh

his half-brother Humphrey Gilbert fit out expeditions to raid Spanish vessels between the Azores and the West Indies. He financed seven expeditions to colonise the Americas, though without lasting success. He was at Court intermittently from 1581 onwards, much favoured by Elizabeth who knighted him in 1584 and appointed him Captain of the Queen's Guard in 1587, subsequently bestowing on him rich properties in five counties. In the summer of 1592 he was imprisoned for marrying Elizabeth Throckmorton (*supra*), without

first seeking permission from the Queen, to whom she was an attendant; but he was soon pardoned, and the couple settled at the finest of his properties, Sherborne in Dorset. He sailed from Plymouth in February 1595 on an unsuccessful expedition to the Orinoco basin in search of the fabulously wealthy city of Manoa ("El Dorado"). On his return later in the year he wrote an account of his explorations up the river, ending his narrative with an appeal to the Queen for the establishment of an English Empire in the Americas. He took part in Essex's raid on Cadiz in 1596 and organised another expedition to Guiana in 1597. In September 1597 a violent quarrel developed between Ralegh and Essex over the tactics to be used against Spanish treasure ships in the Azores, and thereafter Ralegh was a consistent enemy of Essex. Ralegh's arrogance and disdain made him unpopular, and he was widely blamed for Essex's overthrow. James I, already prejudiced against Ralegh, was easily persuaded that he was a dangerous conspirator, and he kept Ralegh imprisoned in the Tower of London from 1603 to 1616, when he was released in order to undertake another expedition to the Orinoco in search of gold. During the expedition he burnt a Spanish settlement at San Tomas, and on his return to London, he found James I seeking to negotiate a Spanish marriage for the Prince of Wales. Protests from the Spanish ambassador led the King to order Ralegh's arrest, and he was executed in Old Palace Yard, Westminster (October 1618). Ralegh's literary gifts enabled him to leave some thirty poems and a work of elegant prose, his *History of the World*, written in the Tower and printed in 1614. His anti-Spanish prejudice, his defiance of the Stuart crown, his championship of intellectual scientific curiosity and his sympathy with religious toleration all contributed to make Ralegh, the former royal favourite, a martyred hero to the

Parliamentarian revolutionaries of the next generation.

A. L. Rowse, *Ralegh and the Throckmortons* (1962)
C. Hill, *Intellectual Origins of the English Revolution* (1965)

RATCLIFFE, Margaret (?–1599), maid of honour to Queen Elizabeth; daughter of Sir John Ratcliffe. She was courted unsuccessfully by Lord Cobham in 1597. After the death of her brother Alexander in Ireland (1599), Margaret died of grief and starvation, and was buried in Westminster Abbey. The funeral was attended by all the Queen's ladies. Jonson wrote an epitaph in the form of an acrostic on Margaret's name, and also addressed a poem to her doubly bereaved father.

REPLINGHAM, William (fl. 1614–15), lawyer: associated with his cousin by marriage, Arthur Mainwaring (q.v.), in attempting to enclose Welcombe, Stratford, in 1614. Replingham drew up the agreement of 28 October 1614 which promised to compensate Shakespeare for losses as a tithe holder if the enclosures went through. He continued to negotiate with the Town Council on Mainwaring's behalf until the following March when the enclosure project was abandoned.

E. K. C., *W.S.*

REYNOLDS, Robert (fl. 1616–40), actor: a player with Queen Anne's Men from 1616-17 but also toured Copenhagen and Danzig in 1616 (v. *Green*). From 1618 onwards he spent most of his life abroad, and it is possible he may have left England for religious reasons since he and his wife, Jane, were both indicted for not attending church in 1616 and 1617. Reynolds was in Strasbourg with Robert Browne (q.v.) in 1618 but his name does not appear again in the company lists until 1626, when he was

back with Green. It is probable that he took over the leadership of Green's company in 1627, and he toured Germany intermittently until 1640. During these German tours Reynolds used the comic name, "Pickleherring", as an alias.

REYNOLDS, William (1575–1633), Warwickshire landowner, friend of Shakespeare: grandson of one of the original Stratford Aldermen. His parents were recusants, living in Chapel Street, and in 1604 they sheltered an escaped seminary priest, who was seen running down the street into their house. In 1606 his mother, Margaret Reynolds, was one of those accused of not receiving Holy Communion at Easter (v. *Susanna Hall*). William inherited from his parents land in Stratford and at Welcombe; and in 1615 he married Frances du Bois, a Frenchwoman from London. Shakespeare in his will left Reynolds two marks to buy a ring. In 1619 Reynolds, John Nash (q.v.) and others were charged in Star Chamber with riot and libel against the new Vicar of Stratford, a Puritan. Part of the charge was that the maypole had again been set up close to Reynolds's house. Reynolds denied being involved in the affair. By 1621 he was recognised as one of the chief landowners in Old Stratford.

M. E.

RICE, John (fl. 1607–29), actor: an apprentice of Heminges (q.v.). Rice was described as "a very proper Child, well spoken", when, on 16 July 1607, Heminges lent him to the Merchant Taylors' Company to recite verses by Jonson at a dinner for James I. In 1610 Rice appeared as the nymph Corinea, representing Cornwall, in the water pageant to celebrate the creation of Prince Henry as Prince of Wales in 1610. Rice must have been the best boy actor in the company since the only adult to perform on both these occasions was the company's leading actor, Burbage. Rice left to join Lady Elizabeth's Men in 1611 but was back in the King's company in 1619 and his name appears in the First Folio list. He is not mentioned in any acting lists after 1625, but he was overseer to Heminges's will in 1630. If he is the "John Rice, clerk of St Saviour's, Southwark" to whom Heminges left 20s in this will, he must have given up acting and become a church official, one of the lay parish clerks authorised by the Book of Canons of 1604 to assist the clergy and help in the general care of a church.

G. E. B.

RICH, Penelope, (1563–1607, née Devereux): elder daughter of the first Earl of Essex and sister of Robert, second Earl, and of Dorothy Percy (qq.v.). Penelope, a golden-haired, black-eyed beauty was considered as a bride for Philip Sidney in 1576 but her father died before the match could be arranged, and her guardian (Huntingdon) married her in 1581 to "the rich Lord Rich", who had no attraction apart from his money. Sidney remained in love with Penelope, and the passionate sonnets of *Astrophel and Stella* are addressed to her as Stella. After Sidney's death (1586), Penelope became the mistress of Sir Charles Blount, later Lord Mountjoy (q.v.), whom she may well have known before her marriage. Mountjoy was a member of the Essex House circle and was frequently there with Penelope, until Essex returned from Ireland in disgrace and Mountjoy succeeded him as Lord Deputy (1600). Penelope wrote a vehement letter to the Queen on behalf of her brother, incurring Elizabeth's anger at her impertinence. She remained Essex's firm supporter: "What I meant I wrote, and what I wrote I meant", she declared. Penelope

was at Essex House in January-February 1601 and engaged in her brother's abortive conspiracy, although not so deeply implicated as his last confession suggested. After a brief spell of house arrest, she was cleared of all charges but remained in retirement until Elizabeth's death. James I's consort, Anne, welcomed her at Court, appointing her a Lady of the Bedchamber; and the King accorded her the place and rank "of the ancient Earls of Essex". She performed in Jonson's *Masque of Blackness* at Twelfth Night 1605. Later that year Lord Rich at last divorced Penelope and she was secretly married to Mountjoy (now Earl of Devonshire) by his chaplain, William Laud, the future Archbishop. This marriage led to renewed disgrace: Mountjoy died in 1606 and Penelope soon afterwards. She left six children by Rich, and five by Mountjoy (Devonshire). In the late nineteenth century Penelope Rich was suggested as a possible "Dark Lady" of Shakespeare's Sonnets.

M. S. Rawson, *Penelope Rich and her Cicle* (1911)

RICHARDSON, John (?–1594), Stratford farmer: witnessed the will of Shakespeare's father-in-law, Richard Hathaway, in 1581. In the following year he and Fulke Sandells (q.v.) were sureties in the bond of 28 November 1582 for Shakespeare's marriage licence (v. *Anne Shakespeare*). When Richardson died in 1594, he was worth £87 and 130 sheep.

M. E.

RIDLEY, Mark (1560–1624), traveller and scientist: son of a first cousin of the Protestant martyr bishop, Nicholas Ridley, burned at Oxford in 1555. Mark Ridley was educated at Clare Hall, Cambridge, where he graduated in 1580. He became a Fellow of the College of Physicians in 1594, travelling with royal recommendation that year to Moscow, where he served as doctor to the Regent, Boris Godunov, for four years and compiled the earliest surviving English-Russian and Russian-English dictionaries (preserved among the manuscript vocabularies of the Bodleian Library, Oxford). After his return to England in 1598 Ridley became interested in the scientific discoveries of Galileo and Kepler, both of whom were a few years his junior. Ridley's *Short Treatise of Magnetical Bodies and Motions* (1613) was a pioneer work in English and was followed by a further essay on electrical bodies, *Magnetical Animadversions* (1617).

A. L. Rowse, *The Elizabethan Renaissance; the Cultural Achievement* (1972)
J. S. G. Simmons and B. O. Unbegaun, "Slavonic Manuscript Vocabularies", *Oxford Slavonic Papers*, II (1951)

RIDOLFI, Roberto di (1531–1612), banker and conspirator: born and died in Florence, settling in England as a banker during the reign of Mary I and establishing financial links with Cecil (Burghley) as well as with the Duke of Norfolk and several prominent Roman Catholics. He acted as a financial agent for distributing money from Rome to the leaders of the rebellion of the northern earls in 1569. He was arrested, interrogated by Walsingham but allowed to go free in January 1570 and it is probable that Cecil hoped to use him as a double agent. Ridolfi spent most of the following eighteen months travelling between the Netherlands, Spain and Rome trying to co-ordinate plots which involved the assassination of Queen Elizabeth, the rising of the English Catholics and the marriage of the Duke of Norfolk and Mary, Queen of Scots, who would re-establish Catholicism in England. This complicated conspiracy, the so-called 'Ridolfi Plot', was revealed to Walsingham from sources in Tuscany and Spain. The principal agents

of the conspiracy in England were arrested and liquidated. Ridolfi settled once more in Florence, where he became a respected and venerable Senator, having confirmed the English suspicion of Italians as arch-conspirators.

Francis Edwards, *The Marvellous Chance* (1968)

ROBERTS, James (fl. 1564–1608), printer, bookseller: became a freeman of the Stationers' Company in 1564 and had shops at the sign of "Love and Death", Fleet Street, by the Little Conduit in Cheapside and in the Barbican. In 1588 Roberts and Richard Watkins obtained a patent to publish all almanacs and prognostications. Roberts married the widow of John Charlewood, printer, and acquired all her late husband's copyrights. In 1598 he registered Shakespeare's *Merchant of Venice* for publication on condition that he should have the Lord Chamberlain's consent; however he eventually printed the *Merchant* for Thomas Hayes, not himself, in 1600. Roberts also printed Titus Andronicus for Edward White (1600) and registered *Hamlet*, but printed only the Second Quarto *Hamlet* for Nicholas Ling (1604), the first being the work of Valentine Simmes (q.v.). His last attempt at publishing Shakespeare was the announcement of *Troilus and Cressida* (1603) with the proviso that he would not print until authorised; apparently he never was. The editions of *Midsummer Night's Dream* and the *Merchant of Venice* bearing Roberts' imprint and the date 1600 were produced in 1619 by William Jaggard (q.v.) and back-dated. Jaggard bought the business in 1608.

ROBINSON, John (fl. 1616), Stratford resident: witnessed Shakespeare's will. The name occurs in the parish registers of Stratford in 1589 and 1605 (for the baptisms of sons) in 1579 and 1609

ROBINSON, RICHARD

(marriages) and as a plaintiff in the local court (1591, 1607 and 1613). Only the 1605 entry shows an occupation, "labourer". There is no positive identification for any of these John Robinsons. The witness may have been someone entirely different, possibly a servant of Shakespeare or Dr Hall. Another John Robinson was tenant of Shakespeare's house in Blackfriars in 1616.

ROBINSON, Richard (?—1648), actor: son of James Robinson, an associate of Evans and Giles (qq.v.) in managing the boys' company at the Blackfriars, 1600; it is likely that Richard Robinson first appeared as one of these boys. By 1611 he was with the King's Men, remaining with them throughout his professional career. He was a Lady in *The Second Maiden's Tragedy* in 1611 and is still called a "lad" by Jonson in 1616 (*The Devil is an Ass*): Jonson also praises Robinson for female impersonation in a practical joke when he was "drest like a lawyer's wife". By 1619, however, he was old enough to witness the will of Richard Burbage, and he subsequently married the widowed Winifred Burbage. In 1619—23 he played the Cardinal in *The Duchess of Malfi*. He lived most of his life in Shoreditch; as Sir Henry Wotton noted, he kept a considerable collection of "pictures and other rarities". His name is in the First Folio list, and he survived the first Civil War to sign the dedication of Beaumont and Fletcher's plays in 1647. He was buried at St Anne's, Blackfriars, on 23 March 1648.

G. E. B.

ROCHE, Walter (c. 1540—post 1582), Anglican cleric, schoolmaster, lawyer, came from Lancashire, graduated from Corpus Christi College, Oxford, in 1559, serving briefly as a Fellow of the college. In 1569 he became Rector of Droitwich,

holding the living while also Master of the grammar school at Stratford, twenty-two miles away. Roche was Master from 1569 to 1571, giving up teaching to practise law and on one occasion acting for Shakespeare's cousin, Robert Webbe, from Snitterfield. From 1574 to 1578 Roche also served as Rector of Clifford Chambers, a village two miles from Stratford, living however not in the impressive rectory (which survives) but in Chapel Street, Stratford, where he was a close neighbour of the Shakespeares (1574—82).

M. E.

ROGERS, Daniel (c. 1536—91), diplomat and poet: born at Wittenberg, son of John Rogers (1500—55), editor of the first complete version of the Bible in English and earliest of the Protestant martyrs burnt at Smithfield in Mary I's reign. Daniel Rogers, who was intended by his father for a preacher, came to England on Elizabeth's accession, graduated from Oxford in 1561, went to Court and wrote Latin verses. He served successive ambassadors (including Walsingham) in Paris from 1565 onwards, travelling about Europe collecting antiquities and writing on the ancient history of Britain and Ireland. As a diplomat he was chiefly concerned with the Netherlands, his mother being an Antwerper, Adriana de Weyden. In 1574, while in the Netherlands, he came into Sir Philip Sidney's circle of literary friends (the "Areopagus") and in the following year became the first of them to address a poem to Sidney. Rogers accompanied Sidney in 1577 on a mission to Don John of Austria, the Emperor Rudolf II and William the Silent. In 1579 Rogers wrote another verse tribute to Sidney. By then Rogers was himself an ambassador to the Protestant princes, but his foreign service came to an abrupt end in 1580 when he was captured by bandits in the pay of Spain, who held him for a ransom which neither Wal-singham nor Burghley were inclined to pay. His literary friends had to collect money in order to buy off his captors, and he was not freed until 1585. As some compensation for his sufferings, he was then appointed Clerk to the Privy Council and permitted to indulge his literary interests at home.

J. A. Van Dorsten, *Poets, Patrons and Professors* (1962)

ROGERS, John (fl. 1605–19), Anglican cleric: came to Stratford as Vicar in 1605, having previously been at St Nicholas Church, Warwick. In 1611 he moved, with his family, to the old priest's house in the chapel precinct, near to the Shakespeares' home. Rogers probably witnessed Shakespeare's agreement with Replingham (q.v.) in October 1614. He was allowed to use the churchyard for pasture and he supported the Town Council against the threatened enclosures. Later, however, the Council deprived him of his burial fees, on the grounds that they were needed to repair the church; and at the same time the Council hoped Rogers would "amend his former faults and failings". These may have included swindling the poor out of a legacy, an action in which he was associated with Thomas Lucas (q.v.). Rogers's replacement in 1619 was blamed on pressure from Puritan elements in the parish and led to riots (cf. *John Nash, Reynolds*).

M. E.

ROGERS, Philip (fl. 1603–4), Stratford apothecary: lived in Chapel Street, close to New Place, selling drugs and tobacco and, after gaining a licence in 1603, ale. The following year he bought, without payment, twenty bushels of malt from New Place, also borrowing from Shakespeare 2s on 25 June. Since he paid back only 6s out of a total debt to the Shakespeares of 41s 10d, it became necessary for Shakespeare to take Rogers to the local court in order to collect the debt.

M. E.

ROLFE, John (?1585–1622), colonialist: by tradition son of John Rolfe, gentleman, of Heacham, Norfolk. There is no evidence of where Rolfe received his undoubted education. He sailed for Jamestown, Virginia in 1609 and was wrecked in Bermuda on the way (v. *Gates, Somers, Strachey*). Rolfe's daughter was born there and baptised "Bermuda"; she died in 1610 before the colonists left the island and Mrs Rolfe was dead by 1613. Once Rolfe had arrived at Jamestown, he started his great enterprise of planting the West Indian variety of tobacco, which was much superior to the native American strain. Rolfe's success was a great contribution to the Virginian economy and broke the Spanish monopoly of the tobacco trade based on the Caribbean. In 1613 Rolfe became interested in the education and conversion of the Indian princess Pocahontas (q.v.), a hostage in the colony; he fell in love with her, went on the expedition of 1614 to her father's territory, and married Pocahontas in April of that year. Rolfe became Secretary of the colony and in 1616 wrote the *True Relation of the State of Virginia*, as well as a letter to James I on the prospects for the tobacco industry. When the Rolfe family went to England in the same year, Rolfe himself was not received at Court with his wife, perhaps because of his enthusiasm for the tobacco so hated by the King, or because of his own low birth. He therefore sent James a copy of his *True Relation*. The Virginia Company appointed Rolfe Recorder-General as well as Secretary of the colony, so he decided to return to Jamestown. After the death of Pocahontas, he left his son, Thomas (*infra*) in Plymouth until he should be strong enough for the voyage. In 1618 Rolfe was on the Governor's Council for the colony, and next year he married again, an English colonist's daughter this time. Rolfe's tobacco plantations continued to prosper. He died between March and October, 1622, probably not in the Indian attack on the colony, as his wife and daughter survived.

F. Mossiker, *Pocahontas, the life and the legend* (1977)

ROLFE, Thomas (1615–?): son of the Indian princess Pocahontas and English colonialist John Rolfe. He was left to be brought up in England from 1617 and did not return to Virginia until some time between 1635 and 1640. Thomas Rolfe inherited large estates from his father and from his Indian relatives. In spite of the hostility between Indians and settlers, Rolfe petitioned the Governor of the colony in 1641 to be allowed to visit his mother's uncle and sister, presumably the aunt who had been his first nurse, and permission was granted. Rolfe remained a colonist in allegiance, however, and by 1646 was a lieutenant in the militia. He married an English settler's daughter and founded a family that spread Pocahontas' blood throughout the U.S.A.

Ibid.

ROOKWOOD, Ambrose (?1581–1606), conspirator: born into a Suffolk family which had remained firmly Roman Catholic throughout the vicissitudes of the Reformation. His youth was spent in Flanders. He inherited a house at Stanningfield, near Bury St Edmunds, on his father's death in 1600 and returned to England to take possession of it, and of the family's excellent horses and stables. Coldham Hall, his home, was a refuge for priests. He was persuaded to take part in the Gunpowder Plot by Catesby (q.v.), his task being to supply horses and support for a summons to arms of the Roman Catholic gentry in the Midlands. For this activity he leased Clopton House, near Stratford-upon-Avon, from George Carew (q.v.). Rookwood, however, was captured at Holbeach in Staffordshire, during the skirmish in which Catesby was killed on 8 November 1605. He was charged with treason and executed in Old Palace Yard, Westminster, with Fawkes (q.v.) on 31 January 1606.

H. Garnett, *Portrait of Guy Fawkes* (1962)
E. I. Fripp, *Shakespeare's Haunts near Stratford* (1929)

ROSSETER, Philip (c. 1575–1623), musician and theatre manager: was a royal lutenist from 1604 until his death. In 1609–10 he joined Keysar (q.v.) as manager of the Children of the Revels at the Whitefriars theatre and was responsible for obtaining a new Royal Patent, restoring the Queen's name to the company. From 1613 to 1615 Rosseter had a financial arrangement with Henslowe (q.v.) by which the Revels was amalgamated with the Lady Elizabeth's (and possibly with Prince Charles's) but the children's company kept its separate identity. The Whitefriars lease expired at the end of 1614 and Rosseter was then authorised to set up a "convenient playhouse" at the Porter's Hall, at Puddle Wharf within Blackfriars precinct. The building was sufficiently advanced for plays to be acted there in 1616, but in January 1617 the licence for the theatre was revoked by the Privy Council under pressure from the civic authorities. Rosseter formed a new Queen's Revels company on 31 October 1617 to replace the combined company after Henslowe's death. This company mainly toured the country. In 1601 Rosseter published *A Book of Ayres* with his friend, the poet and composer, Thomas Campion (q.v.), who left Rosseter all his property on his death in 1620, saying he wished it had been more.

E. K. C., *E.S.*

ROWLEY, Samuel (c. 1575–?1624), dramatist: was with the Admiral's Men in 1597. He remained with that company until 1624, by which time it had become, first, Prince Henry's Men and then the Elector Palatine's. Rowley collaborated with William Bird, another actor in the company, to write the additions for the 1602 production of Marlowe's *Faustus*. He collaborated also with Day and Dekker. Among his own plays, the only survivor is a "chronicle history of Henry VIII" entitled *When You See Me, You Know Me*, first acted in 1603.

ROWLEY, William (?1585–1626), actor and dramatist: first mentioned as a writer in 1607, being one of the authors of *The Travels of Three English Brothers*. From 1609 to 1623 he was with Prince Charles's Men and then joined the King's Company, his name appearing in four lists of its members. He was a comic actor, principally playing fat men. As a dramatist he is associated with Thomas Middleton (q.v.), with whom he collaborated in *The Changeling, A Fair Quarrel*, and *The Spanish Gipsy*; Rowley also wrote verse. He died at his home in Clerkenwell in February 1626.

RUGGLE, George (1575–1622), scholar and dramatist: born at Lavenham, Suffolk, educated at the grammar school there, at St John's College, Cambridge, and at Trinity College, Cambridge (B.A., 1593). In 1598 he became a Fellow of Clare Hall and remained at Cambridge until two years before his death. It is probable he was the author of *Club Law* (c. 1599/1600), a comedy ridiculing the Mayor ("Burgomaster") and other civic dignitaries of

Cambridge ("Athens"). He certainly wrote *Ignoramus*, performed in Latin at Clare Hall before James I in 1615. The play satirised lawyers in general and the Recorder of Cambridge, Francis Brackyn ("Ignoramus") in particular. It provoked lively answers from the lawyers. In 1620 Ruggle resigned his fellowship to become a tutor in the Palavicino family.

G. E. B.
F. S. Boas, *University Drama in the Tudor Age* (1914)

RUSSELL, Anne (1576–1639), maid of honour to Queen Elizabeth: daughter of Lord John Russell and his wife Elizabeth (*infra*). She was a favourite with the Queen, apart from a brief period in 1597 when, together with her friend Elizabeth Bridges, she was banished from Court for flirting with Essex. On 16 June 1600 she married Lord Herbert of Chepstow (q.v.). Lady Russell had at first planned to marry her older daughter, Bess, to Herbert, but he preferred Anne. After some trouble in negotiating a dowry and obtaining the Queen's consent, the wedding was celebrated in very grand style. The Queen dined at Lady Russell's house, and was present at the marriage with all her maids of honour. There was a masque and dancing afterwards. Shakespeare's *Midsummer Night's Dream* was once thought to have been written for this occasion, but is now generally dated earlier (1594–5). Bess Russell, who attended her sister Anne at her wedding, died a week later.

V. A. Wilson, *Society Women of Shakespeare's Time* (1925)

RUSSELL, Elizabeth, Lady (1529–1609): born Elizabeth Coke, third of Sir Anthony's four clever daughters (v. *Ann Bacon, Lady (Mildred) Burghley*). She was married first to Sir Thomas Hoby of Bisham Abbey, Berkshire, in 1558. He died as ambassador in Paris in 1566, leaving one son and his widow pregnant; she hurried back to England so that her child might be born there for fear of legal complications over inheritance later. This son, Thomas Posthumous Hoby (q.v.) caused his mother much anxiety until she saw him safely married to an heiress. Elizabeth gave her first husband a splendid tomb in Bisham church. In 1574 she married Lord John Russell, son of the Earl of Bedford; although she was then forty-six she had two daughters by him, Elizabeth (Bess), the Queen's godchild, and Anne (*supra*). Lord John predeceased his father in 1584, so Lady Russell was disappointed of her hope of being a Countess. As a consolation she insisted on being treated as a peer's widow for the rest of her life, and gave Lord John burial in Westminster Abbey, with Greek and Latin inscriptions by herself on his grave. Lady Russell lived mainly at Bisham Abbey in her second widowhood. There she entertained the Queen in 1592, with a masque by Lyly. She also had a town house in Blackfriars and was one of the leaders in the petition to prevent James Burbage from opening Blackfriars theatre as a public playhouse. Lady Russell busied herself about her nephews' affairs as well as her children's. In particular she tried to reconcile her Bacon and Cecil nephews, and plagued the Bacons (qq.v.), especially Anthony, about their religion and way of life. Robert Cecil also received many petitions from his aunt on behalf of various protégés, most of which he ignored, and she tried to involve him in her lawsuits against Lord Admiral Howard and his servants. This long-drawn out legal battle arose when Queen Elizabeth made Lady Russell custodian of Donnington Castle (1596), infringing the rights of the Lord Admiral. After 1601, when her children were married or dead, Lady Russell devoted herself to translation and litigation. Her version of a French treatise on the Sacrament was published in 1605, and in May 1606 her case against the Lord Admiral was finally heard in Star Chamber. Although Lady Russell (then seventy-seven) made a long speech, she lost the case. All that was left for her to do was to compose her own epitaphs and order the arrangements for her funeral and her monument in the chapel of Bisham church.

Ibid.

D. M. Meads, ed., *Diary of Lady Margaret Hoby* (1930)

A. L. Rowse, "Bisham and the Hobys", *The English Past* (1951)

RUSSELL, Lady Margaret (1560–1616) see CUMBERLAND, Margaret, Countess of.

RUSSELL, Thomas (1570–1634), Warwickshire landowner, friend of Shakespeare: son of Sir Thomas Russell, M.P., who left him the manors of Alderminster and Broad Campden, although he did not live at Alderminster until 1598. He entered Queen's College, Oxford, in 1588. Two years later he married for the first time, his wife being related to Henry Willoughby (q.v.), who was friendly with Russell and may have known Shakespeare. Russell's wife and two daughters were both dead before 1599, when he is known to have begun courting Anne Digges, widow of Thomas Digges (q.v.), at her house in Aldermanbury, near Shakespeare's Silver Street lodging. Thomas and Anne lived together from 1600, officially betrothed but not marrying until 1603 when ways were found of circumventing provisions in Digges's will aimed at discouraging his widow from taking a second husband. Russell's hopes of buying Clopton House near Stratford fell through; in the year of his marriage he purchased the lease of Rushock Manor near Droitwich. His marriage was not altogether happy: Anne had a fortune of £12,000 from her former husband, while Russell was far from rich. Sir Dudley Digges, Russell's stepson, later regretted arrangements to break the trust in his father's will and the ensuing litigation was accompanied by much abuse between the families of Digges and Russell. Thomas Russell was generous with money, especially to the family of his friend John Hanford, with whom in 1613 he contributed to the purchase of new organs for Worcester Cathedral. Shakespeare left Russell £5, asking him to act as overseer of his will.

M.E.
L. Hotson, *I, William Shakespeare* (1937)

RUSSELL, William (c. 1558–1613), soldier: born probably at Woburn, the son of the second Earl of Bedford. He was briefly at Magdalen College, Oxford, but spent much of his youth in travel. In 1581 he saw active service in Ireland, and was knighted. He fought under Leicester in the Netherlands and was Governor of Flushing (1587–8). Subsequently he served in Ireland, where he was Lord Deputy from 1594 to 1597, being succeeded by Essex (q.v.). In 1599 he was appointed Commander in the West, with orders to take the field against any Spanish invasion. James I raised him to the peerage as Baron Russell of Thornhaugh in July 1603. He much admired the abilities of Prince Henry (q.v.). His son, Francis, became fourth Earl of Bedford (q.v.).

RUTLAND, Francis Manners, sixth Earl of (1578–1632): son of the fourth Earl and brother of the fifth Earl, Roger Manners (*infra*). He was educated at Christ's College, Cambridge, from 1595, travelling in France, Germany and Italy (1598–1600). He was implicated, together with his brother, in the Essex

rebellion of 1601 and was briefly imprisoned in the Fleet, before being bailed out for £1,000. In the same year he entered the Inner Temple. James I created him a Knight of the Bath in 1605, with the Garter following in 1616. He succeeded as

Francis Manners, sixth Earl of Rutland

Earl of Rutland in 1612, was sworn of the Privy Council next year, and entertained the King at the family seat of Belvoir Castle, Leicestershire, on six occasions between 1612 and 1620. At the Accession Tilt on 24 March 1613 Rutland carried a device (*impresa*) written by Shakespeare and painted by Richard Burbage (q.v.), each of whom received 44 shillings for the work. Burbage painted another device for Rutland three years later. Rutland was made an Admiral of the Fleet to escort Prince Charles and Buckingham (qq.v) back from Spain in 1623 and kept his position at

Court in Charles's reign through the influence of Buckingham, who had married his daughter, Catherine Manners, in 1620. Rutland died at an inn at Bishops Stortford, Hertfordshire, and is buried in Bottesford church, Leicestershire, where his tomb was built by the sculptor, Gheerart Jansen (q.v.). He was succeeded by his younger brother George (c. 1580–1641), who had already shown himself a critic of the Crown in the Commons, and who opposed Charles I in the Lords in 1640.

RUTLAND, Roger Manners, fifth Earl of (1576–1612): son of John Manners, fourth Earl, who died 1587/8. Rutland was a ward of Lord Burghley (q.v.) and, either in his house or at Corpus Christi College, Cambridge in 1590, he became a companion of one of Burghley's other wards, Southampton (q.v.). He entered Gray's Inn in 1598 after travelling widely abroad (1595–8); Florio (q.v.) was complimentary about his Italian. Rutland and his two brothers, Francis (*supra*) and George Manners were friends of the Earl of Essex (q.v.). He went with Essex on the Islands Voyage of 1597, served under him in Ireland as a colonel of foot and married his stepdaughter, Elizabeth Sidney. He and his brother George were both knighted by Essex in Ireland (1599). Rutland was recalled by the Queen, and while out of favour at Court spent some time in Bath treating swollen legs. By the middle of 1600 he was sufficiently recovered to serve with the Dutch army, but at the beginning of 1601 all three Manners brothers were involved in the Essex rebellion. Rutland gave evidence against his friend Southampton, and had his fine of £30,000 reduced to £10,000. He was imprisoned in the Tower, but released to his uncle's house. James I restored Rutland's honours and sent him to Copenhagen as one of the ambassadors to take the Garter to the King of Denmark (1603). Rutland was succeeded by his brother, Francis, and was buried in Bottesford church, Leicestershire. The theory that Rutland wrote Shakespeare's plays was first aired in Germany in 1906, and has been particularly supported there and in Belgium.

S. Schoenbaum, *Shakespeare's Lives* (1970)

211

S

SACKVILLE, Thomas (1536–1608, from 1567 Lord Buckhurst and from 1604 first Earl of Dorset), poet and Lord Treasurer: son of Sir Richard Sackville, a cousin of Anne Boleyn, who held financial office so effectively from 1538 to 1566 that he was nicknamed "Fillsack" and left a large landed inheritance to his son. Thomas was possibly educated at Hart Hall, Oxford, as well as St John's College, Cambridge, and entered the Inner Temple in 1554. A year later he married Cicely,

Thomas Sackville, first Earl of Dorset

daughter of Sir John Baker of Sissinghurst; and he sat in the Parliaments of 1558 for Westmorland and 1559 for East Grinstead. His main literary work was confined to the early 1560s. He contributed the last two acts to *Gorboduc* (1562), the first English tragedy and the 'Induction' and 'Complaint of Buckingham' to the second edition of *A Mirror for Magistrates* (1563), a collection of verse narratives on the downfall of famous men. His extravagance

forced Sackville to travel in Europe, and he was imprisoned in Rome as a suspected spy. On his father's death in 1566 Sackville returned to England, took possession of his vast patrimony, and was created Lord Buckhurst in 1567. Through the Queen's favour he received Knole in Kent, which he rebuilt in magnificent style. He served as a diplomat in the Low Countries, was appointed to announce her death sentence to Mary, Queen of Scots, and was employed on other discreet diplomatic missions, becoming a Knight of the Garter in 1589 and succeeding Burghley as Lord Treasurer in 1598. James I retained him as Lord Treasurer and created him Earl of Dorset. Although he increased the Crown's non-Parliamentary revenue by fifty per cent in five years, he was forced to borrow heavily at high rates of interest in order to keep up with the King's extravagance. By 1608 the country was near bankruptcy, and Dorset facing charges of misconduct, for he had taken considerable bribes, using his daughter Anne, Lady Glemham, as his agent. He dropped dead suddenly in the Council Chamber while seeking to clear his name.

P. Bacquet, *Thomas Sackville* (1966)
L. Stone, *The Crisis of the Aristocracy* (1965)

SACKVILLE, Thomas (?–1628), actor and merchant: born in Dorset. In 1592 he went to Germany with Robert Browne's company; they played at Arnhem first and then the Frankfurt Fair (v. *Browne*). The company broke up in 1594 and Sackville went to serve the Duke of Brunswick-Wolfenbüttel, who was himself a writer of plays. Sackville served the Duke as head of his company, at least until 1617; he took the name Johan Bouset (or Posset). He did not act all the time, however: in 1604 and

1608 he was selling silk in Frankfurt where Coryat (q.v.) met him in the later year and recognised him as an old servant of his father. (v. Coryat, *Crudities*.) When he died in 1628 Sackville left a considerable library of literature and theology.

E. K. C., *E.S.*
E. Nungezer, *Dictionary of Actors* (1929)

SADLER, Hamnet (?—1624), Shakespeare's friend: came from a family which had lived in Stratford since the reign of Richard II. In 1578 he inherited house property in Church Street and High Street from a relative who was a baker, and he carried on that trade. At some time before 1580 he married Judith, whose maiden name was probably Staunton; Shakespeare's twins were called after the Sadlers, husband and wife. They themselves had fourteen children, seven of whom died young. Sadler's business never recovered from the town fire of 21 September 1595. He bought the right to collect money for fire relief in Wiltshire and was engaged with Richard Quiney (q.v.) for three months of the year 1597 in collecting relief money in Suffolk and Norfolk, as well as accompanying Quiney later to London. Thereafter, Sadler was often sued for debt and by 1611 his house was "much out of repair". In May 1606 the Sadlers were among those charged in the Church Court with not receiving Holy Communion at Easter (v. *Susanna Hall*). Sadler asked for time to clear their consciences, but as the case was later dismissed, they presumably complied with the law and received the sacrament according to the rites of the Church of England. After Judith's death in 1614, Sadler sold the lease of his house. He was a witness to Shakespeare's will, in which he was one of seven old friends left two marks to buy a memorial ring, but his name appears to have been added as an afterthought.

M. E.
E. R. C. Brinkworth, *Shakespeare and the Bawdy Court of Stratford* (1972)

SADLER, Judith (?—1614), Stratford resident: probably born Judith Staunton, marrying Shakespeare's friend, Hamnet Sadler (*supra*), before 1580. She was the mother of fourteen children and suffered much from her husband's impoverishment after the fire of 1595, especially during his long absences from home.

ST ALBANS, Viscount (1561—1626) see BACON, Francis.

SALISBURY, Earl of (1563—1612) see CECIL, Robert.

SALUSBURY, John (1566/7—1612), called "the Strong": son of Sir John Salusbury of Lleweni, M.P. for Denbighshire. The Salusburys were a Roman Catholic family, and John's older brother, Thomas, was executed in 1586 for complicity in the Babington plot. Salusbury was educated at Jesus College, Oxford from 1581 and shortly after his brother's death married Ursula Stanley, the illegitimate daughter of Henry, fourth Earl of Derby (q.v.). The Lleweni branch of the family had a constant feud with their kinsmen the Salusburies of Rûg. In 1593 Salusbury fought a duel at Chester with his cousin Owen and fled to London. He entered the Middle Temple (1594/5) and became a Squire of the Body to Queen Elizabeth, who knighted him on 14 June 1601. This honour may have been a reward for loyalty in the Essex rebellion. The Salusburies of Rûg were Essex supporters and Owen Salusbury was killed in the revolt, defending Essex House. John Salusbury's attitude to Essex is unknown, however. Salusbury wrote poetry (published in 1597) and became acquainted with literary circles in London after entering the Middle Temple. He knew Jonson and Marston and probably Shakespeare, too. These three poets were among the contributors to a collection of "poetical essays" on the theme of the phoenix and turtle-dove which were published in 1601 and dedicated to Salusbury (v. *Chester*). The poems are sometimes thought to celebrate (rather belatedly) Salusbury's love for his wife. In December 1601 Salusbury became M.P. for Denbighshire, after a previous attempt at an election had to be abandoned because of a confrontation at Wrexham between heavily armed supporters of each side. He left London permanently when the Queen died (1603) and led an obscure life of comparative poverty, harassed by creditors and old enemies. Salusbury was in declining health from 1609. His heir, Henry, wrote a poem praising Heminges and Condell (qq.v.) for their production of the First Folio of Shakespeare's plays (1623).

Carleton Brown, *Sir John Salusbury and Robert Chester: Poems* (1914)
J. E. Neale, *The Elizabethan House of Commons* (1949)

SANDELLS, Fulke (c. 1551–post 1594), Warwickshire farmer: was supervisor to the will of Richard Hathaway, father of Shakespeare's future wife, in 1581. With John Richardson (q.v.) he was surety in the bond for Shakespeare's marriage licence (v. *Anne Shakespeare*). In 1584 he travelled to London to testify in a Chancery suit concerning the Earl of Warwick's claim to some land in Shottery. In 1591 he valued his neighbour's goods for probate, performing a similar service for Richardson in 1594.

M. E.

SANDS, James (fl. 1605–17), actor: was apprentice to Augustine Phillips (q.v.) with the Chamberlain's/King's Men, and inherited musical instruments and 40s by Phillips's will (1605). Sands remained with the King's Men for at least three years, since he inherited a further legacy from William Sly of the company in 1608, but by 1617 he had become a member of Queen Anne's Men.

SANDYS, Edwin (1561–1629), colonialist and Parliamentarian: born at Ombersley, Worcestershire, the second son of Bishop Edwin Sandys of Worcester, later Archbishop of York. He was educated at Merchant Taylors' School and Corpus Christi College, Oxford, where he studied under Hooker (q.v.) from 1577 to 1584. While still at Oxford Sandys sat in Parliament, under Leicester's patronage, for Andover (1586) and was returned for Plympton in 1589. He travelled extensively on the Continent, 1593–9, anatomising the religious structure of Europe in a survey which he called *Europae Speculum*. At the same time he established friendly relations with James VI, who knighted him soon after his accession to the English throne. Yet, as M.P. for Stockbridge (1604–13), Sir Edwin was a persistent critic of the Crown's methods of raising revenue, especially the sale of monopolies. From 1606 to 1621 he was an active member of the Virginia Company, controlling it as Treasurer from 1619 to 1621, as well as being for several years a member of the East India Company and the Somers Islands Company. Sir Edwin encouraged the smaller shareholders to invest in trading projects in Virginia and in the foundation of the settlement at Jamestown in 1607. It was during his term as Treasurer that the first representative assembly in the Americas (the Virginia House of Burgesses) convened at Jamestown (1619, v. *Pory*). His younger brother, George Sandys (*infra*) travelled to Virginia as Treasurer to the colony, while the Earl of Southampton (q.v.) succeeded

Sir Edwin at home. Subsequently he sat in the Parliament of 1624 for Kent and of 1625 for Penryn, still a vociferous critic of the Crown.

SANDYS, George (1578–1644), traveller, translator, poet: youngest son of Edwin Sandys, Archbishop of York, and born in Bishopthorpe Palace. Sandys was probably educated first at St Peter's School, York, matriculated with his brother Henry at St Mary Hall, Oxford in

George Sandys

1589, then transferred to Corpus Christi. Sandys took no degree, but entered the Middle Temple in 1596. Between then and 1602 he married Elizabeth Norton, of a noted Roman Catholic family. The marriage was unhappy and ended in separation by 1606. Sandys began his travels in 1610, visiting Italy and the Middle East, including Jerusalem, and in 1615 published *A Relation* of his journey, dedicated to Charles, Prince of Wales, as were all his works. He had been interested from 1612 in the Virginia Company, of

which his brother Edwin (*supra*) became Treasurer. In 1621 Sandys went to Virginia as Treasurer to the colony, with the new Governor Sir Francis Wyatt, who had married his niece Margaret Sandys. Sandys had already published the first five books of his translation of Ovid's *Metamorphoses*. He completed two more at sea and the rest of the work in Virginia, despite the Indian massacre of 1622 and the colonists' revenge on the Indians, in which Sandys took a leading part. His Ovid, the first classic translated in the New World, was published in 1626. Sandys was acknowledged a master of the heroic couplet, and the work was popular enough to go into eight editions by 1690. On his return Sandys was made Gentleman of the Privy Chamber to Charles I and served on several commisions on the administration of Virginia until 1640. When not at Court, he lived with his niece Lady Wyatt at Boxley, Kent and wrote religious verse. His paraphrase of the Psalms (1636) was read by Charles I in his last captivity, but Sandys was dead by then, and buried in Boxley Church.

R. Hooper, ed., *The Poetical Works of George Sandys* (1872)

J. E. Friedman, *Critical Study of George Sandys' "Relation"* (1972)

R. B. Davis, *George Sandys, Poet-Adventurer* (1955)

SANDYS, William, Baron Sandys of the Vyne (ante 1556–1623): son of Henry Sandys, grandson and heir of first Baron Sandys. His father died in 1555 and he inherited the title in 1560, while still in the guardianship of his mother. Sandys was one of the Lords Commissioners at the trials of the Duke of Norfolk (1572) and Mary, Queen of Scots (1586). He went on missions to France in 1572 and 1580, and accompanied the Earl of Derby (q.v.) on the Garter mission of 1585 to Henri III. Sandys was able to offer ten horsemen for defence against Spain in 1588. In February

1601 he was involved in the rebellion of Essex (q.v.), and was imprisoned in the Tower until August. He was fined £5,000 and the manor of The Vyne, near Basingstoke, was seized, along with his house in Berkshire. Sandys was married to two notable women. The first was Catherine Brydges (by 1573), reckoned by the poet Gascoigne the greatest beauty at Court. Towards the end of 1597, Sandys married Christian, daughter of Sir Brian Annesley, whose attempt to have her father certified insane may have contributed a theme to Shakespeare's *King Lear* (v. *Cordell Annesley*). Christian was devoted to her husband's interests and worked hard to have him released from the Tower. With his third wife, Anna, born Baker and twice widowed, Sandys lived a retired life, though he took his seat again in the House of Lords during James I's reign.

SAVAGE, Thomas (c. 1552–1611), goldsmith: born in Rudford, between Preston and Liverpool, in west Lancashire. Although Savage was a member of the Goldsmiths' Company, his main occupation was as an official sea-coal measurer. He was interested in the theatre and, with William Leveson, became one of the nominal trustees for the Globe in 1599. From 1580 until his death he lived in the parish of St Alban, Wood Street, but by 1611 he owned five London houses, one bought from John Heminges, who remained there as a tenant. Another of Savage's houses was in Silver Street, near Shakespeare's lodging, and was purchased by Heminges after Savage's death. A possible connection between Savage and Shakespeare in Lancashire during the "lost years" of his youth depended on identifying Shakespeare with one "William Shakeshaft". This identification, much favoured earlier this century, was effectively disproved by Dr Douglas Hamer in 1970.

S. S.

L. Hotson, *Shakespeare's Sonnets Dated and Other Essays* (1949)
D. Hamer, "Was William Shakespeare William Shakeshafte?", *Review of English Studies*, n.s. XXI (1970)

SAVILE, Henry (1549–1622), Warden of Merton, Provost of Eton, scholar: was born at Bradley, near Halifax, Yorkshire. He entered Brasenose College, Oxford in 1561, but became a Fellow of Merton College in 1565 (B.A., 1566). Savile was a classical scholar, astronomer and

Sir Henry Savile

mathematician; he studied and later lectured on Ptolemy's astronomical treatise *Almagest* in Greek. He spent some time travelling to collect manuscripts in Europe and was in government service in the Low Countries; later he became Queen Elizabeth's Greek tutor. She appointed him Warden of Merton in 1585. In 1591

Savile published his translation of four books of Tacitus' *Histories* and was made the Queen's Latin secretary. He persuaded her to waive the requirement that the Provost of Eton must be in holy orders, and she gave him the post in 1596. Savile managed to preside over both Eton and Merton until his death. He was a friend of the Earl of Essex (q.v.): he became M.P. for Dunwich with Essex's help in 1593, and in 1601 was briefly imprisoned after Essex's revolt. Savile's career flourished under James I. He was knighted in 1604 and was one of the scholars who translated the Authorised Version of the Bible (published 1611); between 1610 and 1613 he produced his great edition of the works of St John Chrysostom, in eight volumes, printed on his own press at Eton, and in 1613 Xenophon's *Cyropaedia*. His last book was an edition of Euclid in 1621. Savile was also concerned with the University of Oxford, first his own college, Merton, where he was responsible for building the Fellow's Quadrangle (1608–10). He helped Sir Thomas Bodley (q.v.) with his new library, providing timber from Merton and devising the arrangement of shelves in bays. He left many of his manuscripts to the Bodleian. Finally, in 1619, he founded the Savilian Professorships of Geometry and Astronomy, stipulating that undergraduates of two years standing were to attend the lectures and that the Professors were to do research. He was himself the first Professor of Geometry. Saville is buried in Eton Chapel, but his monument, with figures of St John Chrysostom, Ptolemy, Euclid and Tacitus, is in Merton College Chapel, Oxford.

M. H. Curtis, *Oxford and Cambridge in Transition, 1558–1642* (1959)

F. Markham, *Oxford* (1967)

SCOLOKER, Anthony (fl. 1604), poet: probably related to the printer, Anthony Scoloker (fl. 1547–8). The poet Scoloker published *Daiphantus, or the Passions of Love* in 1604. In the introductory epistle he says a book should be like "friendly Shakespeare's Tragedies" and "please all, like Prince Hamlet", although he disparaged such general popularity.

SCOTT, Reginald (?1538–1599), writer: son of Richard Scott and related to the wealthy Scotts of Scots Hall, Smeeth, Kent. He was educated at Hart Hall, Oxford, from 1556, and spent the rest of his life in Kent managing his own small estate and helping his cousin and patron, Sir Thomas Scott, with his large one. Queen Elizabeth once refused to visit Sir Thomas because he was already more important in Kent than herself, and she did not wish to increase his consequence. Reginald Scott was twice married, and had one daughter. He may have been a J.P. and was certainly M.P. for New Romney (1588–9). He also held a minor financial post in local government. Scott's first work was *The Hop-Garden* (1574, twice reprinted), a practical treatise on growing the newly-imported hops in England. His famous book is *The Discovery of Witchcraft* (1584) in which he takes a sceptical attitude to the existence of witches and the conjuration of spirits, quite unlike most of his contemporaries. Scott was concerned to show the origin of many superstitions to be the practices of the Roman Church. His book displeased the young James VI of Scotland.

SELDEN, John (1584–1654), jurist and antiquary: born, a farmer's son, at Salvington near Worthing in Sussex. He was educated at Chichester and Hart Hall, Oxford, entering the Middle Temple and being called to the Bar in 1612, by which time he had already published his treatise on the *Duello or Single Combat*. This was followed by *Titles of Honour* (1614) and

Analecton Anglo-Britannicon (1617) in which (like Spelman, q.v.) he found contemporary relevance in pre-Conquest records. His *History of Tithes* (1618) offended the clergy and was suppressed by order of the Privy Council. At the same time he was showing an interest in Oriental studies, which he approached through the traditions of the Bible: a collection of Oriental manuscripts was among his many gifts to the Bodleian Library at Oxford. In 1621 the King imprisoned Selden for having questioned the royal doctrine that parliamentary privileges existed by grace of the sovereign. Selden sat in the Commons for Lancaster 1623–8 and represented Oxford University in the Long Parliament of 1640. Although one of the drafters of the Petition of Right and committed to the Tower in 1629 for championing the rights of parliament, Selden declined to play any direct part in the anti-Royalist movement and retired from public office after the execution of Charles I (to whom in 1635, he had dedicated his important treatise on international law, *Mare Clausum*). His *Table Talk* over the last twenty years of his life was collected by his secretary, Richard Milward, and published some thirty-five years after his death. Clarendon described him as "of stupendous learning in all kinds and in all languages", while regretting the fault in his writings of "a little undervaluing the beauty of a style", Clarendon remembered his conversation as having "the best faculty in making hard things easy, and presenting them to the understanding of any man that has been known".

D. Nichol Smith, ed., *Characters of the Seventeenth Century* (1918)
J. Selden, *Table Talk* (1927)
K. Sharpe, ed., *Faction and Parliament* (1978)

SEYMOUR, Edward, Earl of Hertford (1537–1621) see HERTFORD.

SEYMOUR, William (1588–1660, later Duke of Somerset), courtier: second grandson of Edward Seymour, Earl of Hertford (q.v.), and thus a direct descendant of Henry VII and a great-nephew of the "Nine Day Queen", Lady Jane Grey. Seymour was educated at Magdalen College, Oxford from 1605 to 1607 and was at Court for two years before secretly marrying another claimant to the throne, Arbella Stuart (q.v.), in 1610. Within three weeks both he and his wife were imprisoned for marrying without the King's permission. Seymour escaped from the Tower and reached Ostend but failed to meet Arbella who, although also giving her guards the slip, was recaptured at sea. They never met again. Seymour lived in exile in Paris, supported by his grandfather and by small sums of money from Arbella until her death in 1615. He was later reconciled to James I, created a Knight of the Bath, and married Frances Devereux, daughter of the executed Earl of Essex. In 1621 the Earl of Hertford died and William inherited all the Seymour estates, but not the earldom. His services to the Royalist cause in the Civil War were so great that, at the Restoration, Charles II revived for him the family title of Duke of Somerset, in abeyance since 1552.

D. N. Durant, *Arbella Stuart* (1978)

SHAKESPEARE, Anne (?1556–1623, née Hathaway), Shakespeare's wife: daughter of Richard Hathaway (q.v.) of Shottery. In her father's will of 1581 she was named as "Agnes", and left ten marks as a marriage portion. On 28 November 1582, a bond with two sureties was recorded in the register of Worcester Cathedral, as part of an application for a licence to permit Shakespeare to marry Anne Hathaway. A licence was necessary, as Advent Sunday fell on 2 December, after which banns could not be called until the Sunday following the Epiphany (13 January). Unless an entry of 27 November refers to the matter (v. *Whateley*) there is no record of the licence being granted; nor is the marriage itself entered in the parish register of Stratford. There was a good reason for not waiting to call the banns in January: on 26 May 1583 the Shakespeares' elder daughter, Susanna, was baptised. Anne Shakespeare later gave birth to twins, Judith and Hamnet, who were baptised at Candlemas, 1585. Apart from a reference in the will of Thomas Whittington (q.v.), there is no more to be learned about Anne until Shakespeare's death and his famous bequest to her of the "second-best" bed. Anne may have been automatically entitled to a life interest in a third of his estate, although local custom varied (v. *Shakespeare*). She remained at New Place with her daughter and son-in-law, dying on 6 August 1623, having survived long enough for the Shakespeare monument by Janssen (q.v.) to be placed in Holy Trinity Church in her lifetime. She is buried in the chancel, next to Shakespeare.

E. K. C., *W.S.*
M. E.

SHAKESPEARE, Edmund (1580–1607), actor and Shakespeare's brother: the last of the family, sixteen years younger than William. It is known that he went to London and became an actor but there are no records of his career. He fathered an illegitimate son, Edward, who was buried at St Giles, Cripplegate, on 12 August 1607. Edmund himself died at the end of that same year. He was buried on New Year's Eve in St Saviour's Church, Southwark "with a forenoon knell of the great bell". This must have cost £1; burial outside, with a smaller bell, would have cost no more than 3s. It was suggested by Edgar Fripp in the nineteen-twenties that

Shakespeare paid for his brother's funeral, arranging it in the morning so that his fellow actors might attend.

M. E.
S. S.

SHAKESPEARE, Gilbert (1566–1612), haberdasher, Shakespeare's brother: the second son of the family. In 1597 he was living, and practising haberdashery, in St Bride's, London, where he gave part surety for the bail of a friend from Stratford in the Queen's Bench. He seems, however, to have lived mainly in Stratford, acting on his brother's behalf in 1602, when he received the deed to land in Old Stratford which William had purchased. On 21 November 1609 Gilbert and others were summoned by writ to answer a complaint by Joan Bromley, a widow in Stratford: neither the nature of the complaint nor the outcome is known, but it aroused strong feeling in the town. Gilbert could write; his signature survives as witness to a property lease in March 1610. The register records his burial on 3 February 1612, describing him as "adolescens", a term presumably meaning "bachelor".

M. E.

SHAKESPEARE, Hamnet (1585–96), Shakespeare's only son: baptised with his twin sister, Judith (later Quiney, q.v.) on 2 February 1585. His burial is recorded on 11 August 1596.

SHAKESPEARE, Henry (?–1596), Shakespeare's uncle: farmed at Snitterfield and Ingon in the parish of Hampton Lucy, staying on the land after his father's death, unlike his brother John. Henry was often in trouble or in debt. There are records of three fines imposed on him for minor offences: in 1574 for an affray against the Constable, Edward Cornwell (who was later to marry Shakespeare's mother's sister, Margaret Webbe); in 1583 for presumptuously wearing a hat to church instead of a cap; and in 1596 for not mending his roads and ditches. In 1591 he was imprisoned for trespass and in 1596 for debt. He was also involved in disputes over tithes and caused his brother John to be sued in 1587, as surety for £22 which Henry had borrowed from Nicholas Lane, a wealthy local landowner. Nevertheless, it was said that when Henry Shakespeare died there was plenty of money in his house and much corn and hay in his barn. He was buried at Snitterfield on 29 December 1596.

E. K. C., *W.S.*
M. E.

SHAKESPEARE, Joan, sister of William Shakespeare see HART.

SHAKESPEARE, John (ante 1530–1601), glover and father of Shakespeare: born at Snitterfield, Warwickshire, the son of Richard Shakespeare, a farmer. By 1552 John lived in a house in Henley Street, Stratford (presumably the western of his two houses, now called the "Birthplace") and was trading as a glover, doing well enough to buy the eastern house in Henley Street and another in Greenhill Street by 1556. Probably in the following year he married Mary Arden (v. *Mary Shakespeare*) who bore him eight children between 1558 and 1580. Although John administered the Snitterfield estate on his father's death in February 1561, it was his brother Henry (*supra*) who maintained the farming tradition in the family. John was Constable of Stratford in 1558 and from 1561 to 1563 Chamberlain (in charge of town property and finances; the Protestantising of the Guild Chapel began in his last year of service). He was on the Council, replaced the expelled Bott (q.v.)

as Alderman in 1565, was appointed Bailiff (with the powers of a Justice of the Peace) in 1568, and Chief Alderman in 1571. It was while he was Bailiff, in 1569, that the actors first came to Stratford and were paid by the town: the Queen's Men received 9s, Worcester's Men only 1s. After 1572 John Shakespeare never held office again, but he was in London that year with Adrian Quiney (q.v.) on town matters and brought a case in the Court of Common Pleas at Westminster on his own account. In 1575 he purchased two more houses in Stratford and considered applying for a grant of arms. Thereafter, his fortunes declined and he attended only one more Council meeting after 1576. His fellow Aldermen did their best for him: his taxes were reduced, and he was not fined for non-attendance. By 1586 he was in debt and had enemies, and he was at last replaced by another Alderman. He mortgaged his wife's inheritance at Wilmcote and could not recover it (v. *Edmund* and *John Lambert*) and sold other land belonging to her to Robert Webbe (q.v.), her nephew. John was continually being sued for debt, or suing others. By 1590 he owned only his Henley Street property. In 1592 he appears in a list of recusants, two others in that list having the interestingly Shakespearian surnames of Bardell (or Bardolph) and Fluellen. It is possible that John's apparent recusancy arose from a fear of going to church in case he might be arrested for debt; or he may have died a Roman Catholic. A *Spiritual Testament* was found in the eaves of the Birthplace by a workman in 1757: this was a standard form introduced by the Jesuits. Since the original find disappeared again in the nineteenth century, it is not known whether it was signed by John Shakespeare and it does not therefore provide evidence of his Catholicism. In 1596, with the help of his son William, he obtained the grant of arms from the College of Arms; and thus, technically, at least died a gentleman. He was buried in Holy Trinity churchyard on 8 September 1601. In spite of his misfortunes he was able to leave his son the two houses in Henley Street.

E. K. C., *W.S.*
M. E.

S. S.

SHAKESPEARE, Judith, daughter of William Shakespeare see QUINEY.

SHAKESPEARE, Mary (c. 1540–1608, née Arden), Shakespeare's mother: youngest of eight daughters of Robert Arden, a farmer from Wilmcote, three miles north-west of Stratford, where a large timber-framed house has been known as "Mary Arden's House" since the late eighteenth century, although there is no definite evidence it was the family home. The Wilmcote Ardens may have been related to the Ardens of Park Hall, a family of importance before the Norman Conquest with lands mentioned in the Domesday Book; once again, there is no proof of a connection. Certainly Robert Arden was a prosperous farmer, well able to provide for his children and second wife. To Mary, who was an executor of his will (1556), he left land at Wilmcote, together with ten marks. Some time between her father's death and the baptism of her first child in September 1558, Mary married John Shakespeare. This first child, Joan, died young, as did two other Shakespeare daughters. Of Mary's eight children, four sons and a daughter grew up (v. *Edmund, Gilbert, Richard, William Shakespeare*, and *Joan Hart*). Much of Mary's inheritance from her father was later sold or mortgaged to her cousins or relatives by marriage, because of her husband's need of money. Apart from the litigation involved in these transactions, Mary's only other known appearance was as a witness in the Court of Record at Stratford in 1596. After her husband's death in 1601, she may have lived with her daughter Joan Hart in the Henley Street house or at New Place. She was buried on 9 September 1608.

E. K. C., *W.S.*
M. E.
S. S.

SHAKESPEARE, Richard 1574–1613), Shakespeare's younger brother: baptised on 11 March 1574. Little is known of his life. He must have lived in Stratford since he appeared before the Church Court there on 1 July 1608 for an unstated offence and was fined a shilling, to be given to the poor. He was buried on 4 February 1613.

E. K. C., *W.S.*
S. S.

SHAKESPEARE, Susanna see Susanna HALL.

SHAKESPEARE, William (1564–1616): born at Stratford-upon-Avon, Warwickshire, probably in the Henley Street house now called the Birthplace, oldest son of a glover, John Shakespeare and his wife Mary (Arden). Three other sons (Gilbert, Edmund, and Richard) and one daughter (Joan) survived childhood. William was baptised on 26 April 1564, but of his youth and education nothing is known: it is assumed he attended the local grammar school, the King's New School. At the end of 1582 he married Anne Hathaway, from the nearby village of Shottery, and she bore him three children, Susanna (born May 1583) and twins who were born in January or February 1585, and given the Christian names of family friends, Judith and Hamnet Sadler (qq.v.). Shakespeare's movements and activities before 1592 are subjects of mere conjecture. The persistent legend that he left Stratford because he was caught poaching deer in Sir Thomas Lucy's park at Charlecote does not agree with known facts about the Lucy family (v. *Lucy, Thomas I*). John Aubrey, with some evidence in support (v. *Beeston*), asserted that Shakespeare was briefly a schoolmaster or school "usher"; there is no authority for the tale that he once held horses outside the London playhouses. By 1592 he was certainly known as an actor and playwright in the capital, as is evident from the death-bed verbal attack of the dramatist Robert Greene (q.v.), in which Shakespeare was dubbed an "upstart crow". Shakespeare's long narrative poems *Venus and Adonis* (1593) and *The Rape of Lucrece* (1594), both dedicated to the Earl of Southampton (q.v.), were published by a fellow townsman, Richard Field (q.v.), and established Shakespeare's reputation as a poet. In 1601 Shakespeare contributed two poems to a collection of "poetical essays . . . by the best and chiefest of our modern writers" (v. *Chester*). His contribution, thirteen stanzas and a threnody, is known as *The Phoenix and Turtle*, the general theme of the collection.

It is not possible to date the first appearance of his plays precisely but the most recently agreed dates of production are as follows: *Henry VI*, part 1, *Titus Andronicus* (1590); *Henry VI*, parts 2 and 3 (1591); *Richard III* (1592); *Comedy of Errors, Two Gentlemen of Verona* (1593); *Love's Labour's Lost, The Taming of the Shrew* (1594); *Midsummer Night's Dream, Richard II, Romeo and Juliet* (1595); *King John, Merchant of Venice* (1596); *Henry IV*, part 1 (1597); *Henry IV*, part 2, *Much Ado about Nothing* (1598); *Henry V, As You Like It, Julius Caesar* (1599); *Merry Wives of Windsor, Twelfth Night* (1600); *Hamlet* (1601); *Troilus and Cressida* (1602): *Othello* (1603); *All's Well That Ends Well, Measure for Measure* (1604); *King Lear* (1605);

Macbeth (1606); *Antony and Cleopatra, Coriolanus, Timon of Athens* (1607); *Pericles* (1608); *Cymbeline* (1610); *Winter's Tale, The Tempest* (1611); *Henry VIII*, and possibly *The Two Noble Kinsmen* (1613).

William Shakespeare. Monument with a bust by Gheerart Janssen in Holy Trinity Church, Stratford-upon-Avon

Shakespeare continued to act as well as to write, appearing not only in his own plays but in Ben Jonson's *Every Man in His Humour* and *Sejanus* as well. By 1595 Shakespeare was a recognised member of the Lord Chamberlain's company who appeared mainly in James Burbage's Theatre, in Shoreditch. He settled in London for part of the year, with a house in St Helen's parish, Bishopsgate. In December 1598 the Burbages, disputing the ground lease of the Theatre with their landlord, dismantled the building and the company carried the fabric across the river, rebuilding the playhouse as the Globe on Bankside. As a partner in this enterprise, Shakespeare was entitled to ten per cent of the profits, the value of his holding fluctuating subsequently according to the actual number of partners, and he changed his London residence, moving to the Liberty of the Clink in Southwark, nearer the new playhouse, certainly before 1599 (v. *Gardiner, Langley*).

Although with the death of his son Hamnet by 11 August 1596 Stratford may, for a time, have been less attractive to Shakespeare, he retained links with his birthplace and in 1597 bought New Place, the second largest house in the town. The death of his father in 1601 brought him possession of the Henley Street houses. By now Shakespeare was enjoying the status of a gentleman and he acquired more property in the Stratford area: over a hundred acres in Old Stratford from the Combe family (qq.v.) and a cottage in Chapel Lane (1602); a half-interest in the tithes of Old Stratford, Welcombe and Bishopton, and the small tithes of Stratford parish (1605). He thus became a substantial landowner in his home town.

Meanwhile his position as dramatist and partner in a theatrical company was strengthened by the accession of James I, who particularly favoured his group of players. On 17 May 1603 they received a Royal Patent to change their name from Lord Chamberlain's Men to King's Men, Shakespeare's name appearing near the top of the list of actors on the Patent. By 1604 he moved his London lodging from Southwark to the house of Christopher Mountjoy (q.v.), at the corner of Silver Street and Monkwell Street, Cripplegate. Four years later, in August 1608, the King's Men took over the lease of the Blackfriars theatre (originally part of the Burbage empire) to serve as a winter playhouse, and Shakespeare's income was augmented by the customary share of profits. Possibly it was at this time that he began to visit the Mermaid Tavern in Bread Street and met the landlord, William Johnson (q.v.), who became a friend; but the great days of the

Mermaid as a meeting place for poets came after Shakespeare's retirement to Stratford (v. *Coryat.*)

The year 1609 saw the first edition of the Sonnets published by Thomas Thorpe, with its puzzling dedication to "Mr W.H." (v. *William Hall, Hatcliffe, Hervey, Pembroke, Southampton, Willoughby*), the references to a "Dark Lady" (v. *Jane Davenant, Mary Fitton, Elizabeth Hatton, Emilia Lanier, Lucy Morgan, Penelope Rich*) and a "rival poet" (v. *Barnes, Chapman, Daniel, Drayton, Marlowe*). Shakespeare was beginning to spend more time in Stratford, but he was in London in 1612 to give testimony in a lawsuit between Mountjoy and his son-in-law, Belott, and again in March 1613 for his last property transaction, the purchase of the Gatehouse near King's Wardrobe and Puddle Wharf, Blackfriars. In the same month he obliged the Earl of Rutland by inventing a motto for his shield at a Court tournament, Burbage painting the device and each man receiving 44s for his work.

Shakespeare remained a profit-sharing member of his company but he seems to have spent most of his later years in retirement at Stratford with his family. His older daughter, Susanna, married Dr John Hall on 5 June 1607 and gave Shakespeare a granddaughter, Elizabeth, in February 1608. Judith did not marry until shortly before her father's death, when she became the wife of Thomas Quiney, a son of an old family friend, Richard Quiney. Shakespeare's interest in local events was slight. He sued in Stratford court for small debts in 1604 (v. *Philip Rogers*) and 1608 (v. *Addenbrooke*) and, as a tithe holder, he was involved in a dispute with the Combe family (qq.v.) in 1610–11 and with Mainwaring (q.v.) over enclosures at Welcombe in 1614. His lawyer, Francis Collins of Warwick, drafted a will for him in January 1616, revised on 25 March 1616 when Shakespeare was clearly a sick man. The most famous bequest was "the second-best bed" left to his wife, Anne, who may anyhow have been entitled to a third life-interest in the estate and residence in the family house (the Stratford custom is not known). Provision was made for his daughters and their offspring. Other bequests remembered fellow actors and local friends (v. *Burbage, Combe, Condell, Hart, Heminges, Nash, Reynolds, Russell, Sadler, Walker*).

Shakespeare died on 23 April 1616, of what cause is unknown; there is no supporting evidence for the tale, current fifty years later, that he contracted fever after a drinking party with Jonson and Drayton. The conduct of his unreliable son-in-law Quiney, may have contributed to his illness. He was buried in Holy Trinity Church on 25 April. By 1623 a monument with a bust by Gheerart Janssen had been erected there. In that same year the First Folio of the plays was published, carrying an engraved portrait of Shakespeare on the title-page by Martin Droeshout. This engraving and the Stratford bust are the only authentic images of Shakespeare.

E. K. C., *E.S., W.S.*
M. E.
S. S.

S. Schoenbaum, *Shakespeare's Lives* (1970)
K. Muir and S. Schoenbaum, eds., *A New Companion to Shakespeare Studies* (1974)

SHANK, John (c. 1565–1636), actor: on his own testimony, given in a lawsuit a few months before his death, Shank described himself as an actor who was "an old man in this quality", having served the Earl of Pembroke and "after that, the late Queen Elizabeth and then King James". He played clown's parts and was well known as a dancer and jig maker. His name first appears in company lists from 1610 to 1614, with Prince Henry's/Elector Palatine's Men. He was a King's Man by 1619, remaining in their lists for ten years. He is mentioned in the First Folio actors' list, but he does not seem to have acted much from 1629 to 1631, after which his name disappears. In 1635 he was sued by shareholders of the Globe and Blackfriars theatres for having surreptitiously purchased shares from the son of Heminges (q.v.). Shank complained that he was being victimised by the company, who were keeping him off the stage, although it is probable he was by then a septuagenarian. He lived in the parish of St Giles, Cripplegate, where he was buried on 27 January 1636.

E. K. C., *E.S.*
G. E. B.

SHARPE, Richard (c. 1602–32), actor: with the King's Men from 1616 until his death, and probably played in the company earlier. He may have been the original Duchess in *The Duchess of Malfi* (1614), as no one else is listed for the role and he is known to have played the Duchess in performances of the play between 1619 and 1623. By 1624 Sharpe had a share in the theatres, and finally played young romantic heroes.

SHAW, Julius or "July" (1571–1629), wool trader in Stratford: lived in Chapel Street, Stratford, at the second house from Shakespeare. He was a prosperous man, chosen as Alderman in 1613 with special commendation, after he had served on the Council and as Church warden and Chamberlain. He was Bailiff in 1616, when he witnessed Shakespeare's will, as well as in 1627–8, and he was again Church warden in 1620.

M. E.

SHEFFIELD, Douglas, Lady (?1544–1608), Earl of Leicester's wife or mistress:

the daughter of Lord William Howard of Effingham, Queen Elizabeth's great-uncle. She married Lord Sheffield when she was seventeen (probably 1562). By 1568 she was the mistress of Leicester (q.v.) and her husband was preparing to divorce her when he died suddenly. Rumour naturally had Lord Sheffield poisoned by his wife and her lover. Leicester was then involved with both Douglas and her unmarried sister, Frances Howard. Douglas later claimed that Leicester made a marriage contract with her in 1571 and actually married her at Esher in 1573, just before her son's birth. He always denied this although he acknowledged the boy, Robert Dudley (q.v.), as his own. Douglas gave up hope of Leicester when he married Lettice Knollys in 1578, and became the wife of Sir Edward Stafford (c. 1552–1605) next year. He was a diplomat, then employed on a mission to Paris and later ambassador to the French Court from 1583 to 1588. But he was also a distant claimant to the throne of England, through both his maternal grandparents, and the Queen ordered a full investigation into the alleged Leicester marriage. Douglas now swore that there had been no contract with Leicester. She settled happily in Paris with Stafford, who seems to have prospered in his career until his return to England. He was promised the positions of Chancellor of the Duchy of Lancaster and Secretary of State, but neither was given him, and he held no further public office, though he was M.P. for Winchester (1593), Stafford (1597, 1601) and Queenborough (1604). James I gave him £60 a year as compensation for his disappointment. Stafford died in 1605 during a fresh enquiry into his wife's relationship with Leicester. This time Douglas supported her son Robert Dudley in his claim that she had been married to Leicester, but the Court of Star Chamber dismissed Dudley's case. Douglas survived Stafford by three years and was

buried with him in St Margaret's Westminster.

SHIRLEY, Anthony (1565–?1635), adventurer and traveller: born at Wiston in Sussex and educated at Hart Hall, Oxford, taking his B.A. in 1581 and being elected a Fellow of All Souls. He served under Leicester in the Netherlands (1586) and under Essex in Normandy, where he was knighted. For some years he remained

Sir Anthony Shirley

attached to Essex, participating in the Islands Voyage and receiving his backing for an unofficial mission to Shah Abbas the Great of Persia in 1598. Sir Anthony, with his younger brother, Robert, and twenty-five followers, travelled overland from Aleppo to Isfahan where the Shah granted trading concessions and formal religious liberty for Christian merchants in return for the Shirley brothers' assistance in building up a modern army for war against the Turks. While Robert remained in the Shah's service for some twenty years, Sir Anthony undertook diplomatic missions for the Shah, to Muscovy, to the Emperor in Prague and to Venice, where he appears to have acted as a spy for Robert Cecil. He later (1608–11) served Philip III as a somewhat ineffectual commander in the Aegean against the Turks. His adventures had aroused interest in London from 1600 onwards and provided a thin basis of fact for the play *The Travels of Three English Brothers* (1607), of which John Day, William Rowley and George Wilkins (qq.v.) were joint authors. Shirley's account of his Persian adventures was published in London in 1613. He died in poverty in Madrid. The suggestion by Bishop S.F. Surtees, in 1888, that Anthony Shirley is the true author of Shakespeare's plays is engagingly eccentric. Sir Anthony's elder brother, Thomas (1564–1628), was also educated at Hart Hall, Oxford, but later resorted to piracy in the Mediterranean.

S. Chew, *The Crescent and the Rose* (1937)
B. Penrose, *The Sherleian Odyssey* (1938)

SHORT, Peter (?–1603), printer: became a freeman of the Stationers' Company in 1589 and was admitted to the Livery of the Company in the same year. His shop was at the "Star" on Bread Street Hill. Until 1593 he had a partner, Richard Yardley. Short printed the old play *Taming of a Shrew*, to be sold by Cuthbert Burby, in 1594. This is regarded as the source, or original version, of Shakespeare's *Shrew*. He also printed Shakespeare's *Henry VI*, part 3 for Thomas Millington (1595), and *Henry IV*, part I for Andrew Wise (1598) as well as reprinting *The Rape of Lucrece* for John Harrison the Younger (1598) and *Venus and Adonis* for William Leake (1599).

SHREWSBURY, Elizabeth Talbot, Countess of (?1527–1608) see HARDWICK.

SHREWSBURY, George Talbot, Earl of (c. 1528–90), soldier: fought under Protector Somerset in Scotland. He became fourth Earl of Shrewsbury in 1560. Although his father was a Roman Catholic, he accepted Protestant beliefs. His string of castles and estates across the English Midlands made him one of the wealthiest men in the country, a position of influence intensified by his marriage in February 1568 to Bess of Hardwick (q.v.). She was his second wife and he was her fourth husband; her character was much more formidable than his own. From 1569 until her execution in 1587 Shrewsbury was keeper of the person of Mary, Queen of Scots, in Tutbury (Staffordshire), Chartley and Fotheringay. He treated his captive fairly and honourably, in 1582–3 even arousing the jealousy of his wife by his compassion for the prisoner. Queen Elizabeth found him scrupulously loyal and appointed him Earl Marshal after the Duke of Norfolk's execution in 1572.

A. Fraser, *Mary, Queen of Scots* (1969)

SHREWSBURY, Mary Talbot, Countess of (1556–1632) see TALBOT.

SIDNEY, Philip (1554–86), poet, diplomat, soldier: son of Sir Henry Sidney and his wife Mary (Dudley), Leicester's sister, and godson of Philip II of Spain. He was born and spent his childhood at Penshurst, the family home in Kent, although his father was Lord President of the Welsh Marches (from 1559) and Lord Deputy of Ireland (from 1565). Lady Sidney, a lady-in-waiting, nursed Queen Elizabeth through smallpox in 1562, passing the infection on to her son, who was slightly pockmarked for life. In October 1564 he entered Shrewsbury School, on the same day as his lifelong friend, Fulke Greville (q.v.). Sidney went on to Christ Church, Oxford, in 1568 and was a brilliant student, interested in science as well as the arts, but he took no degree. In the spring of 1572 he was a conspicuous member of Lord Lincoln's mission to France to conclude the Treaty of Blois. The French recognised his importance as heir to the two earldoms held by his uncles, Leicester and Warwick. He received a title from King Charles IX while his personal qualities won him friends among the Protestant intellectuals. Sidney was still in or near Paris during the

Sir Philip Sidney. After a miniature by Oliver

Massacre of St Bartholomew (24 August 1572), probably at the home of the English ambassador, Walsingham (q.v.), an experience which inclined him to accept the view of Leicester and Walsingham, that Protestant Europe should unite against the Catholic powers. Sidney returned home, after travelling in Germany, Austria and Italy, and went to Court where he became one of a circle of poets and philosophers with common interests, the "Areopagus". Prominent in

this group were Dyer, Gabriel Harvey and Rogers (qq.v.) while Spenser was associated with them. They wished to give English poetry the status of the classics, the aim also of Sidney's *Apology for Poetry* (probably completed 1583). Sidney spent some years with his father in Ireland, writing a defence of his administration (*Discourse on Irish Affairs*, 1577) and becoming a friend of the commander of the army in Ireland, Walter Devereux, first Earl of Essex. Sidney fell in love with his daughter Penelope (v. *Penelope Rich*) but, though Essex favoured the match, he died in 1576 before it could be arranged. Sidney served on diplomatic missions in Germany and met William the Silent at Middelburg (May 1577), finding the Prince of Orange shared his vision of a Protestant League. The Queen, however, turned away from this policy, favouring the Duke of Alençon and an alliance with France. Sidney was now the Protestant champion against the papists, as Spenser depicted him in *The Shepheardes Calendar* (1579); he wrote a letter of remonstration to Elizabeth, quarrelled publicly with the Earl of Oxford (Alençon's supporter), and exiled himself from Court (1580–1), living mainly at Wilton, home of his sister, Lady Pembroke (q.v.). Already Sidney had produced some poetry and an entertainment, *Lady of May*, for the Queen's visit to Wanstead in 1578. At Wilton he wrote his two major literary works, the sonnet sequence *Astrophel and Stella*, celebrating his love for Penelope Rich, and *Arcadia*, a prose romance for his sister. *Arcadia*, published four years after his death, became one of the most popular books of the age. By 1582 Sidney was knighted and reconciled to the Queen, who forgave him unenthusiastically. She was again displeased when he married Walsingham's daughter, Frances (q.v.), in 1583 and hesitated over appointing him Governor of Flushing under Leicester in the Netherlands. Eventually, in September 1585, Elizabeth summoned him back from Plymouth, where he was about to sail with Drake for the West Indies, and he crossed to Flushing. A year later (22 September 1586) he was wounded in the thigh at Zutphen, after going to help the encircled Willoughby (q.v.) in such haste that he left off one of his cuisses, according to his friend Dr Moffet (q.v.). The famous incident of Sidney's sending the drink offered him to a dying soldier occurred while he lay on the battlefield. The wound became gangrenous and Sidney died in twenty-six days, with his wife and brother at his bedside, and listening to a song he had composed himself. His best sword he bequeathed to the second Earl of Essex (q.v.). He was given a state funeral in St Paul's in February 1587, grief at his death occasioning some 200 poetic elegies. Personal generosity, commitment to the Protestant cause and artistry with words ensured that Sidney remained a chivalrous exemplar to inspire his own generation and its immediate successors.

R. Howell, *Sir Philip Sidney, the Shepherd Knight* (1968)
J. M. Osborn, *Young Philip Sidney* (1972)

SIDNEY, Robert, later Viscount Lisle, Baron Sidney and Earl of Leicester, (1563–1626): second son of Henry Sidney, younger brother of Philip (*supra*). He was educated at Christ Church, Oxford (1574–8), afterwards travelling in Europe. He visited the German states, including Bohemia, and was everywhere treated with kindness by his brother's friends. Philip wrote many letters of advice to him, even telling him in 1580 to improve his handwriting as it was worse than his own. In 1586 the brothers served together in the Netherlands under their uncle Leicester (q.v.), who knighted Robert. Robert was present at Philip's death-bed. The death of his parents in the same year left him with the problem of settling debts incurred by his father and his brother. Sidney was forced to sell some lands, but kept the main estate at Penshurst in Kent intact. In 1584 he had married a Welsh heiress, Barbara Gamage, celebrated by Jonson in a poem for her housekeeping. Although Sidney was often abroad, the marriage was happy and produced twelve children. He represented Glamorgan, his wife's county, in the Commons of 1584–5 and 1593. Technically Sidney was Governor of Flushing from 1588 to 1616, although both he and his wife begged Elizabeth to relieve him of the post. Twice Essex (q.v.) tried to obtain positions for him in England, as Lord Chamberlain (1596) and as Lord Warden of the Cinque Ports (1597) but he was thwarted by Cecil and the Cobhams (v. *Henry Brooke*), although Sidney was returned as M.P. for Kent in 1597. His career only advanced under James I. The King reappointed him to Flushing, but Sidney spent some time at Court, was Queen Anne's Chamberlain, and was raised to the peerage as Viscount Lisle and Baron Sidney of Penshurst in 1605. He improved Penshurst Place by building the Long Gallery and entertained the King and Queen there. Sidney was interested in colonial expansion, being a member of the Virginia, East India and North-West Passage Companies. James I employed him as escort for Princess Elizabeth and her husband to Heidelberg after their wedding in 1613. He arranged the transfer of Flushing to the United Provinces in 1616 after thirty-one years as an English garrison town. In 1618 he became Earl of Leicester and was one of the commissioners appointed to examine the Order of the Garter, an honour bestowed on him two years before. He died at Penshurst, where he is buried.

R. Howell, *Sir Philip Sidney, the Shepherd Knight* (1968)

SIMMES, Valentine (fl. 1576–1622), printer: son of Richard Simmes, clothworker, of Oxfordshire. He was apprenticed for eight years from Christmas 1576 to Henry Sutton, bookseller, but transferred at his own request to the printer, Henry Bynneman (q.v.). Simmes became a freeman of the Stationers' Company in 1585. He was often in trouble with the law; he was arrested as a compositor of the "Martin Marprelate" Press (1589) and caught printing patented books (1595). On this occasion his press was seized, his type melted, and he lost his apprentice. In 1599 Simmes was one of fourteen printers forbidden to print satire or epigrams and fined 1s. He was also found printing a ballad against Sir Walter Ralegh. Simmes printed several Shakespeare plays: *Richard II* and *Richard III* for Andrew Wise (1597), *Much Ado About Nothing* and *Henry IV*, part 2 for William Aspley and Andrew Wise (1600), the First Quarto *Hamlet* (1603) for Nicholas Ling and John Trundell, *Henry IV*, part 1 for Matthew Law (1604) and *King John* for John Helme (1611). In 1622 Simmes was forbidden to work again as a master printer, but the Stationers' Company gave him a pension of £4 a year.

SINCKLER, John (fl. 1590–1604), actor: was probably with Strange's Men in 1590–1, and with Pembroke's 1592–3. He was certainly a member of the Chamberlain's Men from about 1594 but there is no reference to him after 1604 and he was evidently a hired man rather than a sharer in the company. He appeared as an attendant in *Henry IV*, Part 2. He is said to have been a very thin man who played Aguecheek, Silence and Slender. There appears to be no contemporary evidence for this conjecture which has, however, in recent years won acceptance from Dr Rowse.

E. Nungezer, *Dictionary of Actors* (1929)

SINGER, John (fl. 1583–1603), actor: with the Queen's Men in 1583 and 1588, and with the Admiral's Men 1594–1603, when he was appointed a Groom of the Chamber. Samuel Rowlands (q.v.) in 1600 mentions Singer as a clown, together with Pope (q.v.), and Dekker in 1609 praises him, retrospectively, and couples his name with Kempe and Tarlton (qq.v.). He was certainly dead before 1609.

SLATER, Martin (?1625), actor and manager, also known as Martin Slaughter: described himself in 1608 as "citizen and ironmonger". He was with the Admiral's Men, 1594–7, being described as joint-payee with Alleyn in 1596. He is known to have been with an English company in Scotland in 1599 and was subsequently forced to borrow money from Henslowe (q.v.). In 1603 Slater was with Hertford's Men and in 1606 with Queen Anne's, breaking away in 1608 to manage a boys' company, the Children of the King's Revels, at the Whitefriars, together with Drayton (q.v.). This enterprise was short-lived and Slater was back with Queen Anne's Men before the end of the year, remaining with the company until his death (after 1619 the company was known as the "Late Queen's Men"). Slater was also a manager of the Children of Bristol, a boys' company under the patronage of Queen Anne, 1618–19.

E. K. C., *E.S.*

SLY, William (fl. 1590–d. 1608), actor: was with Strange's or the Admiral's Men 1590–1. From 1598 to 1605 Sly's name appears in all the lists of the Chamberlain's/King's Men, as well in the Royal Patent of 1603 and the First Folio actors' list. He also maintained links with the Admiral's Men, for the company kept one of his stage costumes and on 11 October 1594 the accounts of Henslowe (q.v.) record the sale to Sly of a gold jewel for 8s. Although not an original sharer in the Globe, Sly had a share by 1605. He lived in Shoreditch and was buried in St Leonard's churchyard, but his bastard son was baptised and buried at St Giles, Cripplegate. On 4 August 1608 Sly made a will which was witnessed by several illiterate women; he left bequests to Cuthbert Burbage and James Sands (qq.v.) but his share in the Globe to Robert Browne, whose wife Cecily was Sly's executrix. He also left the remainder of his property to the Brownes, and it is suggested that he lived with the family, and that his legatee was the Robert Browne (q.v.) who toured Germany. Five days after making the will, Sly was given a share in the Blackfriars theatre, but he was by then on his death-bed and was buried on 16 August, Cecily Browne handing back the share in the Blackfriars to Richard Burbage.

E. K. C., *E.S.*

SMETHWICK, John (?–1641), bookseller: son of Richard Smythick, draper, of London. He was apprenticed to Thomas Newman for nine years from Christmas 1589 and became a freeman of the Stationers' Company in 1597. Smethwick was fined several times for printing privileged books, but advanced in the company, being chosen Junior Warden (1631), Senior Warden (1635), and Master (1639). His shops were in Fleet Street, near Temple Gate and then in St Dunstan's Churchyard. In 1609 Smethwick was assigned the copyrights of Nicholas Ling (q.v.) and is known to have published *Romeo and Juliet* (1607) and three quartos of *Hamlet* (1611, 1637, ?). He had a share in both the First (1623) and Second (1632) Folios of Shakespeare's works.

SMITH, John (1580–1631), adventurer, colonialist, writer: son of George Smith, farmer, of Willoughby, Lincolnshire. Smith was educated at Louth Grammar School and apprenticed to a merchant in King's Lynn, but after his father died in 1596 decided to leave England. He went to France in the train of Peregrine Bertie, son

Captain John Smith

of Lord Willoughby, and served in the French and Dutch armies until 1599. After a short spell at home, he travelled again in 1603: Europe, Hungary and Transylvania, the eastern Mediterranean, Turkey and Russia, Spain and Morocco, according to his own account. In 1607 he went with the Virginia Company's first expedition to America, and became a member of the colony's Council, although the other colonists had prepared to hang him on the voyage out. During the winter 1607–8 he went on an expedition for supplies into Indian territory and (as he said) was saved from death by the Princess Pocahontas (q.v.) while actually lying ready for sacrifice on the altar stone. Smith had a special relationship with the Indians, and

Pocahontas in particular. He controlled the colony even before his election as President in 1608 and brought the colonists, whom he called "the scum of the World", through the "Starving Time" in the winter of 1609. After intrigues against him, Smith returned home ill in September 1609. Complaints followed him to England, and he was not employed in America for five years, although taking part in the Virginia Company's work at home. In 1614 he went to Cape Cod with a small expedition. Next year the Plymouth Company (v. *Ferdinando Gorges*) appointed him Admiral of "New England", the name Smith invented for the area. The expedition of 1615 failed and Smith was captured by a French corsair; on board her he wrote his *Description of New England*, published in 1616 after his release. He offered his services to lead the Pilgrim Fathers to New England in 1620, but was rejected. Smith had already produced a history of the Virginia colony's first year and maps of Chesapeake Bay and New England and he now devoted himself mainly to writing. In all he produced eleven books, the weightiest being his *General History of Virginia* (published 1624) and the most entertaining the story of his travels.

John Smith, *Works*, ed., E. Smith (1884)
L. Paine, *Captain John Smith and the Jamestown Story* (1973)

SMITH, Ralph (1577–1621), Stratford resident: hatter and haberdasher in Stratford as well as a member of Stratford's trained band, and nephew of Hamnet Sadler. He is known to have been married before 1605 and often acted as Foreman of the jury at sessions. In 1613 he was accused of adultery with Shakespeare's daughter, Susanna Hall, by John Lane (qq.v.).

M. E.

SMITH (or SMYTHE), Thomas (c. 1558–1625), merchant and colonialist: son of Thomas Smythe, official Customs Receiver of the Port of London, and grandson of Sir Andrew Judd, founder of the Muscovy Company. He became Sheriff of London in 1599 and, for four months, Governor of the East India Company on its foundation in 1600. Essex sought his support in the rebellion of 1601, visiting him in his house in Gracechurch Street on 8 February. Smythe claims to have advised Essex to yield, and slipped out by the back door to warn the Lord Mayor. Nevertheless, Smythe was briefly imprisoned in the Tower and was deprived of his shrievalty. James I knighted him in 1603 and he was re-elected Governor of the East India Company, an office he held until 1621 except for a brief period in 1606–7. He travelled to Russia in 1604–5. There he was received by the Tsar and obtained new privileges for the Muscovy Company, although at a time of such troubles in Russia that they could hardly be implemented. His subsequent *Voyage and Entertainment in Russia* was completed by the dramatist, Wilkins (q.v.). Smythe supported the voyages to seek a north-west passage and Smith Sound, in the northernmost Canadian Arctic, was named after him by William Baffin in 1616. When the Virginia Company received its second charter in 1609 Smythe became Treasurer and was able to obtain the more extensive third charter of 1612 which included Bermuda. Disputes within the Virginia Company led him to resign in favour of Edwin Sandys (q.v.) in 1619, but the internal dissensions continued and Smythe died at his home in Sutton-at-Hone, Kent, during the royal enquiry which withdrew the Company's charter. Smythe was buried in Sutton Church. He was a benefactor of Tonbridge School.

A. L. Rowse, *The Elizabethans and America* (1959)

SMITH, William (1564–?), school-master: youngest son of Alderman William Smith, a mercer, of High Street, Stratford. He was baptised on 22 November 1564 and was thus a contemporary of Shakespeare in Stratford. The Smith family were protégés of the Vicar, Bretchgirdle (q.v.), who in 1565 left books to the five older boys and 1s to William, the baby. By 1579 the family was living in Worcester and William went from there to Winchester College as a Scholar, his uncle (John Watson) being Bishop of Winchester at the time. William entered Exeter College, Oxford, in 1583. On 12 May 1589, a deposition made by William Smith, a schoolmaster of Loughton in Essex, states that he was born in Stratford-upon-Avon, educated at Oxford and had lived for a year at Waltham Cross and a year at Loughton. This led Dr Hotson, who discovered the deposition in the 1940s, to speculate that he is identical with William Smith of Waltham Cross, financial backer of the Burbages. But this William Smith (*infra*) was still described as "of Waltham Cross" in 1601.

M. E.
S. S.
L. Hotson, *Shakespeare's Sonnets Dated* (1949)

SMITH, William (c. 1560–?), theatrical backer: friend of James Burbage and of his son, Cuthbert, whom it is recorded that he had known for fifteen years by 1601. He was present at the pulling down of the Theatre in 1598 and paid the costs of the counter-suit against the Burbages' landlord (v. *Allen* and *Cuthbert Burbage*). In 1601 he was living at Waltham Cross, on the Hertfordshire-Essex border (v. *supra*).

C. W. Wallace, "The First London Theatre", *Nebraska University Studies*, XIII (1913)

SMYTHSON, John (?–1634) architect: son of Robert Smythson (*infra*). Smythson

is known to have been working as a mason under his father at Wollaton Hall for tenpence a day in 1588, by which date he had completed his apprenticeship. By 1597 he was sharing the work of designing and surveying at Hardwick with the elder Smythson. The drawings of father and son are often indistinguishable. John Smythson was still working at Wollaton in 1600, when he married, but after the turn of the century his principal patrons were Sir Charles Cavendish (Bess of Hardwick's third son) and his son, William Cavendish, first Duke of Newcastle. For Sir Charles he began work on Bolsover Castle, only a few miles north of Hardwick, in 1612; it is possible he had his father's help at first, but he was still engaged on Bolsover when he died more than twenty years later. William Cavendish sent Smythson to London in 1618–19 to learn the Italian style, made fashionable by Inigo Jones (q.v.), and his later work shows the influence of this journey. John Smythson died at Bolsover during a visit from Charles I; his son, Huntingdon Smythson, was already associated with the profession, carrying it on to a third generation.

Mark Girouard, *Robert Smythson and the Architecture of the Elizabethan Era* (1966)

SMYTHSON, Robert (c. 1533/7–1614), architect and surveyor. Smythson's name first appears in connection with the building of Longleat House for Sir John Thynne. He arrived there, apparently after the dismissal of Spicer (q.v.), in 1568 with his own team of five masons, recommended by the Queen's Master Mason as having worked for the Queen's cousin, Sir Francis Knollys, probably on his Caversham house. Smythson was not in sole charge at Longleat, and in 1575 Thynne brought in cheaper masons to finish the work, provoking a letter of indignation from Smythson. In 1580 he moved to

Wollaton, near Nottingham, to build Sir Francis Willoughby's house. He spent the rest of his life there and his influence was paramount in the Midlands and the North. Unlike the great houses of the South, with their ample courtyards, Smythson's buildings were tall and compact, with towers, many windows and basement offices. His most famous houses were Wollaton Hall and Worksop Manor, which he undertook about 1585 for the Earl of Shrewsbury (q.v.). Smythson almost certainly drew the plans for Hardwick Hall for the Countess of Shrewsbury (Bess of Hardwick, q.v.) and he appears in her accounts for 1597 as the surveyor, although she closely supervised the work herself. Smythson had introduced long windows into the design of Longleat, Wollaton and Worksop but at Hardwick he excelled himself — "Hardwick Hall, more glass than wall" it was said. But clearly Bess was pleased with his style; he designed her tomb in All Saints Church, Derby, now the cathedral. Smythson paid at least one visit to London, probably two (1602, 1609), leaving many drawings of new buildings, including Somerset House, Northampton House and the Royal Exchange. His last work may have been on Bolsover Castle with his son, John (*supra*). Smythson died at Wollaton, where his monument in the church describes him as "architector and surveyor unto the most worthy house of Wollaton and divers others of great account".

A. L. Rowse, *The Elizabethan Renaissance; The Cultural Achievement* (1972)

Mark Girouard, *Robert Smythson and the Architecture of the Elizabethan Era* (1966)

Mark Girouard, *Hardwick Hall, Derbyshire* (1976)

SOMERS, George (1554–1610), seaman and colonialist: born near Lyme Regis, Dorset, and apparently went to sea when young. He was engaged in buccaneering in 1595 and sailed on the Islands Voyage of Essex (q.v.) in 1597. In 1601 he assisted Mountjoy in Ireland, attacking Spanish vessels supplying the force which had landed at Kinsale. A successful raid off the Azores in the autumn of 1602 marked the end of his naval enterprises. He was knighted by James I in July 1603 and sat as M.P. for Lyme Regis in James's first Parliament. In 1605 he was Mayor of Lyme Regis but his main interest in these years was in the Virginia Company, of which he was a founder member. He sailed for Virginia with Gates (q.v.) in *Sea Venture* in 1609 and was wrecked on the Bermudas. He claimed these islands for King James and they long enjoyed the alternative name, "Somers Islands". On 10 May 1610 Somers and his fellow castaways sailed in two cedar pinnaces to Jamestown, Virginia, where they landed on 23 May. Four weeks later Somers set out again for the Bermudas with a party which intended to bring back meat and fish for the hard-pressed settlers in Virginia. Once again a storm left the party marooned on the islands, and before they could repair their vessels Somers died "of a surfeit of eating of a pig" on 9 November 1610. The saga of *Sea Venture* was soon known in London, thanks to the literary gifts of Jourdain and Strachey (qq.v.), and was used by Shakespeare as source material for *The Tempest*.

SOMERVILLE, John (1560–83), Warwickshire landowner: educated at Hart Hall, Oxford, from 1576, and in 1578 inherited Edstone at Wootton Wawen, six miles north-west of Stratford. He married Margaret Arden of Park Hall, who may have been related to Shakespeare's mother (v. *Mary Shakespeare*). Somerville was a zealous Roman Catholic. On 25 October 1583, he set out for London, with the announced intention of shooting the Queen with a pistol. He was arrested, condemned for treason, and found strangled in his cell at Newgate on the eve of his execution.

M. E.
C. C. Stopes, *Shakespeare's Warwickshire Contemporaries* (1897)

SOUTHAMPTON, Elizabeth Wriothesley, Countess of (1573–?1655/6): the daughter of Sir John Vernon of Shropshire and first cousin to Essex, Queen Elizabeth's favourite. Essex introduced her to the Court and she became maid of honour to the Queen. The Earl of Southampton (q.v.) first noticed her in 1595, and by 1598 was so in love that he pulled out the hair of Ambrose Willoughby for slandering her. In the same year she was pregnant and the couple were secretly married. Southampton was imprisoned for a while and Elizabeth fled to the home of Essex's sister, Penelope Rich, where her baby, Penelope, was born in November. She stayed there again in 1599, while Essex and Southampton were in Ireland. After the Essex rebellion of 1601, Southampton was sent to the Tower, and his wife was not allowed to visit him until the end of the year. With the accession of James I, the family fortunes were restored, and Elizabeth's first son, born in 1605, was named after the King, his godfather; James Wriothesley died in 1624 just before his father. There was a second son Thomas (1608), later Earl of Southampton, and three other children who died in infancy. Elizabeth survived her husband by more than twenty years. She sent all his books and manuscripts as a gift to his former college, St John's, Cambridge, after his death. As an old lady she sheltered Charles I at Titchfield, the family seat, when he fled to the Isle of Wight in 1647.

A. L. Rowse, *Shakespeare's Southampton* (1965)

SOUTHAMPTON, Henry Wriothesley, Earl of (1573–1624), soldier and literary patron: born at Cowdray, Sussex, the son of the second Earl and Countess Mary (*infra*), and baptised a Roman Catholic. His father died on the eve of Henry's eighth birthday; he became a ward of Howard of Effingham and later of Burghley (qq.v.). From 1585 to 1589 he studied at St John's College, Cambridge,

Henry Wriothesley, Earl of Southampton

already showing an interest in drama and literature. He was presented at Court by Essex (q.v.), under whom he later served in Normandy. Writers were eager for Southampton's patronage, believing he would inherit considerable wealth on coming of age in 1594; Shakespeare dedicated *Venus and Adonis* (1593) and *The Rape of Lucrece* (1594) to him; and he has been regarded as the most likely recipient of Shakespeare's Sonnets. It is possible that *Love's Labour's Lost* contains "in" jokes peculiar to Southampton and his circle, including his Italian tutor, Florio (q.v.). Other writers rivalling Shakespeare for Southampton's patronage were Barnes and Nashe (qq.v.). Southampton's income suffered from Burghley's demand that he should pay a large sum as compensation for having declined to marry his granddaughter, Elizabeth Vere (q.v.), in 1590. He incurred displeasure at Court for the aid he had given to Charles and Henry Danvers (qq.v.) after Long's murder, and he was briefly imprisoned in 1598 for having secretly returned from a diplomatic mission in France to marry one of the Queen's ladies-in-waiting, Elizabeth Vernon (*supra*). Southampton shared the royal favours and rebuffs of his friend Essex: he commanded the *Garland* on the Islands Voyage of 1597, and was praised for capturing a Spanish vessel; but he aroused the Queen's fury by accepting the rank of General of the Horse under Essex in Ireland in 1599 without royal permission. Rivalry with Lord Grey of Wilton (q.v.) weakened his standing at Court. He remained loyal to Essex in his disgrace, keeping the Earl in touch with his successor in Ireland, Mountjoy (q.v.). The projected seizure of Whitehall by Essex and his supporters was planned in Southampton's London residence, Drury House; and he was Essex's companion in the futile attempt to arouse London against the Queen's Councillors in February 1601. Southampton was tried for treason with Essex in Westminster Hall, but reprieved from execution after appeals by his mother and the intervention of Cecil (q.v.). He remained imprisoned in the Tower until the accession of James, who reinstated him in his forfeited earldom, appointed him Captain of the Isle of Wight and gave him monetary favours. Southampton was able to resume his literary patronage and live in style in his homes at Holborn, Titchfield and Beaulieu, where he occasionally entertained the King. In politics he opposed the Howard faction and showed great interest in colonisation and maritime enterprise, financing Hudson (q.v.) in 1610 and from 1614 becoming active in the Virginia Company, of which he was Treasurer in 1620. Collaboration with Buckingham (q.v.) secured Southampton's admission to the Privy Council in 1620, but thereafter he turned against the royal favourite and headed opposition to the Crown in the House of Lords during the Parliament of 1621, being imprisoned for a month for allegedly plotting to restrict the King's prerogative. In his last year of life he mollified James by encouraging plans for establishing Virginia as a Crown colony. Southampton died, apparently from plague, at Bergen-op-Zoom in the Netherlands on 10 November 1624 while campaigning against the Spanish; his elder son, who had sailed with him from England three months before, predeceased him by five days. Both were interred at Titchfield where there is an impressive monument.

Ibid.
C. C. Stopes, *Life of . . . Southampton* (1922)

SOUTHAMPTON, Mary Wriothesley,

dowager Countess of (?1553–1607, née Browne): the daughter of Viscount Montague, head of a fervently Roman Catholic family. She married the second Earl of Southampton in 1566. He was sent to the Tower for his involvement with the Duke of Norfolk's treason in 1572, and his wife pleaded for his life to the Queen. Southampton was freed and next year his son Henry, third Earl (*supra*) was born. The couple were gradually estranged, the Earl preferring his servant Thomas Dymoke to his wife. When he died in 1581 he left so much of his wealth to Dymoke that his son was financially dependent on his guardians for his upbringing. The dowager Countess married again twice. On 2 May 1594 she became the wife of Sir Thomas Heneage (q.v.), Vice-Chamberlain and old favourite of the Queen. This marriage has been·

considered a possible occasion for Shakespeare's "Midsummer Night's Dream", less likely because of the age of the couple, although there are appropriate references (e.g. "May Day", IV, i). Heneage died in the following year and left his widow a rich woman. In 1598 she wished to marry a much younger man, the Kentish knight Sir William Hervey (q.v.). Southampton was opposed to the match, and Essex and Lord Henry Howard were called in as arbitrators between mother and son. The marriage was postponed until January 1599. After the Essex conspiracy of 1601, the dowager wrote to Robert Cecil on behalf of her son who had been condemned to death. That she thought he owed his life to Cecil is shown by her letter of gratitude in 1603. The reign of James I relieved all the anxieties of the Southampton family, and the dowager Countess received £600 as a gift from the Exchequer. She died a wealthy woman, able to leave generous bequests to her son as well as her last husband Hervey.

A. L. Rowse, *Shakespeare's Southampton* (1965)

SOUTHWELL, Elizabeth (1586–1631): daughter of Sir Robert Southwell of Norfolk, was a third-generation maid of honour to Queen Elizabeth, following her mother Elizabeth Howard and her grandmother Catherine Howard (q.v.), Countess of Nottingham. In 1605 Elizabeth Southwell eloped to the Continent with her lover and cousin Sir Robert Dudley (q.v.), disguised as his page. The couple became Roman Catholics and, received a dispensation from Pope Paul V to marry. Subsequently they settled in Florence, Elizabeth enjoying the social status of a duchess after her husband was created titular Duke of Northumberland and Earl of Warwick in the nobility of the Holy Roman Empire. The couple are said to have had thirteen children. Elizabeth was buried in the church of San Pancrazio, Florence, now disused.

SOUTHWELL, Robert (1561–95), Jesuit priest and poet: born at Horsham St Faith, Norfolk, distantly related to the Bacon and Cecil families. He left England when he was fourteen, completing his education under Jesuit auspices at Douai and Rome, where he was ordained priest in 1584. After two years as Supervisor of Studies at the English College under Parsons (q.v.), Southwell came back to England in 1586, staying successively with the families of Lord Vaux of Harrowden, Anne Countess of Arundel, and Richard Bellamy of Harrow. His powerfully written prose works were completed in 1590–1; they included *An Epistle of Comfort* and *Mary Magdalen's Funeral Tears*. He was taken prisoner while on his way to celebrate Mass at Harrow-on-the-Hill (20 June 1592) and was brutally tortured by Topcliffe (q.v.) on thirteen occasions. Eventually he was executed at Tyburn on 21 February 1595. Southwell wrote much devotional verse, some of his poems being praised by Ben Jonson. His longest poem (published soon after his death) was *St Peter's Complaint*, a narrative of the closing days in the life of Christ as represented by a repentant Peter. The deep religious feeling of his poetry was sometimes hidden by euphuistic flourishes of style, but his sincerity impressed many Protestants as well as his co-religionists.

C. Devlin, *Robert Southwell* (1956)

SPEED, John (?1552–1629), cartographer and historian: born in Cheshire, but settled in London as a child, eventually becoming a freeman of the Merchant Taylors' Company at the age of twenty-eight and living in Moorfields. His interests in history and genealogy brought him into touch with Sir Fulke Greville, the younger, who secured for him a post in the Custom House (1598). He was encouraged by Cotton, Camden and other scholars to produce from 1607 onwards a series of fifty-four basic maps of the counties of England and Wales, each of them depicting a view of the chief town of the county. These maps were published as *The Theatre of the Empire of Great Britain* (1611) and were followed by his *Historie of Great Britain . . . from Julius Caesar . . . to King James*. Speed's work supplemented the writings of John Stow (q.v.), also a Merchant Taylor. Their fellow antiquarian, Spelman, perpetrated the pun, "We are beholding to Mr Speed and Stow for stitching up for us our English History."

SPELMAN, Henry

SPELMAN, Henry (1564–1641), historian and antiquary: born at Congham, near King's Lynn, Norfolk, educated at Trinity College, Cambridge (1581–3) and entered Lincoln's Inn but never practised as a barrister. In 1590 he married an heiress from his native county, of which he was High Sheriff at the beginning of James I's reign. He was Member of Parliament for Castle Rising in 1597 and, after being knighted by James, for Worcester from 1625 to 1629. He was interested in overseas colonisation, both in New England and in Guinea. In 1612 he left his Norfolk properties and settled for twenty years in Westminster so as to concentrate on his antiquarian studies. His work was mainly concerned with ecclesiastical and legal affairs, and his two principal achievements were left to be completed by others: *Glossarium Archaiologicum* (published 1626–64) and his *Concilia Ecclesiastica Orbis Britannici* (published 1639–64). His scholarship disturbed both James I and Archbishop Laud who found his honest assessment of Magna Carta and the medieval Great Councils politically unwelcome. While Stow and Camden were primarily interested in the materials of history, whether written or archaeological, Spelman was the first scholar to attempt an orderly study of Anglo-Saxon and medieval institutions of government, a significant shift of emphasis from the antiquarian studies of the previous generation.

F.M. Powicke, "Sir Henry Spelman and the 'Concilia' ", *Proceedings of the British Academy* (1930); also printed in L. S. Sutherland, ed., *Studies in History* (1966)

O. L. Dick, ed., *Aubrey's Brief Lives* (1949)

SPENCER, Alice

SPENCER, Alice, later Countess of Derby (?1556–1637): youngest of six daughters of Sir John Spencer of Althorpe, Northamptonshire, and sister of Elizabeth Carey, Lady Hunsdon (q.v.). The poet Spenser (q.v.) claimed relationship with this branch of the family and dedicated *The Tears of the Muses* (1591) to Alice. By 1580 she had married Lord Strange (q.v.), by whom she had three daughters. He died mysteriously soon after becoming Earl of Derby (1594) and Alice retained the title Countess of Derby even when married to her second husband, Thomas Egerton (q.v.). This marriage has sometimes been thought the occasion for the first performance of Shakespeare's *Midsummer Night's Dream*, but the date (1600) is late. In 1601 the Countess bought Harefield Place and its manor in Middlesex from Sir Edmund Anderson (q.v.). Next year the Queen paid an expensive three-day visit there. The Egerton marriage was a stormy one, but Sir Thomas rebuilt Harefield Place and the Countess lived twenty years in it after his death. In 1635 she was still a patron of poetry; Milton wrote the masque *Arcades* for performance at Harefield by the Countess's granddaughters. Her elaborate monument is in Harefield Parish Church, and the almshouses she endowed still stand just off Harefield High Street.

SPENCER, Gabriel (c. 1578–98), actor: probably with the Chamberlain's Men in 1597 and certainly with Pembroke's company by July 1597, as he was one of the actors imprisoned in the Marshalsea for playing in the allegedly seditious *Isle of Dogs* that month (v. *Jonson, Langley*). On release Spencer joined the Admiral's Men and was sued by Langley for breach of agreement. Spencer's career was short and turbulent, marred by his violent and ungovernable temper. In November 1596 Spencer killed James Feake, the son of a goldsmith, by a powerful blow of his scabbard after Feake attacked him with a candlestick. The brawl took place in a barber's house in Shoreditch; a coroner's inquest on 3 December found Spencer had acted in self defence. Two years later Spencer quarrelled with Ben Jonson, for reasons unknown: on 22 September 1598 the two men fought a duel with swords in Hoxton Fields, east of London; Spencer wounded Jonson in the arm, but was himself killed by Jonson's rapier.

E. K. C., *E.S.*

SPENCER, John (c. 1535–1610), merchant and Lord Mayor: son of Richard Spencer of Walfingfield, Suffolk. By the early 1560s he had come to London and begun to trade with the Mediterranean lands and the Levant. Good profits enabled him in 1570 to purchase a country house at Canonbury, where he entertained Queen Elizabeth in 1581. Later he was able to buy, and restore, Crosby Hall, Bishopsgate. He was Master of the Clothworkers' Company, Sheriff of the City of London (1583–4) and Lord Mayor in 1594–5, when he was knighted. His fortune in overseas trade was increased by money-lending on a grand scale, and at ten per cent, to the indigent aristocracy and gentry. The Spencers were the wealthiest family in the parish of St Helen's,

Bishopsgate, at the time when Shakespeare was living there (probably from 1596 to 1599). In 1598 Sir John's only child, Elizabeth, became infatuated with a reckless and free-spending courtier, William, Lord Compton (1568–1630). Since Sir John did not wish his money used to pay off Lord Compton's debts, he restricted Elizabeth's movements and beat her, his behaviour causing the Privy Council to have him imprisoned briefly in the Fleet. According to John Chamberlain (q.v.), Elizabeth eloped with William Compton in the spring of 1599, escaping from Crosby Hall in a basket lowered by a rope from her balcony. Sir John Spencer's anger at their secret marriage is alleged to have prompted the Queen to intervene in an attempt to reconcile father and daughter after the birth of a child, baptised Spencer Compton, in 1601. When Sir John Spencer died (March 1610), no will could be found and, since his widow followed him to the grave within a few weeks, his fortune — which may have been as high as £800,000 — was inherited by the Comptons, causing Lord William to suffer a nervous breakdown from which he speedily recovered. Since it was out of character for Spencer to have died intestate, William Compton may have suppressed his father-in-law's will. William and Elizabeth continued to live extravagantly for the following twenty years; he was created Earl of Northampton in 1618.

S. S.

N. E. McClure, ed., *Letters of John Chamberlain* (1939)
L. Stone, "The Peer and the Alderman's Daughter", *History Today*, XI (1961)

SPENCER, John (fl. 1603–23), actor, alias "Hans Stockfisch": may have played in London in the last years of Elizabeth's reign and appears to have crossed to the Continent to avoid the plague of 1603. He gained an enduring reputation touring the

Netherlands and the German Courts between 1603 and 1623. At different times he served the Electors of Brandenburg and Saxony and the Duke of Stettin. Spencer raised a company which visited Danzig, Königsberg, Nuremberg, Regensburg, Heidelberg, Augsburg, and the Frankfurt Fair as well as several other cities. He was accompanied by his wife and children; while in Cologne in 1615, the whole family and the company were converted to Roman Catholicism by a Franciscan friar, a change of faith which benefitted business. From 1618 onwards Spencer took the humorous alias "Hans Stockfisch", apparently because his rival, Robert Reynolds (q.v.), was calling himself "Pickelherring". The name Stockfisch long survived as a synonym for an English clown in Germany. Despite the intrusion of the Thirty Years War Spencer is known to have continued on the German stage at least until 1623.

E. Nungezer, *Dictionary of Actors* (1929)

SPENCER, Robert (1570–1627), later first Baron Spencer: son of Sir John Spencer of Althorpe, and nephew of Alice Spencer (q.v.). He was M.P. for Brackley (1597) and succeeded to his father's estates in 1600. The Spencers, who were originally sheep farmers from Snitterfield, Warwickshire, were by now one of the wealthiest families in England. Spencer's fortune was not just in land, although his mother Mary Catlin had inherited huge estates accumulated by her Chief Justice father, but in ready cash, his annual income being between £6,00 and £8,000. By 1603, when James I made him a baron, Spencer was paying regular visits to London to sell his wool and mutton by direct contracts with retailers, without going through markets. He adhered to the economical traditions of his family in spite of his new honour, holding no high office

and building no great house. His only government mission was to take the Garter to the Duke of Würtemberg in 1603. Although the Spencers entertained the King and Queen on their progress from the north in 1603, Baron Spencer managed to avoid expensive royal visits again, fleeing to Kent (1608) or going to bed with the ague (1626). He was active in local affairs, however, and in the House of Lords, where he supported the Commons against the King's party. He was insulted in the 1621 Parliament by the Earl of Arundel (*Thomas Howard*, q.v.) who said that his own ancestors had served the country while the Spencers were still keeping sheep. Arundel went to the Tower rather than apologise. In 1618 Spencer, on the advice of Southampton (q.v.), whose daughter had married his son William Spencer, declined to be made an earl and pay £10,000 for the privilege. The Spencer-Churchills, family of the Dukes of Marlborough, are descended from Baron Spencer; so also is Lady Diana (Princess of Wales, 1981).

M. E. Finch, "The Wealth of Five Northamptonshire Families", *Northamptonshire Record Society*, 19 (1956)

SPENSER, Edmund (?1552–1599), poet: probably the son of John Spenser, cloth-worker of London; he was certainly born in London and enjoyed his childhood there. Although his family was not rich, Spenser claimed he was connected with the wealthy Spencers of Althorpe, Northamptonshire, and regarded the Spencer daughters particularly as his patrons (v. *Elizabeth Carey, Alice Spencer*). He was educated as a "poor boy" at Merchant Taylors' School under Mulcaster (q.v.) and began to write poetry even before he went on to Pembroke Hall, Cambridge (1569–73). At Cambridge he met Gabriel Harvey (q.v.) who found him a post in the household of Leicester. Here he made the acquaintance of Leicester's nephew, Philip

Sidney and his literary circle, the "Areopagus". In 1579 Spenser dedicated *The Shepheardes Calendar* to Sidney; it was at once immensely popular. He may have been married for the first time this year, to Machabyas Childe; he certainly acquired a wife and two children fairly early in his career. In 1580 he went to Ireland as secretary to the Lord Deputy, Grey of Wilton, living at first in Dublin. Here he began to write the *Faerie Queene*. Spenser decided to stay in Ireland after Grey's

Edmund Spenser

departure and in 1586 was one of the "undertakers" of Munster, so called because they undertook to resettle the lands with Englishmen. In the same year he wrote *Astrophel*, the elegy on Sidney. Spenser, now deputy to his friend Bryskett (q.v.), Clerk of Munster, was granted possession of Kilcolman Castle, County Cork (formally made over to him in 1590). Meanwhile Ralegh (q.v.), another "undertaker", whose lands bordered Spenser's, persuaded him to return to London, present the first three books of his epic to

the Queen, and publish it. Spenser agreed, and dedicated his work to Elizabeth, with prefatory poems in honour of many courtiers. So successful was the *Faerie Queene* that Elizabeth granted him a pension (which Burghley, who regarded Spenser as a political opponent, is said to have halved), and his early works were collected and printed next year (1591). Spenser returned to Ireland where he wrote *Colin Clout's Come Home Again* (1595), dedicated to Ralegh and describing his London visit. In 1594 he married his second wife, Elizabeth Boyle from Towcester, Northamptonshire, a connection of Richard Boyle (q.v.), Earl of Cork. His courtship of her is described in *Amoretti* and their marriage possibly in *Epithalamium* (both published 1595). They had one son. Spenser was in London again in 1596, with the next three books of the *Faerie Queene* for the printer. He was now patronised by Essex (q.v.) and stayed in Essex House to write his prose *View of the Present State of Ireland* (published 1633). Spenser was at Kilcolman Castle again in 1598 when the victory of Tyrone (q.v.) over the English led to widespread rebellion. The castle was burnt in a raid and the Spensers fled to Cork. The last part of the *Faerie Queene* is said to have been destroyed in the fire. Spenser went to London carrying the despatches of Sir John Norris (q.v.), then commanding in Ireland, to the Court. He arrived on 24 December, received £8 for his service, and on 13 January 1599 died in lodgings in King Street. Essex paid for his funeral in Westminster Abbey, but no monument was erected until Anne Clifford (q.v.) put one up in 1619, with the poet's birth and death dates wrong.

A. C. Judson, *The Life of Edmund Spenser* (1945)

SPICER, William (c. 1534–1604), mason and architect: born in Somerset, probably at Nunney. He worked for Sir

John Thynne on the building of Longleat, originally as a mason but by 1557 he had become the chief executant of Thynne's ideas. Spicer appears to have left Longleat after a clash of temperament with Thynne and was succeeded by Robert Smythson (q.v.). From 1571 to 1584 Spicer undertook work for the Earl of Leicester, principally at Kenilworth. During these years Leicester granted Spicer a lease of the manor of Long Itchington, in Warwickshire, fifteen miles east of Stratford-upon-Avon. Subsequently Spicer was surveyor of the royal manor of Woodstock. He worked on the defences of Berwick and Portsmouth but he remained a Warwickshire man, a resident of Napton-on-the-Hill when he was granted his coat-of-arms in 1591. He was appointed Comptroller of the Queen's Works in 1595 and from 1597 until his death was Surveyor-General, the office later held with distinction by Inigo Jones (q.v.). Although Spicer had responsibility for the royal residences throughout the country, his principal work was undertaken in or near the capital, at the Tower of London, in Whitehall and at Nonsuch in Surrey.

H. M. Colvin, D. R. Ransome, John Summerson: *The History of the King's Works*, Volume III, Part 1 (1975)

STAFFORD, Simon (fl. 1596–1626), printer: was apprenticed for ten years to Christopher Barker, the Queen's Printer. Stafford became a freeman of the Drapers' Company but had his own printing press from 1598. His shops were in Black Raven Alley, Cornhill, Adding Hill (1600), at the "Three Crowns" in the Cloth Fair (1606) and near the "Red Lion" in the Cloth Fair (1607). In March 1598 Stafford was found to have printed the *Accidence*, a patented book, and his press and type were seized by the Stationers' Company. The resulting action was heard in Star Chamber; his press was restored by order of the Privy Council in September. The Stationers, however, insisted that he transfer from the Drapers' Company before he could become a master printer, and this he did in the following year. Stafford printed many ballads and sermons. He also printed Shakespeare's *Henry IV*, part 1 for Andrew Wise (1599) and *Pericles* (1611) as well as the anonymous play of *King Leir and his three daughters*, one of the sources for *King Lear*.

STANDEN, Anthony (fl. 1565–1604), spy: an English Roman Catholic who accompanied Darnley to Scotland in 1565 and then crossed to France. He travelled in Europe and the Turkish Empire and, by 1582, was serving the Grand Duke of Tuscany in Florence, calling himself Pompeio Pellegrini. Standen remained in touch with Catholics in Scotland on behalf of Mary Stuart but after her death he began to work for Sir Francis Walsingham's intelligence service, soon receiving an annual pension of £100 from the Queen. Standen organised the spy network in Spain which sent information of the Armada, at times visiting Spain himself, and among his agents was a servant of the Spanish Admiral, Santa Cruz. In 1590 the French arrested Standen as a Spanish spy and imprisoned him in Bordeaux, but he was released largely through the intervention of Anthony Bacon (q.v.). Standen returned to Spain and continued to forward information to Bacon who, on Walsingham's death, transferred his intelligence service to Essex. In 1593 Standen returned to England and was welcomed in the Essex circle. He was knighted in 1595/6, sailed on Essex's Cadiz expedition (reporting back to Bacon and Burghley), but lay low after Essex's disgrace and death. In 1603 Standen was again active on the Continent, supposedly on a diplomatic mission from James I to the Pope, but it is

241

known that he attempted to set France and Spain by the ears, as well as bringing back secret presents from the Pope to James's consort, Anne. These activities caused Standen to be sent to the Tower on his return in January 1604. There he wrote fanciful memoirs and was released at the end of the year, passing into obscurity although allegedly living "to a great age".

T. Birch, *Memoirs of the Reign of Queen Elizabeth*, Vol. I (1754)

D. du Maurier, *Golden Lads* (1975)

STANHOPE, John (c. 1545–1621), courtier and landowner: born in Yorkshire, although he spent his childhood in Nottinghamshire and had considerable lands in Northamptonshire. He came to Court as a supporter of Burghley and was a friend of Robert Cecil (q.v.). As some of his estates were in north Yorkshire he became *custos rotulorum* of the North Riding, a position of some local patronage; but his chief offices were at Court, where he was Master of the Posts, and, in 1596, Treasurer of the Chamber with a knight-hood. Together with Sir Thomas Hoby (q.v.), Stanhope was a Cecil "Government" candidate in the Yorkshire election of 1597, but was rejected as an absentee landlord and found a seat at Preston, a borough under the patronage of the Duchy of Lancaster, whose Chancellor was Robert Cecil. In 1601 he was appointed Vice-Chamberlain, a post he held at James's accession. He was, however, offended by the new King's pronouncement that such an office should be held by a Scot and he increasingly absented himself from Court. He was returned for Newtown, Isle of Wight, in the 1604 election, receiving a peerage as compensation for the loss of his Court post. But he took little part in James's public affairs.

J. E. Neale, *The Elizabethan House of Commons* (1949)

STANLEY, William (1548–1630), soldier and renegade: born at Hooton in Cheshire and was a cousin of the Earls of Derby. He was a practising Roman Catholic and served under Alva from 1567 to 1570, but then fought intermittently for fifteen years in Elizabeth's Irish conflicts, being knighted in 1579. Subsequently he served with Leicester in the Netherlands, distinguishing himself at Zutphen in 1586. On 28 January 1587 he betrayed the town of Deventer, going over to the Spanish with 1,200 Irishmen under his command. Conscience, and not pecuniary gain, prompted his treason: "Before I served the devil but now I serve God", he declared a few weeks later. He travelled to Madrid, advising Philip II to invade England from Ireland. In 1596–7 he fought for the Spaniards in France and from 1598 to 1603 in the Netherlands. He unsuccessfully sought a pardon from James I in 1604, and he may have been a double agent at the time of the Gunpowder Plot for, in January 1606, Robert Cecil (q.v.), expressly exonerated Stanley from any link with the conspiracy. The Spaniards appointed him Governor of Mechlin but he was in conflict with the Jesuits and spent some of his last years with the English Carthusians near Ostend, dying as a somewhat cantankerous octogenarian in Ghent.

G. Mattingly, *The Defeat of the Spanish Armada* (1959)

STANSBY, William (?–1638/9), printer: son of Richard Stansby, cutler, of Exeter. He was apprenticed to John Windet, stationer, for seven years from 1590 and became a freeman of the Stationers' Company in 1597. He went into partnership with Windet at his shop, the "Cross Keys", St Paul's Wharf. Stansby printed nothing between 1597 and 1611; in 1611 he printed *Hamlet*, Fourth Quarto, for John Smethwick.

STONE, Nicholas (?1587–1647), sculptor and master-mason: born in Woodbury, south Devon, apprenticed to a Flemish refugee stonemason in Southwark (1603–4) and subsequently worked in Amsterdam before establishing a workshop in Long Acre, London, in 1613. He was responsible for many of the ornate Jacobean tombs and, from 1619, he was engaged with Inigo Jones (q.v.) on the Banqueting House at Whitehall. Much of Stone's best work is in Oxford: the monuments to Bodley in Merton College and to Lyttelton in Magdalen College chapel, the Palladian gateway to the Botanic Gardens, and the almost baroque porch to the University Church of St Mary the Virgin.

STOW, John (1525–1605), antiquary and chronicler: born in London, the son of a tailor, and was himself admitted a freeman of the Merchant Taylors' Company in 1547. (v. *Speed*). His amateur

John Stow. From his monument in the Church of St Andrew Undershaft, London

enthusiasm for copying and transcribing ancient documents was noticed by Archbishop Matthew Parker who acted as a patron to Stow while he was editing medieval chronicles, and it was apparently on Parker's intervention that, on three occasions, he was exonerated from charges of being in possession of papist writings. He edited the works of Chaucer (1561), published a *Summary of English Chronicles* (1565), *The Chronicles of England* (1580), and contributed to a second edition of Holinshed's *Chronicles of England, Scotland and Ireland* (1585–7). His famous *Survey of London* (1598 and 1603) combined a contemporary description of the city with his memory of customs going back more than seventy years. Although he died impoverished, his widow erected a fine portrait-bust, which survives in his church, St Andrew Undershaft in Leadenhall Street.

J. Stow, *Survey of London*, ed., C. L. Kingsford (1908)
A. Bonner, "John Stow and his Survey", *Transactions London and Middlesex Archaeological Society*, VIII (1938)

STRACHEY, William (?1567–?1634), colonialist and writer: born at Saffron Walden, Essex, and educated at Emmanuel College, Cambridge. He settled in Blackfriars and was an acquaintance of Ben Jonson, writing some laudatory verse as a Preface for the printed edition of *Sejanus*, the play in which Shakespeare had acted. Strachey became a member of the Virginia Company but had other trading interests, too, for he was secretary of a special embassy to the Sultan in Constantinople in 1606. In June 1609 he accompanied Gates and Somers (qq.v.) in *Sea Venture's* voyage to Virginia, spending ten months as a castaway on Bermuda. He was secretary to the Governor of the Virginia colony (1610–11) and in July 1610 sent home a letter "to a noble lady" — probably Lucy, Countess of Bedford, an active member of the Virginia Company in London — in which he described the wreck of the vessel and his experiences in

Bermuda. Passages in Strachey's account correspond so closely to features in *The Tempest* that it is almost certain Shakespeare read the letter, which was published as *A True Reportory of the Wracke and Redemption of Sir Thomas Gates, a Knight* and printed by Purchas (q.v.). Strachey returned to London, once again to Blackfriars in 1611, and edited the first code of laws for Virginia (v. *Yardley*). In 1613 he completed two volumes of a *Historie of Travell into Virginia Britania*, but this valuable work does not appear to have been printed and published until 1849.

L. B. Wright and V. Freund, eds., *Strachey's Historie of Travell into Virginia Britania* (1953)
A. L. Rowse, *The Elizabethans and America* (1959)

STRAFFORD, Earl of (1593–1641) see WENTWORTH, Thomas.

STRANGE, Ferdinando Stanley, Lord Strange, later fifth Earl of Derby (1559/60–1594), theatrical patron: son of Henry Stanley, fourth Earl (q.v.) and his wife Margaret (Clifford), great-niece of Henry VIII. Strange was educated at St John's College, Oxford, where he matriculated in 1572 at the age of twelve, together with his two younger brothers. Before 1580 he married Alice Spencer (q.v.) and the couple had three daughters. Strange wrote poetry, some of which was printed in the anthology *Belvedere* (1600), and was a patron of poets. He also had a theatrical company, Lord Strange's Men, from 1576 onwards. They appeared in the provinces, and at Court in the early 1580s, as a troupe of acrobats led by the famous tumbler John Symons. By 1589 Strange's Men were performing plays, and some of the company were imprisoned for defying the Lord Mayor's ban on drama in the City of London. Will Kempe (q.v.) appeared with them in 1592. From then until 1594 Strange's Men seem to have joined forces in

London with the Admiral's Men; they played at theatres belonging to James Burbage and Henslowe (qq.v.) as well as at Court, and were led by Alleyn (q.v.). At this period some of Shakespeare's other colleagues joined them and they may have performed his early plays, *Titus Andronicus* and *Henry VI*. In 1594 Strange succeeded his father as Earl of Derby. Almost immediately a Roman Catholic exile, Richard Hesketh, who had served under Sir William Stanley (q.v.) was sent to England to suggest the Earl should claim the throne by right of his mother's descent from Henry VII. Derby denounced the plot and Hesketh was executed as a traitor. It was rumoured that Derby's death was caused by poison or witchcraft, as the "Jesuits' revenge"; but it seems to have been a natural one.

E. K. C., *E.S.*

STRANGE, Henry Stanley, Lord Strange (1531–1593) see DERBY, fourth Earl.

STREET, Peter (fl. 1598–1600), carpenter and theatre builder: employed by the Burbages (qq.v.) to help pull down the Theatre in Shoreditch and to rebuild it as the Globe. For this work he was forced to become chief defendant in an action brought by the Burbages' landlord, Giles Allen (q.v.). Street built the Globe between January and May 1599, although the playhouse may not have been completely finished until the autumn. On 8 January 1600 Henslowe and Alleyn (qq.v.) concluded a contract with Street stipulating that he should build them a new theatre "finished and done according to the manner and fashion of the said house called the Globe". The contract gives detailed specifications for what was to become the Fortune playhouse: it was to be stouter built than the Globe, completed by 25

July, and Street would receive £440. By 10 June Henslowe's accounts show he had paid nearly £300 including 4s to Street "to pacify him" for an unknown grievance. From 13 June until 8 August Street and Henslowe dined continually together. Possibly as a result of these efforts, the Fortune appears to have been finished by August 1600 and was certainly used by the Admiral's Men in the autumn. There is no further record of Street's activities.

E. K. C., *E.S.*
J. Q. Adams, *Shakespearean Playhouses* (1917)

STUART, Arbella (Arabella) (1575–1615): daughter of Charles Stuart, Earl of Lennox, a great-grandson of Henry VII. Arbella thus stood as near the English throne as did James VI. She was probably

Arbella Stuart. Painting by Marc Gheerarts

born in London; her father died when she was a year old and her mother when she was seven, leaving her to be brought up by her grandmother, "Bess" of Hardwick and her aunt, Mary Talbot (qq.v.). Arbella had a sound education in Latin, French, Italian and Spanish. Her grandmother upheld Arbella's claim to be recognised as Countess of Lennox but this was refused her by James VI. She received a small pension from Queen Elizabeth as compensation for the loss of her title and Scottish lands. There were recurring rumours of a marriage between Arbella and her cousin, King James, as well as a proposed match with Leicester's baby son, Robert, who died in 1584. A more serious project, discussed intermittently from 1587 to 1592, was marriage with the Duke of Parma's son, Rainutio Farnese, who had a tenuous link with the English Crown by descent from John of Gaunt. During these years Arbella spent some time at the English Court but when, in 1592, a Roman Catholic plot to kidnap her was discovered, she was returned to the permanent care of her grandmother at Hardwick Hall, Derbyshire. Ten years of frustrating restriction led Arbella to plot a secret marriage with Edward Seymour, elder grandson of the Earl of Hertford (q.v.), and a descendant of Henry VII. The Seymour family revealed the plan to the government, and Arbella was interrogated by the Queen's commissioner, Sir Henry Bronker. Upon James I's accession she was allowed to come to Court, and became friendly with Queen Anne (q.v.), appearing in two of the Queen's masques. James I increased her allowance; she bought a house in Blackfriars and made a semi-royal progress through the shires in 1609. In the same year she was again kept under restraint for allegedly planning to marry. Court life was expensive for Arbella and may have encouraged her in 1610 to conspire with William Seymour (q.v.), Edward's brother, who was thirteen years younger than herself. This time the plan succeeded. The couple were secretly married on 22 June 1610 and arrested seventeen days later. Seymour was sent to the Tower, Arbella detained at Lambeth. In the following summer, while journeying to Durham for a new term of restraint, she disguised herself as a man, eluded her guards at Barnet, and sailed for the Netherlands, where it was intended she would meet her husband who had escaped from the Tower. Arbella's vessel was overtaken and she was herself imprisoned in the Tower (together with her aunt and accomplice, Mary Talbot). In spite of many appeals to the King, Arbella was never released again, and starved herself to death four years later.

D. N. Durant, *Arbella Stuart* (1978)

STUBBES, Philip (?1555–?1610), Puritan writer: probably related to John Stubbes, the Puritan (1541–91), who lost his hand for writing against the Queen's French marriage (1579). Philip Stubbes is supposed to have attended Cambridge and Oxford Universities, but took no degree because he preferred to roam about, studying the lives of his contemporaries. He wrote religious ballads, mostly about terrible judgments on sinners. In 1583, when he had spent (he says) seven winters or more in travelling throughout England, he published his *Anatomy of Abuses*, condemning the evils of the age. The first edition was lenient to some forms of amusement, such as private dancing and useful plays, but subsequent reprints removed such concessions and denounced all popular entertainment. The book had four editions by 1595, and Stubbes was attacked by Nashe, but defended by Gabriel Harvey (qq.v.). In 1586 he married Katherine Emmes, aged fifteen, and wrote no more until her death in 1590, when he produced her biography, *A Chrystal Glass for Christian Women*. This was even more popular, going into six or seven editions. Stubbes went on pamphleteering until 1610.

P. Stubbes, *The Anatomie of Abuses*, ed., F. J. Furnivall (1879)
C. Hill, *Society and Puritanism in Pre-Revolutionary England* (1964)

STURLEY, Abraham (c. 1550–1614), Stratford lawyer: student at Queen's College, Cambridge in 1569; married Anne Hill, who was the daughter of the Bailiff of Stratford in 1575, and settled in the town, having previously lived in Worcester. He was servant, or retainer, of Sir Thomas Lucy of Charlecote in 1573–80. From 1591 onwards Sturley served Stratford in several capacities: as Town Councillor and Church Sidesman (1591), Alderman and Chamberlain (by 1594), and Bailiff (1596–7). In 1610 he played a major role in securing a new charter for Stratford. His house in Wood Street was burnt in the fire of September 1594, but by 1599 he had rebuilt it with sixteen bays. Sturley went on many missions for the town, collecting fire relief money in Cambridge and Bedford (1598), as well as accompanying his friend and colleague, Richard Quiney (q.v.), to see Burghley in 1593 and the Bishop of Worcester in 1601. He kept very full public records and was also a frequent correspondent of Richard Quiney; one letter is in Latin, others partly so, and he advised Quiney to read Cicero's letters. Two of Sturley's letters in 1598 refer to Shakespeare as a man of substance. During his term as Bailiff Sturley paid for four acting companies. He is known to have had at least three sons: the eldest, Henry, was an Oxford graduate who returned to Stratford to serve as undermaster from 1597 to 1604, when he was appointed Vicar of Chipping Camden and Broadway. His second son, Richard, went up to

Balliol College, Oxford, in 1596–7, the year in which a third son died of plague.

E. K. C., *W.S.*
M. E.

STURLEY, Henry (?1576–?), schoolmaster and vicar *see above.*

SUSSEX, Robert Radcliffe, fifth Earl of (1573–1629), soldier and theatrical patron: son of Henry, fourth Earl, whom he succeeded in 1593. A year later he was special ambassador to Scotland for the baptism of Prince Henry, son of James VI. He followed Essex (q.v.) at Cadiz as a Colonel of Foot and was knighted by him (1596). Sussex was Earl Marshal in 1599 and 1601 and was created Knight of the Garter in 1599. In 1601 he was briefly under house arrest because of the Essex rebellion; he was said to have had a letter from the Earl that would have involved him in the plot, had he been in London. Sussex was patron of an actors' company, originally formed in 1585 to serve his father. They played at the Rose under the management of Henslowe (q.v.) in 1593 and 1594, and may have had versions of Shakespeare's *Titus Andronicus* and *Henry VI*. Sussex maintained his minor position in the state during the reigns of James I and Charles I. He was Lord Lieutenant of Essex from 1603 to 1625 and again from 1626, and Governor of Harwich (1626–8), carrying the orb at Charles's coronation. Sussex was estranged from his first wife, Bridget Morrison, daughter of Sir Charles Morrison of Watford, by 1592. After her death in 1623 he married his mistress, Mrs Frances Shute, a widow from West Ham, who was already the mother of his daughter. All Sussex's four legitimate children died young.

SUTTON, Thomas (1532–1611), capitalist: of obscure origin, although he appears to have been at one time a member of Lincoln's Inn. After the suppression of the revolt of the Northern Earls in 1570, Sutton secured the post of Surveyor of the Ordnance in the Northern Parts and began to acquire leases of land rich in coal, especially around Gateshead and Durham. Marriage to a wealthy widow, and a favourable bargain struck with the Earl of Leicester, increased his annual income considerably. By 1580 he was established in London as a usurer, living frugally for many years in Fleet Street. Ben Jonson is said to have based the character of Volpone on the alleged characteristics of Sutton. By 1606, when *Volpone* was first acted, Sutton had become the wealthiest coroner in the kingdom. Five years later he purchased the Charterhouse from the Earl of Suffolk for £13,000. There Sutton established a hospital for eighty patients and a school for forty boys. He became first Governor of his foundation, but died at the end of the year.

SWANSTON, Elliard (fl. 1619–35, d. 1651), actor: he was with Lady Elizabeth's/Prince Charles's Men, 1619–22, joining the King's Men in 1624 and appearing thereafter in all their lists. From 1631 Swanston was associated with Lowin and Taylor (qq.v.) in managing the company and was one of those members who petitioned for a share in 1635. He is known to have played Othello and possibly Richard III. When he retired from acting he became a jeweller and is the only prominent actor to have sided with the Parliamentarians in the Civil War.

G. E. B.

T

TALBOT, Mary (1556–1632, née Cavendish, from 1590 Countess of Shrewsbury): daughter of Elizabeth ("Bess") of Hardwick (q.v.) and her second husband, Sir William Cavendish, was married at the age of twelve to Gilbert Talbot (later seventh Earl of Shrewsbury), son of her mother's fourth husband. Mary Talbot reputedly dominated her husband — Francis Bacon later remarked "The Earl of Shrewsbury is a great man but there is a greater than he, which is my Lady of Shrewsbury." The Talbots helped Bess of Hardwick bring up Arbella Stuart (q.v.) until Gilbert quarrelled with his stepmother after his father's death in 1590. About the same time Mary Talbot became a Roman Catholic. In 1611 she helped Arbella escape after her secret marriage and was herself sent to the Tower. When her case was heard in Star Chamber in 1612, with Bacon as prosecutor, Mary refused to answer because of a vow she had taken; she was fined £20,000 and confined to the Tower until 1615, the year of her husband's death. The enquiry into the murder of Overbury (q.v.) may well have originated at a dinner in the Shrewsbury's house at this time. In 1618 investigations were undertaken to establish whether Arbella Stuart had given birth to a child, but Mary again refused to answer any questions and was returned to the Tower, where she lived in the best lodgings until 1623. The fine was never collected, the Crown seizing Worksop Manor from her instead. She was a subscriber to the Virginia Company, and a benefactor of St John's College, Cambridge, where her portrait hangs to commemorate the building of the college's second court through her generosity.

V. A. Wilson, *Society Women of Shakespeare's Time* (1925)

TARLTON, Richard (?–1588), actor: the most famous comic actor of Elizabeth's reign. After his death there were several disparate accounts of his early life: he was born in Shropshire; or in London, where he was apprenticed to a water-carrier; or had a father living at Ilford, Essex. Tarlton is known to have been a founder member of the Queen's Men in 1583, but he was already an established entertainer. *Tarlton's Toyes* was listed in the Stationers' Register of 1576, followed by *Tarlton's Tragical Treaties* (1578) and *Tarlton's Devise upon this unlooked for Great Snow* (1579); none of these writings have survived. He was a favourite jester with the Queen until he went too far with jokes about Ralegh and Leicester. In 1585 Tarlton wrote a comedy for the Queen's Men, *Seven Deadly Sins*, which became very popular. He was such an able fencer that he became Master of the Fence in 1587. He left his property to his son Philip (named after his godfather, Philip Sidney) and appealed on his death-bed to Walsingham to protect the boy. A Tarlton cult continued long after his death: public houses were named after him, and he appeared on the inn signs in his regular comic costume, a russet coat, sloppy breeches and carrying a big stick. Many pamphlets or ballads, supposedly by or about Tarlton, were published. *Tarlton's Jests*, printed in 1611 but written earlier, contains his alleged life story and includes the episode in which a friend of Tarlton, seeing him smoking for the first time, threw water over him with shouts of "Fire!" (a tale told later of Ralegh). In *Hamlet* the references of the Prince to Yorick have been seen as a tribute by Shakespeare to Tarlton.

E. K. C., *E.S.*
E. Nungezer, *Dictionary of Actors* (1929)

TAYLOR, John (1580–1653), Thames waterman, poet: born in Gloucester and attended Gloucester Grammar School until his Latin proved too bad, and he was apprenticed to a waterman instead. Taylor was pressed for the navy and saw service at Cadiz and Flores (1596–7). On his return he settled to the life of a Thames waterman in London and semi-official collector of wines for the Lieutenant of the Tower. He augmented his income by writing verse, mainly about his travels, but also on public affairs. He provoked a feud with Coryat (q.v.) whose works he parodied, and Coryat succeeded in having Taylor's verses burnt. But after Coryat's death, Taylor became London's chief eccentric poet. Apart from his poems for state occasions, he also organised the water pageant for the wedding of Princess Elizabeth and the Elector Palatine (1613). Taylor's usual method of getting paid for his work was to collect subscriptions before setting off on some ridiculous journey, then write it up in book form for the subscribers. His walk to Braemar, Scotland in 1618 produced *Penniless Pilgrimage*, and 22s from Ben Jonson, whom he met on the way back. Taylor visited Princess Elizabeth in Prague, went to York by sea, and tried to sail to Kent in a brown-paper boat. In 1625 he went to Oxford to escape the plague and stayed in Oriel College, where he wrote Royalist tracts. His collected works were published in 1630. Taylor kept the Crown Inn in Long Acre, London, from 1646 till his death, and is buried in the churchyard of St Martin-in-the-Fields.

TAYLOR, Joseph (?1586–1652), actor: lived most of his life in Southwark. He was first with Prince Charles's Men in 1610, then with the Lady Elizabeth's (1611–15) and back with the Prince Charles company by 1616, until February 1619. He joined the King's Men between 27 March and 19 May 1619, presumably replacing Richard Burbage, who died on 13 March. Taylor certainly took over Burbage's roles of Ferdinand in *The Duchess of Malfi*, and Hamlet. Downes, in the *Roscius Anglicanus* of 1708, claimed that Taylor had been taught *Hamlet* by Shakespeare; this is hardly possible. Wright, however, in his *Historia Histrionica* of 1699 says that Taylor played Hamlet "incomparably well" and also praises his Iago, his Truewit in Jonson's *Epicoene* and his Face in *The Alchemist*. Taylor was sufficiently established by 1623 to be mentioned in the First Folio list of actors and by 1630 he owned two shares in the Globe and one in the Blackfriars, becoming with Lowin (q.v.) a leader of the company. In 1639 he was made Yeoman of the Revels. He was buried at Richmond, 4 November 1652.

G. E. B.

THORPE, John (c. 1563–1655), land-surveyor and writer on architecture: born in Northamptonshire, the son of a mason. He served as a clerk in the Office of Works from 1583 to 1601, for most of the time under William Spicer (q.v.). Subsequently he became — in modern parlance — a free-lance Land Surveyor and Draughtsman, an associate of John Norden and a friend of Henry Peacham (qq.v.). Thorpe was responsible for drawing plans of many great houses in southern England. Much of his work was preserved in what is known as *The Book of Architecture of John Thorpe* in Sir John Soane's Museum, Lincoln's Inn Fields, London. Thorpe was long given credit for having designed houses which he merely surveyed, committing his measurements and detailed notes to the plans that have survived. Only Aston Hall in Birmingham, built by Sir Thomas Holte between 1618 and 1635, is now thought to have been Thorpe's work.

J. Summerson, *Architecture in Britain, 1530–1830* (1953)

THORPE, Thomas (fl. 1584–1625), bookseller: son of Thomas Thorpe, innholder, of Barnet. He was apprenticed to Richard Watkins, stationer, for nine years from 1584 and became a freeman of the Stationers' Company in 1594. He published plays, but is most famous for his edition of Shakespeare's Sonnets (1609) with its enigmatic dedication, probably written by himself, and arousing so much speculation about the dedicatee, "Mr W. H.". Thorpe deserved his own nickname of "Odd".

TILNEY (or TYLNEY), Edmund (?– 1610), Master of the Revels: probably son of Thomas Tilney of Shelley, Suffolk and distantly related to the Howard family. Tilney was M.P. for Gatton, Surrey, a Howard pocket borough, from 1572. In spite of having dedicated a tract on marriage, *The Flower of Friendship* (1568) to Queen Elizabeth, Tilney was appointed Master of the Revels in 1579. He held the office until his death, although in 1581 he was briefly considered as a possible ambassador to Spain. The Master's duty was to provide all entertainment for the Court; he had an allowance of £20 for a house and £15 for the Revels office and wardrobe. After his formal commission in 1581, Tilney gradually extended his rights until by the end of the century he controlled all acting companies and theatres, under the overall jurisdiction of the Lord Chamberlain. In 1583 (the year of his marriage to Mary Bray) Tilney was commanded to enrol actors for the Queen's Men. By 1589 he was advising the Lord Mayor of London to ban all plays in the City, probably because of the dramatists' involvement in the "Martin Marprelate" controversy. In the 1590s Tilney censored *Sir Thomas More*, a play of which Shakespeare is thought to have written part (v. *Antony Munday*). From 1603 much of Tilney's work was done by his deputy, George Buck (q.v.), a connection by marriage. Tilney continued to render the accounts of the Revels, and kept his considerable income from fees, but spent more time at his house in Leatherhead, Surrey, where he entertained the Queen. By 1607 the Master's work included licensing plays for printing as well as performance. Tilney was succeeded by Buck.

E. K. C., *E.S.*
M. Eccles, "Sir George Buck", *Thomas Lodge and Other Elizabethans*, ed., C. J. Sisson (1966)

TOMKINS, Thomas (1573–1656), composer: born into a musical family at St David's, Pembrokeshire, where his father was organist, and moved later to Gloucester. Tomkins received musical tuition from Byrd (q.v.) and became organist of Worcester Cathedral in 1596, a post he held for half a century. He composed a fine collection of madrigals, 1622–30, as well as coronation music for Charles I and many anthems.

TOMKIS, Thomas (c. 1580–1634), scholar and dramatist: educated at Trinity College, Cambridge (1597–1600, Fellow 1604). He wrote two comedies. *Lingua*, dated between 1602 and 1607, is said to have included the first public appearance of Oliver Cromwell, aged four. If so, it formed part of his uncle's entertainment for James I at Hinchingbrook in April 1603 (v. *Sir Oliver Cromwell*). The tradition of Cromwell's acting goes back before the 1657 edition of the play. The other comedy of Tomkis, *Albumazar*, was performed by Trinity men before James I at Cambridge in 1615. It is a satire on astrology; Dryden regarded it, wrongly, as the model for Jonson's *Alchemist*.

E. K. C., *E.S.*

TOOLEY, Nicholas (?1575–1623), actor, alias Wilkinson: with the King's Men from 1605 until his death and is in the First Folio list. He had probably appeared with the company earlier than 1605, as he seems to have been Burbage's apprentice. From 1619 to 1623 he is known to have played Forobosco and a madman in *The Duchess of Malfi*. Tooley lodged with Cuthbert Burbage (q.v.); he left legacies to the Burbage family, and in his will thanked Cuthbert's wife for "her motherly care over me".

G. E. B.

TOPCLIFFE, Richard (1532–1604), interrogator extraordinary: born at Sowerby in Lincolnshire, elected to the Commons as M.P. for Beverley, sitting subsequently for Old Sarum, 1586–1603. He was employed by Burghley as an internal security agent from 1573 onwards, becoming notorious as a torturer of suspected Roman Catholics, especially in the period 1586–96. He maintained a private torture chamber, with a rack and other devices of his invention, in his house in Westminster. His excessive cruelty led to a brief spell of imprisonment on Burghley's orders, but towards the end of Elizabeth's reign he was honoured with a grant of estates at Padley in Derbyshire, where he retired for the last year of his life.

TOTTEL, Richard (fl. 1552–1594), printer: son of Henry Tottel of Exeter. He was an original member of the Stationers' Company and Master in 1579 and 1584. Tottel was granted a patent for printing law books in 1552. This was renewed for seven years (1556) and finally for life (1559). Tottel's shop was at the "Hand and Star", Fleet Street. His most famous production was *Songs and Sonnets* (1557), edited by himself and generally known as *Tottel's Miscellany*. By 1593 he had retired to Pembrokeshire and died soon after; the printer John Jaggard acquired Tottel's shop in 1598.

H. E. Rollins, ed., *Tottel's Miscellany* (1965)

TOURNEUR, Cyril (c. 1575–1626), dramatist: may have been connected with Richard Turner, water-bailiff and Lieutenant of Brill in the Netherlands, but little is known of his early life. Tourneur's first attributed work was an allegorical and satirical poem, *The Transformed Metamorphosis* (1600). He was one of the many poets who wrote an elegy on the death of Prince Henry (1613) but his main literary activity (1607–13) was playwriting. As well as collaborating with other dramatists (notably Fletcher) he wrote under his own name *The Atheist's Tragedy* (1607–11) and *The Nobleman* (c. 1612), a tragi-comedy now lost. *The Revenger's Tragedy*, published anonymously in 1607, was first assigned to Tourneur by the printer in 1656 and is now generally accepted as his. It is the most powerful of the Jacobean tragedies on the theme of revenge, portraying the loathsome corruption of Court and aristocracy. From 1613 onwards Tourneur's life was spent in foreign service, first in the Netherlands and finally as secretary to the Council of War under Sir Edward Cecil (q.v.) in the raid on Cadiz in 1625. Tourneur died in Ireland, with other wounded and sick men who were disembarked there on the way home after the expedition's failure.

E. K. C., *E.S.*

TRADESCANT, John (c. 1585–1638), traveller and botanist: member of a Suffolk family. He accompanied Sir Dudley Digges (q.v.) on a diplomatic mission to Archangel and Moscow, writing on his return *A Voyage of Ambassad* (1618), a work of great interest on the flora and fauna of northern Russia. Tradescant brought back both curiosities and plants. He successfully cultivated in England a *Rosa Moscovita* which he found in the delta of the river Dvina. Ten years later he brought Algerian

John Tradescant

apricots to England from an expedition against the Barbary pirates of north Africa. He also introduced acacia, lilac, and small French willow trees from which baskets were made. Charles I appointed Tradescant royal gardener, and he cultivated a scientific botanical garden at Lambeth. His son and namesake (born at Meopham in 1608, died 1662) succeeded his father as royal gardener, specialising in the botanical study of Virginia, which he visited on three occasions. The collection of the Tradescants, father and son, passed to Elias Ashmole (1617–92) and forms the basis of the Ashmolean Museum in Oxford.

M. S. Anderson, *Britain's Discovery of Russia* (1958)
S. Konovalov, ed., "Two documents concerning Anglo-Russian relations", *Oxford Slavonic Studies*, II (1951)
D. Piper, *The Treasures of Oxford* (1977)

TRESHAM, Francis (1567–1605), conspirator: son of Sir Thomas Tresham, of Rushton Hall, Northants (*infra*). Embittered by the treatment of his recusant father and his family's impoverishment after 1581, he grew up reckless and extravagant and added his own debts to his father's. Tresham became a follower of Essex (q.v.) and joined in his rebellion of 1601. He was fined £2,000 and his father laid out at least £1,000 more in bribes to secure his son's release from prison. Tresham was largely responsible for urging his father to expedite the unpopular policy of enclosing the family's lands. When he inherited what was left of the Rushton estate in September 1605, Tresham made no attempt to cope with the huge legacy of debt. Instead he was persuaded by his second cousin, Robert Catesby (q.v.) to join in the Gunpowder Plot, promising to put up £2,000. Tresham was suspected of writing the letter that revealed the plot to Lord Monteagle (q.v.), his brother-in-law, but he convinced Catesby of his innocence. Tresham was arrested about a week after 5 November and died in the Tower before he could be tried. His mother's efforts to discharge the family debts ended in failure, and his brother Lewis was forced to mortgage Rushton to the wealthy London merchant, William Cokayne (q.v.) who finally obtained possession of the estate.

M. E. Finch, "The Wealth of Five Northamptonshire Families", *Northamptonshire Record Society*, 19 (1956)

TRESHAM, Thomas (1544–1605), of Rushton Hall, Northants: son of John Tresham, (died 1546), succeeded his grandfather in 1559 and was knighted in 1575. The Treshams were an old Roman Catholic family with vast estates centred on Rushton. Until 1580 Tresham prospered in the management of his lands, enclosing and turning to sheep farming.

His direct selling methods were like those of Baron Spencer (q.v.); he even sold rabbits on a large scale to London poulterers. His income, of about £3,500 a year, did not prevent him from running deeply into debt, however. In 1566 he married Meriel, daughter of Sir Robert Throckmorton, by whom he had three sons and six daughters. All the daughters had generous dowries, particularly Elizabeth who married Lord Monteagle (q.v.) and took him £3,800. Tresham, a cheerful man with many friends, always entertained lavishly at Rushton, his other country house Lyveden, and his two London houses. He was a great builder, leaving the triangular lodge at Rushton and the Italian-style market-hall at Rothwell as outstanding examples of his taste for the fantastic. The chief drain on Tresham's income was his recusancy. From 1581, when he was first arrested on suspicion of harbouring a Jesuit, Edmund Campion, he paid nearly £8,000 in fines and spent a total of fifteen years in prison at different times. His religion was a bar to advancement, and he was forced to borrow money on terms which bound his son Francis (*supra*) as well. Tresham also began to mortgage his lands, sell the outlying estates, and enclose the remainder more extensively, an unpopular policy, which caused riots in 1607. He died, owing over £11,000, in September 1605, just before his son became involved in the Gunpowder Plot.

Ibid.

TRUNDELL, John (?–?1629), bookseller: son of John Trundell, yeoman, of Barnet. He was apprenticed for eight years from 1589 to Ralph Hancock, stationer, and became a freeman of the Stationers' Company in 1597. Trundell's shop was at the sign of "Nobody" in the Barbican in 1613. He published mainly ballads,

newsheets and plays. With Nicholas Ling he published the First Quarto *Hamlet* (1603). In 1636 there was a bookseller in Paris named John Trundell, but there seems to be no connection with the London bookseller, who was dead by then.

TURBERVILLE, George (?1540–1610), diplomat and poet: born at Whitchurch Canonicorum in Dorset, educated at Winchester and New College, Oxford. He became secretary to Thomas Randolph (1523–90), accompanying him on a special mission to Ivan the Terrible in Moscow, 1568. On his return Turberville wrote epistolary verses, published in 1587 as *Tragicall Tales* in which he gave the English public a damning picture of Russian life, describing "the Russes" as "a people passing rude, to vices vile inclinde". Turberville was also the author of numerous sonnets, translations from Ovid and contemporary Italian poets, a book on falconry and a book of venery. He was one of the earliest English writers to perfect blank verse.

TYLER, Richard (1566–1636), Stratford resident: son of a butcher, but is not known to have followed any trade himself. He volunteered as a soldier in Armada year and was later described as a gentleman. From 1590 to 1594 he served on the Town Council. In 1607 he and Thomas Lucas (q.v.) were accused of making an affray on each other. Five years later he was bound over to keep the peace, but the Council petitioned for his discharge, as his accuser on this occasion was suspect. After the third of the major town fires in Stratford (1614), Tyler was authorised to collect relief money in Kent. Two years later he was charged with failing to keep account of the money. Originally Tyler was one of the Stratford residents to whom Shakespeare wished to leave money to buy a ring, but in the second draft of Shakespeare's will

Hamnet Sadler (q.v.) replaced Tyler as beneficiary, perhaps because of the embezzlement charge. Tyler was not, however, totally estranged from the family or disgraced. He signed the deed of transfer of Shakespeare's Blackfriars house in 1618, and he served the parish as Church warden in 1621, as did his son four years later.

M. E.

TYRONE, Hugh O'Neill, Earl of (c. 1540–1616), Irish leader: grandson of Con O'Neil (?1484–1559), an Irish chieftain whom Henry VIII created Earl of Tyrone in 1542, hoping he would thereby maintain order in Ireland. Hugh O'Neill's title and estates, at first denied him as a bastard, were confirmed in 1587. In August 1594 he began a Catholic rising in Ulster and appealed for help to Spain. An expeditionary force under Sir John Norris was fitted out to subdue Tyrone's rebellion in May 1595. There was a truce in 1596–7 but in August 1598 Tyrone annihilated an English force at Yellow Ford on the Blackwater River and Essex (q.v.) was appointed Lord Lieutenant in March 1599 to avenge this disaster. Tyrone signed a truce with Essex six months later, but resumed his rebellion in January 1600 by invading Munster in force. Mountjoy (q.v.), Essex's successor, gradually contained the threat from Tyrone, routing an attack he launched in conjunction with a Spanish invading force at Kinsale in December 1601. Tyrone was badly wounded on this occasion. He formally submitted to Mountjoy in March 1603, was pardoned by James I, but continued to intrigue with the Spanish until September 1607 when, together with the rebellious Earl of Tyrconel, he fled from Ireland to France and Spain, fearing arrest for planning yet another insurrection. This "Flight of the Earls" opened the way for the plantation of their forfeited lands in Ulster with English and Scottish protestants. Tyrone died in Rome on 30 July 1616.

C. Falls, *Elizabeth's Irish Wars* (1950)

U

UNDERHILL, William I (?1530–70), lawyer: a Middle Temple lawyer who was Clerk of Assizes in Warwick and acquired considerable property in the county. In 1567 he bought New Place in Chapel Street, Stratford, for £40 from William Bott (q.v.). Underhill married, as his second wife, Dorothy, the sister of Sir Christopher Hatton (q.v.), who was left a guardian to his son, William (*infra*).

M. E.

UNDERHILL, William II (1556–97), Warwickshire landowner: inherited New Place, Stratford, and other neighbouring property from his father at the age of fourteen. Later Underhill and his wife, Mary, lived both in Stratford and at Idlicote; they had three sons and three daughters. Although Underhill had once been imprisoned for recusancy, he held office as Escheator for Warwickshire and Leicestershire. In May 1597 he sold New Place to Shakespeare for £60. On 7 July of the same year he died, poisoned by his son Fulke, who was executed for the murder two years later. The second son, Hercules, retrieved the forfeited estates on coming of age in 1601 and then confirmed the sale of New Place.

M. E.

UNDERWOOD, John (c. 1590–1624), actor: was one of the Children of the Chapel Royal at Blackfriars, playing in Jonson's *Cynthia's Revels* and *Poetaster*, 1600–1. When the King's Men started playing at Blackfriars in 1608 he was taken into their company. His name appears in their acting list for the *Alchemist* in 1610, and in twenty more lists, including the First Folio, until 1624. He played Delio and a madman in *The Duchess of Malfi*, 1619–23. By the time of his death he had acquired shares in the theatres, possibly from Pope (q.v.). He left them to his five children, all under twenty-one, and the shares were held in trust by his executors, of whom Condell (q.v.) was one.

E. K. C., *E.S.*

USSHER, James (1581–1656), archbishop: born near Dublin, ordained in 1601, and was the earliest student from Trinity College, Dublin (founded 1591) to win high academic distinction, becoming the first Professor of Divinity at his college in 1607. Although a Calvinist, Ussher was a man of broad tolerance, who remained on good terms with Laud (q.v.) and was given a state funeral in Westminster Abbey on the orders of Lord Protector Cromwell. Ussher was consecrated Bishop of Meath in 1621 and succeeded his uncle as Archbishop of Armagh four years later. His *Annales Veteris et Novi Testamenti*, completed towards the end of his life, were inserted in later editions of the Authorised Version of the Bible. The pedantically inaccurate fixing of the Creation in 4004 B.C. has tended to discredit Ussher's scholarship. In reality he was a pioneer in patristic studies and a respected authority on the early history of Ireland.

V

VANE, Henry (1589–1655), courtier and Parliamentarian: born at Hadlow, Kent, entered Brasenose College, Oxford in 1604, and Gray's Inn two years later. He was under the patronage of Overbury (q.v.) and was welcomed at Court by James I, by whom he was knighted at the age of twenty-two, given household appointments at Court in 1612 and made Cofferer to Charles, Prince of Wales, in 1617. He held this post until 1630, and was Secretary of State and adviser to Charles I in 1640. Vane turned against Thomas Wentworth (q.v.), Earl of Strafford, for personal reasons and gave important hearsay evidence against him at his trial in 1641. In December 1641 the King dismissed Sir Henry Vane from the royal household and he thereafter supported the Parliamentarian cause as his son, Henry Vane the Younger (1613–62) had done ever since he reached manhood.

VAUGHAN, Rowland (fl. 1570s–1604), inventor: born at Bredwardine Castle, Herefordshire, the second son of Watkyn Vaughan and his wife Joan (Parry), niece of the Queen's gentlewoman, Blanche Parry (q.v.). Vaughan was intended for life at Court with his great-aunt, but his "spirit was too tender" for her scoldings. He next (before 1577) tried soldiering in Ireland under Sir Henry Sidney, but his flesh was too tender for that, and he became very ill. On returning to Herefordshire Vaughan married his cousin, Elizabeth Vaughan, who had inherited Newcourt Manor in the Golden Valley, together with a mill. Landed property — and a legacy of £100 from Blanche Parry — encouraged him to put into practice ideas of his own on irrigation. He was one of the first landowners to construct water meadows and control flooding by means of drains and sluices. Some traces of this work still survive. He developed water power for other purposes, such as turning spits and sawing timber. Vaughan planned what he called a "commonwealth" in the Golden Valley, claiming to have "two thousand mechanicals" of all different trades living together in his model village with its own chapel and eating in a central dining-room. According to John Davies of Hereford (q.v.), they all wore "scarlet caps". Davies wrote an introductory poem for Vaughan's *Most Approved and Long-experienced Waterworks*, which was written in 1604 but published in 1610 and dedicated to William Herbert, third Earl of Pembroke. It is probable that Vaughan's book describes an ideal state of self-sufficiency to which the Golden Valley "commonwealth" had not yet attained. The date of Vaughan's death is unknown; his wife, who died in 1640, was by then a widow who had remarried.

E. B. Wood, ed., *Rowland Vaughan, his Book* (1897)
G. E. Fussell, *Old English Farming Books* (1978)

VAVASOUR, Anne, Gentlewoman of the Bedchamber to Queen Elizabeth see LEE, Henry; KNYVETT, Thomas; OXFORD, Earl of.

VENNAR, Richard (c. 1555–1615), dramatist and confidence trickster: described as a gentleman of Lincoln's Inn. He announced his intention of producing a sensational pageant at the Swan theatre on 6 November 1602. Called *England's Joy*, it would represent English history from Edward III to the ruling Queen, in whose honour the pageant was named. The performers were to be ladies and gentlemen and the playbill promised many special effects: the Queen "taken up into Heaven", while Hell "under the stage" would be "set forth with strange fireworks, divers black and damned souls". Admission was 2s or 18d; but nothing was seen but a prologue, after which Vennar disappeared with the takings and the enraged audience wrecked the theatre. When Vennar was brought before Lord Chief Justice Popham, he was bound over for £5, Popham thinking it "nothing but a jest and a merriment", as Chamberlain (q.v.) wrote. Vennar apparently tried a similar fraud in 1606, securing £500 for a masque for the Lord Mayor; and he finally died in a debtor's prison. "England's Joy" became a catch phrase for comedians and Vennar was the archetypal "cony-catcher" (cheat) who, as a contemporary work said, "drew more conies in a purse-net, than ever were taken at any draught about London" (Day, Rowley and Wilkins, *Travels of Three English Brothers*, 1607).

E. K. C., *E.S.*

VERE, Elizabeth (1575–1627): daughter of the unhappy marriage between the Earl of Oxford and Anne Cecil, Lord Burghley's favourite daughter. Burghley destined her for his ward, the young Earl of Southampton (q.v.) but in 1592 Southampton refused to marry at all. This sequence of events is referred to in Shakespeare's Sonnets urging marriage on his patron, if that patron is indeed Southampton. Elizabeth Vere eventually married William Stanley, Earl of Derby (q.v.) in January 1595. The ceremony was a lavish one, at the Court at Greenwich in the Queen's presence, and has been thought a possible occasion for the first performance of *A Midsummer Night's Dream*. The date would be right.

VERNON, Elizabeth (1573–?1655/6) see SOUTHAMPTON, Countess of.

VERULAM, Lord (1561–1626) see BACON, Francis.

VILLIERS, George (1592–1628) see BUCKINGHAM, Duke of.

W

WALKER, Henry (?—1616), musician: born at Kington, Herefordshire. He was a member of the Musicians' Company and also kept a shop at his house in the parish of St Martin's, Ludgate, London. On 10 March 1613 he sold the Blackfriars Gatehouse to Shakespeare, having previously bought it from Matthias Bacon (q.v.). Shakespeare mortgaged it back for £60 for six months. Walker died a wealthy man, with several apprentices.

L. Hotson, *Shakespeare's Sonnets Dated* (1949)

WALKER, William (1608—80), Stratford resident: son of Alderman Henry Walker, mercer, of the High Street. William was baptised at Stratford on 16 October 1608, and has been identified with probability as Shakespeare's godson. In his will Shakespeare left William Walker 20s in gold. By 1649 he was Bailiff of Stratford.

M. E.

WALKLEY, Thomas (fl. 1618—49), bookseller: became a freeman of the Stationers' Company in 1618 and had two shops in London, the "Eagle and Child" and the "Flying Horse". In 1622 he published Shakespeare's *Othello*. Nothing more is known of Walkley except that he must have been a Royalist, as there was a warrant out against him in 1649 for publishing declarations by the sons of Charles I.

WALLEY, Henry (fl. 1608—1655), bookseller: had a shop in London at the "Hart's Horn", Foster Lane. Walley became a freeman of the Stationers' Company in 1608, was Clerk from 1630 to 1640 and Master in 1655. In 1609 he and Richard Bonian (q.v.) published two editions of Shakespeare's *Troilus and Cressida*.

WALSINGHAM, Frances, Countess of Essex (1567—1632): daughter of Sir Francis (*infra*). In 1583 she married Philip Sidney and had a daughter, Elizabeth, by him. Frances travelled to the Netherlands to nurse Sidney on his death-bed (1586). She proved equally devoted to her second husband, Queen Elizabeth's favourite, Essex (q.v.); they were married in 1589—90 and the Queen never forgave Frances for this. Their son Robert (see under *Essex*) was born in 1591, but the couple were often separated during the years leading up to the Earl's disgrace, and only after this were their two daughters born (1599 and 1600). Frances was allowed to visit Essex while he was ill and under arrest (1599—1600); at the same time she was being blackmailed by John Daniel, the husband of one of her servants to whom she had entrusted some of the Earl's letters from Ireland. Daniel employed Peter Bales (q.v.), the writing master, to copy the letters, but Bales became suspicious and denounced Daniel who was prosecuted in Star Chamber, fined £3,000, pilloried and given a life sentence (from which he was released after the accession of James I). Frances had sold her jewels to redeem the letters (v. *Dyer, Sir Edward*). Her third husband was an Irish peer who had fought for the English, Richard de Burgh, Earl of Clanricarde, created Earl of St Albans in 1628. The marriage took place before 1603 and produced one son and two daughters.

V. A. Wilson, *Society Women of Shakespeare's Time* (1925)

WALSINGHAM, Francis (?1532–90), diplomat and Secretary of State: born at Footscray, Kent, educated at King's College, Cambridge (1548–50) and entered Gray's Inn. His strong Protestantism induced him to spend Mary's reign abroad, mostly at the University of

Sir Francis Walsingham

Padua and in Venice. He was fluent in French and Italian. In 1563 and 1566–7 he represented Lyme Regis in Parliament, and from 1568 until his death was in the royal service, originally as principal organiser of a secret service of spies and informers. He was ambassador in Paris at the time of the Massacre of St Bartholomew's Day (24 August 1572) but became Secretary of State a year later, an office he held for seventeen years. He conducted foreign policy in alliance with Leicester (q.v.) and his party, favouring more active support of continental Protestantism, especially in the Netherlands. A majority in the Privy Council supported Walsingham and Leicester rather than the "peace" policy of the Queen and Burghley (q.v.). Walsingham's greatest service was

as Controller of Intelligence, maintaining more than fifty spies abroad and at least eighteen agents at home. Among these agents were Marlowe, Anthony Bacon and Anthony Standen (qq.v.). On this intelligence network he spent a personal fortune as well as public funds. He was able to ferret out plots against the Queen's person and received early information about the Armada. Walsingham invested in the voyages of Drake and Frobisher, was a literary patron of writers concerned with exploration and colonisation, notably Hakluyt (q.v.), but his cultural interests were constrained by his Puritan zeal. He was knighted in 1577 and for the last three years of his life exercised considerable patronage as Chancellor of the Duchy of Lancaster.

C. Read, *Mr Secretary Walsingham* (1925)

WALSINGHAM, Thomas (1563/8–1630): son of Sir Thomas Walsingham of Scadbury, Chiselhurst, Kent, a cousin of Francis Walsingham (*supra*). He married Ethelred (or Audrey) Shelton, an heiress distantly related to Queen Elizabeth, and succeeded to the Scadbury estate in 1589. Walsingham may have acted as liaison officer for his cousin's spy network, recruiting agents such as Marlowe (q.v.). But he was also a patron of poets, including Chapman and Watson, Marlowe's friend, and acquainted with Blount the publisher. Blount dedicated his edition of Marlowe's *Hero and Leander*, published in 1598, to Walsingham. Marlowe was staying in Walsingham's house just before the fracas in which he died (1593). Frizer, who actually killed Marlowe, was a confidential servant of Walsingham and his wife, as well as an associate of secret agents, and remained at Scadbury till 1597. By then Walsingham had settled down to a country gentleman's life. He was J.P. for Kent, knighted when the Queen visited him in

1597, and three times M.P. for Rochester (1597, 1601, 1604). His estates were increased by a grant of four more manors, Dartford, Cobham, Combe and Chiselhurst, also in 1597. Favours continued to come to the Walsinghams from James I. Lady Walsingham became a friend of Queen Anne, attended her on her progress south in 1603 and appeared frequently in Court masques. She was one of the Keepers of the Queen's Wardrobe and had to take the late Queen's best clothes out of the Tower to be used in the Twelfth Night masque of 1604. Walsingham's tomb, in the Scadbury Chapel of St Nicholas, Chiselhurst, was opened in 1956 by Calvin Hoffman, who hoped to find manuscripts supporting his theory that Marlowe survived the events of 1593 and wrote Shakespeare's works while living secretly at Scadbury. Nothing was found but the coffin.

S. Schoenbaum, *Shakespeare's Lives* (1970)
W. A. Scott Robertson, "Chiselhurst and its Church", *Archaeologia Cantiana*, XII (1880).

WALTER, John (1566–1630), lawyer: born at Ludlow and educated at Brasenose College, Oxford, from 1579 to 1582, when he was admitted to the Inner Temple, being called to the Bar in 1590. Within a few years he was respected as one of the ablest lawyers in London. He became Attorney to the Prince of Wales in 1613 and was knighted in 1619, sitting as M.P. for East Looe in the Parliaments of 1621 and 1624. He attracted much notice through his impassioned speech against monopolies in March 1621 and the crusading Protestant fervour with which he denounced Spain three years later. In 1625 he became a judge, as Chief Baron of the Exchequer, and he showed a Sabbatarian hostility to all plays and other entertainments. Although willing to defend the royal prerogative over money

matters, he was a firm upholder of freedom of speech. His leniency aggravated Charles I, who suspended Sir John in 1629 and formally inhibited him from sitting on the bench in October 1630. He died a few weeks later.

W. J. Jones, *Politics and The Bench* (1971)

WARD, Mary (1585–1645), foundress of a religious order: born of a Roman Catholic family in Mulwith, Yorkshire, and baptised Jane, taking the name Mary at confirmation. At the age of twenty-one Mary Ward entered the Order of Poor Clares at St Omer, but left the convent in 1607 to open a house of the order for English girls. In 1609 she started a teaching order of nuns, the Institute of the Blessed Virgin Mary (known as the "English Ladies"), with a day and boarding school. The nuns were not enclosed; they often accompanied boarders out of the convent and were nicknamed by their detractors "the galloping girls". Mary Ward's ambition was to develop her order so that it rivalled the Jesuits, whose rule she adopted. She succeeded in opening houses in Liège and Cologne (and probably in other cities) but when she travelled to Rome, she found Pope Urban VIII uncooperative. Recognition could come to her order only if she accepted enclosure for her nuns and placed them under the jurisdiction of the local bishop. In 1631 the principal house of the Order, at Munich, was closed, the order suppressed and Mary Ward herself imprisoned as a heretic in the Munich Convent of Poor Clares. She was released in 1632, permitted to reopen her houses on more disciplined lines, and encouraged to go back to England. In 1637 she returned to her native Yorkshire, founding in 1642 a convent near the ruined Fountains Abbey, where she died. The convent moved to York in 1686, Mary Ward's order receiving formal recognition in 1703. The York conventual school is the oldest still existing in England; and there are now four other English schools of the order.

WARD, Samuel (1577–1640), Puritan lecturer: probably a son of John Ward, preacher, of Haverhill, Essex, and educated at St John's College, Cambridge (?1594–7). Ward was one of the original Fellows of Sidney Sussex College from 1599 to 1604 when he resigned to marry. He became a lecturer at Haverhill and from 1603 was Town Lecturer in Ipswich, paid by the Corporation. Ward was often in trouble for Puritan preaching, and in 1621 was imprisoned for setting his name to an anti-Spanish cartoon. His final suspension and imprisonment occurred in 1635, after which he spent some time as a minister in Rotterdam. Ward returned to live in Ipswich about 1638 and is buried there. He published many of his sermons and other treatises separately; the collected editions were printed in 1627/8 and 1636.

WARNER, William (c. 1558–1609), poet: born in London and probably educated at Magdalen Hall, Oxford, becoming a lawyer. He produced a collection of seven prose tales, *Pan, his Syrinx*, in 1585, but his best-known work was *Albion's England* (1586) which indefatigably chronicled in fourteen-syllable verse the legendary history of England from Noah's Flood to the Norman Conquest. A second edition in 1606 bridged five and a half centuries to carry the story down to the reign of James I. Meres (q.v.) in 1598 associated Warner with Spenser as the two leading English heroic poets; Drayton, more judiciously, praised parts of his epic. Warner also published a translation of Plautus's *Menaechmi* (1595), which has been thought an influence on Shakespeare's *Comedy of Errors*. If so,

Shakespeare must have had access to it in manuscript.

E. K. C., E.S., W.S.

WARWICK, Ambrose Dudley, Earl of (c. 1528–1590): son of John Dudley, Duke of Northumberland and Lord Protector, and older brother of Leicester (q.v.). He shared the imprisonment of his family after their defeat by Queen Mary and was condemned to death, but had been

Ambrose Dudley, Earl of Warwick

pardoned and released by 1558. Under Elizabeth he had an active career. He was made Master of the Ordnance for life (1560) and created Baron Lisle and Earl of Warwick (1561). He distinguished himself as a soldier in Normandy, occupying Le Havre for the Protestants from October 1562 till June 1563 and being invested with the Garter there. In the final battle in the town Warwick received the wound in his thigh that eventually killed him. On his return to England he was made Lord President of the North, and in 1565 his third marriage was celebrated with great ceremony in the Chapel Royal in the Queen's presence. The new Countess of Warwick (*infra*), became a favourite with the Queen. Warwick had one more military campaign as Lieutenant-General in the northern rebellion (1569), and many civil positions. He was Lord Lieutenant of Warwickshire (1569–70, and from 1587), Chief Butler of England from 1571, and Privy Councillor from 1573. He was also commissioner at the trials of the Duke of Norfolk (1572) and Mary, Queen of Scots (1586). Warwick maintained an early theatrical company (1559–64) and a more famous one from 1575, which was led by Laurence Dutton (q.v.), played at Court, and was taken over in 1580 by the Earl of Oxford (q.v.). Warwick died of gangrene and the amputation of his leg seventeen years after his wound, and was buried with great state in St Mary's Church, Warwick. Queen Elizabeth praised him as brave, liberal and magnanimous, when she thought of him as a possible husband for her cousin, the Queen of Scots, in 1563; but she wished he had the "grace and good looks of Lord Robert" (Leicester).

WARWICK, Anne Dudley, Countess of (?–1603, née Russell), lady-in-waiting to Queen Elizabeth: daughter of Francis, Earl of Bedford, sister of the Countess of Cumberland and aunt of Lady Anne Clifford (qq.v.). In 1565 she became the third wife of the Earl of Warwick (*supra*) the marriage being arranged by Warwick's brother, Leicester, and celebrated with great festivity at Court. Lady Warwick continued to serve the Queen after being widowed in 1590, and she was present at Elizabeth's death. Quite often she took her young niece, Anne Clifford, to stay at Court with her; the last days of Elizabeth's life are thus recorded in Anne Clifford's diary. It was rumoured that Lady Warwick had been secretly married to Sir Fulke

Greville senior (q.v.) two years or more before the Queen died.

WATSON, Thomas (?1557–92), poet: educated at Oxford, but took no degree, and became a lawyer, but never practised. With Greene, Lyly, Marlowe, and Peele (qq.v.) he was one of the "university wits" literary set in London. He seems to have spent some time in Italy in the 1570s studying law. By 1581 he was in Paris where he met Sir Francis Walsingham, who became his patron, as also did Thomas Walsingham. Watson wrote both English and Latin verse and translated from Italian and Greek into either language; in 1590 he published a collection of Italian madrigals in English, together with their music. His most famous work, *Hekatompathia* (1582), is a collection of one hundred English sonnets. His plays were praised for their wit, but none survive; he also wrote a prose work on memory. On 28 September 1589 Watson was involved in a fight between Marlowe and an innkeeper's son, William Bradley, in Shoreditch. Watson killed Bradley; he and Marlowe were sent to Newgate, but both were pardoned. After the death of Francis Walsingham in 1590 (for which Watson wrote a Latin elegy), he soon left the service of that family, spending the last two years of his life as tutor to William Cornwallis (q.v.).

A. L. Rowse, *Christopher Marlowe* (1964)

WATTS, Richard (fl. 1614–33), Anglican clergyman: Curate of Stratford from 1614 to 1617. It is probable he conducted the marriage service of Judith Shakespeare and Thomas Quiney (q.v.) in February 1616, as he signed the marriage register. By 1633 Watts had married Quiney's sister, Mary, and was Vicar of Harbury. In that year he was one of three trustees who took over the lease of "The Cage" wine shop in Stratford from his brother-in-law.

WAYTE, William (1555–1603), "gentleman": the son of Edmund Wayte, of London. William's mother (born Frances Luce) married William Gardiner (q.v.) on her first husband's death, and it is as Gardiner's stepson that William Wayte is remembered. On Frances's death in 1576 Gardiner defrauded her son of his inheritance, but four years later William Wayte, on his stepfather's advice, married Joan Taylor, an heiress who was under age. Gardiner swindled Joan out of her property, and soon afterwards she died. In a suit brought to recover the property in 1591 Wayte is described (possibly with a pun on his maternal ancestry) as "a loose person of no reckoning or value, being wholly under the rule and commandment of . . . Gardiner." Naturally, he was embroiled in his stepfather's quarrel with Francis Langley (q.v.), and possibly with Shakespeare (1596); and Dr Leslie Hotson has suggested that Wayte is the original of Slender in *The Merry Wives of Windsor*. Despite Wayte's subservience, Gardiner cut him out of his will entirely. Both Wayte and his second wife died in the plague of 1603.

L. Hotson, *Shakespeare versus Shallow* (1931)

WEBBE, Alexander (?–1573), uncle to Shakespeare by marriage: before 1550 he was married to Margaret Arden, sister of Mary Shakespeare. He was also the brother of the Ardens' stepmother, Agnes, from whom in 1560 he leased two houses in Snitterfield (one of which was occupied by Shakespeare's grandfather Richard Shakespeare) and a cottage with some land. By 1569 the Webbes lived in the Shakespeare house themselves, John Shakespeare transferring the copyhold to Alexander Webbe after his father's death. Alexander's son, Robert (*infra*), continued the process of building up property in Snitterfield.

WEBBE, Robert (?–1597), Shakespeare's cousin: son of Alexander Webbe (*supra*) and therefore a nephew of Mary Shakespeare. In 1576 he purchased the lease of the Snitterfield property, obtained from his father, mother and stepfather, as well as their other rights to the estate of Agnes Arden, when she should die. John and Mary Shakespeare sold him their Snitterfield portion for £4 in 1579 and he acquired other shares of Robert Arden's land over the next three years, so as to make himself a farmer of some substance.

E. K. C., *W.S.*
M. E.

WEBBE, Thomas (fl. 1578), Warwickshire farmer: probably one of the family connected by marriage with Shakespeare's mother, Mary. With Humphrey Hooper and George Gibbs, Mary Shakespeare conveyed to Webbe eighty-six acres in Wilmcote in 1578. It was to revert to the Shakespeares for their heirs in 1601. There is no evidence the land was ever restored.

E. K. C., *W.S.*
M. E.

WEBSTER, John (1571/7–1634/8), dramatist: son of John Webster, a member of the Merchant Taylors' Company, but a coach maker by trade. The family probably lived in Cow Lane, Smithfield. Webster senior did business with Alleyn (q.v.) and supplied coaches for City pageants. The dramatist became a freeman of the Merchant Taylors' Company on his father's death (1615). He began writing plays for Henlowe in 1602, though he could have been an actor before then, if he is identical with the John Webster who toured Germany with Robert Browne (q.v.) in 1596. Until about 1624 he wrote infrequently, mainly in collaboration with

263

Dekker. His fame rests, however, on two plays of his own writing: *The White Devil* a tragedy published in 1612 after it had been acted with little success by Queen Anne's Men; and *The Duchess of Malfi* (1613–14), which was presented by the King's Men both at Blackfriars and the Globe, with Richard Burbage as the original Fedinand. Both plays are filled with the hopeless corruption of Court life, as too is Webster's elegy for Prince Henry, *A Monumental Column* (1613). Webster also contributed the sketch in prose, "An Excellent Actor" to Overbury's *Characters*, which was published in 1615. Some have seen in it a portrait of Burbage.

M. C. Bradbrook, *John Webster* (1980)

WEELKES, Thomas (?1575–1623), composer: organist at Winchester College from 1589 and restored the use of the organ in the chapel. Weelkes wrote much church music but was also a very original madrigalist, using different voices to tell different parts of a story in an almost operatic way. He wrote most of his madrigals in his early years of work, the first set appearing in 1597. Next year he published *Ballets for Five Voices*, in imitation of Thomas Morley (q.v.), but an advance on Morley's work. Weelkes produced two more volumes in 1600, and one final song-book *Airs or Fantastic Spirits for 3 Voices* in 1608. Some of his best-known madrigals are *O Care thou wilt despatch me*, *Three Virgin Nymphs*, and *Thule, the period of cosmography*. He took his B. Mus. at New College, Oxford, in 1602, and then became organist of Chichester Cathedral. Here his wife Eliza died, leaving a son and two daughters. Weelkes devoted himself mainly to church music at Chichester, introducing antiphonal effects and independent organ accompaniments.

D. Brown, *Thomas Weelkes* (1969)

WEEVER, John (1576–1632), poet, antiquary: member of a Lancashire family and educated at Queen's College, Cambridge, from about 1594 to 1598. While at the University he began writing epigrams, publishing *Epigrams in the Oldest Cut and Newest Fashion* (c. 1599). The book contains more allusions to contemporary authors than any other work, except Meres' (q.v.). One epigram is addressed to Shakespeare; Weever knew him as dramatist as well as poet, and called him "honey-tongued". In 1601 Weever published a life of Sir John Oldcastle, *The Mirror of Martyrs*, probably in response to Shakespeare's picture of Falstaff in *Henry IV*. In the same year he produced *Faunus and Meliflora*, an erotic and satirical poem which may have been written earlier. By contrast, in 1606, came his *An Agnus Dei*, a history of Christ in "thumb-book size" (one-and-half inches). He travelled to Liège, Paris, Parma and Rome, settling in Clerkenwell, London, on his return, and studying antiquities. For this task he journeyed throughout England, looking for ancient monuments, and made use of Cotton's library. The result was a book of some 900 pages, *Ancient Funeral Monuments* (1631), a valuable source, as many of the monuments described by Weever have disappeared or lost their inscriptions.

J. Weever, *Epigrammes*, ed., R. B. McKerrow (1911)

WENTWORTH, Peter (c. 1524–96), Parliamentarian: probably born at Calais where his father, Sir Nicholas Wentworth of Lillingstone in Buckinghamshire, held an important post. He entered Lincoln's Inn in 1542 and in 1571 was elected M.P. for Barnstaple. His parliamentary career spanned twenty-two years and he was a member of six Parliaments, sitting for Tregony, 1572–81 and for Northampton, 1586–93. With his brother Paul (1533–

93), who was Member for Buckingham in 1571 and for Liskeard (1572–81), he was a critic of government, a stout defender of parliamentary privilege, and an advocate of vigorous measures against Spain and the Catholics and for Puritanism and the English settlement. Peter Wentworth did not hesitate to criticise the Queen for failing to settle the succession, and for limiting freedom of speech in the Commons. He was sent to the Tower briefly in 1576, for a longer period in 1587, and finally in 1593. Although well-treated in his imprisonment and allowed to write "loyal discourses" on the need to determine who was heir to the throne, he remained in the Tower for the rest of his life. By marriage he was well-connected. His first wife was first cousin once-removed to Queen Catherine Parr and his second wife was Elizabeth Walsingham, sister of the Secretary of State, Sir Francis.

J. E. Neale, *Elizabeth I and her Parliaments, 1558–1581* (1953); *1584–1601* (1957)

WENTWORTH, Thomas (1593–1641), created Earl of Strafford January 1640), statesman: born in Chancery Lane, London, into a family with considerable land in Yorkshire (Wentworth Woodhouse). He was educated at St John's College, Cambridge (1607–11) and first sat as M.P. for Yorkshire in the "Addled Parliament" of 1614, inheriting his father's baronetcy at the end of the year. He held offices in Yorkshire as well as representing the county again in two more Parliaments of James I's reign before becoming principal leader of the Parliamentary opposition to Buckingham (q.v.) in 1628. He was created Viscount Wentworth after Buckingham's murder and, from the Lords, served Charles I from 1629 until 1640 successively as Lord President of the North, Lord Deputy of Ireland, Lord Deputy in England and

Lieutenant-General of the Army. His high-handed methods of firm, conciliar government ensured good administration but made him extremely unpopular with his fellow gentry in Ireland and in England. He was regarded as author of the policy of "Thorough", associated also with his friend, Archbishop Laud (q.v.). His offer to bring an army from Ireland to subdue rebellion in Scotland and maintain order in England — an offer corroborated only from hearsay by Sir Henry Vane (q.v.) — led to his impeachment by the Long Parliament under the leadership of Pym (q.v.), his condemnation by Act of Attainder (April 1641) and his execution on Tower Hill, 12 May 1641.

C. V. Wedgwood, *Strafford* (1938)

WESTCOTT, Sebastian (?–1582), choir master: Master of St Paul's Choir School from 1557 until his death. He had started producing boys in plays before Princess Elizabeth at Hatfield as early as 1552. It is probable that they were Paul's Boys. As Master he expanded the theatrical activities of the school considerably. Westcott was in trouble as a Roman Catholic and was imprisoned in the Marshalsea, 1577–8, but he kept his position through his influence with the Queen. Under Westcott the boys performed twenty-seven times at Court, as well as at St Paul's.

E. K. C., *E.S.*

WHATCOTT, Robert (fl. 1587–1616), Stratford resident: may have been a domestic servant in the Shakespeare or Hall household. In 1613 he appeared as a witness for Susanna Hall (q.v.) at the Consistory Court in Worcester during her slander case against Lane. He was also a witness to Shakespeare's will.

"WHATELEY, Anne" (probably nonexistent). On 27 November 1582, the Bishop of Worcester's register shows the granting of a marriage licence to "Willelmum Shaxpere et Annam Whateley de Temple Grafton". On the following day the register records the lodging of a bond as surety against a licence for Shakespeare to marry "Anne Hathway of Stratford" (v. *Anne Shakespeare*). The first entry is probably a clerical error — there are others made by the same clerk. Yet the mention of Temple Grafton, five miles from Stratford and over three miles from the Hathaway home at Shottery, is puzzling, unless Anne Hathaway was living there at the time or the marriage took place at Grafton Church, which is not improbable. "Anne Whateley" has become the central character of much romantic fiction, based only on this single entry in the register.

E. K. C., *W.S.*
S. S.
S. Schoenbaum, *Shakespeare's Lives* (1970)

WHEELER, Margaret (?–1616), resident of Stratford: the mistress of Thomas Quiney (q.v.) who became Shakespeare's son-in-law when he married his daughter, Judith. A month after this marriage, the parish register records on 15 March 1616 the burial of Margaret Wheeler and an infant, she having died in childbirth.

WHITE, Edward (–?1613), bookseller: son of John White, mercer, of Suffolk. He was apprenticed to John Lobley, stationer, for seven years from 1565, was a freeman of the Stationers' Company by 1576, and admitted to the Livery of the Company in 1588. White's shop was the "Gun" near the north door of St Paul's (1577–1612). He published ballads chiefly and was fined 10s in 1600 for selling a ballad called *The Wife of Bath*. White was associated with Thomas Millington in selling Shakespeare's *Titus Andronicus* in 1594 and brought out other editions of the play in 1600 and 1611. He was Junior (1600) and Senior (1605) Warden of the Stationers' Company.

WHITE, John (fl. 1575–95), colonialist and water-colour artist: sailed to Roanoke Island, off the north-east coast of North Carolina, with Ralegh's colonising expedition of 1584. He remained at Roanoke for over a year, making use of his artistic talents as a cartographer and a water-colourist. White returned to England in 1586, with some sixty water-colours of the native Indians and the flora and fauna of Virginia. Twenty-three of these water-colours were published as engravings in 1590, providing the general public with its first visual representation of the New World. White returned briefly to Roanoke in 1587 but was sent back to England with a request for supplies. War with Spain prevented his making a third voyage to the colony until 1590, and by then there was no trace of settlers or settlement. By 1593 White had settled in Ireland, near Cork.

D. B. Quinn and P. H. Hulton, "John White and English Naturalists", *History Today*, XIII (1963)

WHITE, William (fl. 1583–1615), printer: apprenticed to Richard Jugge and presented for the freedom of the Stationers' Company by his master's widow in 1583. White's shops were at the "White Horse", Fleet Lane (1588–96) and Cow Lane near Holborn Conduit (from 1597). In his first business White had a partner, Gabriel Simpson, but set up on his own in 1597. He printed Shakespeare's *Love's Labour's Lost* for Cuthbert Burby (1598), *Henry VI*, part 3, for Thomas Millington (1600), *Richard II* (1608) and *Henry IV*, part 1 (1613) for Matthew Law, and *Pericles* for Henry Gosson (1609).

WHITGIFT, John (c. 1530–1604), archbishop: born at Grimsby, educated at Queen's College and Pembroke Hall, Cambridge, and remained a prominent figure in the University until 1577, serving as a Fellow of Peterhouse, Professor of Divinity, Master of Pembroke Hall (1567–70) and Master of Trinity (1570–7). His hostility to the Puritanism of Cartwright (q.v.) attracted the attention of Queen Elizabeth. In 1577 he was con-

John Whitgift, Archbishop of Canterbury

secrated Bishop of Worcester (the diocese which included Stratford-upon-Avon) and in 1583 was translated to Canterbury in succession to the moderate Calvinist, Edmund Grindal, whose views had become antipathetic to the Queen. Whitgift sought to repress Puritanism (especially after the publication of the "Marprelate" Tracts of 1588–9) by summoning suspects before the Ecclesiastical Commission for interrogation under oath. His theology showed Calvinistic inclinations, but he stood firmly by the principle of episcopacy. When Court intrigues and the half-hearted backing of Burghley weakened his position, he found a strong ally in Queen Elizabeth, and he attended her in her last moments as well as officiating at the coronation of James I. He was a reforming administrator of the Church and an efficient primate. Whitgift founded and endowed almshouses and schools at Croydon.

P. M. Dawley, *John Whitgift and the Reformation* (1955)

WHITTINGTON, Thomas (?–1601), Warwickshire shepherd: known to have been shepherd to the Hathaways, and was left £4-6s-8d in the will of Richard Hathaway (1581) as money owed to Whittington. He stayed in service with Richard's widow and sons and in his own will thirty years later left 40s to the poor people of Stratford. This 40s was in the possession of Anne Shakespeare (q.v.), and was to be paid to the poor by her husband, William. There is no other extant reference to Anne Shakespeare between her marriage and her husband's death. The 40s may have been the shepherd's savings. Whittington has been regarded as a model for Adam in *As You Like It*, the faithful old servant who lent money to his mistress.

E. K. C., *W.S.*
M. E.
S. S.

WILBY (or WILBYE), John (1574–1638), musician and composer: born at Diss, Norfolk, the son of a teacher, became a lutenist and resident musician in the family of Sir Thomas Kytson (q.v.) of Hengrave Hall, Bury St Edmunds. He is best remembered as the composer of sixty-four madrigals (including the well-known "Sweet honey-sucking bees" and "Draw on, sweet night"). These were published in two sets: the first volume was dedicated in 1598 to Sir Charles Cavendish, a son of Bess of Hardwick and a considerable patron of music; and the second set, published in 1609, was dedicated to Arbella Stuart (q.v.). Wilby spent his later years in the household of Lady Rivers at Colchester. Although he published nothing in the last twenty-five years of his life, Wilby was the most accomplished of English madrigalists.

E. H. Fellowes, *The English Madrigal Composers* (1948)
J. Kerman, *The Elizabethan Madrigal* (1962)
A. L. Rowse, *The Elizabethan Renaissance, the Cultural Achievement* (1972)

WILKINS, George (fl. 1604–8), dramatist, novelist, pamphleteer: nothing is known of his life or of his career outside the early years of James I's reign. He wrote plays both for the King's and Queen Anne's Men, collaborating with Dekker and Heywood on works now lost. Wilkins also wrote part of *The Travels of Three English Brothers* (1607) with Day and William Rowley. His tragedy *The Miseries of Enforced Marriage* was published in the same year, apparently while the King's Men were still performing it. The play was based on the case of Walter Calverley, who in 1605 had murdered his wife and children at Wakefield in Yorkshire; the murder aroused wide interest, and many contemporary pamphlets were written about Calverley's crime. In 1608 Wilkins published a novel *The Painful Adventures of Pericles, Prince of Tyre*. It is probable Wilkins used among his sources an earlier version of the play *Pericles*, written partly by himself, as well as Twyne's *Pattern of Painful Adventures*, a novel printed in 1576. The story on which both works are based was an old medieval favourite. References in the prefatory epistle to Wilkins' novel show that "Shakespeare's *Pericles*" had already been played by the King's Men. The first two acts of this play may be by Wilkins rather than by Shakespeare, and some have assigned him a share in *Timon of Athens* as well.

G. Wilkins, *Pericles*, ed., K. A. Muir (1953)

WILLIAMS, Roger (?1540–95), soldier: son of Thomas Williams of Monmouthshire, and may be the Roger Williams who entered Brasenose College, Oxford, in 1552. He is said to have been a mercenary under the Duke of Alva and risen to the rank of Colonel in the Spanish forces. From 1572 onwards, however, he fought for the Dutch rebels against Spain. He was Lieutenant to Sir John Norris in 1577 and eight years later was still serving in the Netherlands under Leicester, who knighted him. Sir Roger Williams returned to England to be a Master of Horse at Tilbury in Armada year (1588). Subsequently he served in France, fighting for Henri IV; he led the attack on the Catholic League at Dieppe under the Earl of Essex, to whom he became much attached. He was left in command of the English contingent in Normandy and spent the last years of his life either campaigning for Henri or acting as his unofficial envoy to Queen Elizabeth. Sir Roger died ("of a surfeit") at his house in London, leaving all his fortune to Essex, who spent much of it in giving his friend a soldier's burial at St Paul's Cathedral. Williams was author of two interconnected books, *The Actions of the Low Countries* (published posthumously in 1618) and *A Brief Discourse of War* (1590). He analysed the opposing forces in the Netherlands and discussed the character of Spanish policy, as well as showing interest in fortification and supporting the new firearms against the old long-bow. Sir Roger was with William the Silent, Prince of Orange, at Delft in July 1584 when he was assassinated. It is possible that Sir Roger served

Shakespeare as a model for Fluellen in *Henry V*.

L. V. D. Owen, "Sir Roger Williams", *Army Quarterly*, XXXIV (1937)

WILLIS, John (?–1628), clergyman and inventor of shorthand: educated at Christ's College, Cambridge, from 1592 to 1596, and subsequently Rector of a city church, St Mary Bothaw on Dowgate Hill near London Bridge (1601–6), finally becoming Rector of Little Bentley in Essex. While he was in London Willis published *The Art of Stenography* (1602), expounding a more practical shorthand method than either of his predecessors, Peter Bales and Timothy Bright (qq.v.). Unlike Bright, whom he criticised, Willis wrote his symbols from left to right in the ordinary Western way and based them on phonetics, not on spelling. His book went into fourteen editions and he followed it up with *The Schoolmaster to the Art of Stenography* (1622). Willis also invented a system of Mnemonics, which he described in Latin in *Mnemonica* (1618).

W. J. Carlton, *Timothe Bright* (1911)

WILLOUGHBY, Henry (c. 1575–?1599), ?poet: of West Knoyle, Wiltshire, entered St John's College, Oxford (1591) but took his degree at Exeter College (1595). He was a connection by marriage of Thomas Russell (q.v.), Shakespeare's friend. In 1594 *Willobie His Avisa*, apparently a narrative poem about the attempts of various suitors to win the chaste Avisa, was published and Willoughby has been generally accepted as the author. The poem went into six editions eventually. There is a reference to Shakespeare as author of *Lucrece* among the commendatory verses and the prefatory epistle describes how "H. W.", presumably Willoughby, talks to his "familiar friend W. S." about his passion; the "new actor" H. W. is compared with the "old player" W. S. Many writers have identified W. S. as Shakespeare; some have decided that the whole poem refers to the events of Shakespeare's Sonnets, that H. W. is "Mr W. H." (possibly Southampton, rather than Willoughby) and that Avisa is the "Dark Lady". G. B. Harrison, however, believed the poem to be an attack on Southampton by the followers of Ralegh. There was obviously some offensive matter concealed in the work, as it was banned and burned in 1599.

S. S.
G. B. Harrison, ed., *Willobie His Avisa* (1926)
L. Hotson, *I, William Shakespeare* (1937)

WILLOUGHBY, Lord (1555–1601, born Peregrine Bertie, known as Baron Willoughby de Eresby from 1580), soldier: born in exile near Cleves, the son of Richard Bertie and Catherine, Baroness Willoughby de Eresby in her own right. He returned to London as a boy of four and spent much of his childhood in the Cecil household (v. *Burghley*), succeeding to his mother's title at the age of twenty-five. In 1582 and 1585 Burghley employed him as a diplomatic envoy in Denmark. Subsequently Willoughby fought in Flanders and was present at the Battle of Zutphen, in the company of his friend, Philip Sidney (q.v.). Willoughby continued to serve in the Netherlands from 1586 to the spring of 1589, taking command of the English expeditionary force after the recall of Leicester (q.v.) and winning popular fame for his defence of Bergen-op-Zoom, an episode commemorated in several contemporary ballads. In the winter of 1589–90 he commanded a force which assisted Henri of Navarre, principally in Normandy. He then spent several years travelling in Europe, mainly in Italy. From 1596 until his death he was Governor of

Berwick, a post that made him an important source of information for Robert Cecil about events at the Scottish Court.

G. Bertie, *Five generations of a loyal house* (1845)

WILSON, Arthur (1595–1652), historian, dramatist: born in Great Yarmouth, Norfolk, son of John Wilson, gentleman. His father destined him for Cambridge, but Wilson longed to travel and in 1609 went to France for two years. On his return, he found his family impoverished and became a clerk in the Exchequer, after learning to write fairly from the best writing-master of the time, John Davies (q.v.). In 1613 he was dismissed for writing satirical verse about his superior's wife. He was very poor, but in 1614 was introduced to the service of the third Earl of Essex (q.v.). Wilson remained an inconspicuous member of the household until the autumn, when he risked his life to save a laundry maid from drowning and so brought himself to Essex's attention. He rapidly became a favourite, and went with Essex to fight for the Elector Palatine (1620–5) and on the abortive Cadiz expedition of 1625. He became a great dueller, but he also began to read history and philosophy. When in 1631 Essex married again, Wilson quarrelled with the new Countess and was dismissed with a pension. He belatedly entered University (Trinity College, Oxford) where he started (and stopped) the study of mathematics, theology and science. At the same time he began to write comedies, performed at the Blackfriars theatre between 1631 and 1633, the most famous being *The Inconstant Lady*. Wilson also embarked on his *History of Great Britain in the reign of James I*, (published 1653). He finally became a Puritan and served Robert Rich, Earl of Warwick, from 1632 onwards. During the Civil War, he protected the Earl's property in Essex and wrote his autobiography.

Wilson is buried at Felsted, Essex.

Arthur Wilson, *The Swisser*, ed., A. Feuillerat (1904)
V. F. Snow, *Essex the Rebel* (1970)

WILSON, Jack (?1585–?1641), actor: believed to have been the son of Nicholas Wilson, "minstrel", and was baptised at St Bartholomew the Less, Smithfield, in April 1585. He is known to have played the role of Balthasar in *Much Ado About Nothing* at some time before 1623 since his name is given in stage directions for the play in the First Folio. It is probable that he was a City "Wait" in 1622, a singer employed on special ceremonial occasions, and it is possible that he was never a full member of any acting company. He has sometimes been identified with the royal lutenist and Professor of Music at Oxford, also John Wilson (*infra*).

E. K. C., *E.S.*
G. E. B.

WILSON, John (1595–1674), royal musician: was already writing music for

John Wilson

the Gray's Inn masque for the Earl of Somerset's wedding in 1613. Wilson, who was a lutenist, violist, singer and composer, wrote other stage music, including settings of two of Shakespeare's songs: "Take, O take those lips away" (*Measure for Measure*) and "Lawn as white as driven snow" (*Winter's Tale*). He may be identical with "Jack Wilson" (*supra*). Otherwise nothing more is known of his career until he became a King's musician (1635), followed Charles I to Oxford in the Civil War, and was made Professor of Music there in 1656. After the Restoration he became a Gentleman of the Chapel Royal and chorister at Westminster Abbey, where he was married in 1671 and is buried. Wilson was known as a great practical joker among his friends at Oxford. His portrait is in the Examination Schools at Oxford.

WILSON, Robert (?–1600), actor and dramatist: a member of Leicester's company in 1572, 1574 and 1581, acting and writing plays. He joined the Queen's Men in 1583 but he does not appear in the acting lists after 1587. Presumably he devoted his time to writing plays, later for the Admiral's company. Stowe (q.v.) says his outstanding characteristic as an actor was his "quick, delicate, refined, extemporal wit" (Stowe, *Annales*, ed. Howes, 1615). His surviving plays are: *Three Ladies of London*, 1581, *Three Lords and Three Ladies of London*, 1589, and *Cobbler's Prophecy*,1594.Wilson also collaborated with Chettle, Dekker, Drayton and Munday.

WINTER, Thomas (1572–1606), conspirator: born at Huddington, Worcestershire, into a family of Welsh descent. He was a kinsman of Robert Catesby (q.v.), with whom he was on close terms of friendship. Winter was a devout Roman Catholic who served for a time in the army in the Low Countries but gave up soldiering because of religious scruples. He visited Rome in 1600, spent some months in Madrid and appears there to have suggested a royal assassination bid in England which would be followed by the landing of a Spanish force at Milford Haven. This ill-considered project developed into the Gunpowder Plot of 1605, in which Winter interested Catesby and Fawkes (q.v.). After Fawkes's arrest, Winter was captured at Holbeach House Staffordshire, tried for treason and executed 31 January 1606.

WINWOOD, Ralph (1563–1617), diplomat: born at Aynho in Northamptonshire. He matriculated at St John's College, Oxford in 1577, transferring to Magdalen College with a Demyship in 1578, graduating four years later and holding a Magdalen Fellowship until 1601, although he left Oxford in 1593 or 1594 and travelled on the Continent. He served as secretary to the ambassador in France, Sir Henry Neville, in 1599 and from 1601 to 1613 held a succession of diplomatic posts, mainly in the Netherlands. He was knighted by James I in 1607, and returned as M.P. for Buckingham in 1614, becoming Secretary of State on 29 March, a week before Parliament met. He was originally a supporter of Somerset (Carr, q.v.) and was present at his marriage, but he was the first of the King's councillors to be suspicious over the circumstances of the death of Overbury (q.v.), beginning the process which led to the indictment of the Earl and Countess of Somerset for Overbury's murder. Winwood sympathised with Ralegh (q.v.), helping to secure his release from the Tower in March 1616, not least because Winwood was consistently anti-Spanish. His health gave way in the autumn of 1617 and, despite the ministrations of the much respected Mayerne (q.v.), he died in December.

WISE (or WYTHES), Andrew (fl. 1580–1623), bookseller: son of Henry Wythes, yeoman, of Yorkshire. He was apprenticed to Henry Smith, stationer, for eight years from March 1580, but in 1581 transferred to Thomas Bradshaw. Wise became a freeman of the Stationers' Company in 1589 and seems to have taken over the business of John Perrin. He set up shop at the "Angel" in St Paul's Church-yard. Wise published several plays of Shakespeare: *Richard II* (1597–8), *Richard III* (1597, 1598, 1602), *Henry IV*, part 1 (1598, 1599), *Henry IV*, part 2 and *Much Ado About Nothing* (1600, both with William Aspley). In 1603 he assigned some copyrights to Matthew Law, and is not mentioned again.

WITHER, George (1588–1667), poet and soldier: was born at Bentworth, Hampshire, and educated at Magdalen College, Oxford from about 1604, sub-sequently entering Lincoln's Inn. Court extravagance, corrupt administration, the purchase of public offices by bribery, and the sale of monopolies so offended Wither's sense of social justice that he satirised them in *Abuses Stript and Whipped* (published 1613); and he was duly imprisoned in the Marshalsea. Here he wrote pastoral poetry, using its harmless conventions to make social and political criticisms which would elude a censor's eye, a practice Wither shared with his friend, William Browne (q.v.). He received some patronage and protection from his fellow Hampshire man, the Earl of Southampton (q.v.) and from the third Earl of Pembroke (q.v.). Wither's most famous song, "Shall I, wasting in despair" appeared in his poetical epistle *Fidelia* (1617, reprinted in 1619). When in 1621 Wither published *Motto, Nec Habeo, Nec Careo, Nec Curo* (I have nothing, lack nothing, care nothing) he was again sent to prison as being "too busy and satirical". His last purely secular poems were printed in 1622. Thereafter he became a Puritan although never a rigid Calvinist. He was deeply shocked by the plague of 1625 which he commemorated in his soul-searching and prophetic work, *Brittans Remembrancer*, printed by himself in 1628 because no publisher would risk the wrath of the censor on his behalf. During the Civil War he became a captain of horse in the Parliamentary army and was commander of Farnham Castle in 1642. After the Restoration he spent three years in Newgate Prison and the Tower. His poetic skills receded under the pressure of events: "God opened my mouth and compelled me, beyond my natural abilities, to speak", he affirmed in 1641. In all, between 1612 and 1666, Wither published more than seventy works. He is buried in the Chapel of the Savoy.

C. Hill, "George Wither and John Milton" in *English Renaissance Studies presented to Dame Helen Gardner* (1980)

WOODALL, John (1569–1643) phy-sician and surgeon: born in Warwick. He was, for a time, a military surgeon under Willoughby (q.v.) in the Netherlands. He lived for many years in Germany and Holland, but by 1603 he had returned to London and was practising in Wood Street, making use of a secret "Aurum Vitae" to fight the Plague. James I employed him on a special diplomatic mission to Poland because of his know-ledge of central European affairs but his greatest service was to medicine. He became Surgeon-General to the East India Company in 1614 and he published the earliest practical manual of surgery and hygiene at sea, *The Surgeon's Mate* (1617), first recommending fruit-juice as an anti-dote to scurvy. For the last twenty-seven years of his life he was principal surgeon at St Bartholomew's Hospital, London.

WORCESTER, Edward Somerset, fourth Earl of Worcester (c. 1550–1628), courtier: son of William Somerset, third Earl. In 1571 he married Elizabeth Hastings, daughter of the second Earl of Huntingdon and thus descended from

Edward Somerset, fourth Earl of Worcester

Edward III. The Somerset family were also illegitimate descendants of the same King. Worcester succeeded his father in 1589. In 1590 he was a member of the Council for the Welsh Marches and ambassador to Scotland to congratulate James VI on his marriage and offer him the Garter. He became a Knight of the Garter himself in 1593. Worcester was deputy Master of the Horse to Essex (q.v.) in 1598, was one of the hostages held in Essex House by the Earl's faction in 1601, and sat on the commission which tried Essex. He succeeded to the post of Master of the Horse, an appointment confirmed for life by James I (1603). Worcester was Earl Marshal for James's coronation, the christening of Princess Mary (1605), and the investiture of Henry as Prince of Wales (1610), and Lord Great Chamberlain for the Coronation of Charles I (1626). He was also Commissioner to expel Jesuits (1603), although a Roman Catholic himself, Commissioner of the Treasury (1612–14) and on several other commissions. From 1607 to 1620 Worcester held the valuable sole licence for the making of gunpowder and saltpetre. He was Lord Lieutenant of Glamorgan and Monmouth from 1602, and Lord Keeper of the Privy Seal from 1616. From 1589 he maintained an acting company, but they did not become famous until 1602, when they appeared at Court. Worcester's Men combined with the company of the Earl of Oxford (q.v.) and both were taken over by James I's consort as Queen Anne's Men from 1604. They included Will Kempe and the dramatist Heywood (qq.v.) and appeared under the management of Henslowe (q.v.) for a time. Worcester was buried at Raglan Castle, Monmouthshire, his principal seat. In his youth, it was said, he was "a very fine gentleman and the best horseman and tilter of the times."

WOTTON, Henry (1568–1639), diplomat and poet: born of an old Kentish family and educated at Winchester and Oxford (matriculated New College, 1584; B.A., Queen's, 1588). He was persuaded to write a tragedy which was performed at Queen's. After Oxford he spent seven years travelling in Austria, Bavaria, Switzerland and Italy, and then entered the Middle Temple. He was a friend of Essex and for a time an agent of his. After Essex's fall Wotton went back to Italy and served Grand-Duke Ferdinand I of Tuscany, who sent him on a secret mission to James VI in Scotland. On James's accession to the English throne, Wotton returned home and was knighted. In 1604 he became ambassador to the Venetian Republic and later to the German Princes and Empire. While in Augsburg Wotton wrote his famous definition of an ambassador, "vir

273

bonus peregre missus ad mentiendum Reipublicae causa", rendered in English by Izaak Walton in his biography of Wotton as "an honest man sent abroad to lie for the good of his country". Wotton returned to England a poor man in 1624, but was appointed Provost of Eton, a post he held until his death. His *The Elements of Architecture* was published in the year of his return from Germany. His poems are more famous, especially the "Character of a Happy Life" and "On his Mistress, the Queen of Bohemia" (a tribute to James I's daughter, Elizabeth), while "Upon the Sudden Restraint of the Earl of Somerset, then falling from favour, 1615" well shows his shrewd judgment of mankind's folly. *Reliquiae Wottonianae*, the collected edition of his works, including letters as well as poetry, was published in 1651, with Walton's *Life* as a preface.

L. P. Smith, *Life and Letters of Sir H. Wotton* (1907)

WRIGHT, Edward (?1558–1615), mathematician and expert on navigation: born in Garveston, Norfolk, and educated at Caius College, Cambridge, from 1580 to 1584. His interest in applying mathematics to navigation first appeared when he published a table of meridional parts. He was elected a Fellow of Caius in 1587, but two years later he was "called forth to the public business of the nation by the Queen" and left his academic life in order to accompany Lord Cumberland (George Clifford, q.v.) on a voyage to the Azores. Wright was thus able to see for himself ways in which the navigation of English ships could be improved. During the voyage he met the celebrated explorer and navigator, John Davis (q.v.). Wright drew on his experiences to prepare two works for publication in 1599: *Certain Errors in Navigation . . . detected and corrected*; and *The Haven Finding Art*. In his works Wright placed greater emphasis

upon making use of the stars for navigation than on the sun's meridian, although from 1594 to 1597 he made observations in London on the sun's altitude. Like William Barlow (q.v.), Wright was for a time a tutor in mathematics to Prince Henry and he made instruments for him. The Prince's early death left Wright in poverty until in 1614 he became lecturer on the art of navigation for the East India Company at £50 a year. Wright died while preparing an English edition of Napier's logarithms. This work was finished, and duly published, by his son and Henry Briggs (q.v.).

E. G. R. Taylor, *Mathematical Practitioners of Tudor and Stuart England* (1967)
D. W. Waters, *The Art of Navigation in Elizabethan and Early Stuart Times* (1958)

WROTH, Lady Mary (1586–?1640, née Sidney), daughter of Sir Robert and Barbara Sidney and niece of Sir Philip. In 1604 she married Sir Robert Wroth, who soon inherited Loughton Hall, Essex, and considerable property. Nevertheless he died in debt for £23,000 in 1613, a month after their son James was born. Lady Mary had often appeared at Court; she took part in Jonson's *Masque of Blackness* in 1605 and he was one of several poets who dedicated their work to her. After her husband's death she retired to Loughton; her son lived only until 1616. She never managed to disembarrass the estate of debt. In 1621 she published *Urania*, a work of prose with songs and verses, clearly an imitation of her uncle's *Arcadia*, but with more satirical intent. The Duke of Buckingham was offended by the satire, to judge by Lady Mary's letters.

Y

YARDLEY, George (c. 1575–1627), colonialist: born in London, his father being a Merchant Taylor. He served as an officer in the Low Countries, and was Captain of the Guard when the *Sea Venture* was wrecked off Bermunda while sailing to Virginia in 1609 (v. *Gates, Jourdain, Somers, Strachey*). He became a member of the Council in Virginia in 1611 and served as Acting Governor from April 1616 until May 1617. He then returned to England with detailed reports of the progress made in the colony. He was knighted by James I in November 1618, arriving back at Jamestown as Governor in April 1619 with instructions to introduce the common law system of England and to summon a representative assembly of planters once a year (v. *Pory*). The first assembly met, under Yardley's presidency, on 30 July 1619. Yardley held office until 1621 and, after a further visit to England, served as Charles I's "Royal Governor" in Virginia, 1626–7.

Z

ZOUCHE, Edward 1a (1556–1625),
eleventh Baron Zouche of Harringworth:
succeeded to the peerage as a child of
twelve and was therefore a "ward of State"
under Burghley. He lived abroad from
1587 to 1593, becoming a friend of
Wotton and of Lobel (qq.v.), the naturalist. He undertook diplomatic missions in
Cecil's interest to Edinburgh in 1593–4
and to Denmark, with Lobel, in 1598.
From 1602 to 1615 he was President of the
Council in Wales, and subsequently Lord
Warden of the Cinque Ports. He was a
patron of the Virginia Company from 1609
and assisted Ferdinando Gorges (q.v.) on
the Council for New England (1620–5).
Lord Zouche was a friend of Ben Jonson. A
physic garden at his home in Hackney was
planned and cultivated under Lobel's
direction, and was more famous than
Zouche himself.

Glossary

Alchemy: the search for a way of turning metals into gold.

Authorized Version: the new translation of the bible, ordered by King James I and printed in 1611.

Burgess: (a) a councillor of a borough, enjoying certain magisterial powers.

(b) a member of parliament for a borough.

Calvinist: a follower of the French-born Protestant, John Calvin (cf. *Huguenot*).

Candlemas: a religious festival celebrated on 2 February, frequently an occasion for the performance of plays or masques.

Civil War: was fought, in England, between the armies of Charles I and Parliament from 1642 to 1646 and ended in defeat for the royalists. Renewed conflict from 1648 to 1651 is sometimes called the Second Civil War.

Clink: an area on the south bank of the Thames under the jurisdiction of the Bishop of Winchester (whose London residence was there, in Southwark) rather than under the jurisdiction of the sheriffs of London or Middlesex. This "Liberty of the Clink" contained a notorious prison, known simply as "the Clink". It was on Bankside, close to the Globe theatre.

Company: (a) *Liveried Company*: a successor to the mediaeval gild or fraternity, controlling a particular trade or industry within the City of London. There were twelve great Liveried City Companies: Mercers; Grocers; Drapers; Fishmongers; Goldsmiths; Skinners; Merchant Taylors; Haberdashers; Salters; Ironmongers; Vintners; Clothworkers. The companies regulated conditions of work and apprenticeship, administered benefactions, provided almshouses and other charities, and encouraged corporate worship in specific City churches. The Lord Mayor of London was elected from among the senior members of a company (known as the "Livery" of the company). The Stationers' Company, controlling printing and publishing, dated only from 1557 and never acquired the prestige or standing of the twelve Liveried Companies.

(b) *Trading Companies*: played a considerable part in the general economic life of the period and especially in colonisation. "Regulated companies", such as the Merchant Adventurers, traded under gild rules and had much in common with the Liveried City Companies. "Joint-stock companies" (Russia Company, East India Company, Virginia Company, Massachusetts Bay Company) were private enterprises in which capital was subscribed by individual merchants who shared risk and profit according to the size of their investment. Some joint-stock companies (notably the Levant Company) enjoyed the protection and privileges of a regulated company.

(c) *Companies of actors*. Groups of players were organised into companies for the sake of protection and patronage. They took the name of a royal person, a court official, or a wealthy courtier responsible for their well-being and working life. They were thus known as "Queen's Men", "Admiral's Men", "Chamberlain's Men", "Leicester's Men", "Strange's Men", etc.

(d) *Boy companies*. Plays were often presented at Court by boy actors from the great choirs. They were known as "Children of the Chapel" (Chapels Royal), "Children of Paul's" (St Paul's Cathedral), etc.

Copyholder: a tenant who held land according to manorial custom through a copy of the original court-roll made by the steward of the lord of the manor. In many instances the rights of copyholders were so limited in law that a determined landowner, who might wish to enclose a number of copyholds for grazing, was rarely defeated if taken by his tenants to a common law court.

Enclosure: The principal change in agricultural methods in sixteenth and seventeenth century England was the replacement of the mediaeval system of cultivated strips of land farmed by peasants. The new pattern of farming led to the enclosure, by means of hedges and ditches, of many strips together so as to create meadows or pastures. This economic change benefited the wealthier landowners, who used much of the pasture-land for sheep farming. It led to unrest in many regions.

First Folio: the earliest collected edition of Shakespeare's plays, published in 1623 and containing, among its preliminary material, a list of the principal actors in the plays.

Fleet: a prison in London, particularly but not exclusively used for debtors.

Huguenot: the name given, from about 1560 onwards, to French Protestants who accepted the beliefs of John Calvin (1509–64). From 1562 to 1594 France was weakened by chronic civil war between the Catholic majority and the Huguenots, many of whom escaped from France to settle in England. Over 5,000 Huguenots were killed, mainly in Paris, during the "massacre of St Bartholomew's Day" (24 August 1572) which marked the end of a twelve months truce in these so-called Wars of Religion.

Impresa: an emblematic device carrying a motto.

Inns of Court: the buildings of four societies in London who alone had the right of calling their members to practise law at the English bar. The four Inns — Gray's Inn, Lincoln's Inn, the Inner Temple, the Middle Temple — provided an academic training in the Common Law together with the social life and activities associated with a university. Numerous plays, revels and other entertainments were first produced or mounted at the Inns of Court.

Islands Voyage: a joint, and largely unsuccessful, expedition to the Spanish-held Azores by the Earl of Essex and Sir Walter Ralegh, July-October 1597.

Justice of the Peace: an unpaid minor magistrate commissioned to keep peace and good order in a specified district. In Tudor and early Stuart England a J.P. was the most important figure in local administration, looking after labour regulations, church attendance, problems of vagabondage, breaches of hunting laws, controversies between masters and servants or between neighbours, and so on.

Lord Admiral: the officer of State responsible for naval affairs — organisation, disposition of squadrons, manning, etc. — and, in time of war, effective commander-in-chief of the fleet. The Lord Admiral was also a prominent figure at Court, patron of a company of actors, the "Admiral's Men", from 1585 to 1604.

Lord Chamberlain: one of the traditional great offices of State. The Lord Chamberlain was responsible for matters concerning the sovereign's day-to-day life at Court, including ceremonial routine, travel and such aspects of entertainment as were not assigned to his deputy, the Master of the Revels. The "Chamberlain's Men" were a theatrical company prominent at Court in the last years of Queen Elizabeth; they came under royal patronage and were known as the "King's Men" from May 1603.

Lord Deputy: the chief executive authority in Ireland (except in 1599 when the Earl of Essex was given the more distinguished title of "Lord Lieutenant").

Lord Lieutenant: the sovereign's appointed representative as governor of a county and thereby head of the magistracy.

Lord Treasurer: Traditionally one of the great officers of State, responsible for financial matters in the sovereign's council and having, as his chief executant, a Chancellor of the Exchequer. By the late sixteenth century the Lord Treasurer had acquired wider powers and privileges, notably as an officer of the law and as controller of customs.

Marprelate Tracts: anonymous Puritan pamphlets, attacking the government of the Church of England by bishops and frequently using violent and scurrilous language. The tracts, which were circulated in 1588–9, owe their name to the pseudonym, Martin Marprelate, assumed by the author.

Masque (or Mask): basically a festive celebration by disguised guests which complimented the person or persons in whose honour the entertainment was mounted. Laudatory speeches were written by poets and scholars of distinction while greater emphasis was placed on dance, music and spectacle than on dramatic content or character. During the opening years of the seventeenth century the masque became increasingly elaborate, actors being occasionally brought into the entertainment when Court poets overtaxed the powers of the high ranking amateurs for whom masques were first intended.

Master of the Revels: head of the Office of the Revels, the body responsible for organising entertainments at Court.

Master of the Rolls: was originally the keeper of the Chancery rolls, the chief records of government administration. By late Tudor times the Master was both a senior civil servant and a leading judicial official.

Overseer of a will: a person appointed by a testator to supervise the activities of the executor of the will.

Patent: a document, licensed under the Great Seal, granting a privilege or an office. The *PATENT OF 1603* was a royal warrant, dated 17 May, authorising William Shakespeare, eight other named actors "and the rest of their associates" to play anywhere in the realm as the "King's Men" rather than as the "Chamberlain's Men".

Privy Chamber: the private apartments at Court or in a royal residence.

Privy Council: the sovereign's inner body of government executives.

Puritan: term applied, from about 1580 onwards, to extreme English Protestants who wished to "purify" the English Church by abolishing bishops, religious ornaments, vestments and other outward forms of public worship. Puritans emphasised the need for strict Sunday observance, for godly preaching and for hard work. They deplored frivolous pastimes, including all dramatic entertainments, and they favoured Church government by members of the congregation.

Recusant: a religious believer, normally a Roman Catholic in faith, who declined to attend the services of the established Church of England. After a month of absence the names of such "recusants" could be displayed on a list posted on the door of the parish church.

Rosicrucian: a Christian believer who belonged to an alleged secret society venerating the twin emblems of the Rose and the Cross and claiming a divine insight into the secrets of Nature, among them being the transmutation of metals.

Secretary of State: a term becoming common in the 1590s to describe the sovereign's principal secretary, the official executant of policy determined by the king or queen in council. Occasionally there were two Secretaries of State, sharing responsibilities. In the earlier sixteenth century the post was known as "Secretary of Estate". From 1573 onwards it was increasingly concerned with foreign affairs and with directing the embryonic diplomatic service.

Separatists: Protestants who wished to separate their congregations from the Church of England and become "Independents" or "Congregationalists".

Sheriff: an officer of the law responsible over a specified area for the custody and punishment of criminals, the carrying out of writs, the summoning of juries, and similar duties. His powers for serving warrants and writs for debt, etc., were frequently delegated to a bailiff.

Star Chamber: an apartment in the royal palace at Westminster taking its name from the gilt stars decorating its roof. The Court of Star Chamber emerged at the end of the fifteenth century and was, in origin, the king's council sitting in a judicial capacity. Its prime function was the suppression of civil anarchy but it also supplemented defects in the common law and was therefore used by plaintiffs with bills of complaint against other private individuals in instances when there seemed no prospect of ready redress from other courts. Star Chamber therefore heard cases of slander, libel, abduction, apparent abuses in the regulation of trade, breaches of ordinances concerning printing or gild regulations, etc. The Court was criticised in the Commons as an arbitrary instrument of conciliar government, and it was formally abolished in 1641.

Stationers' Register: Every book printed in England, apart from those produced on the presses of the universities in Oxford and Cambridge, had to be registered with the Stationers' Company, a corporate body to which all printers and booksellers belonged. Only by entering a book or play in the Stationers' Register could copyright be established.

Thirty Years War: a conflict, extending from 1618 to 1648, fought originally between the leading Catholic and Protestant states on the European mainland. The immediate cause of the war was a revolt in Prague which was both Protestant and Czech nationalist in inspiration, and the first phase of the war (1618–22) was fought around Prague and in the central Rhineland (the Palatinate).

Tiremaker: a person who designed and made women's headdresses.

Tithes: originally rent charges, either in the form of money or crops, paid by the laity to the clergy of a parish, and constituting one-tenth of the produce of land allotted to the church. By the late sixteenth century some pre-Reformation tithes had been appropriated by the gentry and were a recognised form of sound investment.

Trial of Mary, Queen of Scots: took place at Fotheringhay, Northamptonshire, 15-16 October 1586 and, as a major extraordinary treason trial, was assessed by a special commission of twenty-four peers and privy councillors. The trial was concluded, in the absence of the accused, at the Star Chamber in Westminster. Mary was found guilty of planning the death of Queen Elizabeth I and, after a three months' stay of execution, was beheaded at Fotheringhay on 8 February, 1587.

Twelfth Night: the evening of the Feast of the Epiphany (6 January), the last of the twelve days of Christmas, traditionally an occasion for entertainment, either plays or masques. Sometimes the name "Twelfth Night" is given to Epiphany Eve (5 January).

Undertaker (Irish colonisation): someone who, in return for the grant of an estate in Munster or Ulster, "undertakes" to build defensible houses and only to let farms to Englishmen or to Scots and Irish who had been in the Crown's service.